Electronica Dance Music Programming Secrets

SECOND EDITION

Electronica
Dance Music
Programming Secrets

SECOND EDITION

Roger James Brown

and

Martin Griese

Prentice
Hall

An imprint of **Pearson Education**

London · Boston · Indianapolis · New York · Mexico City · Toronto ·
Sydney · Tokyo · Singapore · Hong Kong · Cape Town · New Delhi ·
Madrid · Paris · Amsterdam · Munich · Milan · Stockholm

PEARSON EDUCATION LIMITED

Edinburgh Gate
Harlow CM20 2JE
Tel: +44 (0)1279 623623
Fax: +44 (0)1279 431059
Website: www.pearsoned.co.uk

First published in Great Britain 2000

© Pearson Education Limited 2000

The rights of Roger Brown and Martin Griese to be identified as Authors
of this Work have been asserted by them in accordance with the Copyright,
Designs and Patents Act 1988.

ISBN: 0-13-083696-6

British Library Cataloguing in Publication Data
A CIP catalogue record for this book can be obtained from the British Library

The programs in this book have been included for their instructional value.
They have been tested with care but are not guaranteed for any particular
purpose. The publisher does not offer any warranties or representations
nor does it accept any liabilities with respect to the programs.

10 9 8 7 6 5 4 3

Typeset by Pantek Arts, Maidstone, Kent
Printed and bound in Great Britain by Biddles Ltd, *www.biddles.co.uk*

The Publishers' policy is to use paper manufactured from sustainable forests.

Contents

Chapter 10   The mixing desk, EQ and effects   243

Introduction

Welcome to the second edition of *Electronica Dance Music Programming Secrets*. In the first edition we explored the main styles that constitute Electronica and showed how to produce your own examples. This second edition brings us up-to-date with the latest emergent styles in Electronica, from Trance and Dreamhouse to Big Beat and Nu Skool Electro. One of the best kept secrets of Electronica is the way in which a few, very basic, breakbeats, basslines and melody lines are manipulated via sequencer and synthesiser programming to produce magical effects, and we'll explore more of these secrets in this expanded and revised edition.

Another of the London dance scene's best kept secrets is Newtronic, an expert band of programmers beavering away producing beats and basslines which are sold as building block kits. Many professional Electronica musicians use Newtronic's building blocks and I am proud to collaborate with them on this second edition to bring their secrets to you.

The power of sequencing lies in its empowerment of the individual to produce professional quality music from a modest home set-up. Musical tricks and secrets, previously the preserve of professionals with huge budgets and the time necessary to learn them, become easily understood through a sequencer's graphic displays, paving a much smoother path from musical novice to explorer and innovator. Who hasn't played around on a friend's guitar or keyboard and heard something in their untutored ramblings that sounded great but which they lacked the skill to replicate? With a sequencer your moment of musical genius can be captured, isolated from the dross surrounding it and replicated to form the basis of a new groove.

Beyond the simple process of recording and replaying, sequencers offer a wealth of music processing options that allow you to take your original idea and experiment or generate harmony parts which in the past would have required a studio full of expensive session musicians and years of learning music theory. This opens new avenues of musical exploration and is the driving force behind the continuing development of Electronica. No longer does a composer have to patiently explain to a bass player or drummer just the feel he has in mind and await their understanding of his concept before they can hear their own musical idea – now you can try out the juxtaposition of patterns you had in mind and adjust the results yourself until the required feel is obtained. Once achieved it is there to be replayed perfectly at any time, not just when the musicians are in the right mood. Using the power of computers to capture those precious moments of inspiration leads to faster working and a freedom to experiment which was previously only enjoyed by the classical or jazz musician with years of training and practice behind him.

Electronica Dance Music Programming Secrets is organized so you can simply dip into those areas of Electronica which you are most interested in. There are stylistic links and similarities between the various styles and I hope this book will lead you to explore those links and thus evolve your own, original, style. Along the way, sequencers' music processing features are introduced in context, where they make the most sense. Too often instruction manuals assume you have a degree in computer science and the musical knowledge of a classical musician, introducing powerful features out of context, bewildering novice and expert alike.

Introducing features from sequencer tricks through to sample manipulation and sound effects as they are required will help you unravel many of the mysteries surrounding Electronica music-making. This will free you to create the music we all hear in our head but which most of us have been unable to realize until now. Ultimately the magic that is music depends on that indefinable something that makes a chord sequence or riff transcendental and it would be foolish to say that simply reading this book will make a Derrick May or Goldie of you. What I hope it will do is allow you to discover the magic that is making music and uncover the hidden musician that beats in everyone's breast.

Nothing in this book about the different styles of Electronica is true of course. The very act of creating electronic music denies the existence of formulas. Take the patterns for Garage drums and make a Jungle track with them, try writing a Trip Hop bassline in a Techno style or mash together patterns from all the different styles. Above all else, remember, there are no rules, anything is possible.

The Basics

What is a sequencer?

It may seem an obvious place to start but much of the confusion surrounding MIDI sequencing stems from a misunderstanding of the basic nature of a sequencer. The most common misapprehension is that a sequencer is just like a tape recorder, recording your music and playing it back. Sequencers do *not* record the sounds you hear coming from a MIDI sequencing set up.

What a sequencer does is record and transmit information. In the case of MIDI sequencers this is digital information or data. MIDI stands for Musical Instrument Digital Interface. For a MIDI sequencer to produce sounds it must be connected to at least one sound-producing device. This can be simply a drum machine or, more usually, a synthesizer sound module or keyboard or a sound card inside a computer.

The information that sequencers send out to connected sound-generating devices consists of a series of commands instructing the connected synth or sound card to play a note, what pitch the note is and when to stop playing that note and start playing the next one and so on. The synthesizer receives the instructions and plays the note on whatever sound it is set to produce. In the modern MIDI synths there are a vast number of sounds to choose from – up to 1,600 with the latest generation of GS and XG devices.

Sequencers can be hardware devices, such as the Alesis MMT8, or software, such as Steinberg's Cubase, Opcode's Vision, Emagic's Logic or Twelve Tone System's Cakewalk. Software sequencers are much more common today and offer many more features than do most hardware sequencers. They require a computer to run on.

To understand a little more about how a MIDI synthesizer works let's look at a few simple musical examples. One reason a digital medium was chosen for the MIDI standard is the number-crunching ability of computers. Music itself is a very mathematical process as any classically trained musician will tell you, and the power of computers to process a constant stream of numbers at a fast enough rate to play intricate musical pieces makes them perfect for this process. So let's see how sequencers use numbers to make music.

Four-to-the-floor

To demonstrate how sequencers work we'll start with a very simple musical pattern, consisting of only quarter notes. This simple pattern is actually the basis for most dance music, the 4/4 kick of House, Garage and Techno.

Traditional notation

There are many ways of showing the same data in different formats in various sequencers. Most computer sequencers feature a Score editor which uses traditional music notation and is an excellent place to show how this relates to MIDI sequencing. Here is a simple quarter note pattern in traditional music notation as shown in a Score editor.

ON THE CD-ROM

This pattern can be found on the CD-ROM accompanying this book in the following directory: **chapter1/midifiles/4square.mid**. *Load it into your sequencer if you want to listen as well as look.*

Figure 1.1
Four quarter notes as viewed in traditional music notation.

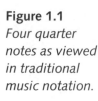

Drum patterns

Other sequencer editors present the same data but in different ways, making it easier to understand the process of understanding music and sequencing. If you don't know anything about traditional music, all you can work out from the above illustration is that there are four notes. You aren't given many clues about the pitch of the notes, when they are to be played or how long they are to be played for. Now let's take a look at the same musical pattern on another of the editors most sequencers feature, a Drum editor.

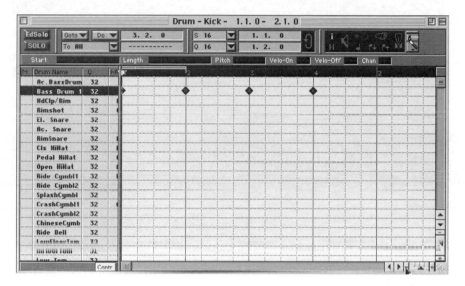

Figure 1.2
A 4/4 kick drum pattern in a Drum editor.

Here we see the same four notes but placed on a grid which graphically demonstrates their relationship to each other in time. The four notes are placed within a bar, each note evenly spaced over the length of the bar. The order they are played in is read from left to right. As they are evenly spaced and all the same pitch, when played on a MIDI drum kit this produces a 4/4 kick drum pattern, the basic beat in dance music.

Move any one of the notes to the right or left and you move the note 'off the beat' to one of the other subdivisions of a bar as used in traditional notation. These smaller subdivisions are known by the number of them in a bar, thus eighths, sixteenths and so forth. The example in Figure 1.3 is the hi hat pattern from 4square.arr, a series of eighth notes. If you move a note to the right it will sound later in time while moving a note to the left will make it earlier. Most sequencers include a 'SNAP' function to force notes onto these time grids relative to a specific note value that you can adjust or turn off completely.

Graphic editing

Although this tells us where in time the notes are played it doesn't tell us anything about for how long each note is sounded. Any note has two qualities that affect its timing, its position in time and its length. This is graphically illustrated in another editor featured in most sequencers, the Grid or graphic editor (see Figure 1.4).

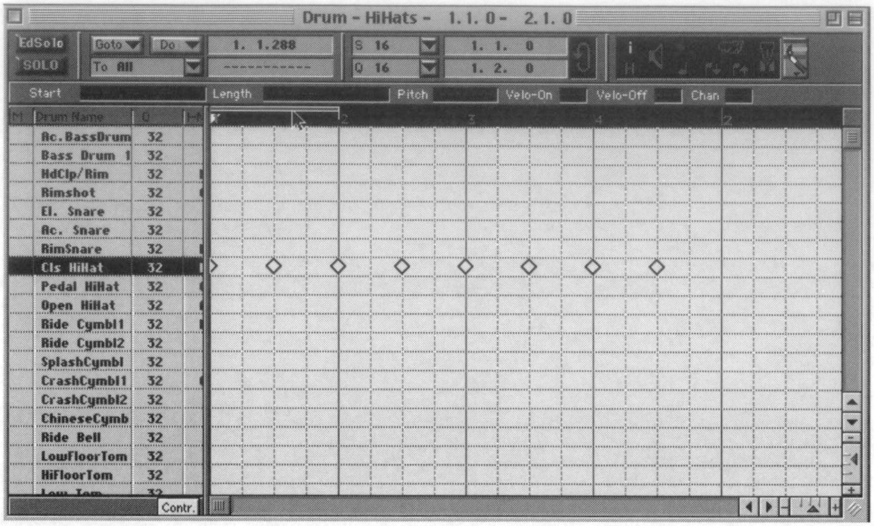

Figure 1.3
Eight hi hats to a bar in a Drum editor.

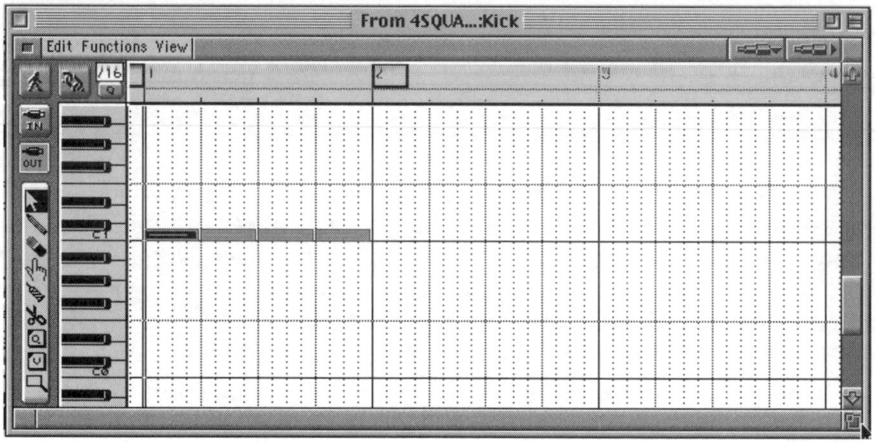

Figure 1.4
The 4/4 pattern in a Grid editor.

The grid here is very similar to the grid in the Drum editor and can be read in the same manner. What has changed is the appearance of the four notes. Instead of appearing as four little dots in time, they are shown as four rectangles, each one occupying a quarter of the bar. This shows us for how long each note sounds. The beginning of a rectangle indicates the point in time at which a note starts sounding and the end of that rectangle is when the note ceases to sound. The eighth note hi hat pattern by contrast looks like Figure 1.5.

To the left of the screen is a representation of a piano keyboard. It is placed upright with the lowest notes at the bottom of the screen and the highest at the top. This indicates the pitch of the notes in the traditional twelve-tone scale used in western music. The notes in the example in Figure 1.6 are easily read as C1, or bottom C on your MIDI keyboard for the quarter notes and F#1 for the eighth notes.

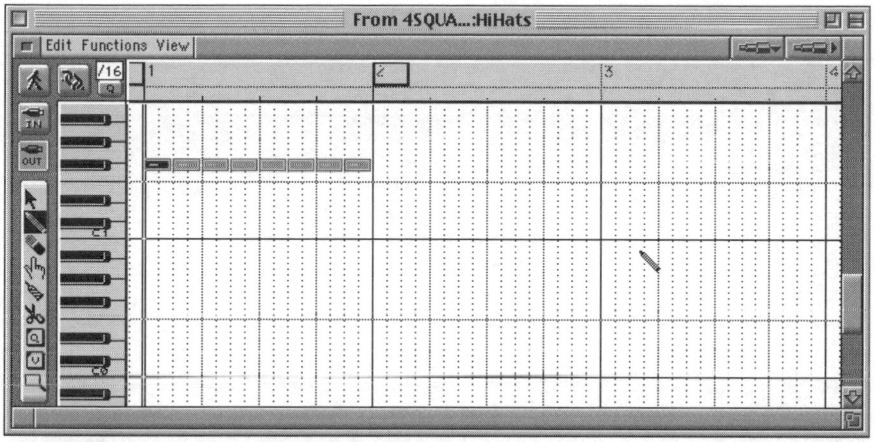

Figure 1.5
*The hi hat
pattern in a
Grid editor.*

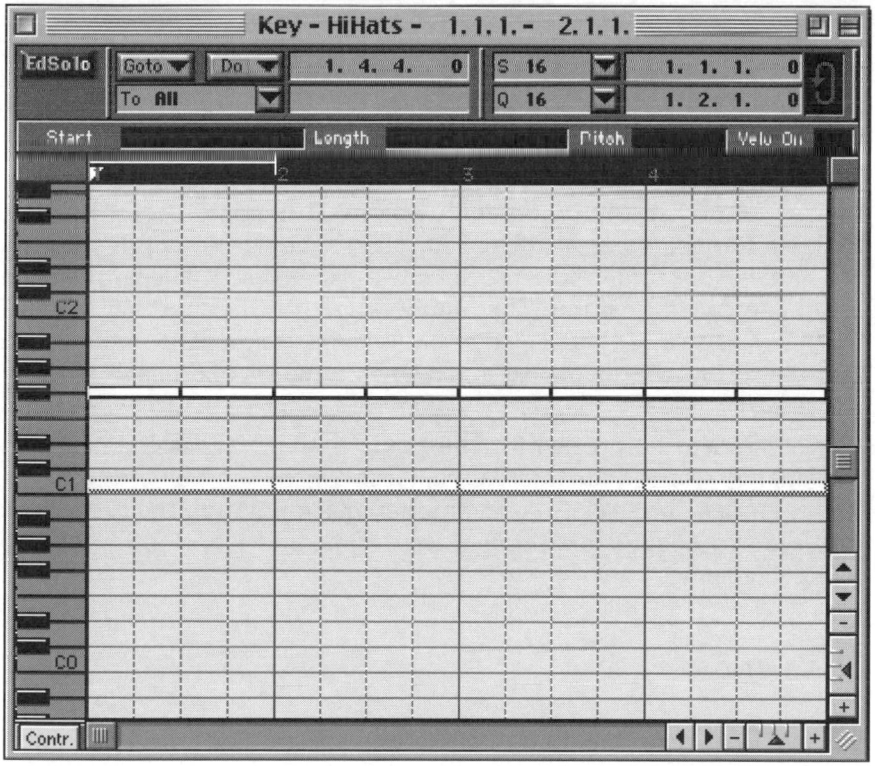

Figure 1.6
*The quarter
notes and
eighth notes
shown together
in a Grid editor
illustrating their
different
lengths and
pitches.*

List editing

To see the notes in a format that is closer to the way MIDI understands
them we must turn to the most common sequencer editor, a List editor.
Here information about the same notes is displayed in the form of a list
of letters and numbers.

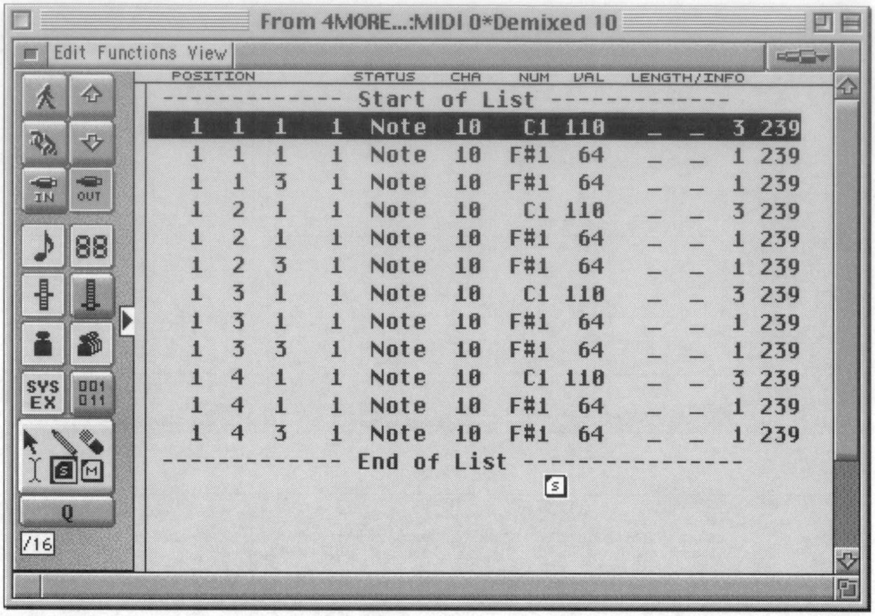

Figure 1.7
The 12 notes in a List editor.

From 4MORE...:MIDI 0*Demixed 10

Edit Functions View

POSITION	STATUS	CHA	NUM	VAL	LENGTH/INFO
-------------- Start of List --------------					
1 1 1 1	Note	10	C1	110	_ _ 3 239
1 1 1 1	Note	10	F#1	64	_ _ 1 239
1 1 3 1	Note	10	F#1	64	_ _ 1 239
1 2 1 1	Note	10	C1	110	_ _ 3 239
1 2 1 1	Note	10	F#1	64	_ _ 1 239
1 2 3 1	Note	10	F#1	64	_ _ 1 239
1 3 1 1	Note	10	C1	110	_ _ 3 239
1 3 1 1	Note	10	F#1	64	_ _ 1 239
1 3 3 1	Note	10	F#1	64	_ _ 1 239
1 4 1 1	Note	10	C1	110	_ _ 3 239
1 4 1 1	Note	10	F#1	64	_ _ 1 239
1 4 3 1	Note	10	F#1	64	_ _ 1 239
-------------- End of List --------------					

Each line in the list represents one note. The first note is, naturally, at the top of the list, the others following in descending order. Reading from left to right along each line is displayed the position of the note on the grid we looked at in the previous two examples. This is arranged in a Column called Position. The numbers 1.1.1 in the first line indicate that the first kick (C1) is played at bar one, beat one; 1.2.1 in the fourth that the second kick is played at bar one on the second beat and so on down the list.

We can see the entries for the notes' pitches and these are self-explanatory. To the far right is a column for the lengths of the notes. These entries don't relate to traditional music notation but are a peek into the way sequencers process the timing and length of notes in a musical sequence.

Time grids

To be able to record and play back music accurately a MIDI sequencer must use a fixed time grid against which to measure the relative timing values of notes. This fixed grid is then 'played' by the sequencer at a speed relative to a fixed time signal from a quartz timing chip inside your computer or hardware sequencer which vibrates at a set frequency.

Although different resolutions are used, most sequencers use a compatible resolution which divides each bar in a piece of music into 384 'ticks' and uses this as its base grid against which all other timing values are measured. With this resolution sequencers can play back MIDI data accurately at tempos ranging from 30 to 250 beats per minute.

Note lengths

Using this grid your sequencer measures the length and placement of notes on its timing grid in divisions of 384. So a quarter note will occur every 96 ticks and will be that number of ticks long (384/4 = 96) whereas an eighth note will occur every 48 ticks and be 48 ticks long.

The table below gives the major note lengths as used in traditional notation and their equivalent number of ticks using the basic resolution of 384 ticks per bar.

Traditional name	Length of note	Number of ticks
Whole note	One whole bar	384
Half note	Half a bar	192
Quarter note	Quarter of a bar	96
Eighth note	Eighth of a bar	48
Sixteenth note	Sixteenth of a bar	24
32nd	32nd of a bar	12
64th	64th of a bar	6

The table below gives the major note lengths as used in traditional notation and their equivalent number of ticks using the higher resolution of 960 ticks per bar.

Traditional name	Length of note	Number of ticks
Whole note	One whole bar	960
Half note	Half a bar	480
Quarter note	Quarter of a bar	240
Eighth note	Eighth of a bar	120
Sixteenth note	Sixteenth of a bar	60
32nd	32nd of a bar	30
64th	64th of a bar	15

Some sequencers use an even higher resolution of 1536 ticks to the bar. The table below gives the major note lengths as used in traditional notation and their equivalent number of ticks using this resolution.

Traditional name	Length of note	Number of ticks
Whole note	One whole bar	1536
Half note	Half a bar	768
Quarter note	Quarter of a bar	384
Eighth note	Eighth of a bar	192
Sixteenth note	Sixteenth of a bar	96
32nd	32nd of a bar	48
64th	64th of a bar	24

NOTE

For more information about timing grids please refer to Chapter 9, GM, GS and XG Programming.

Odd notes and timings

There are other values in traditional notation and a resolution of 960 also allows sequencers to deal with these. Dotted notes and triplets are used in traditional notation to describe notes that don't fit into this relatively simple scheme. Dotted notes are simply notes that are half as long again as their normal equivalent note. Thus a dotted half note (**2.**) is 720 ticks long and occurs at intervals of the same number of ticks. This is illustrated in the example below

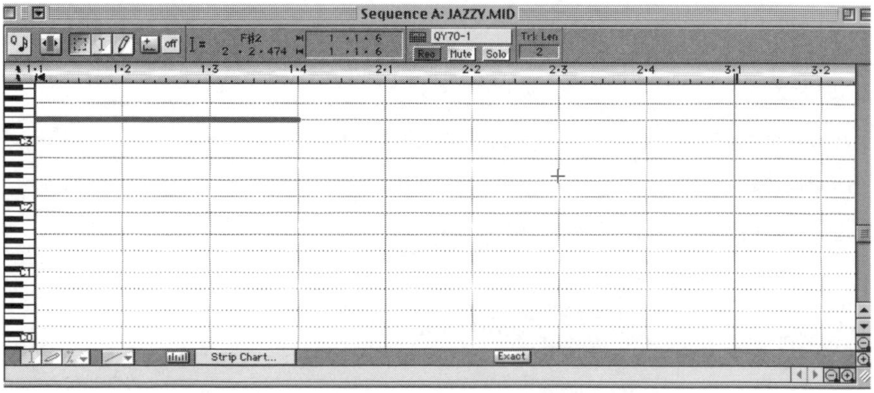

Figure 1.8
A dotted half note in a Grid editor.

Triplets are slightly more complex. They are half as short again as a normal note and occupy corresponding positions on the grid. Sixteenth triplets (the most common triplets used in electronic dance) are 40 ticks long using a base of 960 and, as they are placed on the grid in the equivalent time positions, there are 24 sixteenth triplets in a bar as opposed to 16.

Triplet and dotted notes' values occupy 'out of time' positions on the standard 4/4 grid and thus make for more complicated rhythmic patterns than the mechanical patterns of regular notes. Often a piano or bass part will use straight sixteenths for most of its length and switch to triplets for the last beat to bring a 'swing' to the end of a bar or series of bars.

Have a look at the jazzy piano part here for an example of this:

ON THE CD-ROM
This pattern can be found on the CD-ROM accompanying this book, in the following directory: **chapter1/midifiles/jazzy.mid**.

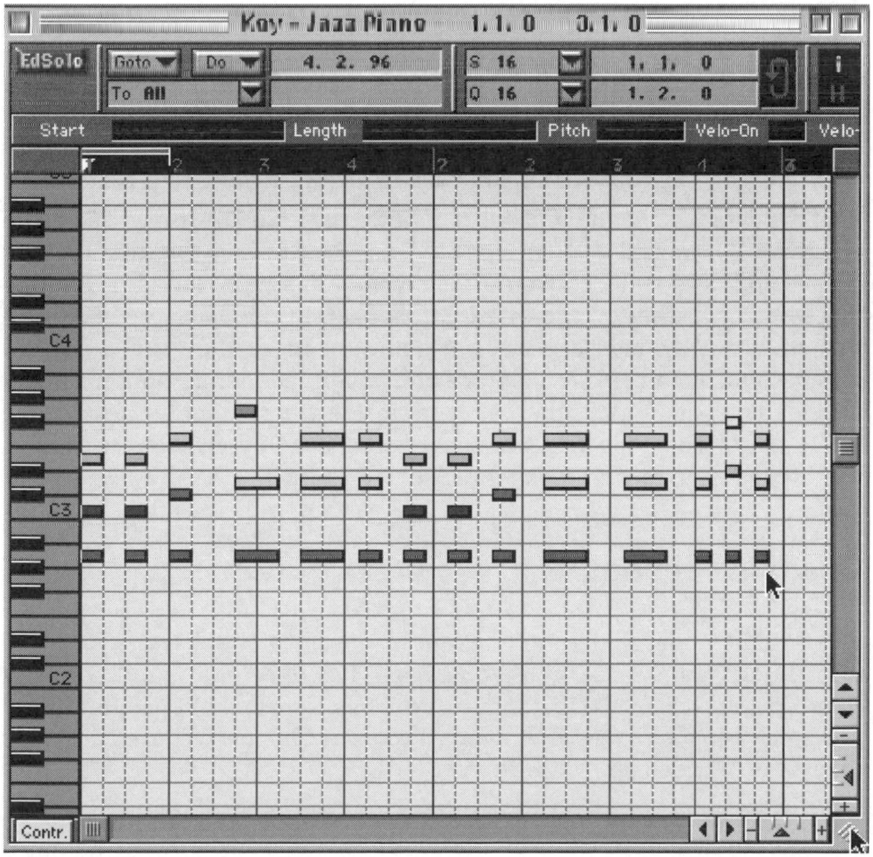

Figure 1.4
A piano part ending in 16th triplets.

The process of aligning notes to a given note value in terms of their length and timing is known as quantization. Human players don't play strictly to a musical grid, of course, and the subtle differences in this give what is known as a 'human' feel to live music. With a resolution of 960 ticks to a bar your sequencer is able to record these subtle nuances of feel. There are several ways to quantize music and we'll cover those as they arise.

Measuring pitch

To deal with the different pitch values in the twelve-tone musical scale MIDI gives each note a number. The number 60 represents middle C, 61 is a semitone above that and so forth. There are up to 128 numbers available in the MIDI data format and consequently 128 notes. This gives us a range of 10 octaves to play with, larger than most piano keyboards.

MIDI channels

There are 16 MIDI channels on which to transmit all this data. Each of the 16 MIDI channels can be considered as akin to the channels on your TV set. Data sent out on MIDI Channel 2 will only be received by a synth set to respond on that channel. This allows you to connect a series of synths, all set to different channels and all playing different parts.

MIDI data is transmitted using a series of five-pin DIN plugs and sockets, the MIDI In, Out and Thru ports. Only the Atari has MIDI ports built in as a standard feature, even if their wiring is a non-standard one that employs MIDI Thru on the MIDI Out socket. PC and Mac owners must either buy a MIDI interface that plugs into the modem or printer port, or purchase a sound card. A sound card is a very economic option as they provide you with a multi-timbral synth inside your computer besides the MIDI interface and the best sound cards are, in addition, samplers, giving you all you need to start making music.

Changing sounds

The MIDI standard encompasses more than just simple note information. MIDI synths usually have at least 128 different sound settings, called patches. The MIDI standard provides a means of changing these remotely using another MIDI event, Program Changes. These allow you to choose between up to 128 sounds.

Your sequencer displays Program Changes as decimal numbers from 1 to 128. The actual range used by computers and MIDI is from 0–127. Some synths use this numbering system and so Program Change 1 will call up Program 0 on the synth. This is fairly simple to deal with but you will come across some synthesizers that use other numbering systems such as banks of 16 (A1–16, B1–16, C1–16, D1–16). A conversion table for the most common systems can be found in Appendix 2.

Modern synths often offer more than 128 sounds, so the manufacturers of MIDI equipment have devised the Bank Select command to enable you to access more than the standard 128 programs from a sequencer. The maths involved is rather complicated but essentially the bank select command allows you to access 16,384 banks. Within each bank you then address 128 Program Changes. This means you could address a total of 2,097,152 programs if your synth had enough memory to hold so many different sounds. The bank select command is actually a combination of two special MIDI messages called Control Changes and the MIDI Program Change event and entering them in a sequencer can be rather confusing.

Figure 1.10
The Bank change box on Cubase's Inspector set to choose Bank 353.

General MIDI

The General MIDI standard, or GM, was devised to solve a problem that arose almost as soon as the MIDI standard was established. Picture this. You finish your arrangement and whip around to the recording studio to put it all down on DAT. You stick your floppy disk in the studio's computer and load the song up into their sequencer. As soon as you hit playback your masterpiece is reduced to trash. A demented drummer is playing the piano part and a maniac is playing the drums on a hundred pianos! What has happened is that the sounds and program changes you used do not match the sounds in the sound modules in the recording studio's set-up.

In an effort to avoid this happening, the GM standard specifies a common set of 128 sounds, all with matching program change numbers. Sounds are assigned to categories such as piano, strings, etc. Whatever manufacturer made your GM device, a similar set of sounds are allocated to the GM program numbers. This means your Program Change commands will call up these sounds, whatever the sound module, though of course no two modules from different manufacturers will sound identical. The General MIDI sound set is shown in Appendix 3.

The General MIDI specification also calls for synthesizers to be addressed on all 16 MIDI channels and to be at least 16 note polyphonic. 'Polyphony' defines the maximum number of notes a synth can play at the same time. Thus the GM specification calls for up to 16 notes to be played simultaneously.

The GM drum kit

So that the drum track doesn't sound awry, with bongos playing the hi hat pattern and the kick drum pattern sounding on a glockenspiel, the GM standard also specifies a standard drum kit, with each individual drum sound assigned to a specific note. This is always on MIDI channel 10. The General MIDI drum kit is reproduced in Appendix 3.

MIDI controllers

MIDI performance controllers are the most powerful yet underused aspects of sequencing. They replace the sliders and knobs on analogue synthesizers, changing various parameters of their sounds in real time. Most synthesizers have at least two of the most common controllers, Pitch Bend and Modulation. Wheels on the front panel of a keyboard usually control these.

The wheels that alter these values also send out the appropriate MIDI data so you can record them from your MIDI keyboard. Modules don't feature Modulation and Pitch Bend wheels of course, but most respond to Pitch and Modulation messages sent from your MIDI keyboard or your sequencer. As with all MIDI data, Control Change events are specific to one channel and will not affect sounds on neighbouring channels.

Pitch Bend

Pitch Bend raises or lowers the pitch of a note just as bending a string on a guitar does. The amount of pitch bend is determined by settings in your synth. If Pitch Bend sensitivity is set to a value of 12 semitone steps in the sound module, then the pitch will increase by an octave when you push the pitch wheel all the way up. If you set the maximum to two semitone steps, pushing the pitch wheel all the way up moves the pitch up by only two semitones. This can also be set in your sequencer by adding controller data in the setup measure, which we'll look at in more detail in Chapter 9.

> **NOTE**
> *You can usually alter this from the front panel of your synth, commonly within the voice parameters for an individual sound, although sometimes the pitch bend setting may be global, i.e. all voices will use the same setting.*

Modulation

The Modulation wheel on the front of your keyboard is used to control the amount of modulation applied to a synth sound. This can produce warbling effects and can be used to introduce variation and 'feel' to things like string patches or lead voices. Like all MIDI controllers it can be recorded and played back. Not all voices respond to modulation; a dry slap bass usually has little or no modulation, but most do. Some voices use modulation to affect other settings in a synthesizer's sound, like filter frequency, replicating the knob-twiddling effects of classic dance synths like the Roland TB-303.

Aftertouch

When you play a sound on your synthesizer the modulation of the sustain portion of the sound may be controlled by Aftertouch. Aftertouch is sometimes called Channel Pressure, as it affects every note on a specific MIDI channel. Like all the MIDI data described here it can be recorded into a MIDI sequencer. Many MIDI keyboards output Aftertouch by default, yet not many voices respond to it. It also generates a lot of data and consequently is a real memory hog so it is usually best filtered out of the recording chain.

Poly Pressure

A variation on Aftertouch is Poly Pressure which also affects the amount of modulation applied to the sustain part of a synth sound. Unlike Aftertouch it is note-specific, i.e. each note in a chord can have differing amounts of Poly Pressure applied to its sustain section. Only the most expensive synths support Poly Pressure. Like Aftertouch, Poly Pressure gobbles up memory and should really only be used if absolutely necessary.

Volume, Pan and other Control Changes

As well as Pitch Bend, Modulation, Channel Pressure and Poly Pressure, MIDI offers a further set of controllers called Control Changes. There are 128 MIDI Control Change numbers. Some of these have been assigned specific functions like Volume level and Panning (the position of a sound in the stereo spectrum) while others perform different actions on different synths. The full list of Control Changes and their functions where agreed is reproduced in Appendix 4.

In an ideal world your sound module should be able to support all 128 MIDI controllers but this is not always so. Many early digital drum machines don't respond to the MIDI Control Change event for Volume, for example. With the growth of electronic dance music throughout the

Figure 1.11

A MIDI implementation chart showing which MIDI controllers this synth responds to. This chart is also clear about what synth parameters these controllers address; some, unfortunately, are not.

Function		Transmitted	Recognised	Remarks
Basic Channel	Default Changed	1 - 16	1 - 16	Memorised
Mode	Default Messages Altered	x ************	4 x	
Note Number	True Voice	24 - 72 ************	12 - 120 12 - 120	
Velocity	Note ON Note OFF	o 9nH,v=1-127 o	o v=1-127 o	
After Touch	Keys Ch's	x x	x o	
Pitch Bender		x	o 0-12 semi	7 bit resolution
Control Change	1	x	o	Modulation Wheel
	2	x	o	Breath control
	7	x	o	Volume
	105	o	o	Filter frequency
	106	o	o	Filter resonance
	107	o	o	Filter mod depth
	108	o	o	Env1 Attack
	109	o	o	Env1 Decay
	110	o	o	Env1 Sustain
	111	o	o	Env1 Release
	112	o	o	Env1 Velocity
	114	o	o	Env2 Attack
	115	o	o	Env2 Decay
	116	o	o	Env2 Sustain
	117	o	o	Env2 Release
	118	o	o	Env2 Velocity
Program change	True *	o 0 - 99 ***********	o 0 - 99	
System exclusive		o	o	Voice parameters
System Real Time	:Clock	x	o	Start,Stop, Continue
Aux messages	:Local ON/OFF :All Notes OFF :Active Sense :Reset	x x x x	x o x x	

```
Mode 1  : OMNI ON,POLY      Mode 3  : OMNI ON,MONO
Mode 2  : OMNI OFF, POLY    Mode 4  : OMNI OFF,MONO
```

80s and 90s, synth manufacturers have begun to address this problem and many synthesizers now make extensive use of MIDI controllers to alter the sound parameters.

You can find out to which of these MIDI commands a module responds by consulting its MIDI implementation chart, which should be contained in the instruction manual. Unfortunately the manufacturer's foresight in making extra controllers available doesn't always extend to providing clear information as to what parameters are addressed by them and you may need to read the manual thoroughly before understanding which controller does what.

Making connections – MIDI

Setting up MIDI connections is often a daunting project the first time you set about it. The confusion arises from not understanding the important distinctions between the three types of MIDI port, In, Out and Thru. MIDI connections are not sound or audio connections but must be considered as data flow connections just like the cables that connect your PC to a printer or modem.

There is a crucial difference between MIDI and those other computer connections and that is that MIDI was not designed primarily as a computer controlled data format but was created to allow instruments to talk to each other, enabling a keyboard player to play other MIDI instruments connected to his master keyboard, as in Figure 1.7. This is why three MIDI ports are used and it is important to understand the differences between them before making any connections.

MIDI Out

The MIDI Out port on your computer's MIDI interface or at the back of your synth sends MIDI data out to other connected instruments in the chain, *after* it has been processed by the originating device. On your keyboard this simply means that every time you press a key the note information is sent out to any other connected devices. If their MIDI channel corresponds to the transmitting channel on the master keyboard, a note will sound. On your computer this is where note information is sent out from your sequencer to connected instruments. All information sent out from a MIDI Out port must be sent to its twin on the connected instrument, the MIDI In port.

MIDI In

This is where a device receives and processes MIDI data. A synth receiving MIDI data from a sequencer will play those notes if the MIDI channel corresponds. The MIDI In port on your computer is for receiving MIDI note information from your keyboard, enabling you to record this for editing and playback. The MIDI In and Out ports comprise the basic MIDI/Computer connections. A module's MIDI In must be connected to a keyboard's MIDI Out for the keyboard to control the module, as shown in Figure 1.12.

Figure 1.12
Basic MIDI connection between a keyboard and module.

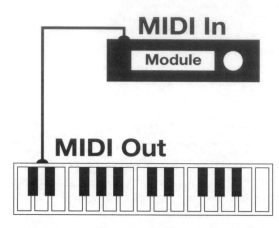

A computer's MIDI Out must be connected to a keyboard's MIDI In and the keyboard's MIDI Out to the computer's MIDI In for a computer MIDI set-up to work. See Figure 1.13 shows a diagram of a basic computer/keyboard connection.

Figure 1.13
The basic MIDI connections to a computer.

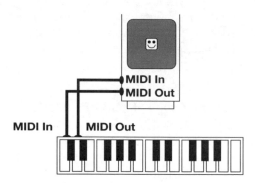

What is happening in the computer set-up is that, when you press a note, MIDI information is sent from your keyboard's MIDI Out port to the computer's MIDI In port. Your sequencer passes the data back to your synth via the computer's MIDI Out port, which is connected to the synthesizer's MIDI In port.

MIDI Thru

If there were only In and Out ports you'd be stumped as soon as you wanted to connect a second MIDI device to your sequencer. This is where the Thru port comes into its own. In contrast to the Out port, which sends out MIDI data from the originating device, the MIDI Thru port sends an exact copy of anything arriving at its In port straight back out again. This enables you to chain a second device to your basic set-up as shown in Figure 1.14. The first synth connected to the sequencer receives MIDI information, plays only those notes that are on the MIDI channel it is set to receive on, while simultaneously passing a copy of everything on to the next device, which does the same, passing a copy through its Thru port to the next device in the chain and so on. Using this 'daisy-chaining' method, enough synths can be connected to use all 16 MIDI channels.

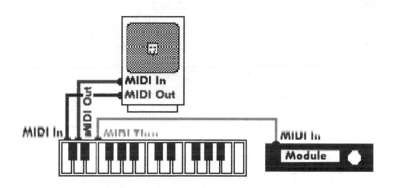

Figure 1.14
A multi-instrument MIDI set-up.

That's all the MIDI you need to know for now. Any MIDI facts relevant to operation with sequencers are covered as and when they occur in the process of programming. Now that you have your MIDI connections all done it's time to look at the final bit of cabling, the audio connections.

Making connections – audio

All these MIDI connections are useless without audio connections, so the sounds lurking inside your MIDI synth can get out and be heard. If you're only working with one tone module, computer sound card or MIDI keyboard then you can plug straight into your home stereo. Be very careful when doing this as most synths output a much broader range of frequencies than home equipment is designed to cope with. Push the volume level up too high and you may blow your speakers or amplifier.

If you're serious about making music, you'll need a mixer through which to mix together the audio outputs from your various synths and drum machines. Mixers take the output from various sound sources, feed them in through separate channels and mix them down to a stereo signal that is fed to an amplifier. Some mixers, called powered mixers, come with in-built amplifiers but these are really intended for live use and are generally too noisy for recording purposes.

Once you have a mixer it's a relatively simple matter of taking the mono or stereo outputs from the back of your synth or synths and patching them into the desk as in Figure 1.15.

Figure 1.15
Basic audio connections.

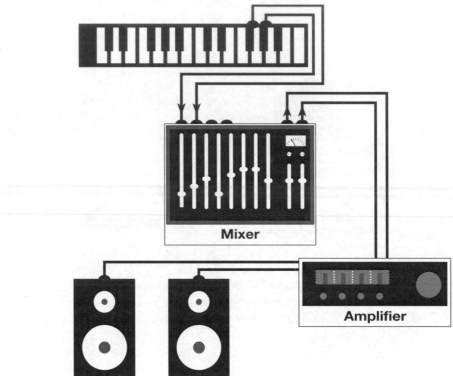

Professional synths and mixers use $\frac{1}{4}$" jacks for carrying sound and your only concern is how many jacks a synth has. If it's a mono synth there will only be one $\frac{1}{4}$" jack at the rear and that can be plugged straight into a mono channel on the mixer. Synths with stereo outputs (which includes most modern synths) must be patched into a stereo channel on your mixer, or two mono channels panned left and right if your mixer has no stereo channels. Computers fitted with sound cards often output their sound on RCA phono connectors or mini-jacks and you will have to purchase special cables for these, but the principle is the same. Figure 1.16 is a diagram of a typical set-up, including MIDI connections alongside the audio ones.

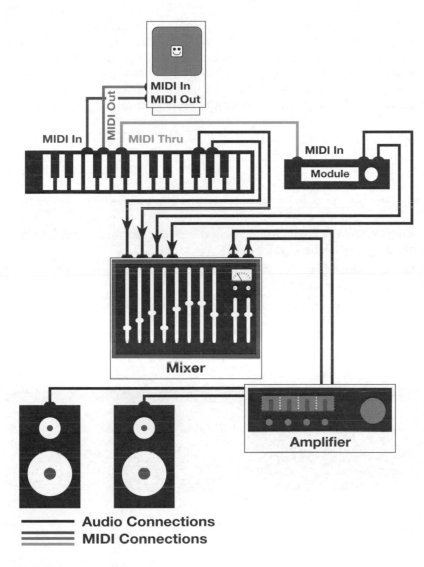

Figure 1.16
*A mixer is
essential if you
have more than
one synth.*

Sequencer basics

Now you have your MIDI and audio connections set up, it's time to look
at the basic layout and functions of a typical sequencer.

Initial settings

As soon as you have installed your sequencer on your computer's hard
drive you're ready to go. However, there are some initial settings that it is
wise to consider before starting your first recording. Personalizing your
set-up will make future recordings and day-to-day operation much simpler.

Good sequencing starts, as in all computer applications, with good housekeeping. Normally in computing terms this means keeping your files in order and so on. When MIDI is brought into the computing environment, these ground rules are even more important. MIDI, for all its perceived magic, is a serial medium with its own set of protocols, and a little work at this stage will save a lot of tears later on.

Who's in control?

The first step, once you have all your synths connected and your sequencer booted up, is to set Local Control to Off on your master keyboard and Soft Thru to On in your sequencer. If these two settings aren't as just described, note-doubling will occur as you play, with both the sequencer and the keyboard sending the same information to the sound-generating part of the keyboard.

Local Control is the connection from the keyboard to itself we must turn off to prevent this happening.

This can also lead to note stealing, with sound devices losing polyphony as all the doubled notes use up their quota. You'll have to consult the manual on your synth for this. Local Control is usually to be found under Global or MIDI parameters in your synth's menu hierarchy.

NOTE

Some of you may be using a master keyboard that is dumb, i.e. it has no internal sounds of its own and is only for transmitting MIDI information to the other devices in your set-up. This kind of keyboard often has no Local Off as it has no need of one and so you can proceed straight to your sequencer's MIDI set-up page with no further ado.

MIDI set-up

Remember talking about MIDI In, Out and Thru? In our explanation of a basic MIDI set-up we explained how a computer MIDI set-up works. When you hit a key on your keyboard a note message is sent from the keyboard's MIDI Out port to your sequencer. Your sequencer then sends the note message back to your synth via its Out port.

To allow all this to happen, something known as soft MIDI Thru must be set to On in your sequencer. The term 'soft' refers to the fact that the *soft*ware is handling the MIDI data while it's in your computer. MIDI Thru is usually set to On by default but is worth checking.

If you look at Figure 1.17, you will see MIDI Thru checked as active, and you will also see a box below, for THRU OFF CHANNEL, set to OFF. This little function is very handy if you have an older synth in your set-up, with no Local Control Off. Setting this to the MIDI channel on which the rogue synth is transmitting will eliminate the phenomenon of doubled notes.

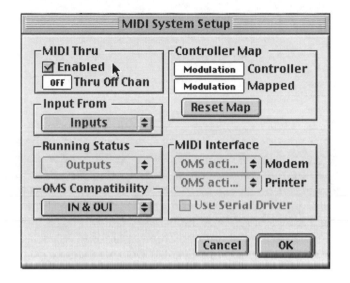

Figure 1.17
MIDI set-up page with MIDI Thru active.

MIDI filter settings

Most sequencers feature a MIDI set-up page with filter section featuring all 128 MIDI controllers, allowing you to filter out specific controllers which may be causing problems, such as stuck notes on older synths. This is very useful for locating problem controllers and filtering them out of the data stream. Of course, you'll have to resort to the manual of your synth but the information in Appendix 4 is there to assist you in this process.

It makes a lot of sense to read the manual of each and every synth in your set-up, and make sure the settings are as advised for operation in a multi-timbral, sequencing set-up. As you are configuring the synths and modules, it also makes sense to think about planning a working set-up which makes full use of the MIDI channels available to you, and set Performance patches so that you have a ready set of voices to work with.

2 Programming House and Garage

What is House music? This question was hotly debated in the early days of the dance explosion. The music called 'House' encompassed many styles and came from the four corners of the world. The name originated in Chicago where the 'House Party' was a long established institution. But this music wasn't the rhythm and blues the J Geils Band had celebrated in their cover of an early tune, 'Ain't Nuthin' but a House Party'. R'n'B was in there somewhere but Chicago House music, as played in the Warehouse Club by DJs like Frankie Knuckles, encompassed a variety of styles, from the disco flavourings of Adonis to the Acid House of DJ Pierre's 'Acid Trax'.

As well as music from Chicago labels like Trax and Prelude, House DJs were playing tracks from Detroit, New York, Germany, Belgium, London and all the nightspots of Europe. A 'House' record could just as easily be Mandy Smith intoning 'I Just Can't Wait' to a Euro-beat as the jazzy piano tinkling of Mr Fingers. What united these records was, in the refrain of the tub-thumping holy roller who had inveigled against rock'n'roll in the 50s, 'the beat, the beat, the beat'.

The 80s saw the appearance of affordable drum machines on the market, the Roland TR808 and TR909 most notably. Usually they were in second hand shops, discarded by rock musicians as being 'not realistic enough'. A new generation of musicians took to these machines, falling in love with their electronic thumps and hisses and ability to play all manner of complicated patterns. The first musical style to use this was Electro out of which grew both House and Hip-Hop. Many of the tracks played in the early days were actually Electro tracks by luminaries like Juan Atkins, whose project Cybotron was the first to integrate the mechanical rhythms of European electronic music masters Kraftwerk with the funky basslines of funk masters like Bootsy Collins.

We'll start our exploration of Electronica by laying down a very basic four square beat and then adding to that. Once we've built it up, we'll knock it down, deconstructing it to explore all the various flavours of Electronica around today. In this chapter we'll look at programming some of the main drum patterns used by the various styles of House and Garage. Then we'll explore the foundations of House and Garage basslines. This will lead us on to exploring some of the piano and melody lines often used in House. Finally we'll take all these pieces and put together a track in a Dream House style.

Programming House drums

Let the bass kick

Create a four bar part and activate your sequencer's Cycle function so you can loop around these four bars. House music is usually in the tempo of the human heartbeat at peak exercise rates which is approximately 120–132 beats per minute so set the tempo to one you find comfortable within that range. Set the track's output to MIDI channel 10, or whichever channel your drum machine is set to receive on, then open the Drum editor.

The first dance programmers often used the Roland TR808 and 909. If you're after that authentic early sound look for these presets on your drum machine before trying out the patterns in this section. On the GM drum kit they're usually to be found in the preset named 'Analogue Kit'.

NOTE

While most GM sound modules include a Roland TR808/909 drum kit, this shouldn't necessarily be your first choice when programming House and Garage drum patterns. The extensive use of strong melodic elements in these two forms demands punchy snares and kicks which will 'cut through' the melodic overlay.

For House and Garage drums try using the Electronic Kit (Program 25) as the drum sounds used in the style are often heavily processed. The electronic kit produces a quite respectable 80s drum machine sound. Even the 'Standard' and the 'Rock' or 'Power' kits can yield surprisingly good dance drum sounds. Try using two or three kits on separate MIDI channels to mix'n'match the drum sounds you find the most effective.

One of the peculiarities of the Roland TR808 and 909's sequencers is that they only allow you to work on up to four bars at a time in pattern mode. Limiting as this may seem, it is actually a very effective way of building a basic pattern then making variations of the original. We'll start by setting our editor to loop internally around one bar and build up the first pattern in the same way.

- Go to the loop indicators on your sequencer. The first should already be set at 1.1.0. Leave it there and set the other one to 2.1.0.

- Now activate looping so your sequencer loops around this single bar.

- Selecting the drumstick from the toolbox, move it until it rests on the first beat of the first bar, on the line marked Bass drum, then click to enter your first kick. Repeat this process at beats 2, 3 and 4.

You now have a 4/4 beat, the basis of house music. Press play on the Transport bar and cycle around the first bar so you can hear your kick looping. It probably sounds a little dull though. Most sequencers automatically assign notes a fixed velocity value when you enter notes with this method. This is fine for most sounds but often produces a very quiet drum kick. The solution is to alter the velocity levels of each note so your 4/4 kick has some movement to it. An accent on the first kick is the most obvious, signalling the beginning of a bar in imitation of human drumming.

Offbeat hi hats

A 4/4 beat on its own is still pretty lifeless so let's turn our attention to the offbeat to introduce a little life into our groove. Move the cursor down to the Open hi hat and insert four notes on every second eighth position. Setting quantize to 8 on your sequencer ensures you can only enter notes on eighth note positions on the grid. Experiment with different velocity levels on the four Open hi hat notes so your loop doesn't sound completely mechanical.

You now have the basic building block of a house drum pattern. It still sounds a little dull so add some accents on other drum sounds to spice up the basic groove. Placing other drum sounds on the same beats as the 4/4 kick is the most common method of laying the foundations for a groove. Try placing four Closed hi hat notes on the beat and two snares on the second and fourth beats as in our illustration.

Figure 2.1
A basic House groove.

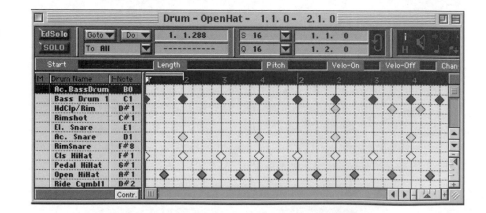

Now you have a basic pattern, copy that over the remaining three empty bars so you can try out some variations. Select all the notes and copy them all. Now move the cursor to the first beat in bar two. Once the Song Position cursor is located at 2.1.0 paste the notes in. You now have two bars of the same loop.

Hand claps

With our pattern copied over two bars it's time to add some fills to define a pattern. Perhaps the most defining sound in House music is the electronic handclap. In our illustration we've added some fills with these at the end of bars two and four. Two bars is the most common length of a musical 'phrase' and fills and breakdowns are often used here to add some variation and define points of movement. This isn't a hard and fast rule of course. Experiment with breaks and fills at various points in your own drum patterns.

Set the Drum editor to loop around bar two by setting the loop indicators to 2.1.0 and 3.1.0. You can proceed to try out some fills with the handclaps as your sequencer cycles the second bar. You'll notice that the first handclap is on the second beat but the next three claps are placed where there are no other drum sounds. It's the spaces between sounds that make music what it is. If there were no gaps between sounds it would all just be noise.

Programming drum patterns is an ideal exercise to learn the meaning of this fundamental truth. When programming drum patterns, always look for the unoccupied slots in the drum grid, as they are your most likely candidates for introducing new grooves. If everything were placed on the beat it would all sound pretty dull and plodding.

Having found a fill that works, select everything and copy it again, just as you did before. Now move the cursor to bar three and paste your first two bars in there. You can now move to bar four and add a little more variation, 'signing off' your four bar pattern. In our example Figure 2.2 only one note has been added. It's an accent note so the velocity value on the snare sound on the same beat has been lowered to push the claps to the forefront at the end of our four bar loop.

Cycle this in the Arrange page and press play. The single note, coupled with the lowered velocity on the snares, adds just enough rhythmic variation to make a more expressive phrase.

Figure 2.2
'Signing off' a loop.

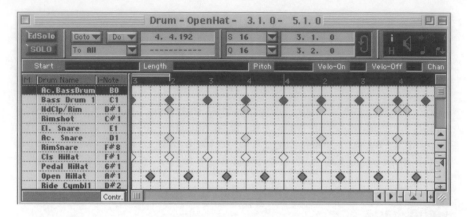

> **NOTE**
>
> *It's a good idea, once you have a loop running which you like, to make a copy of that and then work on the copy to try out variations, otherwise you'll end up with a stunning new loop and will have forgotten how the original was constructed.*

The loop you have is fine as a basic House pattern but will rapidly begin to sound boring unless you add some variations to spice up the basic rhythmic push. It may also be beginning to sound a little slow to your ears by now. What makes any drum track pump along is not really the bass kick thumping away but the hi hat and snare patterns. Ours is fairly four square at present, as only the open hi hat is adding any rhythmic push on the offbeats. Remembering what we said earlier about looking for spaces in a drum pattern as our first choice to add new patterns, let's try adding some side sticks or 'Rimshots' in the spaces between our closed and open hi hats.

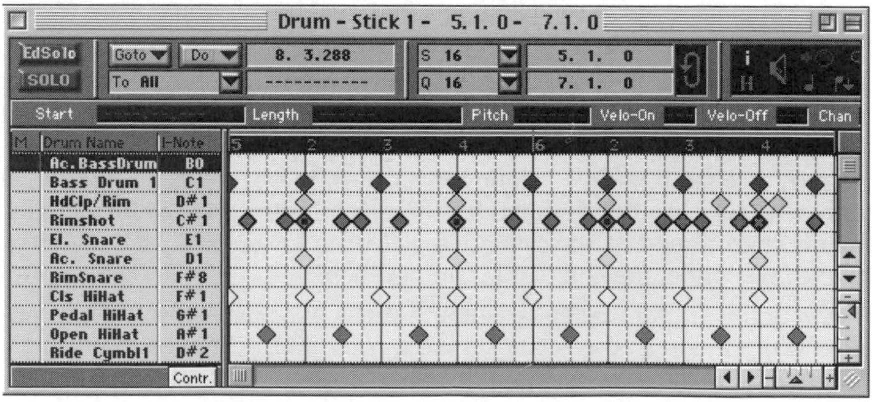

Figure 2.3
A sidestick pattern adds to the House rhythm.

Adding those side sticks has pushed the rhythm along a bit and made our loop a little livelier. We've added some side sticks on the beat as well. Now all we need is to program up a few more fills and variations and we'll be ready to start on a tune.

Making another copy as before, this time of our second loop, go into the drum editor and set the internal loop to cycle around the last bar in this pattern. The figures in the top bar of the drum editor tell us this part extends from 7.1.0 to 9.1.0 so we know that entering 8.1.0 and 9.1.0 here will cycle around the last bar. This is where we want to introduce those little fills and rolls which we can use later in putting together an arrangement.

The first one is perhaps the least obvious but is a device widely used to add interest throughout a track or to mark the transition from one musical phase to another. Just add one bass kick on the last offbeat as shown below, loop and listen. You can experiment with the placement of this kick. It doesn't have to be in the last bar but could work equally effectively in the second or third bars; and it doesn't even have to be on the offbeat but can be placed on a sixteenth beat as we've done in the first eight bars.

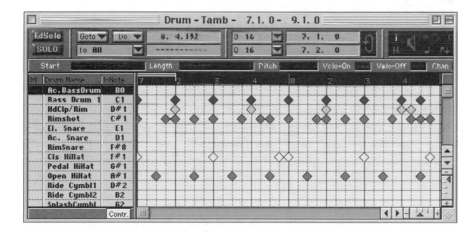

Figure 2.4
An offbeat kick drum signals a change.

You can use this final offbeat kick throughout a tune or simply at points where you want to signal a change from straight bassline accompaniment to the introduction of chords – it's up to you. It's a very simple trick but surprisingly effective. Have another listen to your favourite House tunes and see just how often they use it. Stripping out some of the side stick notes, we've also added in a tambourine to replace the side stick notes that we removed and added more accents to the beat again.

Snare rolls

Snare rolls are a more obvious means of signalling a change and adding those tension-building moments that fill the dance floor. Listening to them you'd be forgiven for thinking 'I could never program that in, only a drummer can play like that' but you'd be wrong.

A snare roll is simply a series of sixteenth notes with building intensity as the drummer strikes increasingly harder on his kit. Velocity is the tool the MIDI musician has at his command to emulate this technique. All you need to do is fill four bars with snares, making each successive beat progressively more intense, using the different velocity levels available.

- Fill the four bars with sixteenth snare notes.

- Ramp the velocity of the notes from nothing to 127.

Figure 2.5
Ramping velocity.

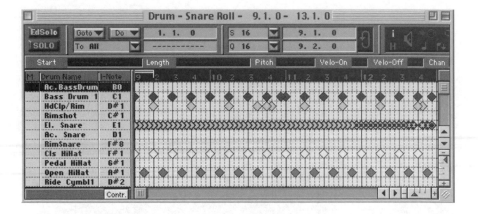

As snare rolls go this one is pretty mechanical, more suited to Techno than House or Garage. In electronic music less is often more. If we look at our pattern and see where we can sculpt away some notes to bring some space back into what is becoming a very cluttered last bar, we can see there are a lot of notes all happening at the same time.

ON THE CD-ROM
This file can be found on the CD-ROM accompanying this book in the following CD-ROM directory: **chapter2/midifiles/drums/house/clubroll.mid**.

We could remove the claps entirely but that would still leave us with a mechanical snare roll and the basis of House is more akin to R'n'B than Techno, so let's hack away at that and make it interact with the claps for a more 'human' feel. There are three accented notes on the last beat in the bar: the kick; one of our snare rolls and a closed hi hat so let's remove that snare note. Now our snare roll sounds pretty realistic and adds a lot more interest to the last bar. Set your sequencer to cycle mode and listen to your efforts so far. Sounds a bit more like a track now, doesn't it?

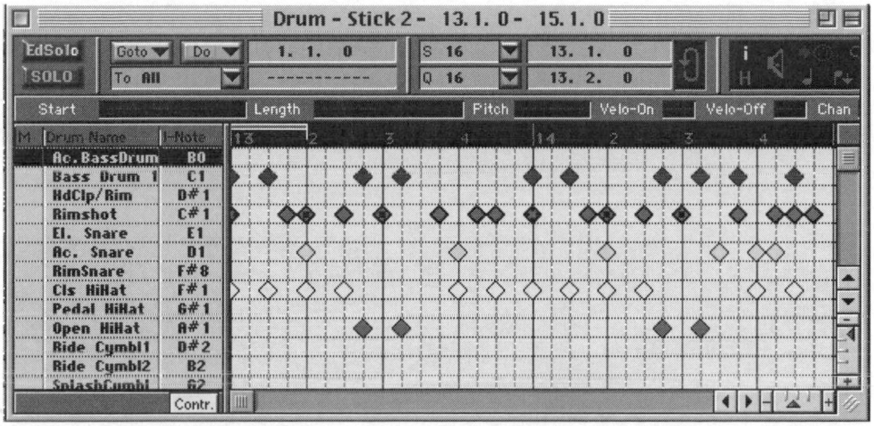

Figure 2.6
A simple breakdown of our groove.

We now have a kicking little House pattern and can start breaking it down. In the next example I've shifted the clap pattern up to the snare voice to make a breakdown of the drum track. The tambourine pattern has been merged with the hi hats to further simplify the rhythm. Then I've sculpted away some of the hi hats to produce a stop-start effect to the rhythm. Finally the kick drum has been thinned out and the notes kicked around to add to the disrhythmic effect. This was all done with copies of the original loops, cycling around four bars and adjusting notes as the loop played until the desired effect was achieved.

ON THE CD-ROM
This file can be found on the CD-ROM accompanying this book in the following CD-ROM directory: **chapter2/midifiles/drums/house/clubreak.mid.**

You've probably noticed how the stick adds its own little pattern that stands out from the rest of the drum track owing to the nature of the sound. The other sounds that add a similar textural relief to House tracks are often to be found in the bongos and congas in your drum kit. These are quite conveniently grouped together in the GM drum map and can be found on the following keys on your synth keyboard:

C3	Hi bongo
C#3	Low bongo
D3	Mute hi bongo
D#3	Mute hi conga
E3	Low conga

This makes it very easy to groove along with them from the keyboard and record a bongo fill 'live' from your keyboard. Recording bits 'live' like this can often bring just enough 'human feel' to make even the most mechanical loop sound grooving. That's what been done to add the final touch to this House breakdown, perfect for a middle section before launching back into the main theme.

Figure 2.7
Conga and bongo fills are easily played live from the keyboard.

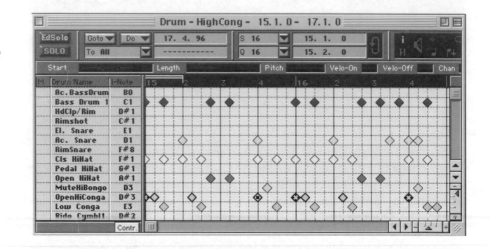

ON THE CD-ROM
This file can be found on the CD-ROM accompanying this book in the following CD-ROM directory: **chapter2/midifiles/drums/house/congas.mid**.

Garage drum patterns

Garage music developed alongside House and Techno and came out of the legendary Paradise Garage in New York; hence the name. From the outset there was a large interplay between House and Garage, most noticeably in the pioneering work of Frankie Knuckles who moved from New York to Chicago in 1977, taking New York disco grooves with him.

Disco is the basis of Garage, and Garage drum patterns are similar in many respects to House grooves. The 'four to the floor' kick drum originated in disco music and many of the features which appear in House patterns, like the use of claps for accents and highlights, made their first appearance in Disco. Garage is distinct from House, however, in its strong reliance on melody and what identifies the best Garage grooves is the strong melodic element in the drum grooves. Cowbells, High and Low Agogos and Bongos are all pulled into play here to produce drum tracks which play a melody all on their own. Often Garage relies on elaborate percussion acting as a counterpoint to simple basslines and sweeping, soaring strings over which the vocal line rides as a heavenly chorus.

Because of the busier percussion of Garage grooves, the offbeat open hi hat that identifies House music is not so much in evidence here. That space is frequently occupied by syncopated bongos and congas. The bass kick too often gets busier, as do the snares, particularly during the chorus when more emphasis is placed on the melody of the vocalist by the drum patterns.

Disco, on which Garage is based, draws its inspiration in turn from funk and soul. Accordingly syncopated patterns are used. If we take our original House groove and move the snares to the right that House pattern suddenly takes on an ever so slightly syncopated feel. In the example below, the first snare has been moved backward in time by three sixteenths while the second snare has moved backwards in time only two sixteenths, or one eighth.

Figure 2.8
Out of the House and into the Garage.

Syncopating the snare works so well some extra closed hi hats have been added to syncopate the closed hi hat pattern, working the offbeats. This gives the groove that 'disco swing'. Now it only remains to add some more swing and develop other percussive fills to give us a set of patterns to manipulate into an arrangement.

ON THE CD-ROM
This file and the following examples can be found on the CD-ROM accompanying this book in the following CD-ROM directory:
chapter2/midifiles/drums/house/ *There are three files,* **houseg01/2/3.mid**.

Adopting the 'filling in the gaps' approach described in the last section you can add other syncopated patterns. In the example below, the swing has been moved on to the fourth beat by adding an Electro snare drum just before the beat. A final accent note has also been added to shift the emphasis forward on the last sixteenth of the second bar. Finally there are some extra beats in the fourth bar. This gives the final bar a little snare roll for a useful accent.

The final touch is to introduce some percussion using congas, bongos or similar. Bongo and conga fills can often be programmed in visually and that's what has been done here, creating a simple visual pattern that actually works very well. If you aren't happy with it simply delete it and try another pattern or play in a live one.

Figure 2.9
Visually program bongo and conga fills to make a pattern.

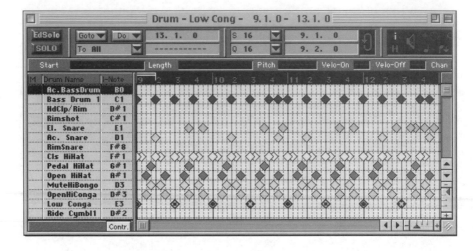

Our loop now has quite a syncopated feel to it. You can keep on in this way, building up a series of variations to provide a series of starting block loops for building your tune. The examples below were all programmed by copying a loop, stripping parts out and adding in percussion. Working this way, you can take any of the new parts you program and marry them to the original loop for further variations. Try the Ride Cymbal pattern with the original loop for instance. The first

Figure 2.10
Strip away some kick drums to break down a groove.

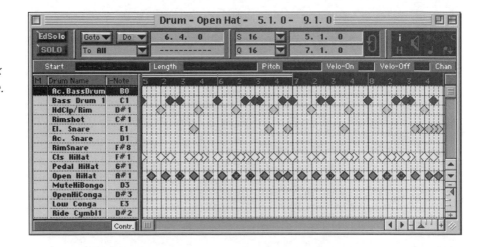

variation provides a simple breakdown, merely by stripping out some of the kick drums and hi hats.

Adding a fast tambourine and some sixteenth bongos plus some syncopated kicks makes for a more rhythmic breakdown.

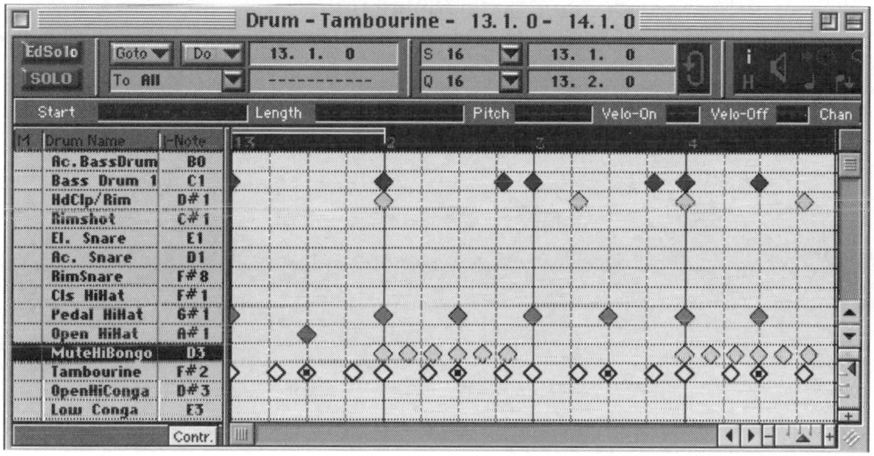

Figure 2.11
Sixteenth bongos.

Finally some snare judders (using the same sixteenths pattern as the bongos above) dissolve into a series of claps for complete rhythmic breakdown.

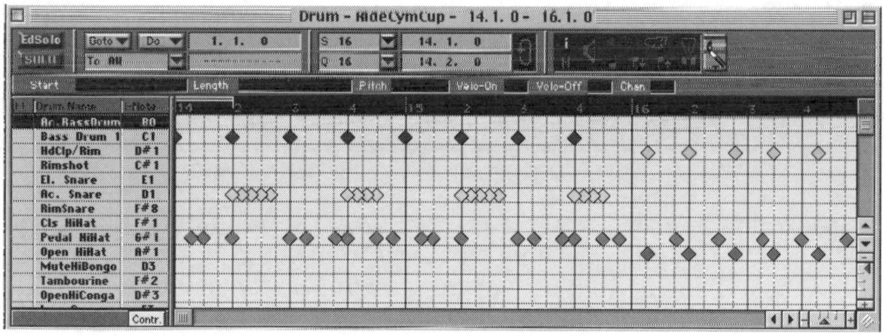

Figure 2.12
Juddering snares.

ON THE CD-ROM
The final two breakdowns here can be found on the CD-ROM accompanying this book in the following CD-ROM directory:
chapter2/midifiles/drums/house/. *There are three files,* **gar_01/2.mid** *and* **gar_fl.mid**.

Programming House basslines

Bass is the heart of the pulsating rhythm of House. The interplay between this and the low pulse of a pumping bassline creates the pulsation in the bass frequencies that emulates the human heartbeat in a lot of dance music. As we're laying the foundations for so much of what follows let's start right at the beginning of the bassline, the walking bassline.

Figure 2.13
A walking bassline is the most basic of basslines.

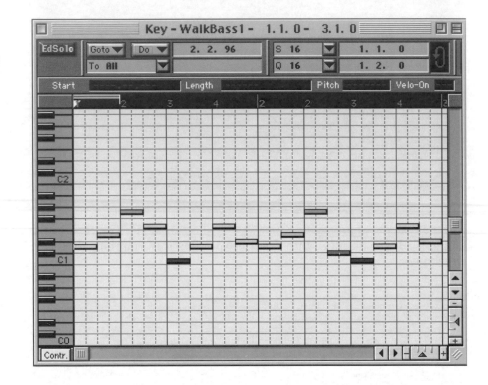

Consisting of a simple 'walk' up and down five semitones, this simple but effective pattern forms both an accent to the bass kick and an offbeat to it. The walking rhythm derives from the third note that doesn't follow the simple pattern of the first two notes with two semitones between them. What would logically be the third note becomes the fourth, giving a slight swagger to the walk. The addition of semitone shifts instead of two semitone shifts lends a slight funkiness to the proceedings at the eighth, twelfth and sixteenth notes. Basic as this pattern is, it provides a fine example of the underpinning role of the bassline in most modern music.

ON THE CD-ROM

The basslines demonstrated here can be found on the CD-ROM accompanying this book in the following CD-ROM directory: **chapter2/midifiles/bass/house/**. *There are four files,* **walkfnk1/2/3/4.mid**.

The trouble with the walking bassline is its static nature. It possesses all the urgency of a quiet stroll down a country lane. House music draws its basslines from a rich heritage of R'n'B basslines of which this is one, but somewhere along the line the bass player started 'leaning forward' into the rhythm and dropping the pitch of a few notes along the way. Funk was born from this shift in emphasis and it is to funk that House, Garage and Techno owe their basslines.

The first thing to do is drop the pitch by an octave of a couple of notes in the pattern. In our example here this has been done on the second off-beat and the fifth beat in the second two bars of the first part, Walkbass2. The second and third beats are good places to start adding twists and shifts to a bassline in House, as the first and fourth beats are often busy with something else. Straight away there's a slight funkiness to the rhythm in the second two bars.

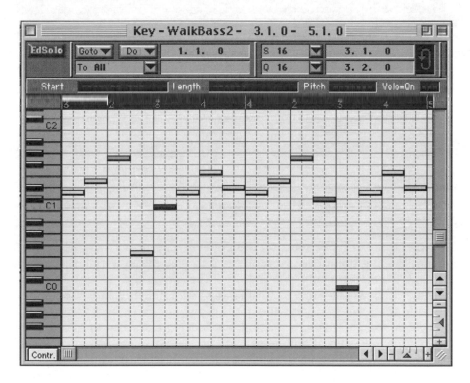

Figure 2.14
Dropping the pitch to raise the funk.

Funking up a bassline

Shorten the notes to sixteenth note lengths, half an eighth, so the part sounds a lot funkier with some space between the notes to allow the rhythm pattern more space in the mix. It only remains to kick some notes around and play with the bassline to see if we can turn that walk into a strut.

We want to make the bassline lean into the beat rather than lope along behind it so we'll move all the notes after the first bar forward in time by 96 ticks or one sixteenth note length. First select all the notes after the first quarter note in the first of our two bars.

Figure 2.15
Lean into the rhythm by moving notes forward in time.

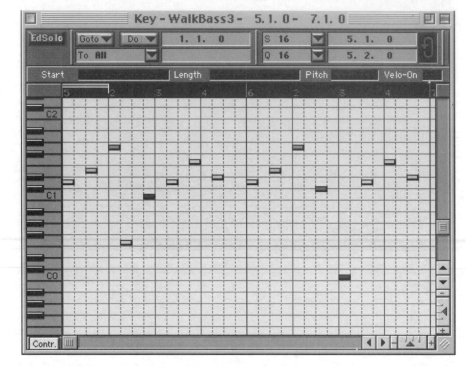

Now drag the notes back on the grid. Moving notes forward in time means moving them backward on the grid – as the time reads from left to right, the closer a note is to the left of the screen the earlier it happens in time. Repeat the process for the second, third and fourth bars and listen to the results. Moving the notes of the last three bars forward has lent an urgency to the bassline that was lacking before and has begun to really funk things up. It only remains to fill in some gaps that have begun to appear in the rhythm as a result of altering the time pattern.

TIP

Looping around one bar at a time is accomplished by setting the cycle function within the editor in the same way as done previously. You can change the loop points as your sequencer is looping, so stepping through the bars of your pattern.

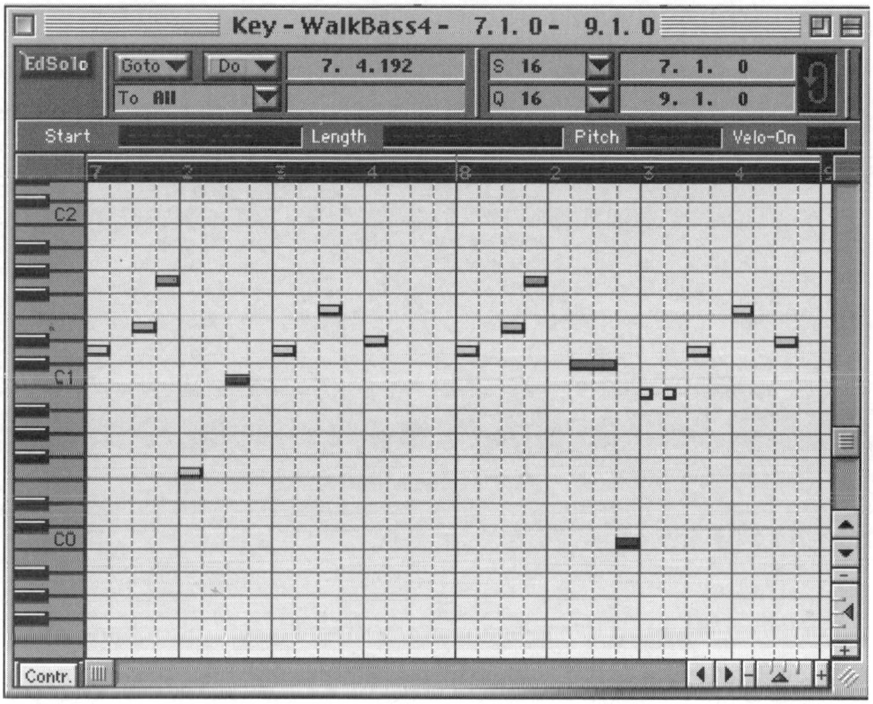

Figure 2.16
From walk to funk in four easy steps.

In our example the pitch of a couple of notes has been altered and their position in time shifted to create a more rhythmic section. You might want to alter different notes than we have changed here; a lot will depend on the drum pattern you're running. The aim is to achieve a syncopated push between the bass and snare pattern and the rhythm of the bass notes.

NOTE

Basses in House tend to move on and around the harmony and can be synth or real type sounds. Original House basses were played by real players so bear this is mind when programming. A good bass sound to recreate is the stopped note. Take a Picked / Fingered bass sound (GM Program 34 or 35).

Shortening certain notes to be half as long again is a useful way of breaking up the bassline and creating more room for the percussion and melody lines to breathe. A live bass player adopts the same practice when he slaps notes rather than plucking or picking them, using the bassline to follow the percussion as opposed to the melody line. Don't forget the velocity of your new notes. They need to be lower than the surrounding notes to create a 'live' feel to your bassline.

Finally you can delete notes to create more room for the percussion parts. House basslines are fascinating things and the main focus of a

House track after the drum and percussion. They are very loosely based on funk basslines from the 60s and 70s but with a lot of the 'widdlyness' taken out, resulting in a cross between the smooth sliding syncopation of the walking bassline we started with and the overtly funky bassline we've ended up with here. Now let's try some more variations.

> **NOTE**
>
> *A good trick when you start to work on a bassline for a House track is to select all the drum parts and the bassline before activating the editor. Then when you go into the editor the drum parts are shown as short notes that you can easily distinguish from the bass notes. With all the notes in view you can get a clearer picture of which bass notes are helping the drum pattern and which are hindering it.*

Making variations

Figure 2.17
In basslines less is often more.

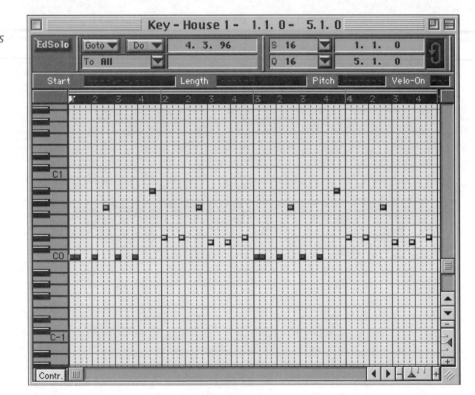

Simplicity is the key to good House music and this example takes the bassline we've already been simplifying and knocks even more out of it.

Instead of five semitones we've now only got four and consequently more use is made of repeated notes. This gives less of a funk feel and more of a House groove to the bassline.

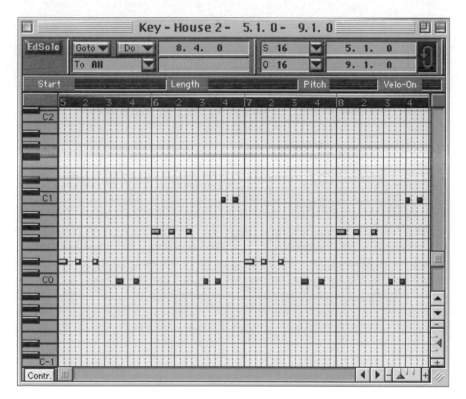

Figure 2.18
Octave shifting to create a melodic and rhythmic motif.

We're getting even simpler here with only three semitones used, albeit with a little pitch shifting on the C note. This gives a rhythmic signature to the end of the each bar. This process is called octave shifting and is often used in both House and Garage. In fact it is the basis of one of the most recognizable basslines used in Disco from which both House and Garage grew. Before we look at that we'll strip this bassline right down to provide a complete House breakdown.

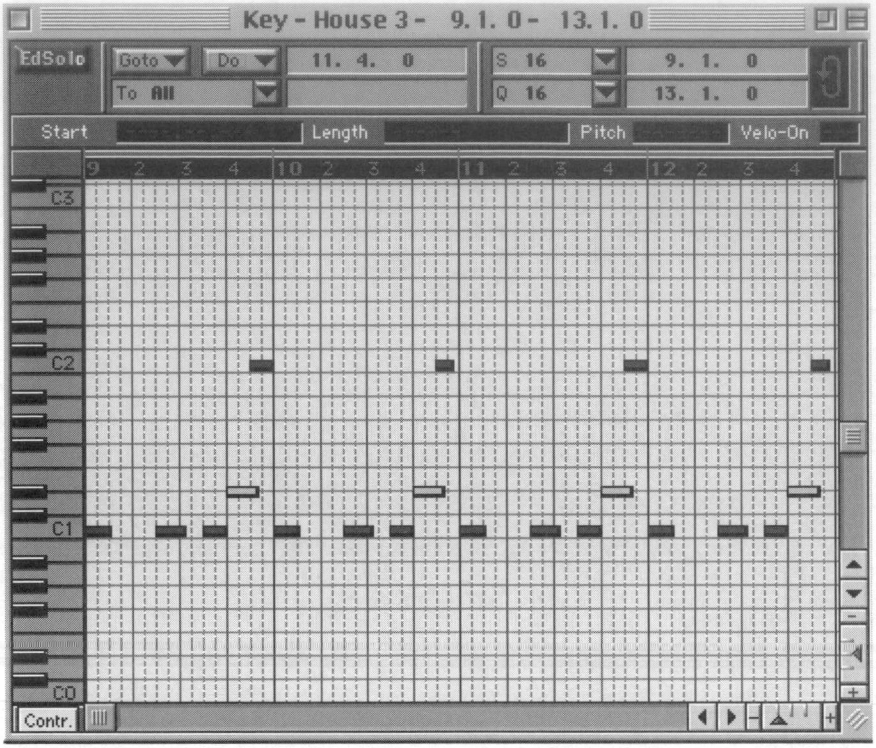

Figure 2.19
Syncopated basslines make more out of even less.

Now we are really getting simple! The notes have been reduced to three semitones only with no octave shifting and, instead of the eighths and sixteenths of the last example, we're using quarter notes. Don't be fooled by their length: they might look like eight notes but there's really two quarter notes here played on beats one and four and three syncopated quarter notes played in eighth positions at beats two and three plus a final syncopated note in the last beat. Using syncopation as our guide we can reduce that even further for the final breakdown (see Figure 2.20).

One note, played on offbeat, or eighth note positions, two to a bar provides as complete a breakdown as you could wish. You may decide to change the bass sound here. Up until now we've been using a picked bass sound but these notes are so sparse it's probably time to introduce some resonance to fill up the spaces we're creating in the mix.

TIP

The more resonant TB303 soundalikes and Moog basses are what you're after here. Synbass 1 and 2 (Programs 39 and 40 in the GM set) are good choices. If you have a GS or XG synth you have even more variety to choose from. I've used an XG variation of Synbass 2 (Bank 40 Program 40) on this bassline for some resonant funk.

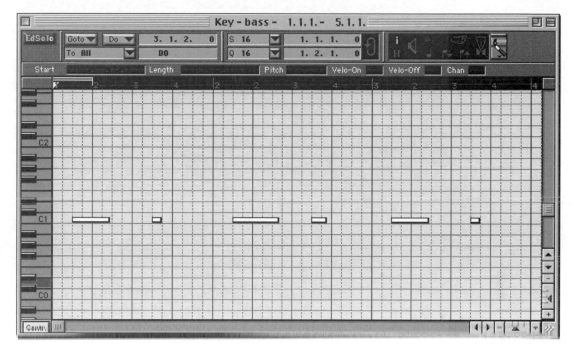

Programming Garage basslines

Garage, in contrast to House, is very concerned with melody, usually the soulful melodies of the Disco classics. The bassline therefore is more often written after the chord pattern, as the progression of the melody will determine the bassline. There are two approaches you can adopt here; play or program a chord or melody line and extract a bassline from that, or program a bassline and then pitch shift sections of it to provide a melodic basis for developing a chord pattern. Both methods can yield interesting results so we'll look at both of them. First let's look at the basic Garage bassline and see if we can work it up into something approaching a tune.

The bassline in Garage is usually a Disco bassline, as that is where Garage draws its prime inspiration. Disco pioneers like Giorgio Moroder developed the octave shifting and one note stuttering basslines and New York added the soulful melodies which resulted in such early disco classics as 'I Feel Love'. Octave shifting basslines are very simple to write but have a beguiling feel which belies their programmed rigidity and the rhythmic pattern they produce is the basis of that most identifiable of all Garage trademarks, the pumping piano riff.

Figure 2.20
As basic as you can get, one note resonates.

Step writing a Disco bassline

> **NOTE**
>
> *Octave shifting basslines have another important effect on synth bass patches too. Many synth bass patches will produce vastly different timbres with each shift of twelve semitones and the alternating timbres add a lot of interest to, and can even become the focus of, a track. The synth and electric bass patches are a good place to start looking for interesting sounds. Synth Bass 2 (Program 40) from the GM set-up has been used here as it has a nice shifting filter frequency dependent on pitch which gives the bassline some movement.*

The basic shifting octave, or Disco, bassline can be easily and quickly entered by the following method:

- Create an empty part one bar long.

- Set 'Snap' to '8' and 'Quantize' to '16'.

- Now go to your synthesizer keyboard and play eight notes alternating between two notes an octave apart.

The result should look something like this:

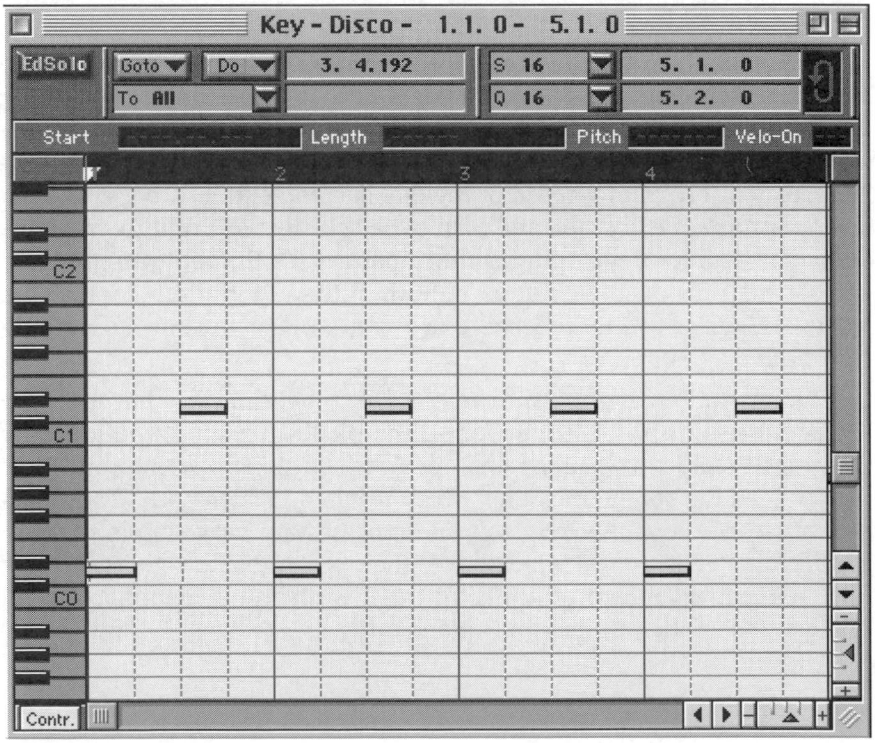

Figure 2.21
The basic disco bassline.

Now make three copies of the bassline you've just recorded, select the second of the four parts you now have and raise its pitch seven semitones. Repeat this for the third bar part raising it by only five semitones and then finally raise the last bar by seven semitones again. Now loop the whole four bars, set the tempo anywhere from 123 to 132 bpm and press play for that Disco fever feeling.

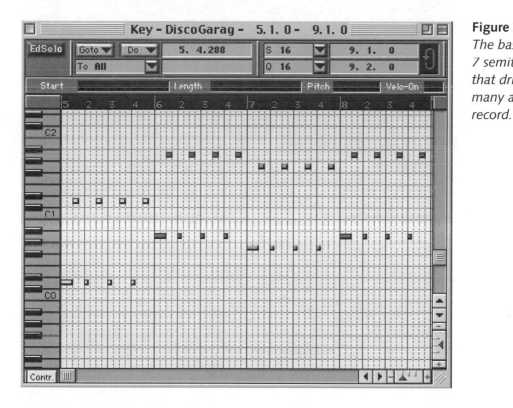

Figure 2.22
The basic 7, 5, 7 semitone shift that drives many a dance record.

This 7, 5, 7 semitone shift is the disco interpretation of a musical pattern, which is used throughout the different musical forms in Western music. Basically, shifts of 3, 5 and 7 semitones produce a harmonic progression from any original notes. Rock and pop music frequently use this 3, 5, 7 pitch progression and if you alter the transposition on the second bar in our example to '3' instead of '7' you will hear the melodic shift which is used in many chart records.

ON THE CD-ROM
The basic Disco bassline shown here can be found on the CD-ROM accompanying this book in the following CD-ROM directory:
chapter2/midifiles/bass/garage/disco1.mid.

NOTE

*The Disco/House/Garage twist on this process of harmonic progression is to
turn the progression back on itself, alternating between a higher and lower
transposition over the last three bars. Stylistically there's an obvious link with the
approach we took to turning the classic R'n'B walking bassline into a funk one,
with the emphasis on lateral patterns rather than the linear progressions
favoured by Rock and Pop. You don't have to stick to the 7, 5, 7 pattern either,
as differing patterns of 3rd, 5th and 7th semitone shifts produce equally usable
melodic progressions.*

Putting Garage into the Disco

The standard, octave shifting bassline we have programmed here suffers
from the same problem we encountered with our walking bassline;
there's no rhythmic movement within the course of its one bar progression. What we need to do to turn what is essentially a robotic,
Euro-Disco pattern into a danceable New York Garage one is to do the
same thing we did to the walking bassline – funk it up.

As we discovered in the previous example, moving the notes in the
second and third bars forward in time produces a leaning into the rhythm
which produces a funky, housed up feel. Using the same method as
before we can start to explore this computer bassline and find the funk

Figure 2.23

*Move the notes
in the second
and third bars
forward to
create some
urgency and
danceability in
the rhythm.*

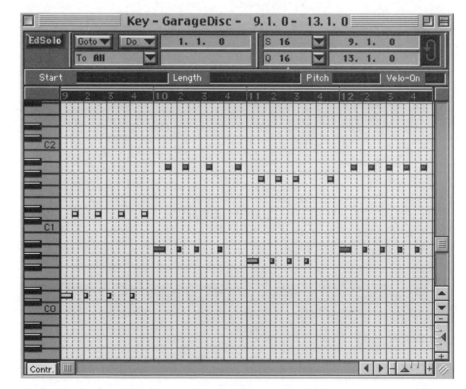

hidden within it. The secret of House, Garage and Techno lies in their marriage of the European electronics of Euro-Disco with the funk basslines of Detroit, Chicago and New York, and finding the funk in the robotic rhythms of Europe is a theme we'll keep returning to.

In the example above, the fourth, fifth, sixth and seventh notes have all been selected and moved forward in time by one sixteenth. Playback reveals that this process has introduced the requisite push to the second bar but the fourth and fifth notes in the third beat now sound decidedly late. These notes are therefore highlighted and kicked forward another sixteenth.

ON THE CD-ROM
These variations on the disco bassline can be found on the CD-ROM accompanying this book in the following CD-ROM directory:
chapter2/midifiles/bass/garage/. *There are three files,* **disco2/3/4.mid**.

Now the first three bars sound all right but moving their notes forward so much has produced a gap in the rhythm. Fill that with a copy of the last two notes you moved forward and see how the whole thing sounds then.

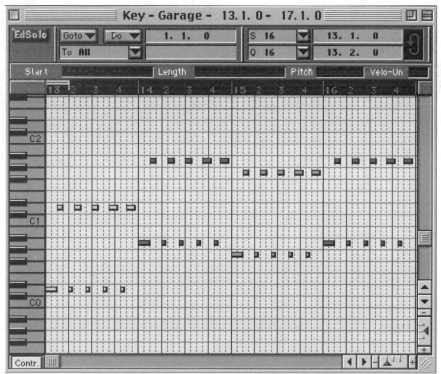

Figure 2.24
Move forward and fill the gaps to funk up the disco.

Already the pattern sounds more like a typical Garage bassline. The two extra notes add a little more movement while shifting the notes in the centre beats forward in time has created that sense of urgency and funky twist to the rhythm which is the cornerstone of danceability. If all the notes were the same length a robotic feel would be impossible to disguise.

In this example the first note has been doubled from its original length to produce a distinct 'twang' from Synth Bass 1 at the beginning of each bar. Playing around with note lengths and velocities is an integral part of programming a good Garage bassline, exploring the different timbres produced as filter frequencies are opened and closed on your bass patch.

You can funk it up even more, of course. Our final example has been raised up an octave for that real high and dry funk bass effect and this works best with a picked or slap bass sound. It couples the walk up and down semitones we first saw in the walking bass with the octave-shifting riff of the Disco bass. Here the octave shift alternates between very short and long notes for that real slap-bass effect.

Figure 2.25
*Slap the bass
for some real
funk.*

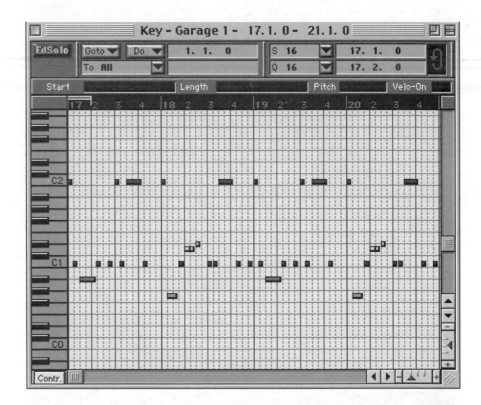

ON THE CD-ROM
This final bassline can also be found on the CD-ROM accompanying this book in the following CD-ROM directory: **chapter2/midifiles/bass/garage/ garage1.mid**.

> **NOTE**
>
> *GM Programs 37 and 38 provide two real dry slapped bass sounds (called Slapbass1 and 2) and work well on basslines like this. You might want a warmer sound, in which case the Finger bass, Fretless or Picked bass sounds (GM Programs 34, 35 and 36) are the ones to try.*

Programming piano parts

Piano sounds play a large part in House and Garage with the piano break from James Brown's '(Get up I feel like being a) sex machine' often used as a template. Once House took a foothold you couldn't get away from this rocked minor piano chord being heard. Here we'll look at producing the classic House and Garage piano riff from our Disco Garage bassline and then apply that to some of the other basslines we've produced so far to produce piano chords with a similar rocked chord effect.

> **NOTE**
>
> *For those James Brown type rocked piano chords try experimenting with adding a chorus effect, either from your tone modules internal effects or from the effects unit on your mixing desks (see Chapter 9 for more about effects and how to use them). Quite a lot of the effect makes the piano sound detuned but this will help add to the style. The rocking effect is created by playing (in eighths) the 3rd and 5th of a chord together and then playing the root. You can then explore other thirds in step with the 3rd's and 5th's or with small jumps.*

Making a piano part from a bassline

Garage is a very melodic musical form, based as it is on soul and Disco. If we now take our bassline and form the notes into chords we will have a melodic riff which can be used to build up an arrangement or simply as a basis to vamp around. Make a copy of the original one bar bass part. If we go into the editor we can see that the bass part is actually two bass lines, one an octave lower than the other. Piano riffs are commonly played using the left hand to play a leading bass note while the right hand follows it playing chords, resulting in a pattern like the one we have here.

First transpose the whole part up to a pitch more suitable for a piano part. One or two octaves higher will give the right sound. Now with the notes in the right octave we can start to make some chords out of the top line of notes. Select them all, then hold down the Alternate key on the keyboard and drag the cursor up three semitones.

When you release the mouse button you should have a copy of the original line of notes three semitones higher in pitch. Repeat the process, this time dragging the notes another four semitones higher. The finished result should look like the screen shot below.

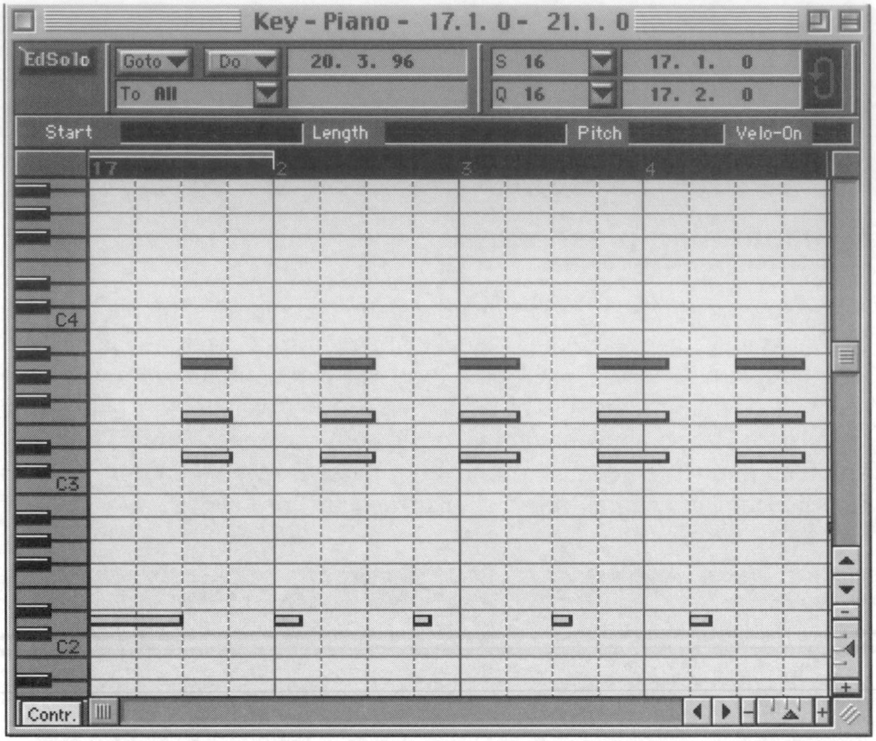

Figure 2.26
The classic garage piano chord pattern.

![Key - Piano - 17.1.0 - 21.1.0 sequencer window showing the classic garage piano chord pattern with notes arranged between C2, C3 and C4](figure-2.26)

This chord pattern is a minor chord progression, with the extra notes forming the chord. If you make copies of this part and transpose them by the same 7, 5, 7 pattern as the bassline you'll have the classic Garage piano which has graced a thousand records. Loop it and listen. Try making an arrangement of the single bar transpositions into other melodic arrangements. You can quite effectively repeat some transpositions for two bars or more and build up interesting basic chord patterns from this.

ON THE CD-ROM
This example can be found on the CD-ROM accompanying this book in the following CD-ROM directory: **chapter2/midifiles/chords/garage/ dpiano1.mid**.

NOTE
*If you want to produce a **major** chord pattern simply reverse the transposition sequence. Transpose the first copy of your bassline up four semitones and copy the next up three semitones and you'll produce major chords instead of minor ones. A chord pattern doesn't have to be all majors or minors and many a hook hinges on that change from major to minor, especially in House and Dream House so remember the golden rule – there, are no rules, experiment freely!*

Extracting notes from a bassline

Now listen to the bassline. It drives the whole thing along and the echoes of it in the bass notes of the piano pattern actually work together to produce some interesting changes in the overall timbres making up the new groove. We can now turn our attention back to the bassline and try simplifying it or even splitting the two basslines we observed in the process of generating the piano part.

Make another copy of the original bassline and drag that to the beginning of the next bar, keeping it on the same track. We're going to separate those two bass lines onto separate tracks.

* Select all the notes below E1 in the editor and execute a 'cut' command.

* Return to the arrange page and create a new part the same size as the original.

* Go into the editor and select 'paste' to place the notes you cut from the original part in this new track.

* You now have two basslines, each playable by a different synth.

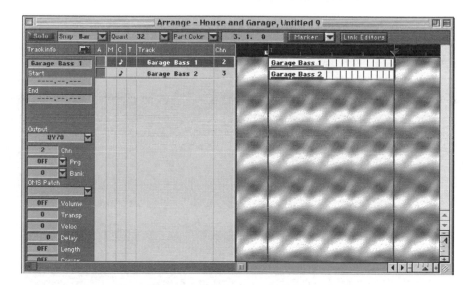

Figure 2.27
A new track and a new part from our original.

Set the output of your new track to a new MIDI channel and try playing back your two new parts together, experimenting with different synth sounds on the new part as your sequencer cycles. You may want to make three ghost copies of the two bass line parts and transpose them in the same manner as we have done for the original bass and piano parts to gauge the full effect of new voices on the second part. Just select the two parts and follow the same procedure as before, remembering to make the transposition adjustments on both tracks.

Depending on the voice you choose for this new part you may also want to transpose it up or down an octave so it stands out from the original bass sound now playing the top notes from our original bassline. This is an entirely subjective matter at this stage; you now have all the basic building blocks of a storming Garage dance floor filler. Before you race off to work up an arrangement let's just look at the reverse process – extracting a bassline from a piano chord pattern.

Taking the bass out of a chord pattern

The opposite process is even simpler; all we need is a chord pattern to start with. The piano pattern we finished the last example with is an easy one to play and you can learn to bang out quite respectable variations of it by playing along with the original while your sequencer cycles. Once you get the rhythm going you can branch out into your own spontaneous improvisations. For the purposes of this next exercise you may want to do that and try our instant bassline method on your new recording. Using a variation of the piano riff we used last time we'll see if this method will yield a new variation on the original bassline.

NOTE
The variation of the piano riff has the same chords but they are moved to form what is known as an inversion of the original chord. In inversions the root note and the next note of the chord are an octave higher than the original while what was the highest note in the three notes of the chord becomes the lowest note in the inversion. This won't affect the bassline as that stays the same but inversions are an interesting way of playing the same chord while adding brightness to a riff. Listen to the whole arrangement and see if you can spot the inversions.

- Take a copy of the piano part and place it on a new track.
- Select the notes of the bassline and cut them.
- Create another new part and paste the cut notes into it.

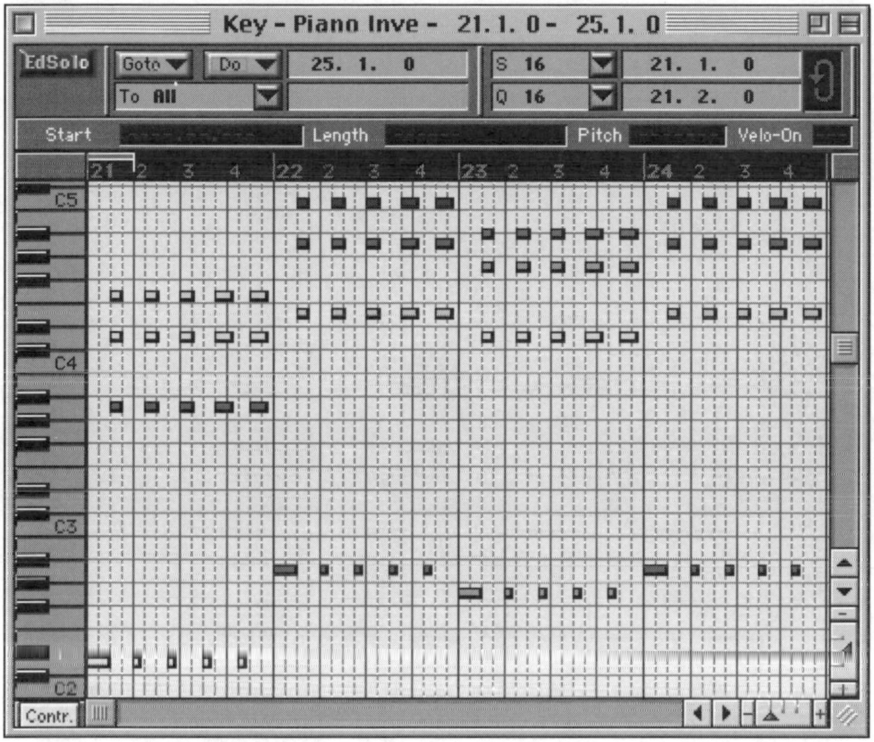

Figure 2.28
The same piano part as before but the chords are inverted.

- Transpose the notes in the new part down 12 semitones or one octave.

- Copy the transposed notes and raise the copies back up an octave while moving them backward in time by an eighth.

Cycle your sequencer and listen to the new bass part. It's similar to the funkified disco bassline but with its own rhythmic pattern.

More rocking pianos

Some more rocked piano chords can be produced from the other basslines we looked at earlier in the House basslines section. These basslines don't feature the same simple octave-shifting pattern and so a little more has to be done to produce those rocked minor chords.

- Take a copy of the bassline and transpose it up two octaves

- Move the notes backward in time an eighth. (Remember backward in time is *forward* on the edit grid)

- Now perform the same three-four semitone copy as we did on the disco bassline.

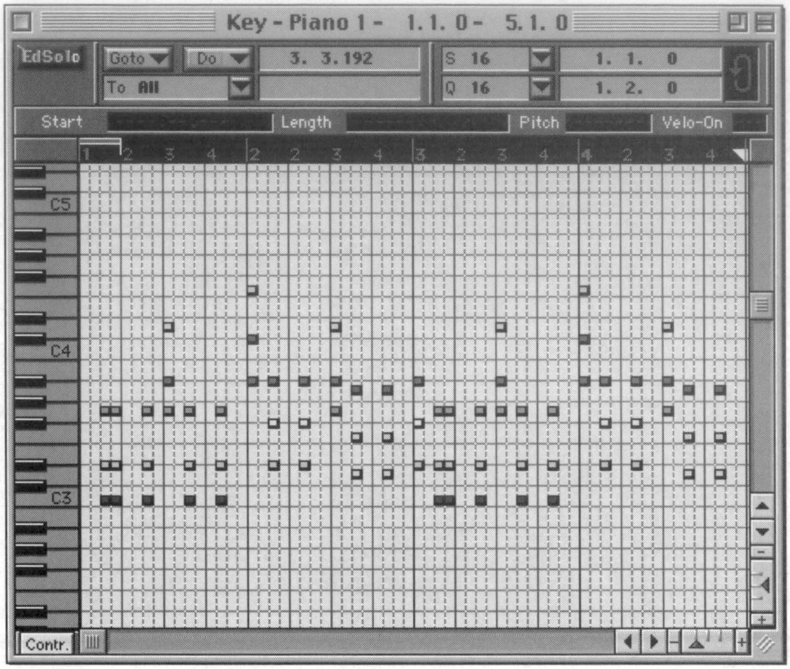

Figure 2.29
Another rocking piano.

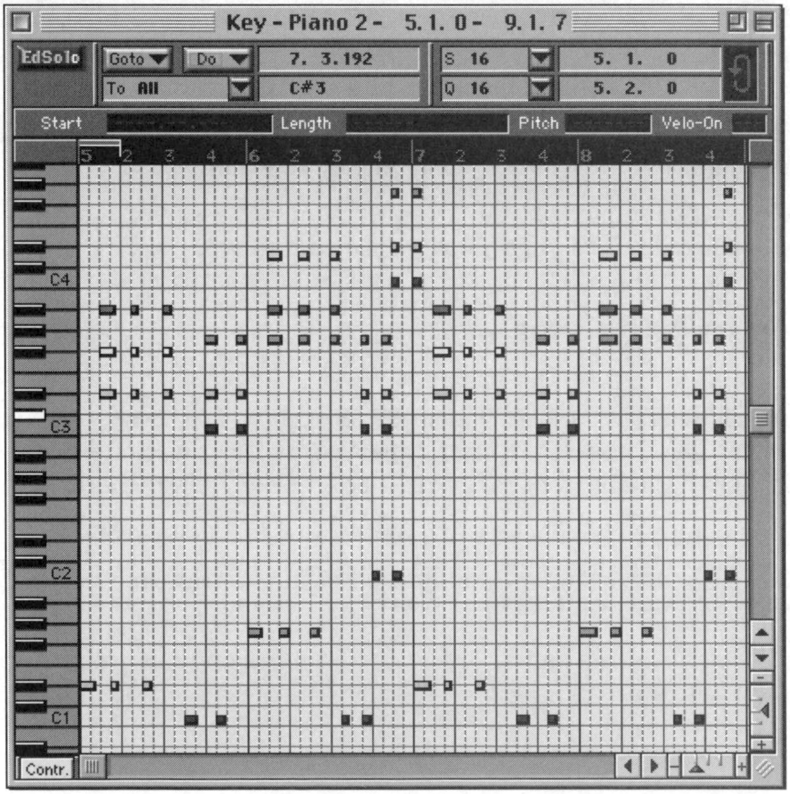

Figure 2.30
A rocking piano with bassline.

In this example I've left the bass guitar to carry the bass line on its own, rocking against the chords. It's entirely up to you whether you do this of course. Sometimes this sounds better; sometimes it sounds more rocking to have the piano playing a left-hand bassline alongside the bass guitar as in Figure 2.30. Let your ears decide.

You can perform the 'rock' the other way of course, playing first the chord and then the bassline as in the James Brown riff mentioned earlier. Simply move the notes forward in time by an eighth as opposed to backward in time from the bassline before adding the transposed notes.

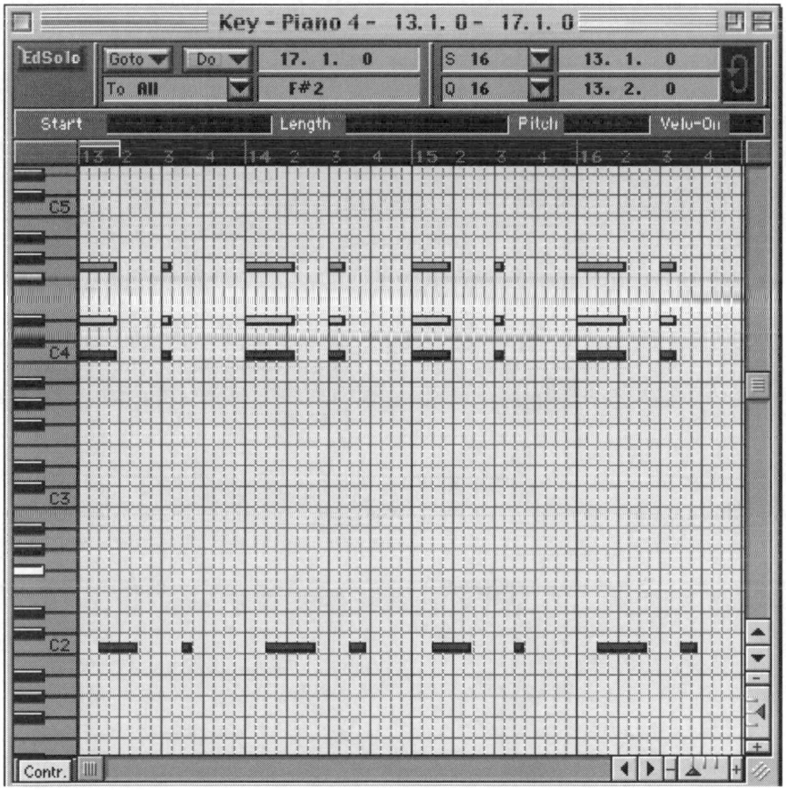

Figure 2.31
Rocking the bassline after the chords.

Finally the funky octave shifting slap bassline which evolved out of that Disco-based Garage bassline provides a real Italian House style piano track. This time the chord notes have been moved backwards in time by only a sixteenth instead of an eighth as with the previous examples. This is because this bassline was much busier and made much more use of syncopated sixteenths than the other examples that relied more on syncopated eighth notes.

Figure 2.32
A busy piano groove for that real Italian House feel.

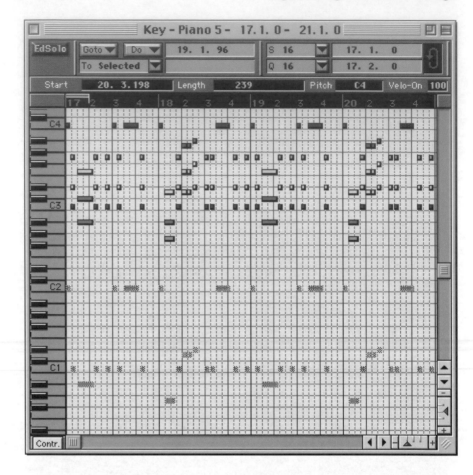

ON THE CD-ROM
These piano grooves can be found on the CD-ROM accompanying this book in the following CD-ROM directory: **chapter2/midifiles/chords/garage/ pgroove1/2/3/4/5.mid**. *Marry them up to the basslines they were extracted from which are all to be found in the following CD-ROM directory:* **chapter2/ midifiles/bass/house/house01/2/3/4/5.mid**.

Arranging a Dream House track

Now that we have a selection of parts and loops it's time to look at producing an arrangement of them all. So far we've been looking at Chicago style Garage and New York style House because that's where it all began. However, House music really took off when it reached European shores and it has developed apace since the early days when Frankie Knuckles first spun Donna Summer tracks over a heavy bass kick. In this section we'll program a track in one of the newest European styles, Dream House.

Viva the Italian Dance music scene! That's the country we have to thank for this particular style. Lots of people are writing Dream House now, as it represents the respectable face of Electronica at the moment. Dream House puts together electronic music production with harmonic and melodic movement: in other words, tracks in this style are more like structured songs with tunes. The music is more aurally accessible, which is why 'Children' shot to the top of the UK charts. The good news is that MIDI gear was *made* for Dream House – almost everything you need for the style nestles in your module's innards (with a little tweaking).

First the drums

By stripping away at the House and Garage drum tracks we've been programming so far we can assemble a few basic building blocks to start playing around with the other parts of our arrangement. In the screen shot below, some of these drum loops have been sampled and looped so we can play around with some basslines. Although we've only been using the sequencer to play MIDI up until now, most modern sequencers are capable of handling digital audio as well. Chapter 8 gives a complete rundown on digital audio, what it is and how to use it, but we'll also introduce the use of digital audio throughout these style chapters and examine the different ways of using it in context.

TIP

Dream House drums are almost exclusively Drum Kit Program Number 26 (Analogue Kit). The patterns used are also quite simple and easy to program, 4 to the floor bass drum, snare and/or claps on the 2nd and 4th beats, open or closed hi hat on eighths offbeats: in other words, a very stripped down version of the House and Garage drumbeats we've already been looking at.

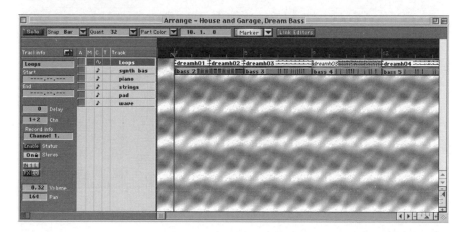

Figure 2.33
Recording MIDI instruments as audio tracks frees up MIDI channels.

What we've done here is record some of the drum loops directly onto a hard drive as two and four bar loops. This frees up MIDI channels on connected modules and allows us to experiment with different drum sounds, layering the sampled sounds with MIDI ones to get just the drum sound we want. Programming electronic music is just as much about programming your synthesizers and layering samples to get the sound you want as it is about programming musical patterns.

TIP

Sampling your own MIDI modules is a good way of freeing up some polyphony or MIDI channels if you're running out of either. You can either just record it straight into your sampler or sound card or direct to your hard drive if you have an audio sequencer as we have done here.

ON THE CD-ROM

The various drum loops used in the construction of this tune can be found in MIDI file format on the CD-ROM accompanying this book. There are various files in the directory: **chapter2/midifiles/drums/dreamho**. *The main riffs are called* **dreamho1/2/3/4.mid** *while the breaks and fills are named* **dreambr1/2/3.mid**. *The audio files can also be found on the CD in the path* **chapter2/samples/drums/dreamho/** *and they share their names with their MIDI file equivalents. Only the extension is different,* **.wav**.

Dream House fills tend to come in the form of fast snare drum rolls that increase in volume towards the climax of the fill, much like the snare roll we programmed earlier in this chapter. The difference is that these can last for up to 16 bars gradually climaxing to send us to the next song

Figure 2.34
Adding excitement to a snare roll with some extra kick drums.

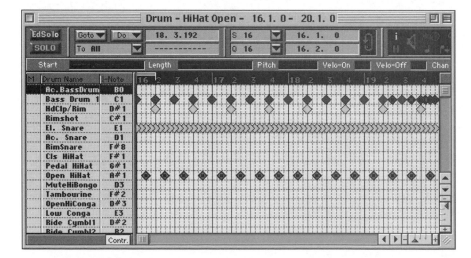

section. Dream House fills often contain crash cymbals and bass drum playing at the same time, also increasing in volume and speed. Our example here uses some extra kick drums to add to the excitement. Try adding some cymbal crashes at appropriate moments to generate even more tension.

A simple bassline

Once you have assembled your drum loops, whether in MIDI file format or audio files or a combination of both, it's time to start working on the melody. Like Garage, Dream House relies on a distinctive melody. There are many ways to achieve this. You may already have a melody worked out, in which case you can start to work out your basslines according to the melody.

Sometimes Dream House bass will play on the eighths offbeat with an onbeat note at the beginning of a phrase. Or maybe the bass will play alternating octaves with the onbeat note quieter than the offbeat. In any case, the bass line will tend to follow the root note of whatever chord is being played above it so that the harmony is never unapproachable. If you don't have a melody line at this stage then you may prefer to work up some basslines first and then jam up a melody from there. Whichever way you work is up to you: remember there is no right or wrong way to write music!

> **NOTE**
> *Dream House basses are synth sounds with lots of resonance so you can tweak the filters as the bassline is playing. On the GM program set these are Program Nos. 39 and 40. If you have a GS or XG kit there are more bank variations which are well worth exploring.*

In the example above, a series of basic basslines have been laid down so that we can start laying down the real meat of a Dream House track; the melody. By laying down a simple bassline you provide a harmonic root to experiment with as you tinkle the ivories. Dream House basses use synth basses so you can tweak the filters as the bassline is playing for breakdowns and to build up to climaxes. In our example an XG sound set has been used and MIDI controllers 71 and 74 have been used which control the sound's resonance and filter cut-off frequency respectively.

> **ON THE CD-ROM**
> *The basslines laid down here can be found on the CD-ROM accompanying this book in MIDI file format. They're in the directory:* **chapter2/midifiles/bass/ dreamho/dhbass1/2/3/4/5.mid** *are the files you're looking for.*

Laying down a melody

The piano sound (GM Programs 1–3) is used a lot in Dream House as the main melody instrument. It doesn't tend to play chords but just single note lines. These are best generated by laying down some basslines, as we have done here, and then vamping around the notes of the bassline an octave or two higher.

The piano sound in Dream House often has an echo of some kind on it, usually onto the next beat. If your module has effects you can set up a delay and experiment with the settings so that the piano themes interfere with themselves pleasingly as the delay acts on them. Try setting this up before you start playing around and see what develops.

> **TIP**
>
> *You can also create MIDI delay using your sequencer's MIDI processor. This is a good idea because it frees up your module's effects processor for some other effect. If your sequencer doesn't have a MIDI processor you can create your own delays quite easily. Select your piano theme, go into your key editor, select all the notes and then copy them somewhere else like the next beat. Then reduce the velocity of those notes by about 30 or 40. Repeat the procedure for multi delays.*

The melody of a Dream House track often has spurts of movement then slower notes. Using sixteenth arpeggios usually creates these spurts. The melody also tends to have small sequences of notes that rhythmically repeat but change notes depending on the chords. You can lay some basic melodies down and work up a chord progression from them or lay down some chord progressions and then evolve a melody from them: once again it's up to you.

Programming string pads

You should have plenty of material by now to start making an arrangement of all the different parts. You might want to add some simple string parts before embarking on that venture though, the chord shifts of the string pattern echoing the chord pattern of the piano riff. This can be very simply accomplished so let's finish off by making a simple string pattern.

- Take a copy of the piano riff you want to use as the basis for a string pattern and move it to a new track.

- Set that track's MIDI channel to a new one and select one of the string patches on your synth or sound card. Now go into the Key editor.

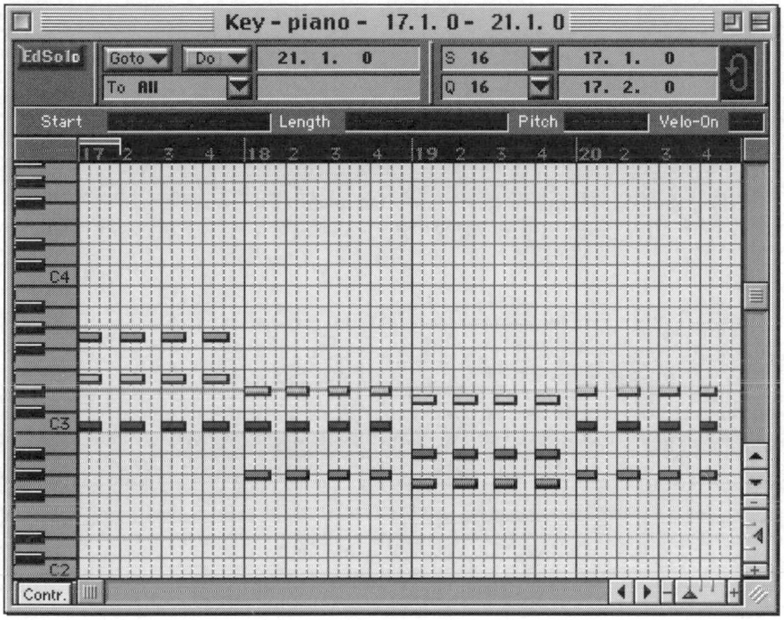

Figure 2.35
A dreamy piano riff changing from major to minor.

- Select all the notes in each bar except for the notes on the first beat. Our chord pattern changes chords each bar, and so what we are doing is leaving those chords that are the first in each change.

- Now delete all the selected notes, leaving a very empty looking pattern indeed. Set 'Quantize' to '1' and activate the 'Quantize' function in your sequencer.

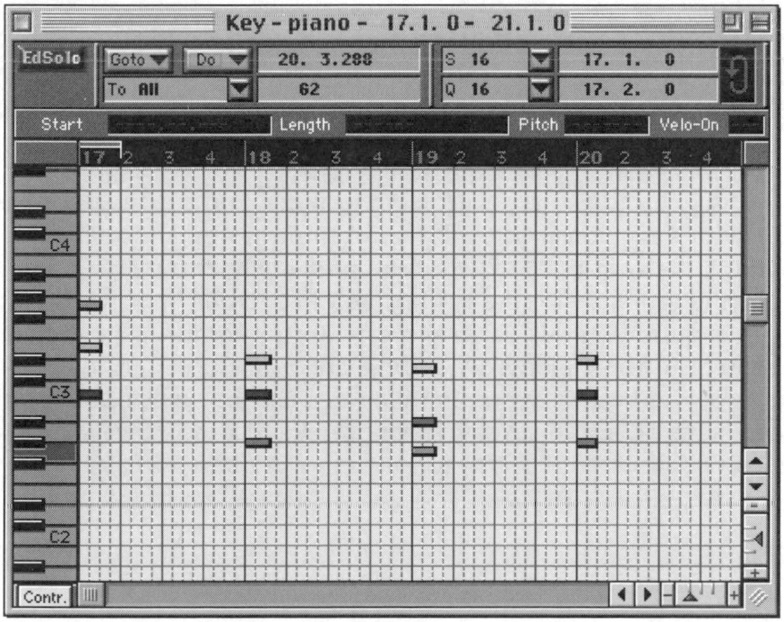

Figure 2.36
The essential chords in our pattern.

- Finally fix the length of the chords at one bar. Now the edit grid is filled with chords, each a bar long, making a very basic string section.

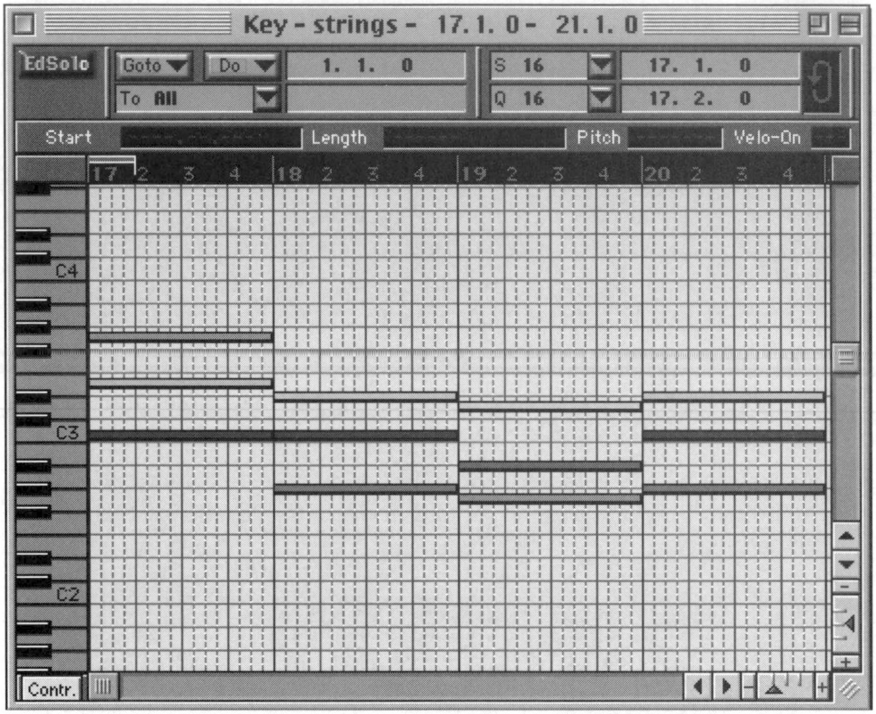

Figure 2.37
With their length fixed at one bar long the chords provide the basic pattern for a string section.

With this basic chord progression in place you can start to experiment with variations, either by shortening notes and kicking them around in the Grid editor as we have previously done for basslines, or by playing around with the riff. In the next screen shot we can see a simple variation on this basic chord pattern introduces an element of movement to the melody. By setting the new string pad to a sharper sound we can hear the variation play against the basic chord pattern. Once you've produced several variations like this, your basic chord pattern can be discarded or kept for use in a very basic breakdown – it's up to you.

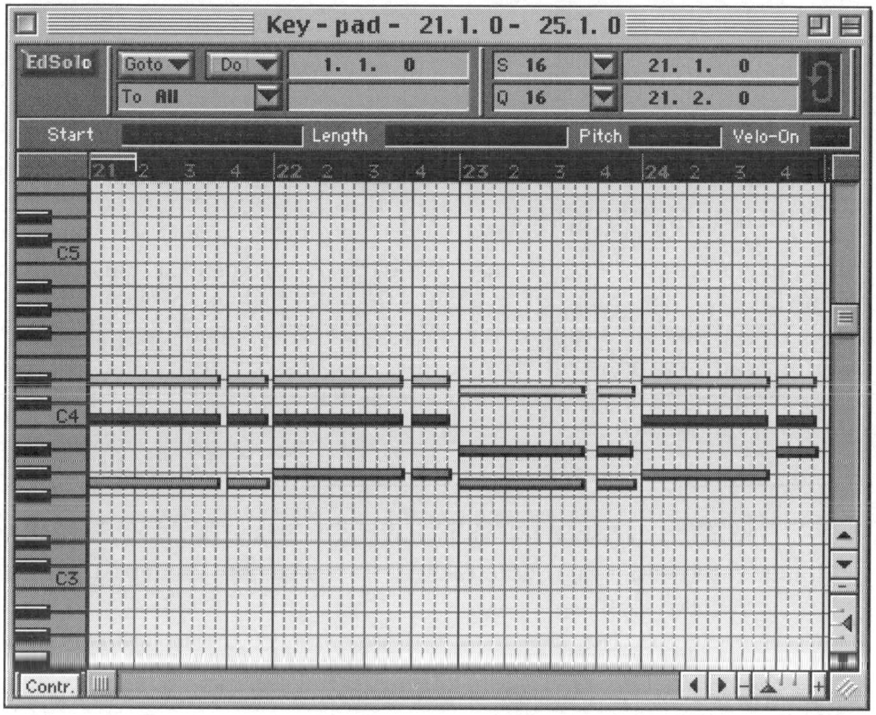

Key - pad - 21. 1. 0 - 25. 1. 0

Figure 2.38
Subtle variations make all the difference when programming string pads.

ON THE CD-ROM
These two string parts can be found on the CD-ROM accompanying this book in the following CD-ROM directory: **chapter2/midifiles/chords/dreamho/dreamp2/3.mid**.

TIP
Frequently used chords in Dream House include 1sts, 4ths and 6ths (e.g. in the key of C minor: Cm, F (major or minor) and A flat respectively). Chords with common notes are often played in succession giving an evolving feel to the chordal progressions, thus in C minor the 1st chord would be C minor (C, E♭, G) then A♭ (A♭, C, E♭, often keeping the G) then Fm7 (F, A♭, C, E♭).

NOTE
Pads and string sounds are used a lot for the chords, so try to choose a sound with some movement e.g. Sweep Pad (GM Program 96) or variations on this.

You can of course reverse the process we've used here and generate these chord sequences first then spin out basslines and melodies from the pad sequences. Many House producers actually prefer to work this way, laying down a basic chord sequence using a drifting pad sound, then working up melodies and basslines over that. As ever, it all depends on how you feel most comfortable working. Sometimes you may begin by playing a chord sequence that inspires you, other days it may be a bassline that fires your imagination. The key is to keep an open mind.

Synthesizer arpeggios

The final element in Dream House writing is the synthesizer lines. These can be little phrases/tunes or arpeggios that add feel and movement to a track. Arpeggios are simply the notes of a chord played one after the other instead of together. If your sequencer doesn't feature an arpeggiator to produce these for you, simply take a chord track and follow the procedure below.

- Reduce all the note lengths to sixteenths.

- Move the second note of each chord forward in time by one sixteenth.

- Similarly, move the third note forward two sixteenths and you have a basic arpeggio.

Figure 2.39

A basic arpeggio

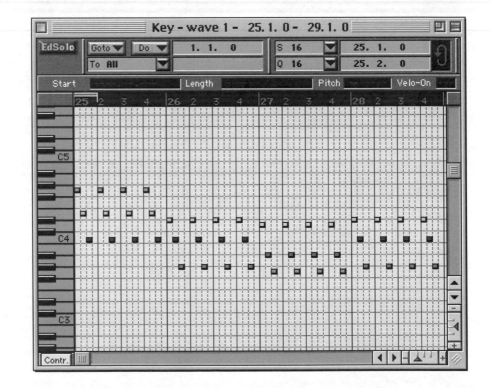

Once you have the basic arpeggio laid down, try experimenting with other note lengths to get the sound you want. Sixteenth triplets, 32nds or even 32nd triplets will work well, depending on the synthesiser patch you are using.

NOTE

If you start from the highest note in the chord you have a descending arpeggio as in our example. Conversely, if you start from the lowest note, you have an ascending arpeggio. Introduce rhythmic and harmonic variation by repeating and/or adding notes.

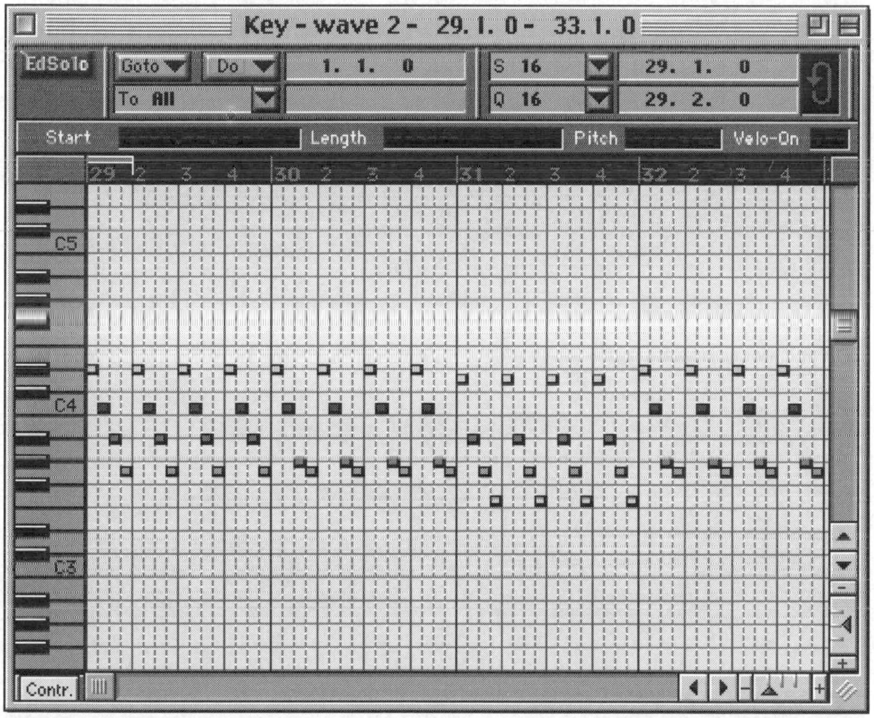

Figure 2.40
House and Garage/Dream bass/arpeggio 2. Rhythmic and harmonic variations transform a simple arpeggio to a melodic feature.

ON THE CD-ROM

These arpeggios can be found on the CD-ROM accompanying this book in the following CD-ROM directory: **chapter2/midifiles/seqs/dhseq1.mid** *and* **drmarpi.mid**.

TIP

Sounds used should be taken from Programs 81+82 plus bank variations if possible. Make sure you put some real time filter/panning/volume changes in to add movement.

Putting it all together

Once you have all the basic elements of your track, chord sequences, basslines, melodies and drum loops, it only remains to put them all together in a mix. Different sequencers offer various ways of working and it is a matter of finding the way that works best for you. The basic principle remains the same, however, lining up a series of looped sections and chopping and changing between them to build up an arrangement in much the same way as a DJ cuts between records to produce a mix.

In the screen shot below we see a basic arrangement laid out on Cubase's arrange page. This approach is what is known as linear sequencing and may be the approach you prefer if you already have a rough idea of the way you want to put all your different parts together.

Figure 2.41
The 'building block' approach to laying out an arrangement.

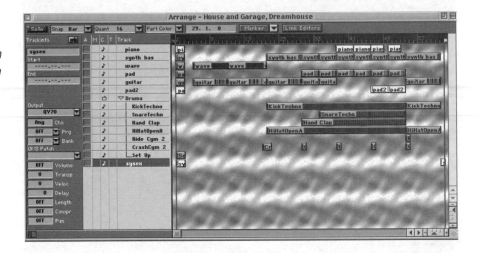

ON THE CD-ROM

This final arrangement can be found on the CD-ROM accompanying this book in the following CD-ROM directory: **chapter2/midifiles/songs/dreamh.mid**.

Some sequencers let you view all your assembled loops as a list and move the various loops about from there. This has the same effect as moving parts on an arrange page but is another way of experimenting with the arrangement of the various parts. Many dance producers favour this approach, as it is more intuitive. Once again it's entirely up to you. In Figure 2.42 this has been set down in Emagic's Logic.

```
┌─────────────────────────────────────────────────────────────┐
│ □                    From DREAMY.MID#2                   ▣ 冒 │
├─────────────────────────────────────────────────────────────┤
│ ▣ Edit Functions View                                 ◄▣▶   │
│             POSITION        NAME        TRACK   LENGTH    △  │
│ 人 ⇧      ------------- Start of List -------------        │
│            1  1  1  1 piano1        10   8  0  1   0        │
│ ▨ ⇩       1  1  1  1 synth bass1   11   8  0  1   0        │
│ ▭         1  1  1  1 wave1         12   8  0  1   0        │
│ IN  OUT    1  1  1  1 pad1          13   8  0  2   0        │
│ ♪ 88      1  1  1  1 guitar1       14   8  0  2   0        │
│            1  1  1  1 pad2          17   4  0  1   0        │
│ ┋ ┇       1  1  1  1 Set Up        25   1  0  0   0        │
│            1  1  1  1 sysex         32   1  0  0   0        │
│ ▨ ▨       5  1  2  1 pad3          17   4  0  1   0        │
│ SYS UUT   9  1  2  1 piano2        10  43  3  3   0        │
│ EX  011   9  1  2  1 synth bass2   11  53  3  3   0        │
│ ◥ ◤       9  1  2  1 wave2         12  12  3  3   0        │
│  S M      9  1  3  1 pad2          13  44  3  2   0        │
│            9  1  3  1 guitar2       14  52  3  2   0        │
│ Q         9  1  3  1 pad4          17  45  3  2   0        │
│ /16      21  1  1  1 CrashCym 2    24  34  0  0   0        │
│          22  1  1  1 KickTechno    19  40  0  0   0        │
│          22  1  1  1 HiHatOpenA    22  40  0  0   0        │
│          30  1  1  1 Hand Clap     21  24  0  0   0        │
│          30  1  1  1 SnareTechn    20  20  0  0   0        │
│          54  1  1  1 Ride Cym 2    23   1  0  0   0        │
│          ------------- End of List -------------    ▽      │
│                                                             │
└─────────────────────────────────────────────────────────────┘
```

Figure 2.42
Logic audio/mix list.

Most hardware and many software sequencers also let you assign sequences to a MIDI key so you can call up a loop from your MIDI keyboard and 'play' your arrangement into being. In the screen shot below you can see this in Opcode's Vision.

```
┌─────────────────────────────────────────────────────────────┐
│ □ ▽                         DREAMY                       ▣ 冒 │
├─────────────────────────────────────────────────────────────┤
│ ⇕ •   Name      Key        MIDI      References    Comments  │
│ ▽ Sequences                                                  │
│ • DREAM 1      A    ♪ C1      DX11    11    INTRO            │
│ • DREAM 2      B    ♪ D1      DX11    11    MAIN THEME       │
│ • DREAM 3      C    ♪ E1      DX11    11    VARIATION 1      │
│ • DREAM 4      D    ♪ F1      DX11    11    GUITAR THEME 1   │
│ • DREAM 5      E    ♪ G1      DX11    11    GUITAR THEME 2   │
│ • DREAM 6      F    ♪ A1      DX11    11    PIANO THEME 1    │
│ ▷ DREAM 7      G    ♪ B1      DX11    11    PIANO THEME 2    │
│ ▷ Segments                                                  │
│ ▷ Templates                                                 │
└─────────────────────────────────────────────────────────────┘
```

Figure 2.43
Vision sequence window.

You could also record everything as an audio loop and trigger the resulting loops from your MIDI keyboard to record the result 'live' straight to your hard drive, DAT or simply as a MIDI arrangement. Whichever method you choose is entirely up to you and the limitations of your studio set-up. Whatever you choose, remember to have fun!

We've now studied how to program House and Garage drum loops and then add basslines to them. You should by now be familiar with creating a bassline from a chord sequence and with the converse, creating a chord sequence from a bassline. The relationship between chords, basslines and arpeggios should also now be clear to you if it wasn't already and you should, by now, have discovered an optimum method of working within your personal studio set-up. In the next chapter we'll delve further into the depths of synthesizer programming as an integral part of sequencing as we look at the intricacies of programming Techno and Trance.

3 Programming Techno and Trance

If everyone was confused about what House music really was, the arrival of the term 'Techno' created even more confusion. Some claim that all electronic music is Techno music because it is technological in origin, while dance aficionados point to House, Garage and Acid as being forms of Techno. Techno purists would scoff at this latter claim, regarding Techno as a development from those earlier forms.

The truth lies somewhere in the middle of all this confusion as House, Garage and Techno developed simultaneously. People like Derrick May and Kevin Saunderson produced classic House tracks like 'Rock to the Beat' and 'Strings of Life' even as they were recording pioneering Techno tracks like 'The Dance' and 'The Groove That Won't Stop'.

The uniting factor remains the love of space age funk like George Clinton and European electronic music like Kraftwerk. The early Detroit and Chicago pioneers were united in exploring the marriage of these two forms. Where Techno emerged was in exploring the process of stripping something back down to the simplest elements, and seeing just how far you could take this process while keeping the groove intact.

Trance and Techno are respectively the oldest and newest forms of Electronica and are very similar in terms of instrumentation and style. In fact Techno has been an umbrella term for various dance music styles since the early Detroit days. Trance developed in Europe and grew out of Eurobeat, which tends to be a faster style with lots of energy while Techno is more sonically experimental, but now styles have split into the other categories discussed throughout this book.

In this chapter we'll look at programming the basic building blocks, drum patterns, basslines, melody and chords. Finally we'll put together a Trance track to examine how all the pieces work together and look at how Techno programmers develop a track.

NOTE

Techno and Trance use mostly synthesized sounds, which is good news for MIDI programmers. Older analogue gear is also used a lot in Techno music so bear this in mind when selecting sounds.

Programming Techno drums

In this section on programming Techno drum patterns we'll look at the early patterns, originating in Electro, then their evolution to Old School Techno and modern, minimalist Techno. Next we'll look at the evolution of breakbeats to the faster Eurobeat style and finally we'll look at the drum grooves used in the most upfront of Techno styles, Trance.

Electro

As House and Garage have their roots planted firmly in Disco so Techno owes its origins to Electro, that sci-fi mix of breakbeats and munchkin voices which had a whole generation spinning on squares of linoleum in the phenomenon known as break dancing. Breakbeats take their name from the 'breakdown' employed by drummers to signal a change in pace in a song. They do this by simply omitting beats from the regular pattern thus 'breaking down' the groove.

ON THE CD-ROM

You'll find a selection of Electro grooves on the CD-ROM accompanying this book in the following directory: **chapter4/midifiles/drums/electro/ electro1/2/3.mid**.

TIP

Because Techno is so groove-based far more use is made of breakdowns and breakbeats as a main groove rather than just a fill, as in House or Garage. If you've been programming your own House and Garage grooves after reading the last chapter, you may want to experiment with 'breaking down' some of those grooves to provide your own breaks.

Because Techno ignores traditional song structure, attention is focused far more on the beats. This approach requires the use of a lot more breakdowns to prevent a track becoming monotonous and led to the invention of 'breakbeats' where a string of breakdowns are played end on end rather than simply once every 4, 8 or 16 bars. **electro1.mid** is a good example of this.

This groove shifts the second kick forward a sixteenth before the beat has broken up the foursquare kick pattern. The third and fourth kicks have been moved a sixteenth later, after the beat, and doubled notes have syncopated the beat in the third beat and at the end of the fourth bar. This is far more rhythmically dynamic than the simple four/four kick that House and Garage are based on.

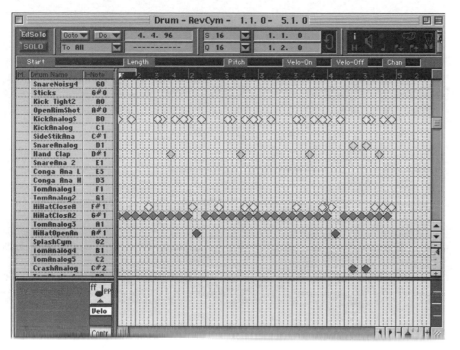

Figure 3.1
A classic Electro groove.

> **NOTE**
> *Techno drum sounds are almost invariably TR 808/909 type sounds (Drum Kit 26, often called Analogue Kit by non-Roland programmers). Some tinkering with the drum sounds may be needed to produce a nice punchy sound so experiment. If you have an XG module there are two variations, Analogue 2 (Program number 27) and Dance Kit (Program number 28) which are versions of the Analogue kit with punchier kicks and snares already programmed for you.*

Old school

Old school Techno grew straight out of these Electro beats, upping the tempo and stripping the beats down to even more basic grooves. Our next example is a straightforward Techno groove that clearly shows its Electro origins. Once again the four square kicks are gone, with two beats on the first and third bars only, followed by syncopated kicks on the first eighth and third eighth in the first bar. The second bar breaks the groove down even further with only two kicks, one on the first eighth and another right at the end of the bar on the last sixteenth.

In this groove the snare is carrying the rhythmic weight, falling on the second and fourth beats and shifting the emphasis back on the beat. A simple sixteenth hi hat pattern provides the ticking, mechanical rhythm that so often identifies a Techno track and is a direct link to early Kraftwerk grooves.

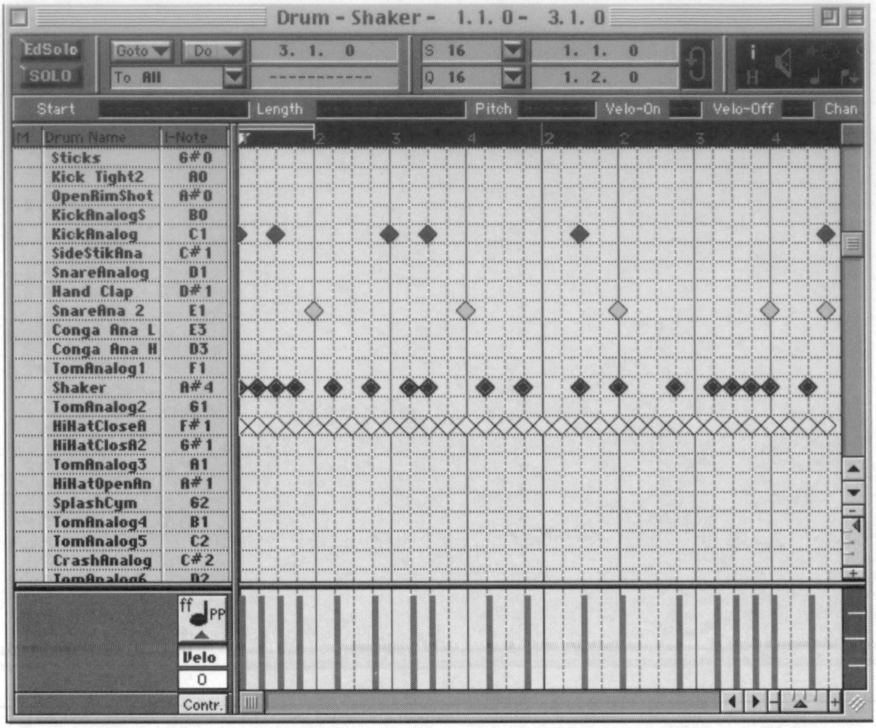

Figure 3.2
Old Techno grooves use mechanical rhythms.

ON THE CD-ROM
You'll find these old school Techno grooves on the CD-ROM accompanying this book in the following directory: **chapter3/midifiles/drums/oldtechno/ drums/oldtechno/oldtec01/2/3.mid**.

This leads nicely into a more familiar four/four groove like our next example. Here only the ticking hi hat remains to carry forward that old Techno feel and the four square kicks have returned. The ticking hi hat is broken up by deleting a couple of notes in each bar and replacing them with open hi hats, introducing some syncopation to the essentially robotic groove. Claps on the second and fourth beats provide the classic dance groove.

TIP
If all the notes in a hi hat pattern like this are of the same velocity, everything starts to sound pretty monotonous. You can vary the velocity on each note in your sequencer's Drum or Grid editor. There may be a Randomize function to do this on a selected range of notes.

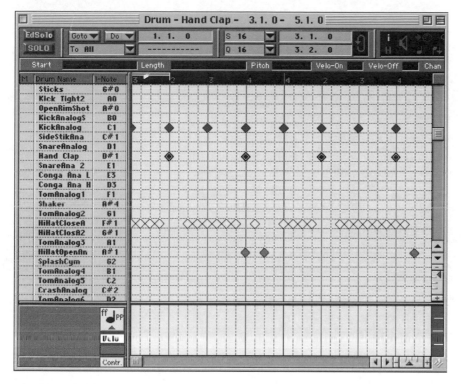

Figure 3.3
*Four to the
floor for a
classic Techno
groove.*

Our final old Techno groove returns to a more syncopated Electro feel. There are only three kicks over two bars, the first on the beat at the beginning of bar one, the second on the third eighth and the final one on the same position in the second bar. What carries the beat here is, once again, the snares on beats two and four. These are accented with claps as well to emphasize the rhythm. The ticking hi hat is similarly supplemented with a shaker shuffle of four sixteenth notes starting on the first and third beats (see Figure 3.4).

TIP

Don't just stick to the 808 and 909 kits: experiment with electronic and other drum kits in your tone module. They're all electronic drum sounds after all, even if they do purport to be jazz, rock or something else. As long as they sound metallic or robotic they're perfect for Techno.

Modern Techno

Modern Techno has evolved into an extremely minimal beast with very sparse beats underpinning even barer bass and melody lines. These beats are often used in the other styles as raw Techno tends to be a development ground for new beats and many of the grooves heard in minimalist

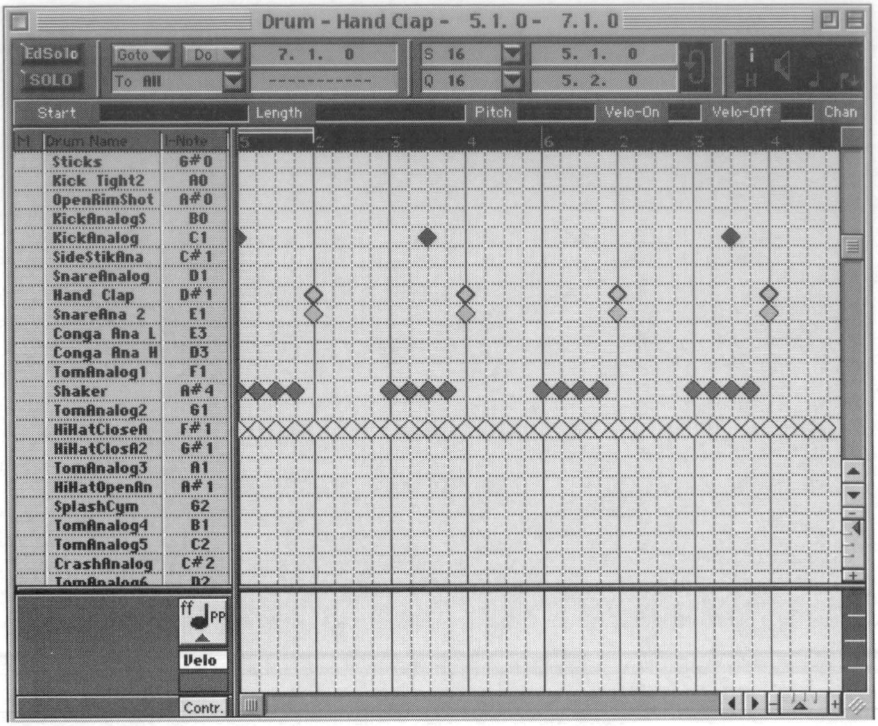

Figure 3.4
*Minimalism is
the heart of
Techno.*

Techno find their way into Eurobeat and Trance, usually with more
beefed up drum sounds and busier percussion elements.

TIP

*Once again our old friend GM program number 26 is the first drum kit of choice
for this minimalistic style. Some of the more basic GM machines may leave this
out so you may need to look elsewhere. If you have old analogue machines or
samples of machines like the Korg KPR 77 or Roland CR78 try loading them
into your sampler and playing these loops using them.*

Our first example is the classic Techno beat, and this pattern has
found its way into virtually all styles of dance music, especially Trance.
The feeling of fast movement it generates gives any track it's used in an
urgency that translates well to the dance floor.

The basis of the beat is immediately recognizable. The four square
kick supported by snares on beats two and four should be familiar by
now as the basis of most dancefloor styles. The urgency in this groove
comes from the hi hats – two sixteenth closed hi hats starting on every
beat, leading to an open hi hat on every eighth. This simple hi hat pattern
seems to zip along at whatever tempo you play it and immediately ups
the apparent speed of a simple four/four kick.

Figure 3.5
The classic Techno drum pattern with fast hi hats.

ON THE CD-ROM
You'll find these Techno grooves on the CD-ROM accompanying this book in the following directory: **chapter3/midifiles/drums/techno/techno1/2/3.mid.**

Breaking it down, as in our next example, does little to remove that sense of urgency but does introduce some space into the beat. This is simply accomplished by removing or muting the closed hi hats of the previous groove, leaving the offbeat open hi hats to carry the rhythmic push. Little variations in the kick beats, an extra beat on the eighth of beat four or the last sixteenth of a bar provide just enough rhythmic variation to prevent the beat from becoming totally monotonous.

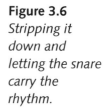

Figure 3.6
Stripping it down and letting the snare carry the rhythm.

Our final example introduces a spacier feel by the simple stratagem of using the ride cymbal instead of open hi hats, and spacing out the pattern from the close knit one used for the closed hi hats. The kick stays the same and the snare is changed to a clap on beats two and four. The spaciness of the ride cymbal sound works well with a more open rhythmic pattern like this and complements the simple percussion of the accompanying toms.

Figure 3.7
Ride cymbals introduce a spacier feel.

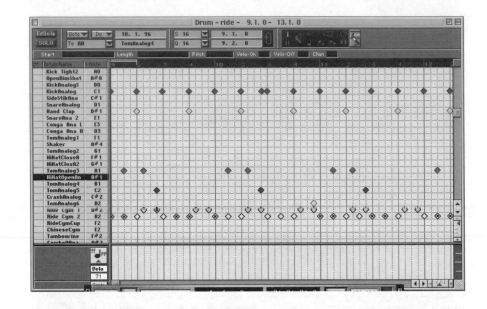

TIP

Try revoicing elements within drum patterns onto other drum sounds or even a synth sound or bass patch. The essence of Techno is using mechanical sounds to catch that futuristic feel and you'll find many a weird and wonderful robotic ping coming from the unlikeliest sounding synth patch. Experiment, experiment and experiment some more – that's Techno.

Eurobeat

Often derided as the cheesy face of Techno, Eurobeat takes the basic Techno beats and speeds up the tempo, starting at 145 beats per minute. Our first example demonstrates how this change of tempo means that a minimal beat can be made even simpler yet still retain its essential momentum.

Here we have the same pattern as our first Techno beat but with the second of the two sixteenth closed hi hats deleted. Because the tempo is faster we don't notice this absence and the beat sounds very similar to

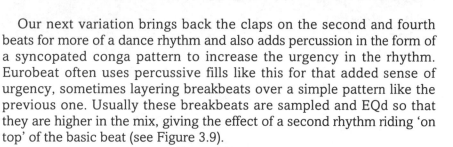

Figure 3.8
An increase in tempo and a decrease in hi hats.

the original Techno groove. Notice the other very simple accent used here: an analogue conga on the first beat in every bar. This adds a resonance to the first kick beat in every bar and helps to introduce some sonic variation to a very basic drum pattern. The offbeat eighth kick at the end of every bar also adds movement to this very simple pattern.

ON THE CD-ROM
You'll find these Eurobeat grooves on the CD-ROM accompanying this book in the following directory: **chapter3/midifiles/drums/eurobeat/ euro01/2/3.mid**.

Our next variation brings back the claps on the second and fourth beats for more of a dance rhythm and also adds percussion in the form of a syncopated conga pattern to increase the urgency in the rhythm. Eurobeat often uses percussive fills like this for that added sense of urgency, sometimes layering breakbeats over a simple pattern like the previous one. Usually these breakbeats are sampled and EQd so that they are higher in the mix, giving the effect of a second rhythm riding 'on top' of the basic beat (see Figure 3.9).

Our final Eurobeat example (Figure 3.10) brings back the two sixteenth hi hats per beat pattern for what constitutes a breakdown or fill in Eurobeat. This just makes the beat sound faster, of course, and is exactly the effect that the Eurobeatmeisters are after. This is music that thrives on adrenaline and any little trick to pump that up is employed without mercy. Although Trance programmers probably won't admit it, many of their best tricks come from the Eurobeat songbook and this is one of them.

Figure 3.9
Claps and congas make a syncopated Eurobeat.

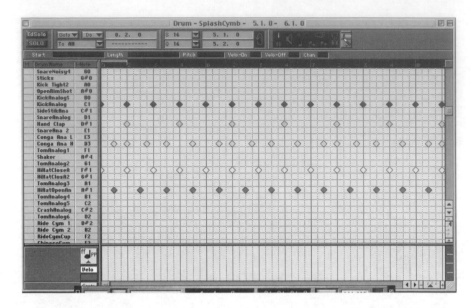

Figure 3.10
A Eurobeat breakdown that just goes faster!

Note the use of a shortened kick drum to add punchiness to the onward movement and allow the open hi hats and crash cymbals space to reverberate in the mix. The crash cymbal pattern builds over two bars, from two crashes on the first and third beats in the first bar to four crashes, one on each beat, in the second bar.

TIP

This little trick is one you can use in any four beat pattern and is one you can usefully experiment on with voicing. It works fine with any crash cymbal of course but why not try it on a second, heavier kick drum or echoing tom or even a synth sound?

Trance

Eurobeat led directly to Trance, dropping the cheesy vocals and synth lines for a more groove-based approach where a rhythmic chordal section is set up and repeated with variations. Trance also uses breakbeats less than Techno or Eurobeat, relying on strict four-to-the-floor patterns with the snare playing mainly on beats two and four with breakbeat notes. The hi hats tend to play variations on sixteenth notes with the open hi hats on every eighth as in the screen shot below.

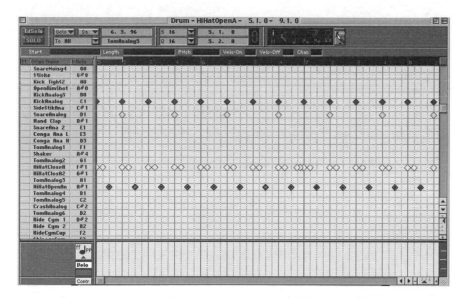

Figure 3.11
Trance uses similar patterns to Techno, adding a 'human' feel.

This is almost the same pattern as our first Techno groove, only the little 32nd hi hats at the end of the second bar identifying it as Trance. These were played in 'live' and left unquantized, so they don't fit any strict quantize grid, being neither 32nds or even sixteenth or 32nd triplets. They add that essential 'human' feel that Trance, for all its roots in Techno and Eurobeat, brings to the Techno canon. Perhaps Trance's origins in the hippie-ish Goan Trance scene are responsible for this but it is certainly a defining, albeit subtle, characteristic of Trance drum patterns.

ON THE CD-ROM

These Trance drumbeats can be found on the CD-ROM accompanying this book in the following CD-ROM directory: **chapter3/midifiles/drums/trance/**. *There are four Trance grooves,* **trance1/2/3/4.mid** *and two fills,* **trncfl1/2.mid**.

Our next Trance example continues the trend for 'human' drum patterns laid over a metronomic beat. Here a ticking hi hat on every eighth offbeat provides the mechanical beat while a programmed series of rolling bass drums lends the air of Indian drums to the rhythm. Indeed, in the sequencer's grid pattern it looks like the pattern on a hippie's headband! Some programmed toms underscore this 'Indian' beat.

Figure 3.12
Rolling bass drums make an 'ethnic' sounding beat.

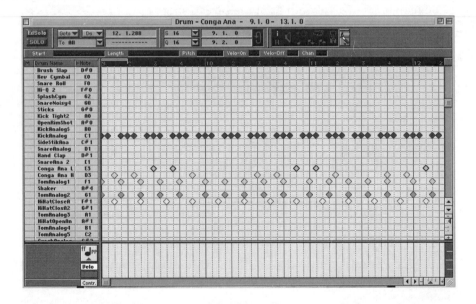

The real 'human' element comes in the percussion pattern, played live from the keyboard on the congas and left unquantized. The congas are to be found at E3 and D3 on your synthesizer keyboard, making it a very simple matter to 'play' a conga pattern on them with two fingers, just like a beatnik banging on a pair of bongos.

You don't have to stick to congas and bongos either. Our next example is played live from the keyboard in the same way, using three different ride cymbals to build a spacey percussive pattern over the familiar four/four kick drum coupled with snare hits on beats two and four. Note too the use of two separate closed hi hat sounds to make a very simple hi hat pattern sound intricate and 'live'.

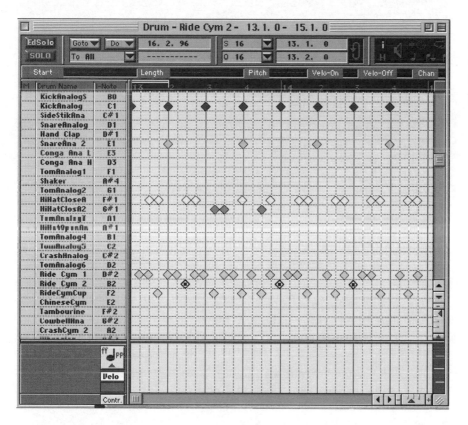

Figure 3.13
Ride on the cymbals for a spacey percussive fill.

Trance breakdowns tend to be similar to the Eurobeat breakdown we've just looked at, as they are usually designed to link from one fast-paced section into another. The ubiquitous snare roll is used in Trance of course but far more use is made of fast-paced fills like this one with a galloping double-beat bass drum providing the underlying rhythmic push.

Four-to-the-floor claps provide excitement while a fast snare consisting of two sixteenth notes, played on a different snare to the main riff, signs off this one bar fill with a ride cymbal providing the final flourish. This too has been played in 'live' and left unquantized for that 'human' feel.

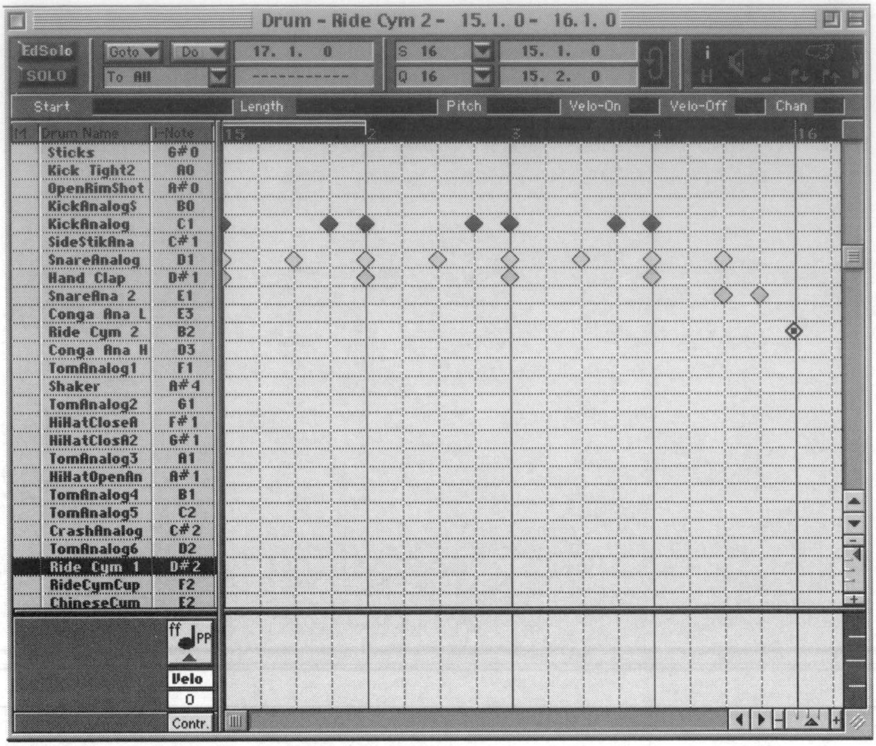

Figure 3.14
Trance fills are usually quite busy.

Figure 3.14
Trance fills are usually quite busy.

The next fill uses parts from the ride cymbals used earlier as a spacey riff and adds them to the galloping bass drum to excellent effect. The snare pattern uses sixteenth offbeats to sign off another one bar fill (see Figure 3.15).

Our final Trance breakdown (Figure 3.16) is far more of a real breakdown. It still uses the galloping bass drums but thins everything else right out, utilizing a series of percussive effects to add drama to the breakdown. You could even cut this one up and make four separate breakdowns out of it.

First there's a very simple break where the galloping kick drum carries a minimal hi hat pattern which uses progressively lowered velocities to fade out the hi hats. This is an effect that is natural for leading into a quieter section where the drums drop right out and a pad or simple melody line comes in (see Figure 3.17).

The next section just uses the side stick and kick drums to beak the rhythm right down. Note the way the side stick pattern moves around the kick drum pattern, echoing and evolving it at the same time (see Figure 3.18).

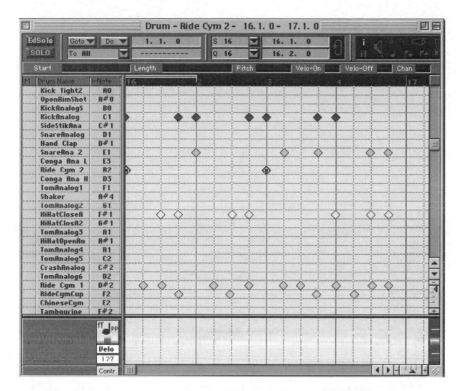

Figure 3.15
Re-purposing parts from other drum patterns to make a whole new groove.

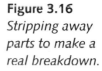

Figure 3.16
Stripping away parts to make a real breakdown.

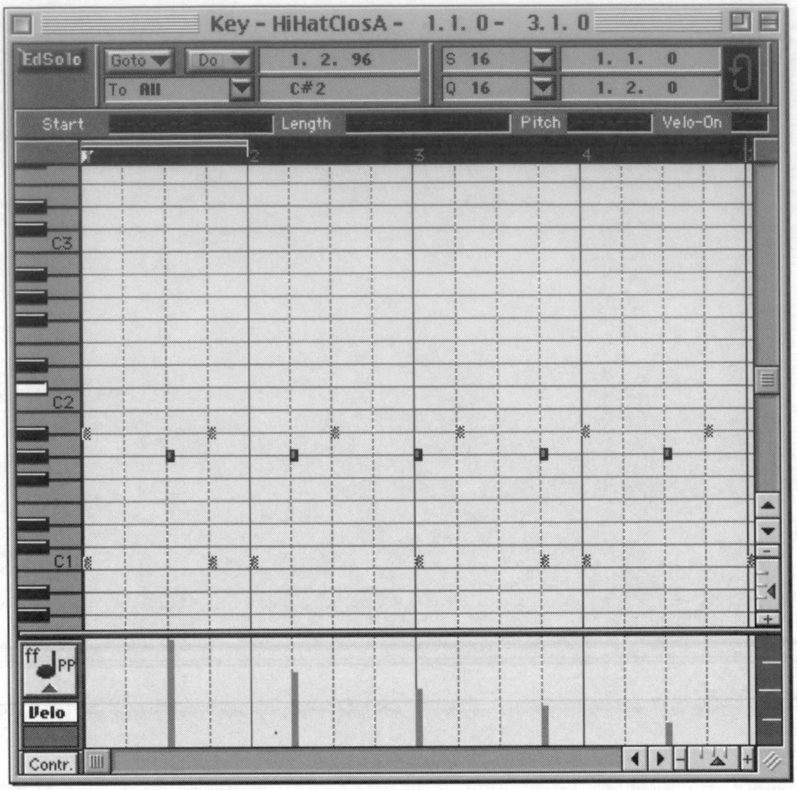

Figure 3.17
*Velocity
fades produce
dramatic
effects.*

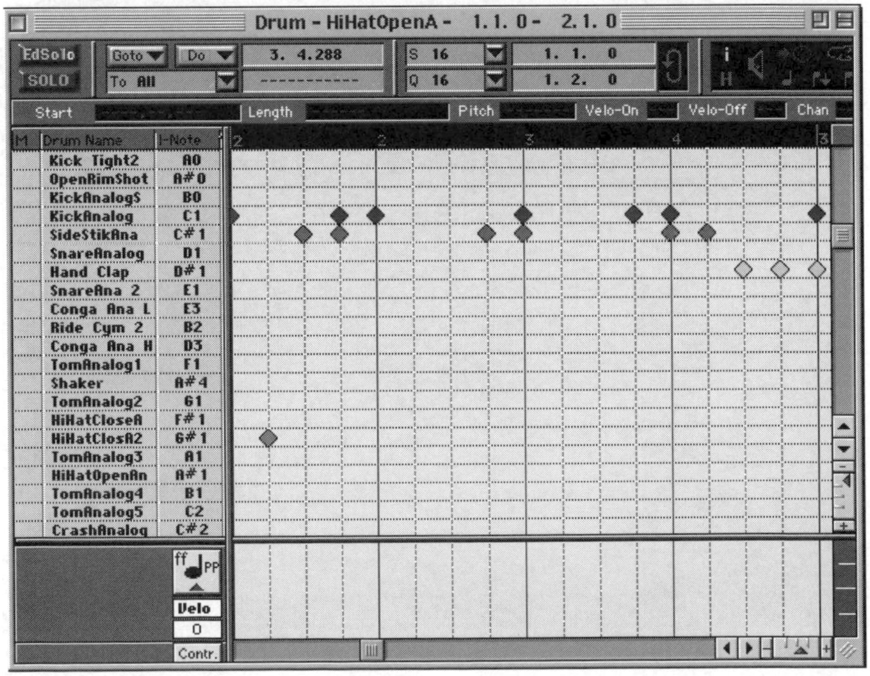

Figure 3.18
*Sticks and kicks
for minimal
grooves.*

The third section just uses claps and the kick drum but manages to build intensity by the simple trick of increasing the velocity and density of the claps over the course of a bar. This section would be perfect for leading back into a faster bassline or melodic riff.

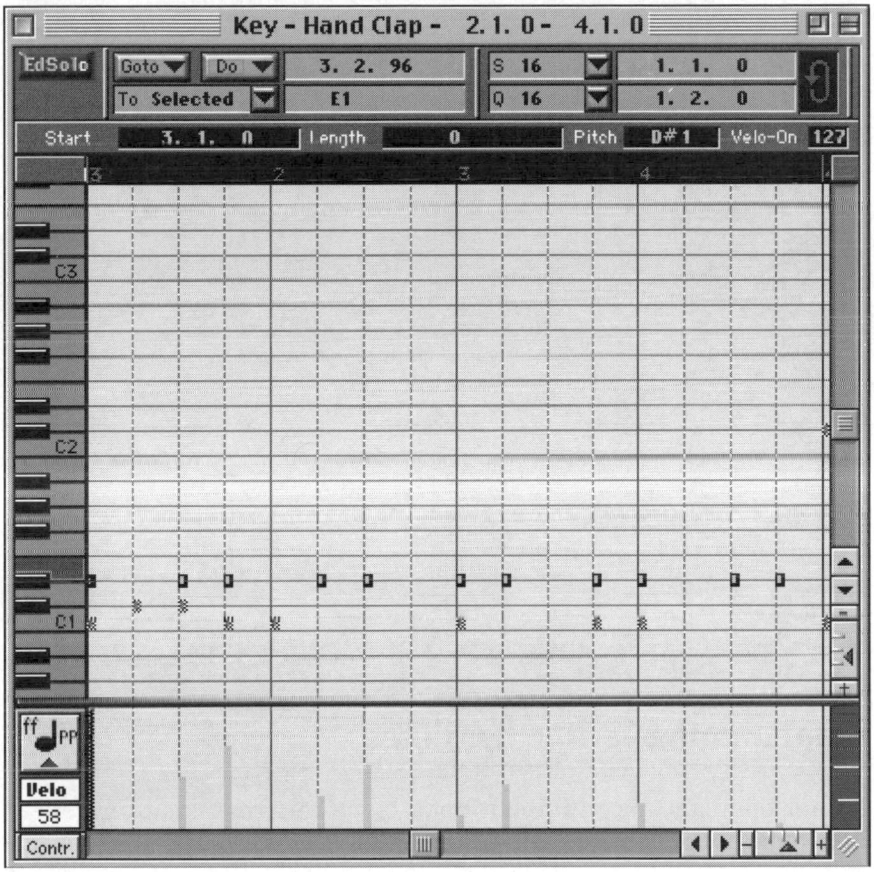

Figure 3.19
Reducing velocity on the claps to breakdown a groove.

Finally the last bar uses the simple but effective trick of ramping the velocity down twice over the course of the bar on a crash cymbal. This has the effect of sounding as if a drumstick had hit the cymbal and left to bounce on its surface, once again, providing a very 'human' feel.

Figure 3.20
Bouncing hi hats from velocity ramps.

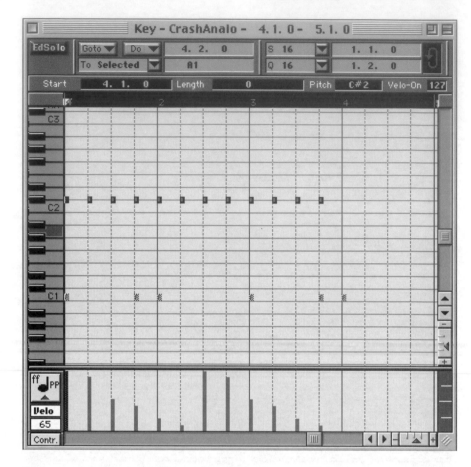

Programming Techno basslines

Rather than starting with the robotic electronic rhythms of European Electronic musicians like Kraftwerk, Techno often takes funk rhythms as a starting point and strips them right down to their essential elements to transform them into robotic yet funky grooves. Sixteenth quantized notes are the most commonly used and stem from the use of early step write sequencers that couldn't handle anything finer. What European electronic musicians found was that by manipulating the filters of the bass synths they could introduce variations into the sound which compensated for the mechanical rigidity of the patterns the sequencer forced the synth to play.

NOTE

Bass sounds used in Techno are always synth sounds and do not exhibit the characteristics of an electric bass. Pick a sound from program 39 or 40 and don't forget the bank variation sounds. Techno basses aren't afraid to go much lower than electric basses and they can jump around a lot more, often leaping up and down octaves.

Techno, Techno

Our first example is a simple two-note pattern played live from the keyboard but strictly quantized to sixteenths so it retains its funky rhythm but adopts the mechanical approach of European basslines. If we now start playing that pattern on a livelier bass patch we will arrive deep at the heart of Techno.

NOTE

Quantizing to sixteenths means the notes all sit on the grid. Make sure you leave the note lengths intact and your sequencer doesn't reduce them all to sixteenth lengths.

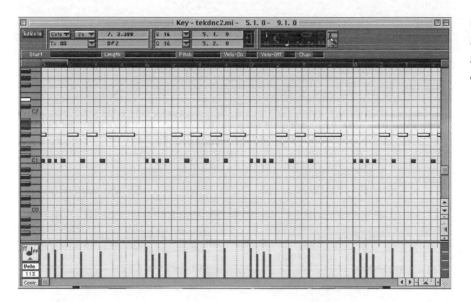

Figure 3.21
In Techno, simple basslines are the best.

The squelchy sound of GM patch 39 shows how important the choice of sound is in Techno. It could even be said to be its very *raison d'être*, exploring the different harmonics thrown up by filter sweeping sounds. If you cycle the sixteenth pattern and listen to it with GM patch 39 or similar you'll hear all manner of harmonic overtones as the end of the notes abruptly cuts off the filter. Programming Techno basslines is largely concerned with manipulating two parameters that make a huge difference to a sound's pitch and timbre, the Filter Cut Off Frequency and the Filter Resonance.

ON THE CD-ROM

You'll find the all the Techno basslines described in this section on the CD-ROM accompanying this book in the following directory: **chapter3/midifiles/bass/ techno/tekdnc1/2/3/4/5.mid**.

Filter Frequency

The Filter Cut Off Frequency controls the pitch at which the filter on a sound is closed. Turning this up to maximum means all the frequencies from the sound will be audible as the filter will allow them all through. This parameter was traditionally used to control the overall harmonics of a sound. Adjusting the cut-off frequency in real time produces rising and falling harmonics as the filter frequency is swept.

On analogue synthesizers there is always a knob that you can use to adjust this parameter. Recording those sweeps into a sequencer has always been a problem; any such manipulation of a bassline had to be done live as the tape rolled. Fortunately many modern synths now provide a controller for this parameter. Have a look at the MIDI implementation chart and see if there is a controller listed for Filter Frequency as there is in the chart for the Novation BassStation reproduced in Figure 3.22

If nothing is listed there, have a look in your synth manual in the sound programming section. You may find that the modulation wheel controls the filter frequency setting as on the Deep Bass Nine, in which case try moving the modulation wheel as the part cycles. Alternatively most GS and XG synths respond to MIDI controllers 71 and 74 for Resonance and Filter Cutoff respectively. You'll find this covered in more detail in Chapter 9, which looks at GM, GS and XG programming.

Function		Transmitted	Recognised	Remarks
Basic Channel	Default Changed	1 - 16	1 - 16	Memorised
Mode	Default Messages Altered	x •••••••••••	4 x	
Note Number	True Voice	24 - 72 •••••••••••	12 - 120 12 - 120	
Velocity	Note ON Note OFF	o 9nH,v=1-127 o	o v=1-127 o	
After Touch	Keys Ch's	x x	x o	
Pitch Bender		x	o 0-12 semi	7 bit resolution
Control Change	1	x	o	Modulation Wheel
	2	x	o	Breath control
	7	x	o	Volume
	105	o	o	Filter frequency
	106	o	o	Filter resonance
	107	o	o	Filter mod depth
	108	o	o	Env1 Attack
	109	o	o	Env1 Decay
	110	o	o	Env1 Sustain
	111	o	o	Env1 Release
	112	o	o	Env1 Velocity
	114	o	o	Env2 Attack
	115	o	o	Env2 Decay
	116	o	o	Env2 Sustain
	117	o	o	Env2 Release
	118	o	o	Env2 Velocity
Program change	True *	o 0 - 99 •••••••••••	o 0 - 99	
System exclusive		o	o	Voice parameters
System Real Time	:Clock	x	o	Start,Stop, Continue
Aux messages :Local ON/OFF :All Notes OFF :Active Sense :Reset		x x x x	x o x x	

Mode 1 : OMNI ON, POLY   Mode 3 : OMNI ON, MONO
Mode 2 : OMNI OFF, POLY   Mode 4 : OMNI OFF, MONO

Figure 3.22
MIDI implementation chart for the Novation BassStation showing the MIDI controller which Novation has assigned to open and close the filter.

Filter resonance

If the results of all your filter sweeping are altering the timbre from nothing more than a low thud to a 'natural' bass sound you probably need to turn the resonance up. The amount of resonance applied to the filter makes a huge difference to the amount of extra harmonics generated by the filter. If the filter's resonance setting can be controlled by a MIDI controller then just remap the modulation wheel, or even perhaps another controller on your synth like the volume slider, to the new MIDI controller and record the data as before.

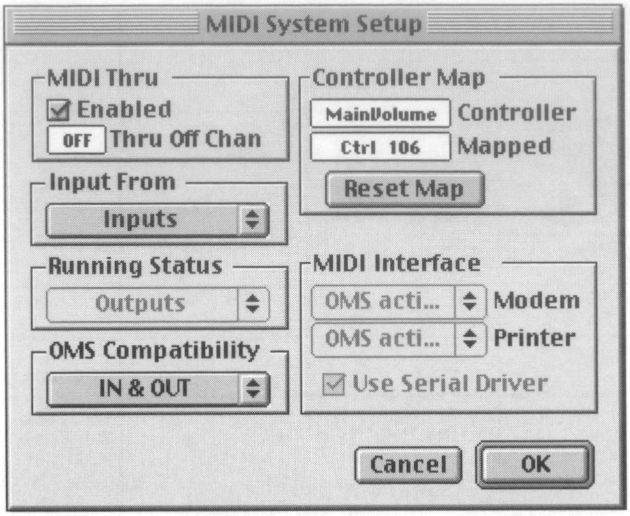

Figure 3.23
Remapping the Volume slider on a keyboard to control Filter Resonance (MIDI controller 106) on the BassStation.

> **TIP**
>
> *Often the resonance setting only needs to be turned up once to allow the filter frequency some input to sweep. This can be done from the front of your synth of course but, once you know which MIDI controller this is, you can create a MIDI controller event and type in the appropriate value. Then you only have to save that part as a MIDI file and you can load it in to an existing arrangement whenever you want to reset the resonance.*

Velocity control

If your synth doesn't respond to MIDI controllers or SysEx data you can often alter its timbre using an integral part of the MIDI note protocol, the velocity value. Many digital synth patches are programmed to respond to different velocity levels in the same way as analogue synths do to filter settings. Try programming a smooth velocity sweep on a bassline as shown in Figure 3.24 opposite.

As the velocity sweep spans the full extent of the velocity levels you can hear how each level sounds. If the bass sound doesn't respond in any way besides growing in loudness, try other sounds, since not all synth patches respond to velocity levels with different timbres.

> **TIP**
>
> *A sweep up like this is very useful for gradually bringing a new pattern into a mix, the timbre becoming louder and more distinct as the velocity levels rise.*

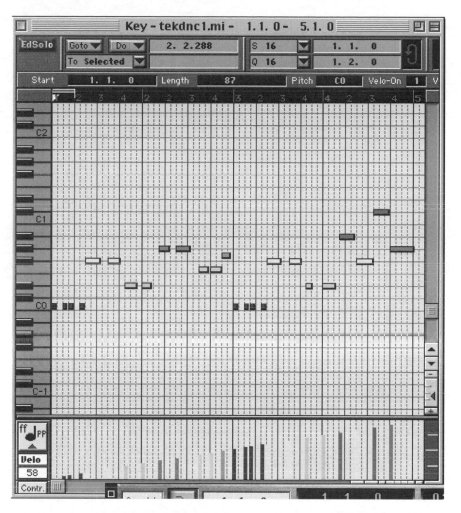

Figure 3.24
A smooth velocity sweep.

Once you've found a sound that does change radically you can try programming effects in using the velocity levels in exactly the same way you did on the controller data (see Figure 3.25).

We looked at octave shifting in Chapter 2 and discovered it provided a real jumping House or Garage bassline. The same effect can also be very useful in playing or programming a Techno bassline. This example jumps back and forth over two octaves with a third octave jump in bars one and three at sixteenth offbeats at the end of the second and fourth beats. These provide a minimal 'acid' effect as the higher pitch triggers a different timbre on GM patch 39. The notes here are very short as played, roughly 32nd notes in length and this adds to the 'acid' effect. As the sound is triggered and almost immediately closed the resonance becomes predominant. See Figure 3.26

Figure 3.25
Sawtooth velocity sweeps.

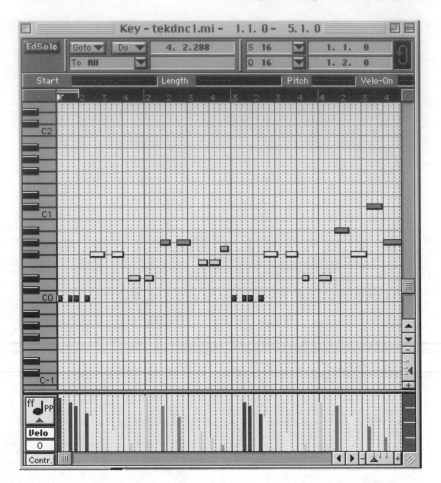

Figure 3.26
A one note bassline using octave shifting to make it sound more 'acid'.

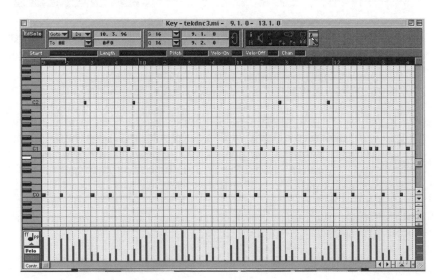

Once again, using only three notes, our next example relies on a portamento effect. You probably won't notice the overlapping notes if you're playing it on a General MIDI synth patch unless you've switched the sound to portamento. Once you've done this, however, you'll notice the sound sliding up and down between those overlapping notes as the sound is bent into the next note rather than being retriggered. Once again this is a classic 'acid' effect. The effect is especially noticeable in the last bar where the overlap is the largest.

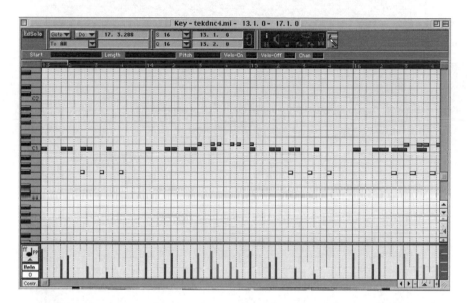

Figure 3.27
Portamento produces the infamous 'acid slide' when used on mono bass patches.

Our next example (Figure 3.28) is more complicated and demonstrates the use of the lower registers of a bass sound. Normally these wouldn't be used, as their timbre is rather dark and can sound strange. But this is Techno and Techno is about strange if nothing else. Other than its use of more notes this bassline follows the pattern we've already looked at, alternating between very short notes and longer ones to play with the opening and closing of a sound's filter. Once again the portamento effect is invoked in the last beat for that 'acid' slide. Note too the use of sharps, another Techno favourite.

Our final Techno bassline (Figure 3.29) makes extensive use of the portamento effect with a long note at the beginning of every bar which overlaps the beginning of the next note for that 'acid' slide mentioned above and also completely overlaps a grace note in bars one and four. This has a weird pitch-shifting effect as the note jumps up to the grace note and slides back down to the original. Extensive use is also made of portamento in the rest of the bassline. This is really a Eurobeat or Trance bassline and shows just how far you can take Techno. From minimal basslines to octave jumping business the essence of Techno basslines is, like so much else in Techno, all about breaking the boundaries and playing with all the different timbres to be found within a bass sound. The popularity of the Roland TB303 bassline, with its wildly different pitches, is testament to this.

Figure 3.28
How low can you go? Techno basslines go lower than your synthesizer manual advises.

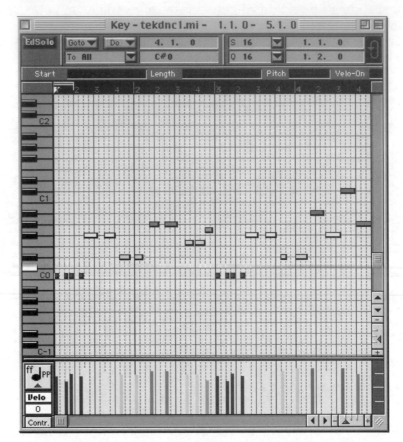

Figure 3.29
This example uses portamento and octave jumping to produce a busy bassline.

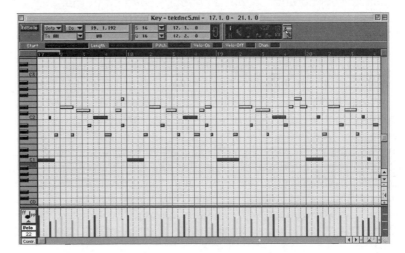

Trance

Whereas Techno basslines can be stately, everything tends to move fast in Trance, with more use being made of sixteenth notes. The bass can play sixteenth and also offbeat sixteenth notes (a Dream House crossover). Chords and melodies too, are often gated to create a fast moving effect. Speedy 'analogue' lines are also played and are reminiscent of early analogue sequencers with only eight or 16 notes of memory. Trance is usually much faster in tempo than Techno, usually starting at 145 bpm and going up sometimes as high as 175 bpm.

> **NOTE**
>
> *The basis of programming Trance and Techno basslines is experimentation with the sounds and patterns. There are a wealth of basslines in different styles on the CD-ROM accompanying this book and you could feasibly make a Trance or Techno bassline from any of them. Remember it's as much about playing with the sounds in your synth as it is about writing musical patterns.*

Minimalism plays a large part in Trance as well as Techno, and our first Trance bassline is as minimal as you can get, using just one pitch and octave shifts for sonic effect. Offbeat sixteenths are in evidence here and these mark this bassline out as Trance or Dream House. There is no use made of portamento here, in contrast to Techno, mainly because Trance tends to leave more room for all the melodic elements of a bassline and accompanying arpeggios to interact with each other. However, differing note lengths have been used to play with the sound and provide scope for filter tweaking.

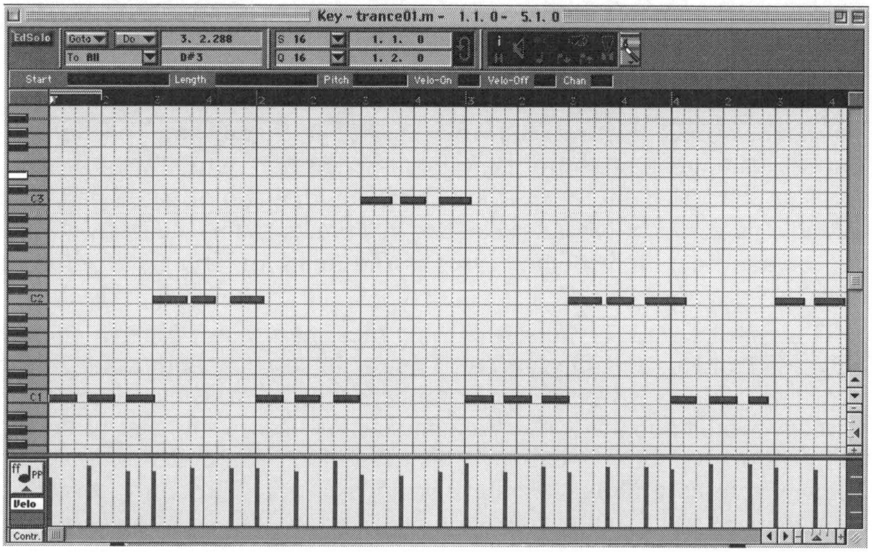

Figure 3.30
Trance uses one note basslines and octave jumping as well.

ON THE CD-ROM
You'll find the all the Trance basslines described in this section on the CD-ROM accompanying this book in the following directory: **chapter3/midifiles/bass/ trance/trance01/2/3/4/5.mid**.

Although we said that Trance basslines tend to move fast there is always an exception to the rule, and our next example is just that. Essentially a stripped-down version of the previous example, it adds a semitone shift to C sharp at the end of each bar and could be used in conjunction with the first bassline if played on a different voice and possibly transposed up an octave or two.

Figure 3.31
Semitone shifts and stripped down basslines can be used on their own or in conjunction with other basslines.

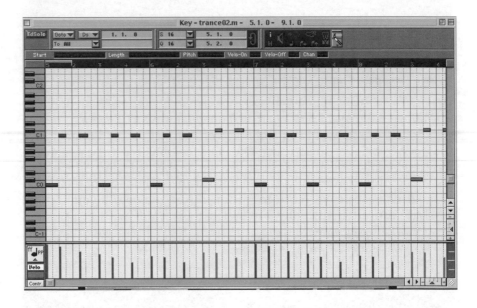

Once again alternating a natural with a sharp, the two note bassline in our next example (Figure 3.32) would sound pretty dull at a Techno pace but begins to generate some excitement at 135 bpm plus. This is another bassline that cries out to be layered with an arpeggio or gated pad. You actually need lots of basslines like this in Trance, as the successive layering of basslines and melody lines is the heart of Trance. If all your basslines are busy everything's going to get cluttered very quickly.

Our next example is the sort of thing most people envisage when they think of Trance, particularly Goan Trance: lots of sixteenth notes laying down what sounds like a very complicated pattern. Closer inspection reveals it to be minimal: only three pitches are used, with great use being made of octave shifting and portamento in direct contradiction to everything we've said about Trance basslines so far. This only serves to demonstrate that Trance is exactly like Techno, all about breaking the

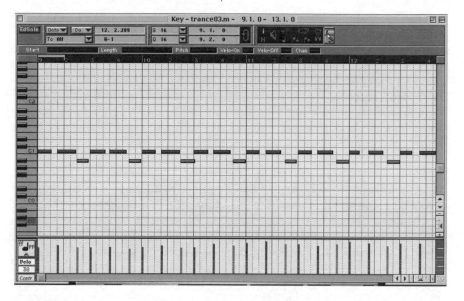

Figure 3.32
Alternating between a natural and a sharp is a classic Trance bassline style.

rules. This bassline makes extensive use of portamento by the simple trick of layering sixteenth notes on top of each other and shortening one so that a brief slide comes out as an acid squeal. Make sure you set your synthesizer to mono for this one or the whole thing will sound too cluttered.

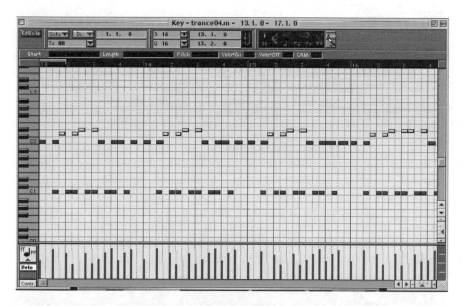

Figure 3.33
This bassline looks very busy but there are really only three notes in it! Octave jumping and portamento are used to great effect.

TIP

If you're using a GM, GS or XG synthesiser, Portamento can be adjusted from your sequencer using MIDI controllers 65 to turn it on and off (on = 127, off = 0) and 5 to control the portamento time. See Chapter 9 for more details.

Our last example returns to basics, contrasting long notes and short notes without overlapping portamento notes to confuse things. This bassline could be layered with any of the others in this section or used on its own as an intro or breakdown section. The trick in programming a Trance track is to build up a lot of contrasting basslines as we have done here and then experiment with layering and revoicing them to achieve a synthesis of simple elements that sound more than the sum of its parts. That's exactly what we'll do when arranging our Trance mix. It only remains to generate some chords and arpeggios and we're ready to put our Trance track together.

Figure 3.34
The contrast in texture produced by long and short notes produces a trance bassline.

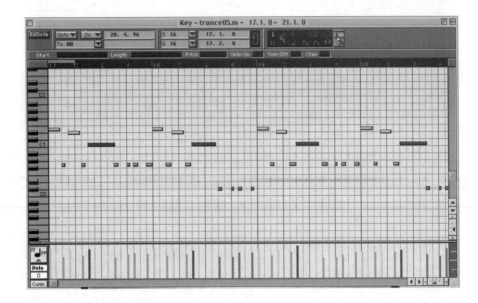

Programming Techno chords

Chords used for Techno are mostly simple without many added notes. The best way to generate chords is to load up your basslines and play around on the keyboard until you find a pad sound that suits you. For Trance and Techno you should look to more synthetic sounds, i.e. anything that sounds like a synthesizer as opposed to 'real' sounding patches. In general MIDI terms this is any program between 81 and 91. If you have a GS or XG synth then there are even more exciting variations available. Consult your synthesizer's voice listing.

TIP
Early Techno music was known for its root position chord stabs that were sampled and then played as one finger rhythmic themes. This is now seen as a little old-fashioned but is part of the style's heritage. If you do want to recreate this technique just make sure that whatever chord you play has the same intervals.

We've only generated one example here: a simple chord with a semitone shift after two bars. This could be used as is or made even more Trance-y with the addition of one of Techno's most-used tricks, the volume gate.

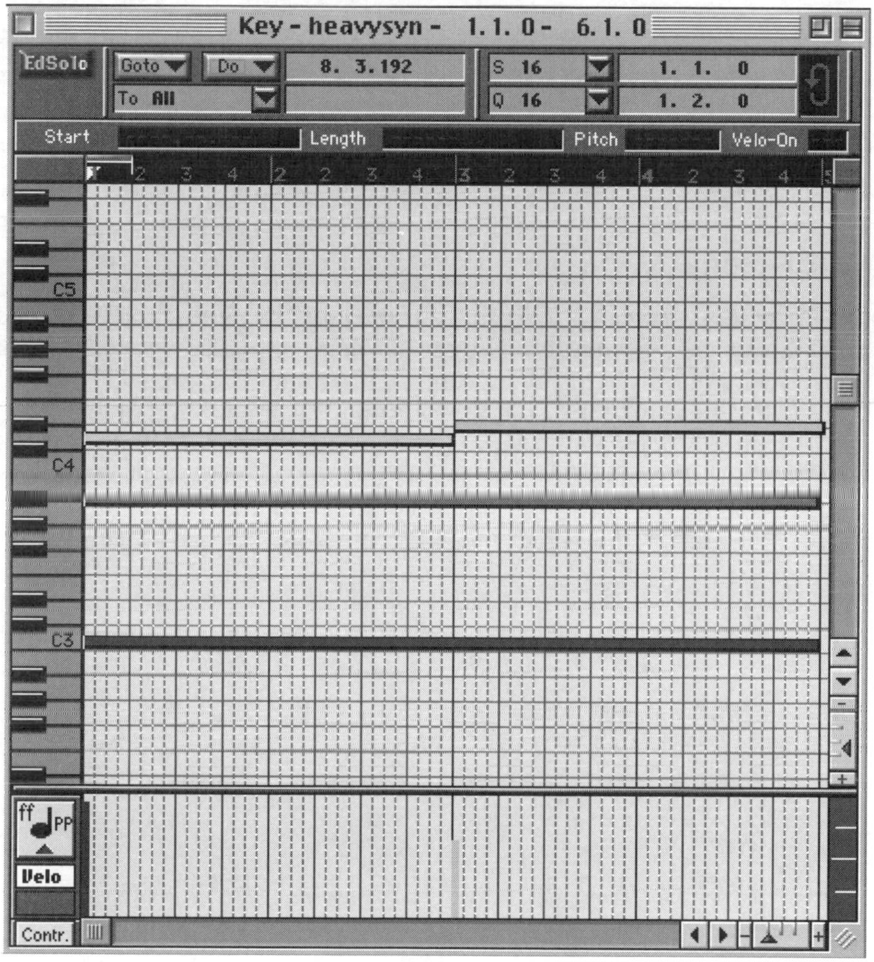

Figure 3.35
A simple chord using a semitone shift, the essence of Techno.

Volume gating is an old studio trick that is usually achieved with the help of an external device known as a volume gate. This takes an incoming signal from one source, say a ticking hi hat beat, and uses that as a trigger to open and close the volume on another sound. It is really effective on pad and synthesizer sounds like this one and works best on sustained chords. You don't need an external box of tricks to achieve this with MIDI, however; you can easily program up a MIDI volume gate.

TIP

Generally trance tracks are minor in tone because this gives the music much more instant credibility. Some Trance tracks are in a major key e.g. 'La Primavera' by Sash but there is a very fine line between sounding good and sounding twee. Dance music in major keys is much more difficult to pull off.

MIDI gating

MIDI gating is used a lot in Techno. When a held note or chord is played and the volume is rapidly changed it seems that the chord is being played very quickly. This effect can sound spectacular especially if coupled with some real time controller changes, e.g. panning, filtering etc. MIDI gating is achieved using either controller 7 (main volume), or 11 (expression). Either will work but the current vogue is to use 11 (the thinking being that once set, main volume shouldn't be changed too often). The table below shows the elements of a simple MIDI gate.

Basic MIDI gate

Beat	Controller	Value
Note or chord	11	127
next sixteenth	11	0
next sixteenth	11	127
next sixteenth	11	0
next sixteenth	11	127
next sixteenth	11	0
next sixteenth	11	127
next sixteenth	11	0
next sixteenth	11	127
next sixteenth	11	0
next sixteenth	11	127
next sixteenth	11	0
next sixteenth	11	127
next sixteenth	11	0
next sixteenth	11	127

Try varying the values for different effects. In a typical Grid editor the result will look something like the following figure.

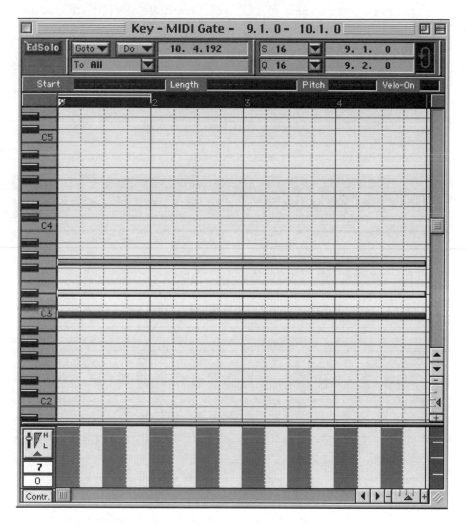

Figure 3.36
The volume gate programmed above as seen in a Grid editor.

You can also transform notes from other events into a MIDI volume gate in imitation of the original effect.

- Take a hi hat part and use your sequencer's transform function to change the notes in the hi hat pattern into volume or expression events.

- Once they are transformed into volume events you can either manually set each alternating event to zero and 127 as in the above example or perform the following operation:

- Copy the events, moving them a sixteenth forward in time as you copy them.

- Set the copied events to 127. You now have a MIDI volume gate based on the hi hat pattern.

NOTE

The second half of this operation should only be performed if your pattern features events spaced an eighth or more apart. If it is already a sixteenth hi hat pattern you may find that the alternating values are already enough to perform a gate-like function. If not you'll have to manually set them to alternating values.

TIP

The alternating values don't have to be zero and 127. Try experimenting with different values that will open and close the volume gate by varying amounts for a more 'organic' effect.

The completed MIDI gate directly imitates the effect of a hardware gate which takes the sound signal from something like a drum pattern and uses that to open and close the volume gate.

**Figure 3.37
A Dynamic
MIDI Volume
Gate.**

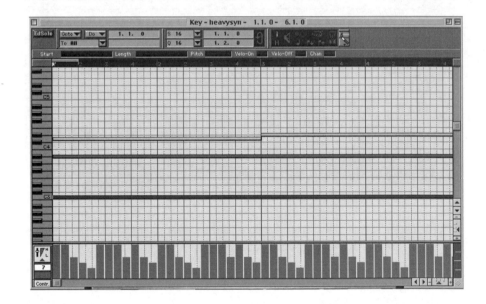

Programming melody motifs

Repetitive analogue type sounds playing little motifs and sequences are a characteristic of both Trance and Techno. You can program these using the technique for originating arpeggios described in Chapter 2 or simply play them 'live' into your sequencer. Two-finger playing is the essence of Trance and Techno styles and the only rule is: keep it simple; as simple motifs sound much more dramatic than musically busy ones.

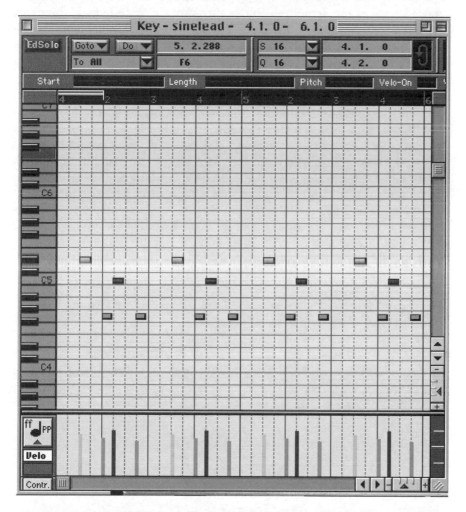

Figure 3.38
A simple arpeggio provides a melodic motif to decorate a Trance track. See TranceTechno/ SEQS/ TrSeq2.mid.

ON THE CD-ROM
You'll find this Trance arpeggio on the CD-ROM accompanying this book in the following directory: **chapter3/midifiles/seqs/trseq02.mid**.

TIP
Arpeggios and melodic motifs like this can be made more interesting by adjusting the cut-off and resonance filters in real time. The way to get the most extreme filter effects is to set the resonance at its maximum at the start of a sequence and then adjust the cut-off in real time. This makes the most of the filters to produce ringing and whistling sounds.

Arranging a Trance track

All Techno is groove-based with movement in the music caused by variations of texture and instrumentation rather than chord changes and verse–chorus type structure. Putting together a Trance track involves grouping together lots of basslines, beats and a few simple elements like the pad and arpeggio we've just generated, then playing around with the instrumentation and voicing to find combinations of sounds which have a pleasing effect.

Trance tracks follow a set pattern with a series of combinations of bass and synth sounds building up to a climax of some sort. There usually follows an abrupt change to another section which may be related thematically to the first or may not: the essential thing is that it should have a different mood. After this the main theme is usually brought back again with even more rhythmic and textural variations. This is similar to the composing technique used in pop where a 'middle eight' provides the change of pace. In Trance the middle section is usually much longer, sixteen bars or more, and usually goes on so long that the main theme is all but forgotten when it comes crashing back in, adding to the surprise.

Figure 3.39

The Trance song featured on the CD-ROM.

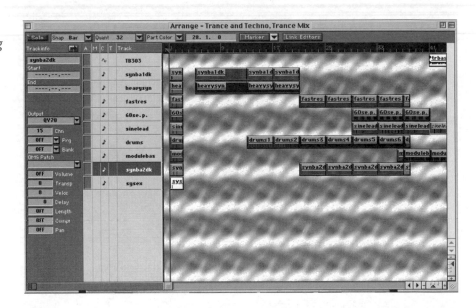

In our example mix here, that's exactly what been done. The piece kicks off with an intro produced by marrying one of the basslines with the gated synthesizer part. Next a simple beat is added to bring in the beats. This is progressively built up until the standard Trance groove kicks in. At this point the first abrupt change is made.

ON THE CD-ROM

The MIDI file of the mix shown here can be found on the CD-ROM accompanying this book in the following directory: **chapter3/midifiles/songs/**. *There are two files, one for the mix itself,* **trance1.mid** *and another setting up the program changes and effects settings for an XG synth,* **tranceset.mid**.

In this mix a little experimentation with different synthesizer bass sounds has produced a marriage of two different sounds playing the same bassline. The XG patch, FastResBass, a TB303-style sound, plays the line simultaneously with a deeper patch; an XG patch called SynBass2Dark. This second bass patch is pitched lower than the FastResBass and so is actually playing the bassline an octave lower than the first bass. If necessary you can transpose basslines up and down for this effect but in this case that is not necessary.

Once this groove is kicking along nicely the arpeggio is brought in. This has been played here on a sine wave sound, the basic building block of synthesized sounds and consequently the most synth-sounding. Sine waves are useful for all sorts of things, from high-pitched arpeggios to low down bass rumbles. The XG sound helpfully provides a few of these patches but you can usually locate them in most sound sets.

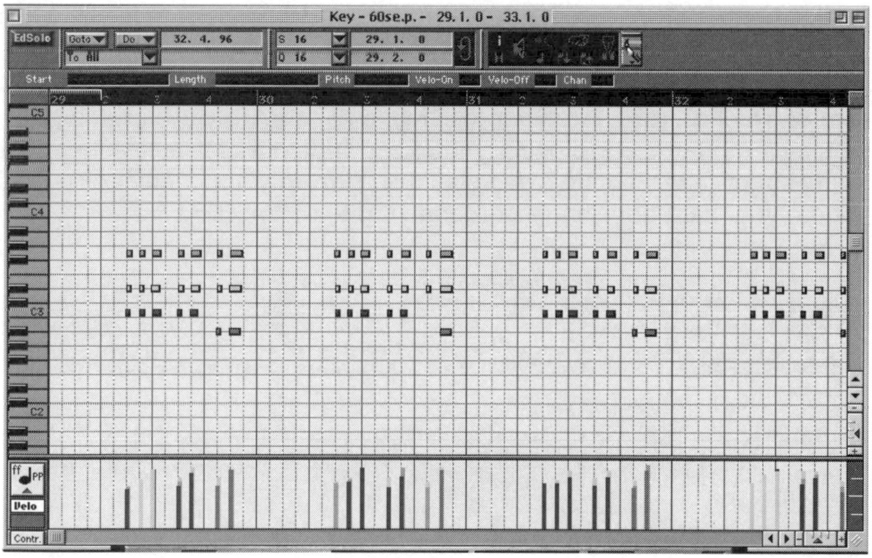

Figure 3.40
A simple chord pattern played on an electric piano.

To accompany the arpeggio a simple chord pattern has been played in live on an electric piano sound. Electric piano patches on the GM, GS and XG sound sets offer some surprisingly expressive sounds. It's always worth having one or two of these loaded up and ready for you to tinkle around with when looking for that extra something as an arrangement starts to come together. Because the piano sound is sharp and clear it will usually cut through all your other sounds, thus making your jamming easier.

> **TIP**
>
> *Once you've played a few chords that you like you don't have to have the pattern playing with the electric piano sound; try changing the sound to a synthier one or even a staccato string patch. Often this will expose a whole new dimension to the part you've played. You may be able to use a series of such program changes to produce different parts of your mix.*

This electric piano part, with the addition of a single low bass note, produces a nice breakdown, ready to swing back into any of the main sections. Once you've built up a series of sections like these, it's a simple matter of 'playing' your various sections to produce a mix, as described in Chapter 2. The method you choose will depend on your sequencer and the way you prefer to work.

Don't forget audio tracks either. When putting together a Trance or Techno track you may want to incorporate sampled sounds and riffs played on old analogue gear. It's usually best to sample riffs on old analogue synthesizers as they're notoriously prone to drifting out of tune. There's nothing more frustrating than coming up with a killer bassline on such a beast, only to lose it as the synthesizer drifts out of tune just when you're ready to record.

Even if your old synth does have stable tuning, you still have the problem of synchronizing it to your MIDI gear. There are ways of doing this but, all too often the analogue synthesizer drifts out of sync as often as it drifts out of tune. Sample it and play the riff from your sampler or record it onto your hard drive and incorporate it into the mix that way.

Figure 3.41
Analogue sounds are best sampled or recorded digitally.

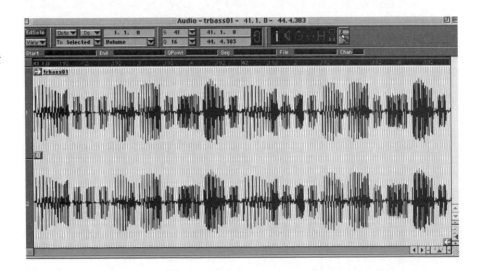

ON THE CD-ROM

The audio file of this TB303 bassline is on the CD-ROM accompanying this book in the following directory: **chapter3/samples/bass/**. *For PC users the file is called* **trbass06.wav** *while Mac users will find a version called* **trbass06.aiff**.

As we mentioned earlier, you can sample all the bits of your Trance track and then either load them into your sampler and play the various parts 'live' from the keyboard to build up a track, or produce an arrangement of them using your sequencer's audio tracks. This is the way that many Techno musicians work.

Alex Patterson of The Orb marks up the keys on his keyboard naming the sample that is triggered by each key and uses that as a guide when mixing and playing live. Richie Hawtin, better known as Plastikman, sets up a series of loops and then records everything from his sequencer onto a DAT tape while he experiments with filter sweeps and the like. He then chooses the best parts from hours of taping to produce his final mix.

You might also want to use other audio software to put together your final mix. ProTools, Audio workshop and many similar programs offer advanced audio editing facilities and are the choice of many professional studio engineers when it comes to putting together a final mix of the various elements of a track. You'll find a description of these software applications in Appendix 6, Other Music Software.

Another program that is now very popular among Techno fiends for putting together a mix of audio parts is Acid. This program automatically calculates the bpm of a loop and adjusts it to sync with whatever tempo you have chosen for your mix. Acid is also described in Appendix 6 and a demo version of the program can be found on the CD-ROM accompanying this book.

ON THE CD-ROM

To assist you in putting together a mix of this Trance track we've included audio loops of all the main parts in the track, recorded at 135 beats per minute. You can take these audio loops and simply load them into the audio tracks of your sequencer to create an instant mix. You'll find the audio loops in the following directory: **chapter3/samples/**.

Inside the samples directory are folders for drums, melody and bass, all named appropriately and containing sampled loops of the building blocks of the Trance track. Remember that the basis of Techno is experimentation. Whichever way you choose to put together your Trance or Techno track, don't forget to have fun while you're doing it!

We've now studied how to program Techno drum loops and then add basslines to them. You should by now be comfortable delving into the depths of synthesizer programming as an integral part of sequencing. In Chapter 4 we'll look at various aspects of programming the constituent parts of the latest style of Electronica, Big Beat, which has recently been storming up the charts.

4 Programming Big Beat

Where House, Garage and Techno ultimately rely on four-to-the-floor beats, Big Beat and its sister styles, Drum'n'Bass and Trip Hop, replace these rhythms with breakbeats, the more cut up the better. Of these three, Big Beat in particular has opened up dance and Electronica to a whole new audience of people who found the unrelenting rhythms of House and Techno too cold and mechanical. Fusing the gurning idiot grins of acid house with Hip-Hop, funk and rock beats and riffs, Big Beat is the party animal of Electronica, more at home with a belly full of beer than a head full of pills.

Because of the big hip-hop, grunge and heavy metal influences, Big Beat is a raw and brutal sound with a really Lo-Fi feel essential to the groove. The use of heavily effected guitar is almost mandatory giving a kind of heavy metal meets Electronica sound. Big Beat tends to sound like there is a rock band playing together; but this is an illusion. The familiar rock instruments are present (guitar, bass, drums) but they are mostly put together from samples. Scratching is another influence from Hip-Hop, making tracks sound like they've been mixed by DJs.

In this chapter we'll look at programming Big Beat grooves with particular emphasis on getting that essential 'human' feel to the patterns. We'll explore the different type of drum sounds essential for the Big Beat sound and show you how to get them from GM modules and samples, then we'll look at basslines and guitar riffs, once again exploring the different ways of bringing a 'live' feel to these parts. Once we've done that we'll look at the different ways of adding the final elements of raw dirt to a mix with scratches, sirens and sound effects. Then, with all the elements in place, we'll put together a Big Beat track.

Programming Big Beat drums

Like all dance styles, Big Beat is very groove-based and the changes in instrumentation and texture are what make a track. The drums are the most important part and they play breakbeat patterns that are either played on a real kit, sampled from existing music or sample CDs or programmed. When the beats are programmed they must be created in a way that sounds like a real drummer. Care needs to be taken over this, as a heavily quantized drum part won't sound right. The human rhythmic imperfections should be present or even manufactured by the programmer to give a loose feel to the part. It's worthwhile programming Big Beat grooves rather than simply relying on sampled loops as you can more easily cut up your own MIDI files and manipulate the resultant loops.

Drum sounds

Getting the right sounds is the first step in programming Big Beat drum patterns. The following is a guide to the sort of sound you should be after, whether you're programming your drum machine or loading up the sampler.

Kick

Unlike House and Techno, where heavily compressed drum sounds are the norm, Big Beat requires either a hard sound without the clicking of compressed kick drums, or a boomy kick drum. The 808 kick drum is useful here, mimicking as it does the boominess of a natural kick drum. You can always emulate this effect with the judicious application of reverb from your mixing desk. The kick drum isn't as important in Big Beat as it is in House or Techno; because of Big Beat's rock and hip-hop emphasis, snares play a far more important role.

Snare

Snare sounds are the main focus of Big Beat and you can't really have enough variations on that essential, the big loud, dirty snare. There are two types of snare sound which predominate in Big Beat, metallic and woody. Metallic snares can be found in both the Rock (Program 17) and Electronic drum kits (Program 25) on GM modules while 'real' woody sounding snares mainly reside in the Rock kit. Try layering snares to get an even bigger sound.

Hats

Like snares, the bigger and brighter more and in-your-face the hi hats the better. As with snares, don't fight shy of adding crustiness with dirty reverb or layering crackly samples – anything to get that essential Lo-Fi effect.

Crash

As with snares and hats, crash cymbals in Big Beat tend to be as bright and thin as possible. Once again judicious use of dirty reverb adds to the Lo-Fi effect and don't be afraid to cut the sounds unnaturally short.

Clap

Claps aren't used as much in Big Beat as they are in House or Techno. If they are they tend to be used with loads of chorus for a 'real crowd' effect.

Toms

If toms are used in Big Beat it tends to be for their boominess. Try layering them with kick drums for a cartoon Big Beat sound.

Percussion

Anything goes here. From Latin style percussion to sampled loops, the cheesier and crustier the better. If you're using sampled loops don't get too hung up on getting the timing tight as the Big Beat style is loose and messy.

Using a drum machine

Because of the extensive use of sampled loops and individual drum sounds in Big Beat, the drums used are not always drum machine sounds. The feel is funky in nature with many breakbeat notes and hi hats in unquantized sixteenth patterns. If you don't have a sampler, how do you create the raw drum sounds needed for Big Beat just using sound modules? Several tricks are involved:

- Take some time to work on the drum sounds before you start programming grooves. Experiment with different kits like the Rock kit (Program 17) and the Electronic kit (Program 25) for harder snares.

- Edit individual drum sounds if possible by adjusting filters and the ADSR.

- Don't quantize too heavily as you're trying to create a feel produced by a live drummer who *never* plays exactly in time.

- Experiment with iterative or groove quantizes.

- Use a one or two bar drum 'loop' for your drum track so that you're mimicking a re-triggered sample.

- Try adding effects like distortion or phasing to your drum track to provide more sonic rawness.

Sampling sounds and loops

If you do have a sampler try sampling as many different hits of a sound as your sampler has memory for. Snare rolls and loops, using three or four different hits, sound more convincing than do those composed of single hits.

Don't trim the samples too much; try and leave the vinyl crackles and atmosphere that are an essential part of the Big Beat sound.

When loading your samples into the sampler don't use one-shot mode. Although this is normal for drum sounds, a common element of the Big Beat sound is abruptly cut-off cymbal and snare samples. By leaving the note length to cut off the hit you can program this effect by the length of note you program or play a hit with.

Program as much response to velocity as you can into each hit. If possible make 0 = silence and 127 the maximum. This gives you far more control over programming dynamics and getting variation into your grooves.

Filter frequency

Another absolutely essential element of Big Beat drums is filter frequency manipulation. Where Techno plays around with the filters on bass and synth sounds for dynamics, Big Beat does it all over the place, particularly on drum sounds. If you're using a sampler use the modulation wheel to filter cut-off and squash the sounds with the filter.

If you're using a drum machine try routing it through a filter from your mixing desk. Cheap guitar pedals can provide all sorts of filtering effects so experiment with those if you don't have a dedicated filter unit. Some analogue synths like the Novation BassStation let you route external sounds through their filters so try sending your drum loops through there and manipulating the synthesizer's filters.

If you're recording direct to disk you should be able to use a filter effect from your sequencer's array of in-line effects. The Cubase plug-in standard is now used on most sequencers and there's a nice free plug-in filter called North Pole that has just the requisite dirty sound. You can download it free from the Internet.

Once you have a selection of sounds ready it's time to start programming. The first place to look for Big Beat grooves is on funk, R'n'B and Hip-Hop records. Hip-Hop usually samples its grooves from funk and R'n'B anyway or they program them up on early, electronic beatboxes. We'll look at some classic hip-Hop grooves first, then we'll deconstruct a couple of Electro grooves before getting stuck into some classic Big Beat loops.

Hip-Hop

Beats per minute range from 96 to 140 in Big Beat and it's Hip-Hop beats that you'll find at the lower end, as this is the natural tempo for most Hip-Hop. Hip-Hop beats are very sparse, relying on the interplay between the kick and snare for most of their impact, with the hi hats occupying a very minor fill-in role. This is primarily to allow the rapper room to display his vocal prowess. In the context of Big Beat this usually allows room for fast bass or guitar riffs or an extremely silly or even annoying vocal sample.

ON THE CD-ROM

The following Hip-Hop beats can be found on the CD-ROM accompanying this book in the following directory: **chapter4/midifiles/drums/hiphop/hiphop01/2/3.mid**.

Our first Hip-Hop example is a classic Hip-Hop beat with the ubiquitous snare beats on beats two and four, as in most dance music. The kick drum interplays with this with two kicks before the first snare, one on the first beat and another on an offbeat. In our example here it's on the last sixteenth offbeat in each bar, only moving onto the eighth offbeat in the last bar. The hi hats are minimal, accenting the offbeats rather than adding anything to the tempo as they do in House or Techno. Note that most of the beats are not strictly quantized, which adds to the human feel of this loop. Using the Electronic kit, a heavily gated kick drum has been used along with a very noisy snare. Although the kick drum is heavily gated it is a 'natural' sounding kick with plenty of boominess and so doesn't have the 'thud' of a gated 909 kick as used in House and Techno. The noisy snare is an almost 'rock' sound.

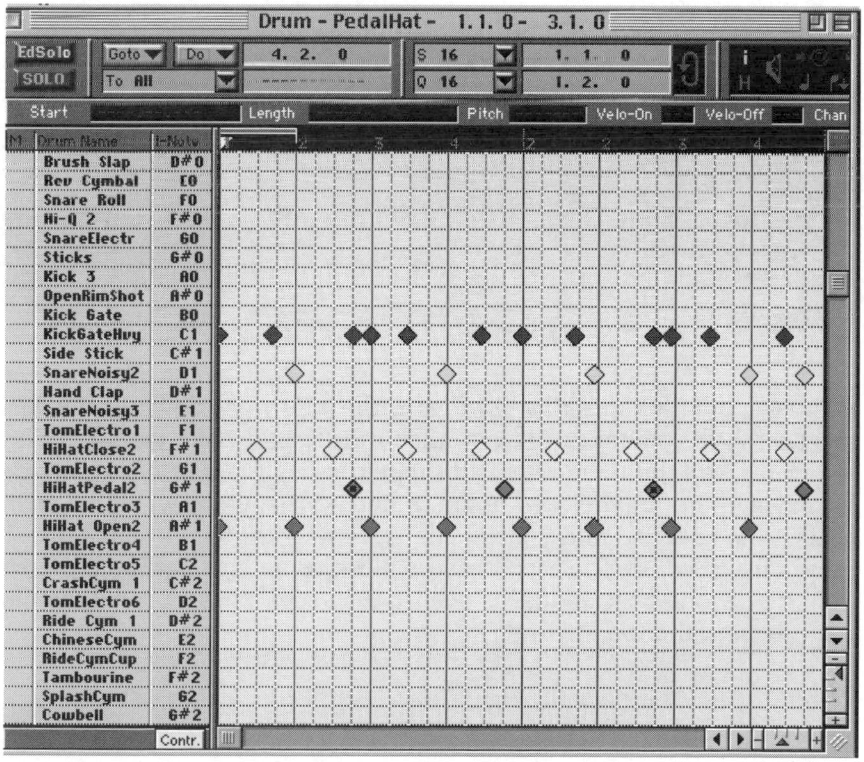

Figure 4.1 *Hip-Hop beats provide the basis for many Big Beat loops.*

The second Hip-Hop loop is an even simpler beat with fewer open hi hats and the same ticking closed hi hat. The snares play essentially the same role as the last loop with a little flourish at the end of the second bar while the kick drum gets busy there too. The kick drum moves into the classic Hip-Hop beat for the first bar of one onbeat followed by an eighth offbeat and then relies on sixteenth offbeats thereafter, building to the interplay with the snare at the end of the second bar. This makes the last beat very busy.

Figure 4.2
Stripped to the bone, Hip-Hop beats are paragons of minimalism.

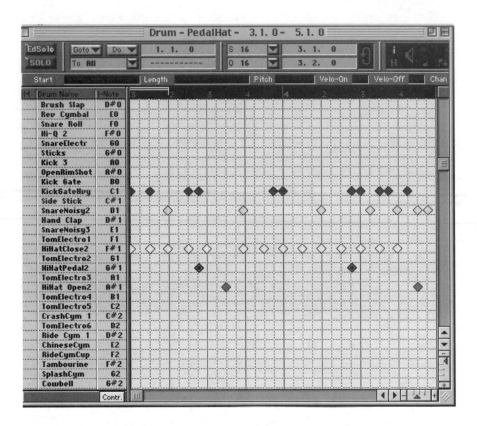

Finally, our last Hip-Hop loop pares the beat right down to one kick per beat (still unquantized) and adds a little laid back business on a second snare. The open hi hats disappear completely, leaving only the ticking eighth offbeat closed hi hat to carry the rhythm while the snare beats on the second and fourth beat move forward to the sixteenth offbeat in the first bar. The second snare picks up an eighth offbeat pattern from the second beat and takes over in the second bar, pushing the first snare even further off the beat.

Figure 4.3
*Beat this!
How low can
you go?*

Electro

Electro beats up the tempo to around 120 bpm and provide most of the source and inspiration for Big Beat loops in this tempo. Once again the Electronic drum kit is the favoured GM program for this sound, evoking the early beatboxes on which most Electro beats were programmed. The Electronic kit features very 'natural' sounding gated kick drums and our first loop makes maximum use of this sound (see Figure 4.4).

Aside from the familiar ticking offbeat hi hat, here played on an even more laid back pedal hi hat sound, the snares are almost entirely absent from this loop, only making a brief appearance at the end of the fourth bar. Claps occupy the fourth beat and the second beat is left free, disrupting the normal pattern. Note the use of two crash cymbals at the end of the fourth bar, layering these two sounds together with a noisy snare for a dirtier sound. The closed hi hat is used in a similar way, layered unquantized with the pedal hi hat to dirty up the loop.

ON THE CD-ROM
The Electro beats featured here can be found on the CD-ROM accompanying this book in the following directory: **chapter4/midifiles/drums/electro/electro01/2/3.mid**.

Figure 4.4
Electro also provides some excellent Big Beat loops.

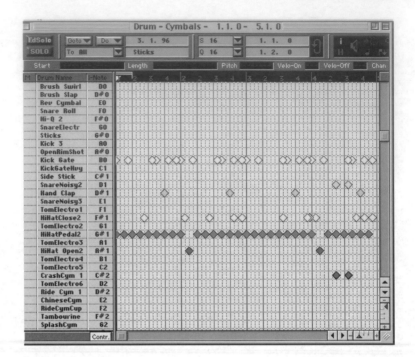

In a similar fashion two kicks are layered in our second Electro beat for a really dirty bottom end to this classic Electro loop. The Hi-Q, an electronic 'blip' of a sound, makes its appearance in the fourth bar

Figure 4.5
The Hi-Q immediately gives that Electro feel to a loop.

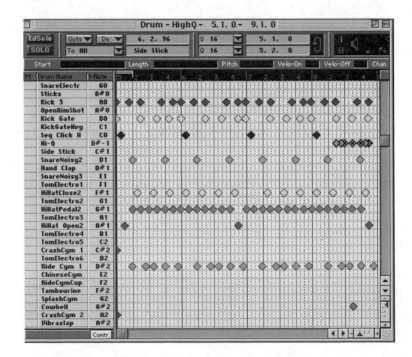

and along with the Seq. click, immediately gives the loop its Electro flavour. Elsewhere the classic snare on beats two and four makes a reappearance interacting with the kick drums and providing the basis of the beat.

Everything else in the loop is decoration. The heavily layered closed and pedal hi hats are played at a very low velocity so they just provide a dirty shuffle. The only other trick to note is the doubled crash cymbal at the beginning of the bar leading to an open hi hat, the whole thing programmed to sound like a sloppy open hi hat hit.

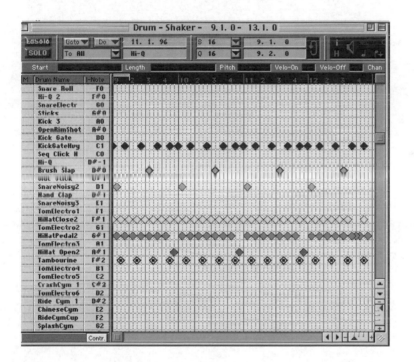

Figure 4.6
Building an Electro beat to a climax: start with a basic beat...

The final Electro beat builds over 12 bars in a classic manner. This obvious build is a favourite of Big Beat programmers and this loop could be broken up into three parts and each used individually, the three parts only being brought back together when the build is needed.

The first four bars establish the basic rhythm, which consists of a sixteenth offbeat kick drum pattern with a single sixteenth offbeat snare at the beginning of each bar. The layered hi hats play the same shuffling underpinning role as in the previous examples with a tambourine added for rhythmic emphasis.

Figure 4.7
*...build the
intensity of the
kicks and snares
then...*

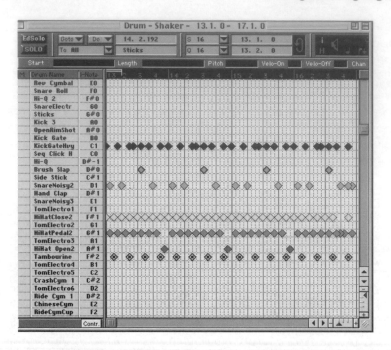

The next four bars build up the intensity of the snare rhythm by adding the familiar snare pattern on beats two and four. Everything else stays the same yet the contrasting business of the snares and kick drums makes the loop sound completely different when played in isolation from the preceding four bars.

Figure 4.8
*...pile
everything on
for a final
flourish!*

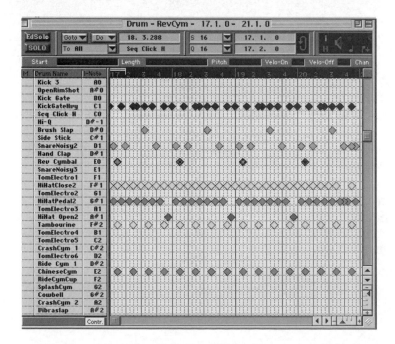

Everything gets really busy in the last four bars, with a reverse cymbal muddying up the open hi hat pattern and a Chinese cymbal performing the same honours on the tambourine pattern, which has remained unchanged throughout the previous eight bars. What makes the last bar sound busier is the gated kick drum which has been getting progressively busier throughout the whole 12 bars. Because this is a gated 'natural' sounding kick the effect is actually more like a drummer getting progressively busy on a couple of snare drums and the whole build has an organic progression to it.

The complete absence of quantization is an integral part of this natural feel. Loops like this are usually best played 'live' from the keyboard, building them up in layers and leaving the quantize button alone. If you have a set of MIDI drum pads and are a keen drummer you might like to play a loop like this live in one take.

Big Beats

Most Big Beat loops are sampled from 70s funk and Hip-Hop records and as such are essentially R'n'B breaks which are all variations on the funky drummer type of loop. This, in its most basic format, consists of a kick on beat one, two snares on beats two and four and a shuffle on or around beat three. The shuffle is usually made up of a few sixteenth snares and some offbeat kicks and that's exactly the pattern our first example follows.

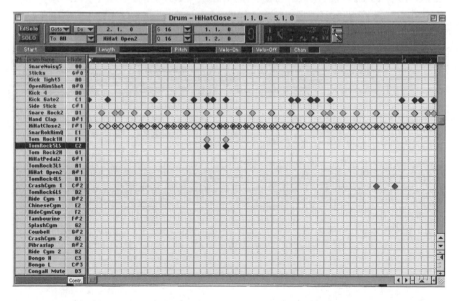

Figure 4.9
The basic Big Beat: kicks, snares and a shuffle.

The metronomic ticking hi hat is unquantized and has actually had a degree of this added by the use of Cubase's 'Groove' feature. Once again a mixture of low and medium velocities makes this pattern one that is almost subliminal in its dirtiness, mimicking the sound of a badly sampled loop. In our illustration the XG Rock Kit 2 (Program 18) has been used, as this features a wonderfully noisy snare and very bright hi hats. This loop works equally well with the standard rock kit and even the electronic kit if you're feeling really brave.

ON THE CD-ROM

The three Big Beats featured here can be found on the CD-ROM accompanying this book in the following directory: **chapter4/midifiles/drums/bigbeats/ hbigbeat1/2/3.mid**.

The only other things to note about this loop are the use of the two toms, doubled up in the second bar to muddy up beats one and two on the kick drum and thus emulate the dirtiness of a sampled loop. These tom hits use a very low velocity setting so they don't actually override the kick drum. The two crash cymbals in beat four of bar three perform the same function for the snare sound, adding variety to the texture.

A machine gun snare makes an appearance in our second Big Beat loop. This pattern breaks the mould of the previous example, moving the emphasis to the last beat of a bar with the rapid volley of sixteenth snares providing the 'machine gun' effect, mimicking the breakdown a real drummer might use to signify a change of beat. A ride cymbal is used instead of a high hat, as this is exactly what a 'real' drummer would do when playing a breakdown of this sort.

Figure 4.10
Machine gun snares are a Big Beat staple.

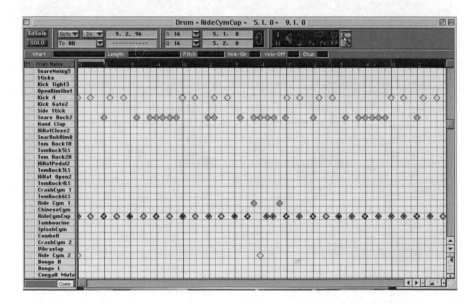

The kick drums in this loop are busy in the first two beats of every bar and then effectively hand over to the snares the business of keeping the groove intact. Once again a second ride cymbal is used at a low velocity to vary the texture of the ride cymbal pattern which features wide variations in velocity to emulate the 'human' variation a live drummer would bring to this part.

Our third example is an almost textbook example of the classic R'n'B loop referred to in our first Big Beat loop, featuring the classic snares on beats two and four, a kick drum at the beginning of every bar and a shuffle on the snares around beat three. The closed hi hat plays a very open eighth offbeat pattern with an open hi hat at the beginning of every bar on the first eighth offbeat for a syncopated feel.

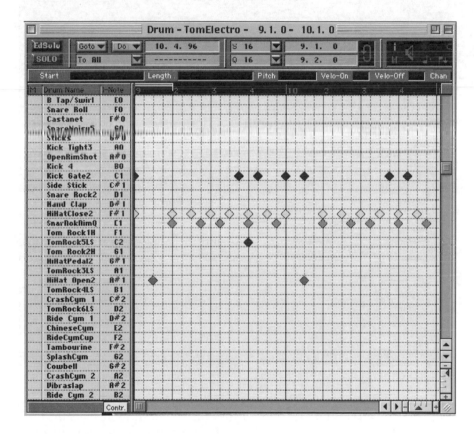

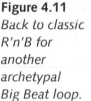

Figure 4.11
Back to classic R'n'B for another archetypal Big Beat loop.

This beat is perhaps the most useful of all the Big Beats we've programmed here and could be used in a variety of ways. Try revoicing it on various drum kits on your GM or XG module or playing it on drum kits of your own devising, made up of samples. You could also try playing the two snares around beat three, which play the shuffle, on a different snare sound or sample to the other snares.

We'll finish off our Big Beat programming with a couple of fills. The first is a classic snare roll as played by a drummer, not the mechanical rolls we've looked at in the House and Techno chapters.

ON THE CD-ROM
These Big Beat fills can be found on the CD-ROM accompanying this book in the following directory: **chapter4/midifiles/drums/bigbeats/**. *There are two files* **bigbe_fl.mid** *and* **bigbro.mid**.

Figure 4.12
Four-to-the-floor does feature in Big Beat sometimes!

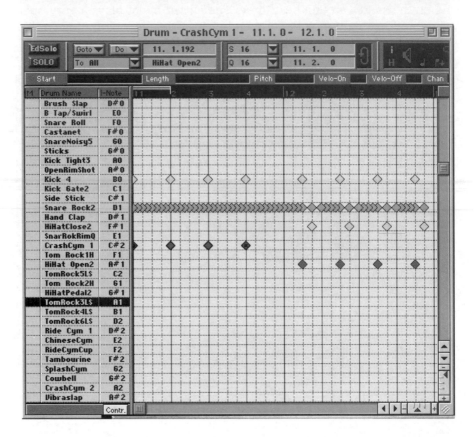

The kick drum starts off playing something we've not seen so far in Big Beat programming, a four-to-the-floor kick emphasized by four crashes on the beat. This prevents it from sounding anything like the disco beat of House and signals a breakdown in the groove to any rock fan. The kick moves to the offbeat in the second bar echoed this time by an open hi hat to emulate the effect of the drummer hitting a cymbal less harshly as he concentrates on breaking up his snare roll. A closed hi hat is placed on the sixteenth after every offbeat as an echo of the open hi hat and that, combined with the break up of the sixteenth snare roll, makes for a very human sounding fill.

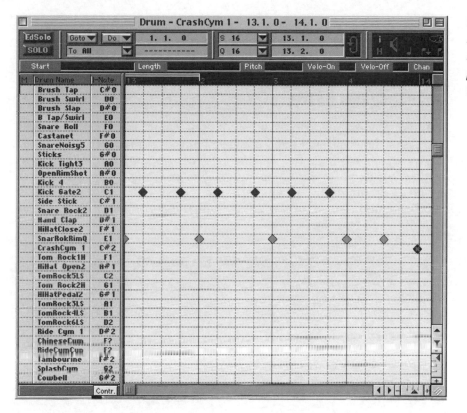

Figure 4.13
A classic 'rock' breakdown provides our final fill.

Our final fill is a classic rock breakdown. The snares occupy the four square on the beat pattern we've previously seen occupied by the kick drum while the kick drum stutters around on sixteenths offbeats like a drummer struggling to bring it all back on to the beat. A crash signs off the bar with a flourish and we're ready to roll back into any one of our main grooves.

Programming Big Beat basslines

Once you have a series of kicking drumbeats, whether sampled or programmed, the bass part is the next most important part in Big Beat. Big Beat basses are all about riffs. Whether sampled from an old rock record or boogie blues album, the bigger and badder the better. The attack of a real bass helps to give a Big Beat track its punch as R'n'B basses play continuous eighths or sixteenths, driving the music along. If you don't have access to a real live bass, or any samples of one, either use a really dirty synth or electric bass sound. The best results usually come from layering one sound against the other, a dirty synth sound against a hard, picked bass sound.

Emulating live bass

Our first programmed Big Beat bass is a classic R'n'B progression, familiar from a thousand blues and boogie albums. It's a fast variation on that classic of all basslines, the walking bassline, stepping its way through a scale with lots of forward momentum. This bassline really drives a beat along. Try matching it up with the classic Big Beat drum loop (**BigBeat3.mid**). This loop works best with the dry sound of a picked bass (GM Program No. 35).

Figure 4.14
Fast offbeat eighth notes for a boogie bassline.

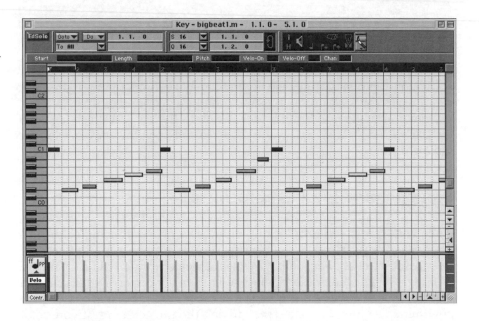

Another variation on the walking bassline, our second example walks its way up through the scale in offbeat eighths and sixteenths, returning to a third above the root note for its turn. Once again this bassline has a driving boogie rhythm and works best with a dry picked, fretless or finger bass.

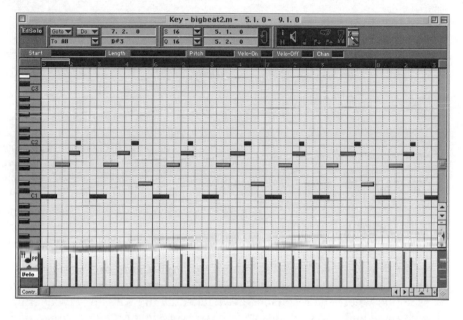

Figure 4.15
Combine offbeat eighth and sixteenth notes for a driving bassline.

TIP

The finger bass (GM Program 34) and the fretless bass (GM Program 36) are also excellent choices for a 'real' bass sound.

Octave jumping is another favourite trick of boogie bassists and our next example combines the walking bassline with octave shifting for a 'jump up' bassline. In contrast to the previous examples this bassline sounds better on a big dirty synth bass sound.

TIP

Synthbass1 (GM Program 39) and Synthbass2 (GM Program 40) are good starting points for a dirty synth sound. If you have a GS or XG synth, the variations on these two will provide some wonderfully crusty synth bass sounds.

Figure 4.16
Combine the walking bassline with octave shifts for a pumping bassline.

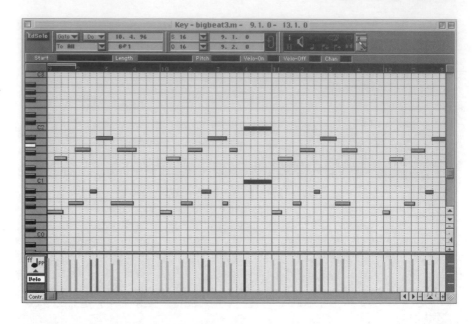

Figure 4.16
Combine the walking bassline with octave shifts for a pumping bassline.

Using Techno basslines

Our next bassline, in direct contrast to the preceding examples, comes straight from the world of Techno. A simple three-note affair, it alternates between long and short notes and thus works best with a synth bass sound where the resonance is whacked all the way up. Try layering this bassline with a fast boogie style bassline played on a dry bass sound for a classic Big Beat mayhem effect.

Figure 4.17
Techno and acid basslines are used just as much in Big Beat as boogie ones.

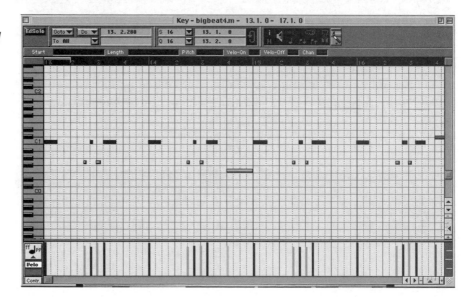

NOTE

Make sure you set your bass sound to mono mode for Techno basses or you'll lose the portamento effect essential to the sound.

Another Techno-style bassline completes our quintet of Big Beat basses. This one uses octave shifting in a more minimalistic Techno fashion than the walking boogie bassline and sounds better on a dirty synth sound, as in our previous example. If you want to go all out for the funk try the Slapbass patches for a real 'out there' sound.

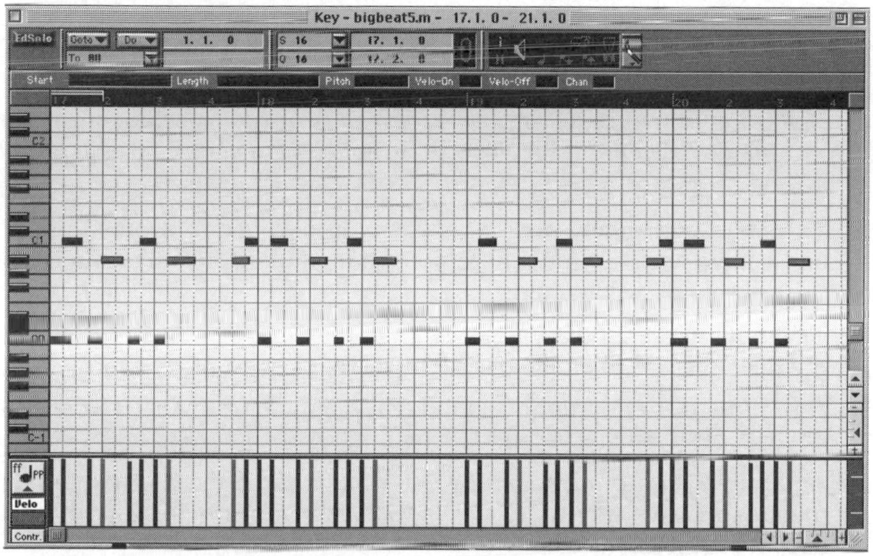

Figure 4.18 *Octave shifts and minimalism in a Techno bassline.*

TIP

Slapbass1 (GM Program 37) and Slapbass2 (GM Program 38) provide very funky slapped bass sounds.

NOTE

Big Beat basses often move quickly following the movement of the fast hi hat sixteenths. Sometimes the bass is use to create a reggae feel by dropping from the root note to the fifth. There is also a lot of octave jumping in Big Beat bass writing. When a bass line leaves its root notes it will often be a funky line with lots of syncopation.

Programming Big Beat Guitars

The other essential elements of a Big Beat track are guitar parts, noises, dirty vocal samples and repeated synth riffs. All of these add the muck, dirt and industrial sound which form an important part of Big Beat. The trick is to experiment with weird sounds/instruments and if it sounds bizarre use it! We'll have a look at the guitar parts first and then explore a few of the more unusual noises found in Big Beat tracks.

> **TIP**
>
> *Big Beat tracks usually groove around one chord (usually a minor) or a sampled riff that is repeated* **ad infinitum.**

Electric guitars are a very important part of the Big Beat style and unfortunately they are difficult to reproduce using sound modules. The following tricks work well though:

- To create convincing power chords only play the root plus the fifth and octave above, as any more notes added muddy up the sound and start to sound uncharacteristic.

- Try moving the individual notes in a chord progressively further off the quantize grid to emulate the way a real guitarist plays chords.

- Add some distortion on the sound (Amp Simulator tends to work well on an overdriven guitar sound (Program 30).

- Add movement to the sound by entering cut-off filter information, the most expressive way to do this is to assign your modulator wheel to output cut-off information.

Figure 4.19
Syncopated rhythms make funky basslines.

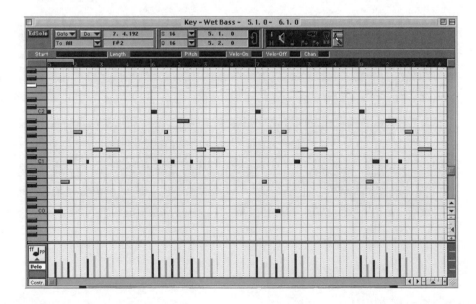

Filter wah wah effects

Starting with the last trick first we'll use filter cut-off frequency to add some guitar style funkiness to a bass groove. Our bass groove is not a bassline as such but more of a funk-style riff, using lots of syncopation. See Figure 4.19.

By mapping the modulation wheel to Control 74, which is Filter Cut-off Frequency, or 'Brightness' in XG terminology, we can manipulate the bass sound and make it sound like a guitar played through a wah wah pedal.

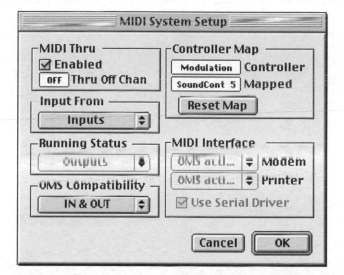

Figure 4.20
Mapping the modulation wheel to control MIDI controller 74 (listed as Sound Controller 5 in Cubase).

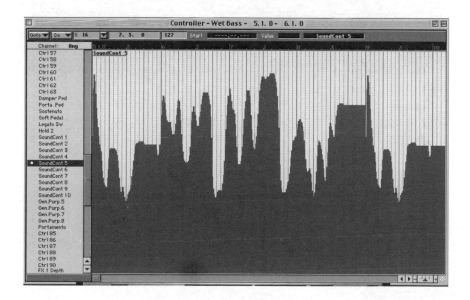

Figure 4.21
The filter frequency control change events are recorded as part of the track.

Programming guitar chords

The simplest way to program realistic-sounding guitar chords on a MIDI module is to play a one-note riff first then 'chord it up'. Our example here is s simple riff, played on two notes, fading out toward the end as the progressively lower velocity values played in produce a MIDI echo effect.

Figure 4.22
*A simple
two-note riff,
played on either
mute guitar
or guitar
harmonics.*

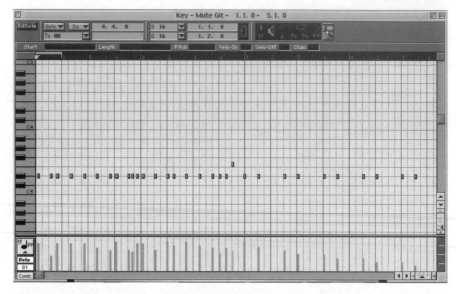

NOTE

This has been played using the GM patch, Guitar harmonics (GM Program 32), for a reasonable simulation of a guitar sound. The other alternative is the Mute Guitar patch (GM Program 29). Sadly the guitar patches don't sound very realistic on single-note riffs such as this and so may ruin your concentration as you struggle to visualize a guitar sound.

To turn this one note riff into a guitar-style chord it is now only necessary to copy the track twice onto succeeding tracks. Set the copies to a more regular guitar sound and then transpose the first copy up by a fifth and the second copy up by an octave.

TIP

GM Program 31, Distorted Guitar and Program 32, Overdrive Guitar usually sound more realistic than the other guitar patches in the GM set, especially for this type of riff.

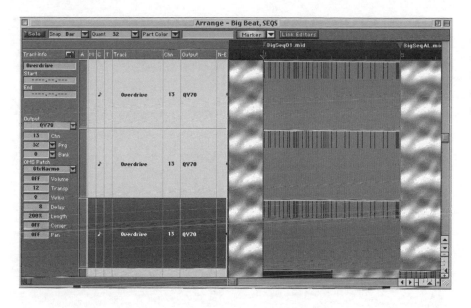

Figure 4.23
Copies of the one note riff, transposed up one fifth and an octave.

It probably still doesn't sound like a guitar riff, as the notes are all playing at the same time. A guitarist strikes the strings on a guitar either up or down and hence each successive string is struck slightly later than the preceding one. To emulate this effect add a delay to each track. You only want to add a small amount, 4–6 ticks or you'll end up with an arpeggio which is not what you want.

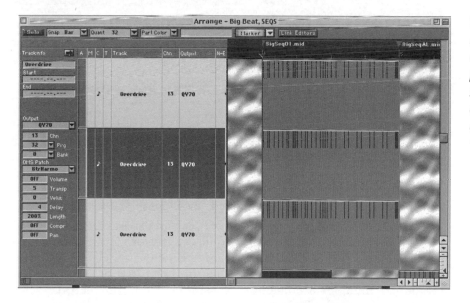

Figure 4.24
Add delay to each track to produce a staggered series of sounds, emulating a 'real' guitarist.

Once you're satisfied with the result, mix the various tracks down to one complete track.

Figure 4.25
The Grid editor showing the mixed down track with each successive note slightly later than its predecessor.

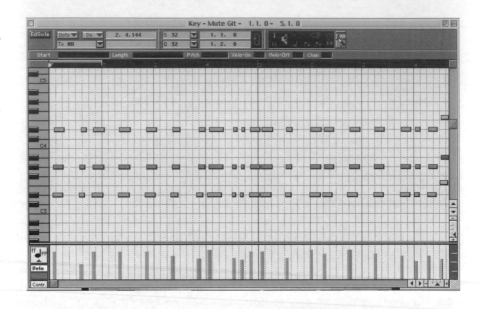

Programming bells, whistles, scratches and sirens

With the basic building blocks of your Big Beat band in place, all that remains is to assemble a collection of weird sounds to add the icing to your Big Beat cake. Lots of dirty screams, sirens and gritty saw waves playing single note patterns grace Big Beat tracks. Use the filters in real time, set sounds to monophonic, and play with the module's effects and use portamento to recreate these sounds (see Figure 4.26).

This is where it's time to get adventurous and experimental. Try playing a hi hat pattern on a monophonic saw wave synth sound or a bassline on the GM SFX kit, pitched up or down to trigger the weirdest sounds in the kit. If you have a sampler, or direct to disk recording set-up, gather together a collection of samples from old records, sci-fi movies and even the Internet! Don't be afraid of dirt in your samples either. Sometimes it's the weird background noise in a sample that adds the right effect to a track (see Figure 4.27).

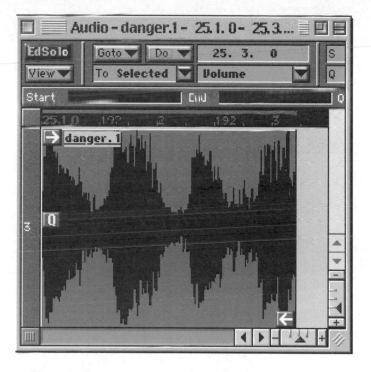

Start Position	Length	Val1	Val2	Val3	Event Type	Chn	Comment
1. 2.228	-------	0	0	---	BankSel.MSB	14	Bank Select
1. 2.228	-------	32	6	---	BankSel.LSB	14	Bank Select LSB
1. 2.230	-------	82	---	---	ProgChange	14	Saw Wave
1. 2.234	-------	7	100	---	MainVolume	14	Volume
1. 2.236	-------	10	44	---	Pan	14	Pan
1. 2.237	-------	11	127	---	Expression	14	Expression
1. 2.240	-------	91	40	---	FX 1 Depth	14	Ext FX Depth
1. 2.240	-------	93	0	---	FX 3 Depth	14	Chorus Depth
1. 2.242	-------	94	0	---	FX 4 Depth	14	Celeste Dpth
1. 2.244	-------	71	127	---	SoundCont 2	14	(Control 71)
1. 2.256	-------	126	1	---	MonoModeOn	14	Mono On

Figure 4.26
Set-up for a monophonic saw wave for Big Beat effects.

Figure 4.27
This sample from a TV show has a strange whistle in the background that adds to, rather than detracts from, a Big Beat track.

The GM, GS and XG drum kits and SFK kits also include lots of scratching noises and these can be applied liberally for a touch of old school Hip-Hop flavour. Check out the telephone rings, car crashes, helicopter and other weird sounds gathered together between Programs 123 and 128 of the standard GM Programs.

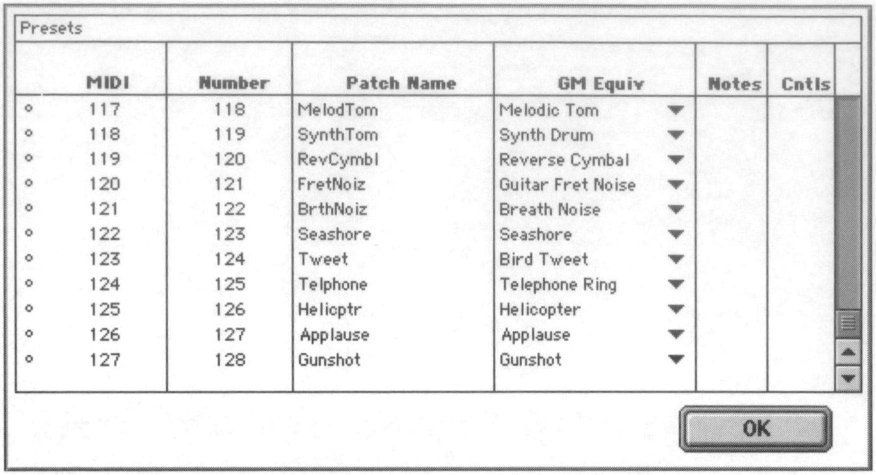

Figure 4.28
*GM Programs
123–128 are
the weird ones.*

	MIDI	Number	Patch Name	GM Equiv		Notes	Cntls
○	117	118	MelodTom	Melodic Tom	▼		
○	118	119	SynthTom	Synth Drum	▼		
○	119	120	RevCymbl	Reverse Cymbal	▼		
○	120	121	FretNoiz	Guitar Fret Noise	▼		
○	121	122	BrthNoiz	Breath Noise	▼		
○	122	123	Seashore	Seashore	▼		
○	123	124	Tweet	Bird Tweet	▼		
○	124	125	Telphone	Telephone Ring	▼		
○	125	126	Helicptr	Helicopter	▼		
○	126	127	Applause	Applause	▼		
○	127	128	Gunshot	Gunshot	▼		

Presets

OK

If you have a GS or XG synth there's an even wider selection of weird noises at your disposal. Don't be afraid of the obvious, as Big Beat thrives on cheesiness and using obvious noises. If you think something is too obvious or clichéd try sampling it and playing around with the sound, reversing it or squashing the sound with the filters. Be bold!

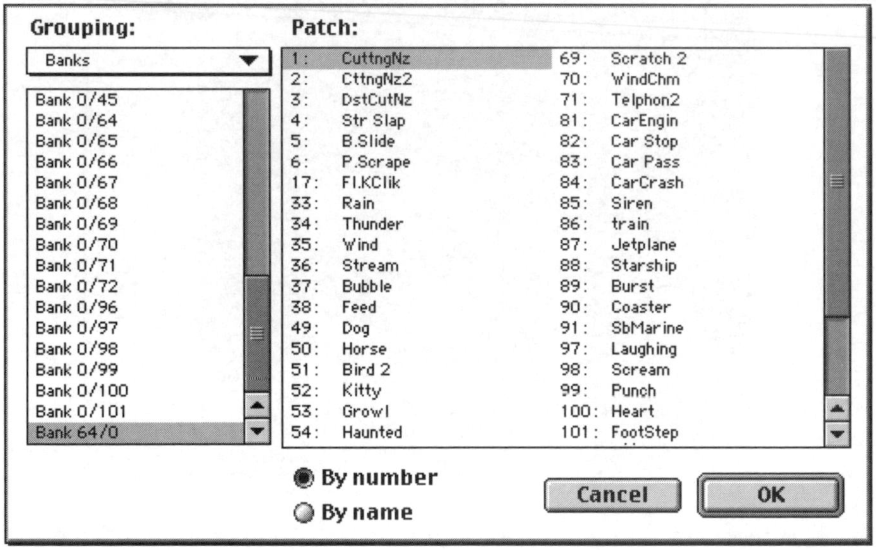

Figure 4.29
*Program map
showing XG
'Noise'
Programs.*

Grouping: Banks

Bank 0/45, Bank 0/64, Bank 0/65, Bank 0/66, Bank 0/67, Bank 0/68, Bank 0/69, Bank 0/70, Bank 0/71, Bank 0/72, Bank 0/96, Bank 0/97, Bank 0/98, Bank 0/99, Bank 0/100, Bank 0/101, Bank 64/0

Patch:

1: CuttngNz	69: Scratch 2
2: CttngNz2	70: WindChm
3: DstCutNz	71: Telphon2
4: Str Slap	81: CarEngin
5: B.Slide	82: Car Stop
6: P.Scrape	83: Car Pass
17: Fl.KClik	84: CarCrash
33: Rain	85: Siren
34: Thunder	86: train
35: Wind	87: Jetplane
36: Stream	88: Starship
37: Bubble	89: Burst
38: Feed	90: Coaster
49: Dog	91: SbMarine
50: Horse	97: Laughing
51: Bird 2	98: Scream
52: Kitty	99: Punch
53: Growl	100: Heart
54: Haunted	101: FootStep

◉ By number   ○ By name   Cancel   OK

Arranging a Big Beat track

When it comes time to put together your Big Beat track you'll want to gather together all the parts in as easily accessible a mode as possible.

Big Beat, for all its sounding like a 'real' beat combo is arranged in a DJ style. Everything is mixed like a DJ would mix, cutting from one obvious riff to another, often mid bar. Of the methods we've looked at in arranging tracks for House and Techno the obvious ones are those where you can 'play' your parts from a keyboard. This style gives you the most flexibility in making a DJ style mix.

Those methods are:

- Sampling everything and loading all the parts into a sampler, then 'playing the track from the keyboard.

- Arranging all the parts in a sequencer so an external device, as shown in Figure 4.30, can trigger them.

- Recording everything to disk and arranging the parts in a dedicated digital mixing program like ProTools or Acid (see Figure 4.31).

- Arranging the parts in blocks and playing around with the arrangement in the arrange page. Cubase has a Group function that allows you to group parts into 'Groups' and make your arrangement from these blocks (see Figure 4.32).

- Using the traditional arrange page or sequence editor to fine-tune your arrangement (see Figures 4.33 and 4.34).

Figure 4.30
Our Big Beat parts all lined up and ready to mix in Opcode's Vision.

Figure 4.31
The big beat parts being arranged in Sonic Foundry's Acid.

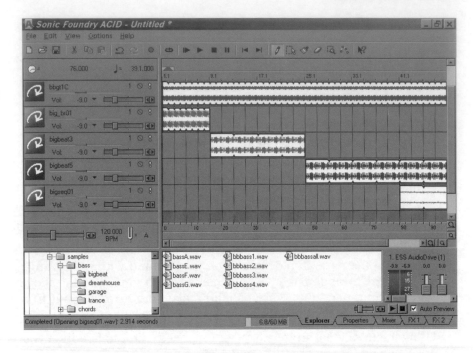

Figure 4.32
The Big Beat track in Cubase 'Groups' being arranged on a separate arrange page.

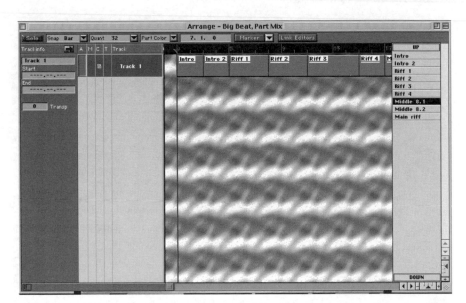

Whichever method you choose, the arrangement should follow the Big Beat pattern of jumping from one obvious riff to another. Link together the sections with obvious builds like ramped velocities and fast cuts between contrasting sections. In Figure 4.35 our arrangement jumps

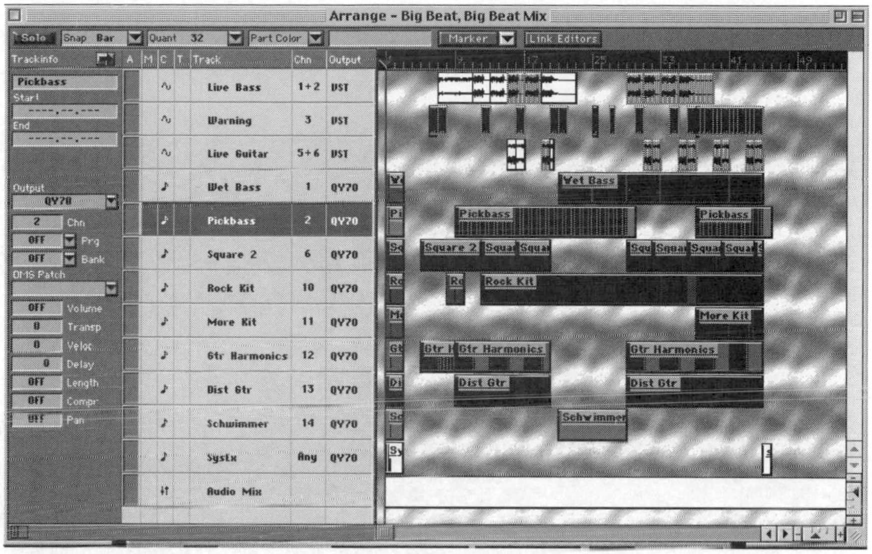

Figure 4.33
The Big Beat track as laid out on Cubase's arrange page.

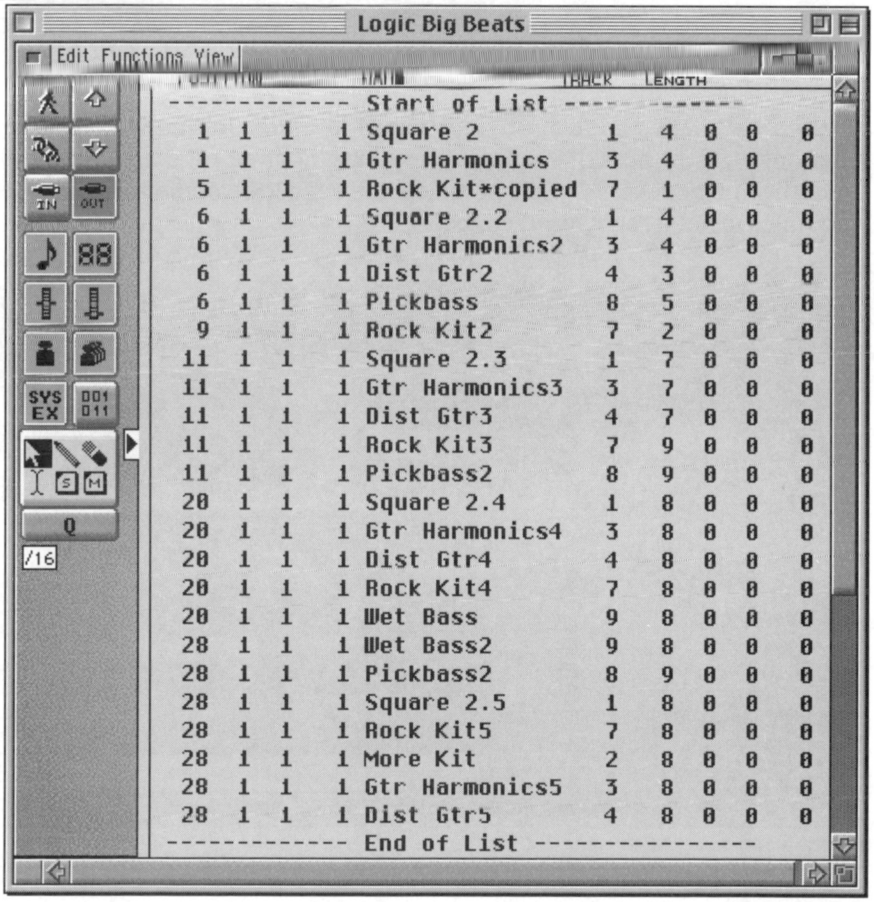

Figure 4.34
The Big Beat track as laid out in Logic's sequence editor.

between the programmed guitar riff we made earlier and a sampled guitar riff, placed in the gaps.

Figure 4.35
Chopping between sampled and MIDI guitar parts.

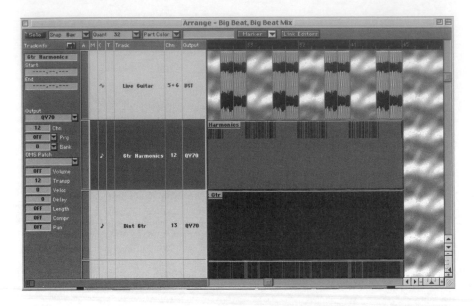

Big Beat makes a lot of obvious tricks like this, jumping from quiet sections straight into riffs where everything is piled together for maximum bad boy effect. Don't be afraid to over-egg the pudding; in Big Beat too much is not a recognized concept!

Figure 4.36
The intro jumps from a very quiet section to one where lots of sounds are piled on.

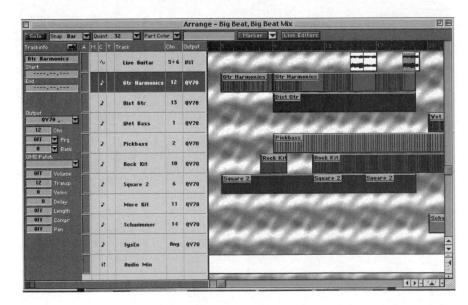

Go for the obvious, layering together basslines and guitar riffs with scratching noises, whistles, sirens and whatever other samples take your fancy. Big Beat is all about having fun and creating a frathouse party atmosphere – let the big kid in you come out to play!

The kick drum isn't as important in Big Beat as in other dance styles so don't put it too high in the mix. Where kick drums are boosted in Big Beat is when you want a booming bass drum that sounds more like a bass guitar and takes the place of that instrument. Normally you would boost the bass drum around 50Hz but for a booming bass drum add some boost around 90–200Hz. You'll probably find you need to cut bass drums rather than boosting them in these ranges or else they'll dominate the mix too much.

Snares are where you do need to add boost, normally around the 400–800 Hz range, which is where most of their solid mid-range frequencies lie. When adding reverb to snares don't use too much brightness or top end, as that is not the area you want to emphasize. Try a short reverb, no more than 1.5 seconds. If you have a compressor try a ratio of around 10:1 with a relatively slow release time of 5–10ms for real dirty sounding snares. You may need to shorten the release time if the snares are crowding the mix.

Much use is made of panning in Big Beat. Try panning two hi hat patterns (or the same pattern copied) hard left and right for a spacious top end. If you have an auto-panner this can be very effective, applied to vocal samples or guitar riffs for maximum excitement.

Figure 4.37
Make maximum use of obvious effects like this plug-in auto-panner effect.

Figure 4.38
Whether a plug-in effect or real, a fuzz box and other guitar pedals are an integral part of the Big Beat sound.

Cheap guitar pedals are an almost essential element of the Big Beat sound, providing nice and dirty reverbs and the other similar sounds. The ultimate 'dirty' sound effect is the fuzz box. This is especially effective applied to bass and guitar riffs, as is the ubiquitous wah wah pedal (see Figure 4.38).

This chapter has looked at cutting up breakbeats to make Big Beats, pushing sixteenth basslines to produce driving riffs and programming killer guitar riffs. Putting together a Big Beat track is the easy part and you should be confident enough by now to do this. Chapter 5 looks at cutting up breakbeats and breaking down basslines even more as we dive deep into the junglist heart of Drum'n'Bass.

5 Drum'n'Bass

Drum'n'Bass is the evolution of Jungle. It was Jungle that first took breakbeats and sped them up to tempos that had never been heard before in Electronica. The result was frenetic and aurally new. Breakbeats are sampled and retriggered to create rhythmic variations. Layer a healthy sub-bass sine wave sound over the beats, add some string chords and you've got Jungle.

Of course there's more to it than that but it was from this that Drum'n'Bass grew. This music has evolved into a well respected style with the likes of Bowie and Madonna grabbing a slice of the Drum'n'Bass pie. The sped up loops are still there but are now complemented with extra, programmed drums and well thought out chords and textures.

Drum'n'Bass is a groove-based style, as there is a lot going on rhythmically. With performers such as Goldie and Roni Size, Drum'n'Bass has broken into the pop chart scene featuring tracks with a stronger song structure and lyrics. Drum'n'Bass is still evolving and is becoming a certain sound or feel that can be added to any song at almost any speed.

Now Techno has embraced breakbeats again, the evolution is coming full circle as many Techno practitioners rediscover their roots through exploring the creative use of breakbeats. If you want to explore this fascinating new musical venture, check out early Electro and Techno just as much as current Jungle classics. There's a whole new musical landscape being explored in this process and in true Techno tradition it exists with one eye focused firmly on the future and the other on the past.

In our exploration of Drum'n'Bass we'll first look at programming some drum loops in various Drum'n'Bass styles. Next we'll examine the process of programming dub basslines to go with those beats. Finally we'll program up jazzy chords and create our own Drum'n'Bass track.

Programming Drum'n'Bass drums

If Techno can be said to have begun the process of deconstructing drum beats, Drum'n'Bass takes the process to its logical extreme, cutting up drum patterns into ever smaller sections, shifting their pitch and timing to transform them into unrecognisable blurs of rhythm. Where Techno uses the sequencer to achieve this, Jungle initially relied heavily on the time-stretching capabilities of samplers to perform this process.

At first no one thought it possible to program Jungle beats, so fast were the time-stretched snare rolls and hi hat patterns resulting from this. The evolution of Jungle into Drum'n'Bass has seen Techno programmers get to grips with this new musical form, analyzing the beats of pioneers such as Roni Size and Goldie to produce their own, programmed Jungle grooves. Early Electro and Techno used breakbeats almost as Jungle does now, only the speed was slower and their use less frequent.

The process of programming breakbeats involves extensive cutting up of parts and much manipulation of musical data. The drums are the most important part of Drum'n'Bass and recreating them represents a challenges for the MIDI programmer. If drums are sampled and then played at a faster BPM two things happen: the drum pitch goes up and the beat sounds quicker. To mimic this process in MIDI all you need to do is pitch up the drum kit by an appropriate amount. Sometimes a loop is played back more slowly so a pitched down drum kit is also useful.

The term Jungle arose from the idea of life being an urban jungle in which people must struggle to survive. Drum'n'Bass describes the musical emphasis of the music far better as the focus is on booming sub-bass tones in the kick section and bright pitched-up drum sounds in the snare and hi hat section of a Jungle groove.

The use of those booming sub-basses with their long delays precludes any busy kick patterns and accordingly the emphasis is on rattling snare rolls and swishing hi hat patterns. We'll start our exploration of Drum'n'Bass beats by looking at the rattliest of styles, Hardcore. Next we'll look at some true Junglist loops and finally we'll examine some Drum'n'Bass loops.

Breakbeats

Jungle and Drum'n'Bass both started by time-stretching and pitching up funky R'n'B drum patterns like the infamous 'Funky Drummer' or 'Amen Brother' beats, then breaking down the various parts to transform the groove. Our first examples, drawn straight from the earliest style of Drum'n'Bass, called Breakbeat or Hardcore use these funky beats as a starting point.

Our first example sounds like an authentic Hardcore beat but quickly betrays its origin if we slow it down to its original 96 bpm, then the basis of most funky loops is plain to see. First and most obvious are the two hits on beats two and four. These are played on the electric snare and doubled up on the handclaps for added emphasis. The next element of the funky groove is the shuffle around beat three. Here it is played on first the electric snare and then the kick drum to break up the pattern. This is a common pattern and one that we'll encounter in several variations throughout this section.

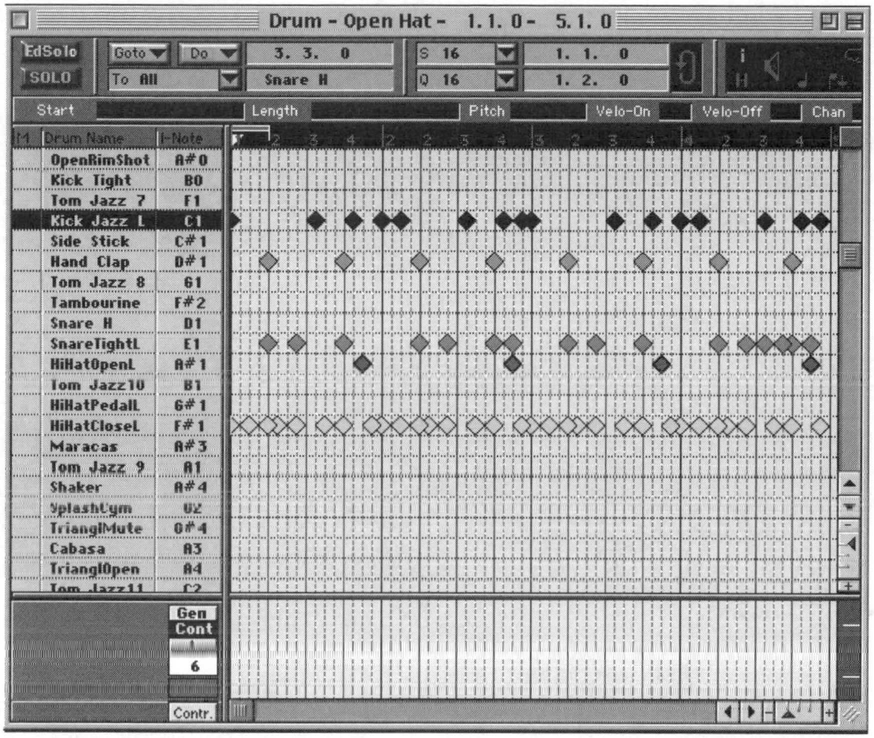

Figure 5.1
Most breakbeats started life as funky R'n'B loops.

The loop features a further shuffle at the end of each bar, once again alternating the kick and snare. This is further emphasized by the open hi hat at the end of each bar. This plays in the gap left by both the kick and snare and the closed hi hat pattern, mimicking the playing of a live drummer. Live drummers played the original funky loops and you should bear this in mind when programming up your starting beats. You can ignore this once you start cutting up and layering the loops later but for maximum authenticity now is the time to think like a 'real' drummer.

ON THE CD-ROM
The breakbeat loops featured in this section can be found on the CD-ROM accompanying this book in the following directory: **chapter5/midifiles/ drums/breakbeat/breakb01/2/3.mid**.

Breakbeat number two is more of a cut-up loop with the first two beats being relatively 'natural' while the second two beats in each bar act like retriggered parts of the first two beats. The kick drum has been 'time-stretched' so that it plays in double-time. What has happened is that the kick drum now occupies all four beats, taking over the work of the snare on beat four, and has extra, syncopated sixteenth beats added in before the second and fourth beats. This gives the loop a double-time effect commonly found in Hardcore.

Figure 5.2

A four square kick drum under breakbeats makes for a classic Hardcore loop.

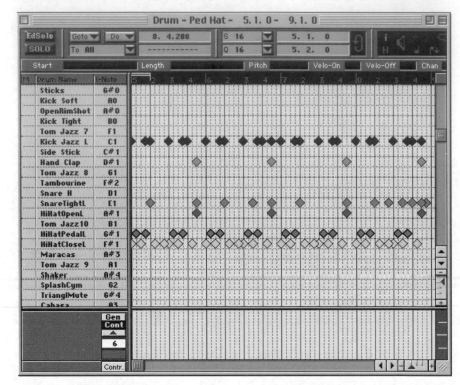

The closed/open hi hat pattern is nearly identical to the first break-beat but has had a shuffling pedal hi hat added to underline the syncopated double-time beat of the kick drum. The kick drum was 'time-stretched' by using a transform function to double the tempo of the kick drum. Most sequencers offer some form of function like this which enables you to multiply the placing of the notes of a piece so that it plays in double time.

Time-stretching MIDI drum loops

In Cubase you perform this in the Logical editor while Logic calls it the transform function. Vision allows you to alter this aspect of a piece directly with its 'Scale Time' function while Cakewalk has a 'Length' function that you access from the 'Edit' menu in order to alter the tempo of a part.

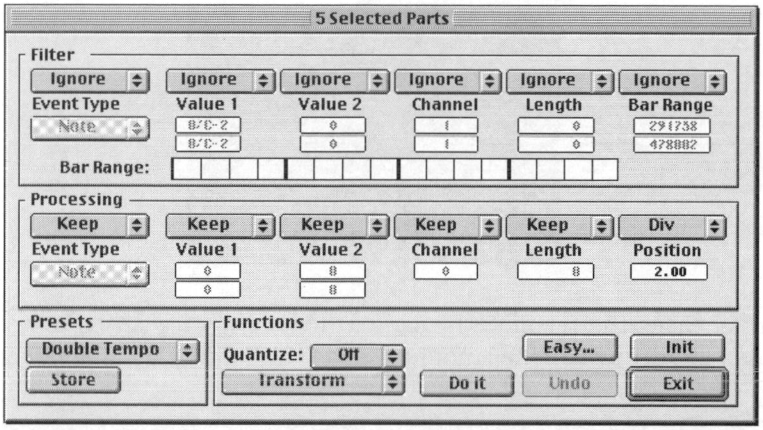

Figure 5.3
Cubase's Logical editor set to divide the notes in a piece to play in double tempo.

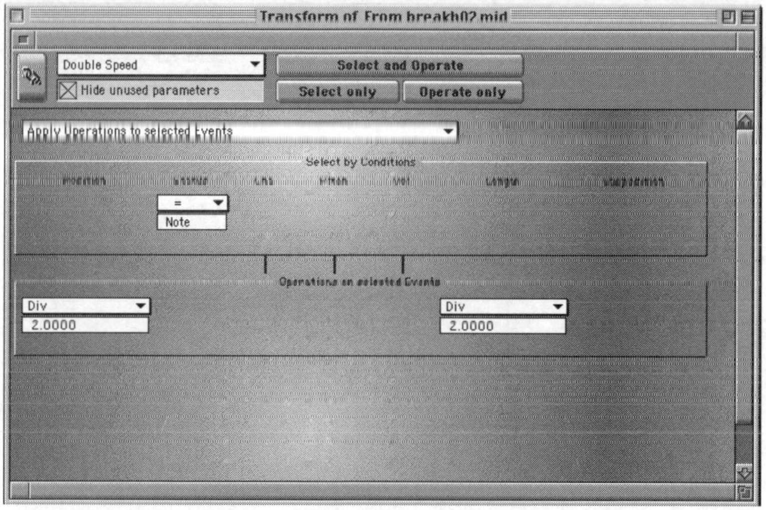

Figure 5.4
Logic's Transform function set to do the same.

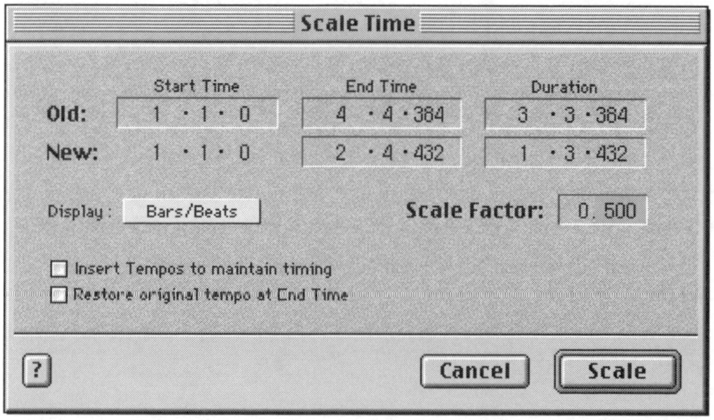

Figure 5.5
Opcode's Vision set to double the tempo within its Scale Time function.

Figure 5.6
*The Length
function in
Cakewalk can
double the
tempo of a part.*

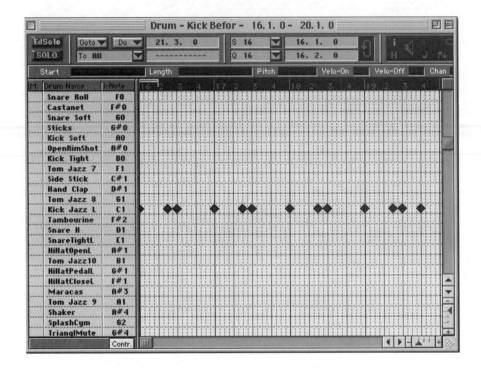

In all cases the result is the same: the timing of a series of notes is divided to occupy half the amount of space and thus play in double time.

Figures 5.7
*Kick drums
before tempo
doubling.*

Our last breakbeat is a regular funky loop played at double tempo. In the first bar of each two bar section we see the familiar pattern of a snare on beats two and four. The following bar then 'breaks' up this pattern by moving the second snare forward in time, placing it a sixteenth before the fourth beat. Extra snares are added on the third beat and after the fourth beat for that all-important funky shuffle (see Figure 5.9).

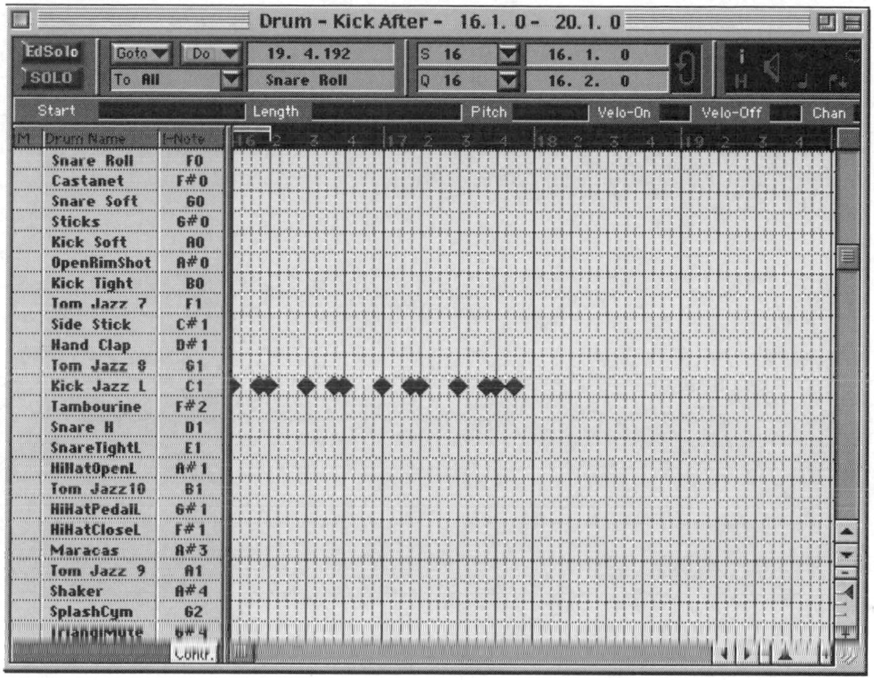

Figure 5.8
Kick drums after tempo doubling.

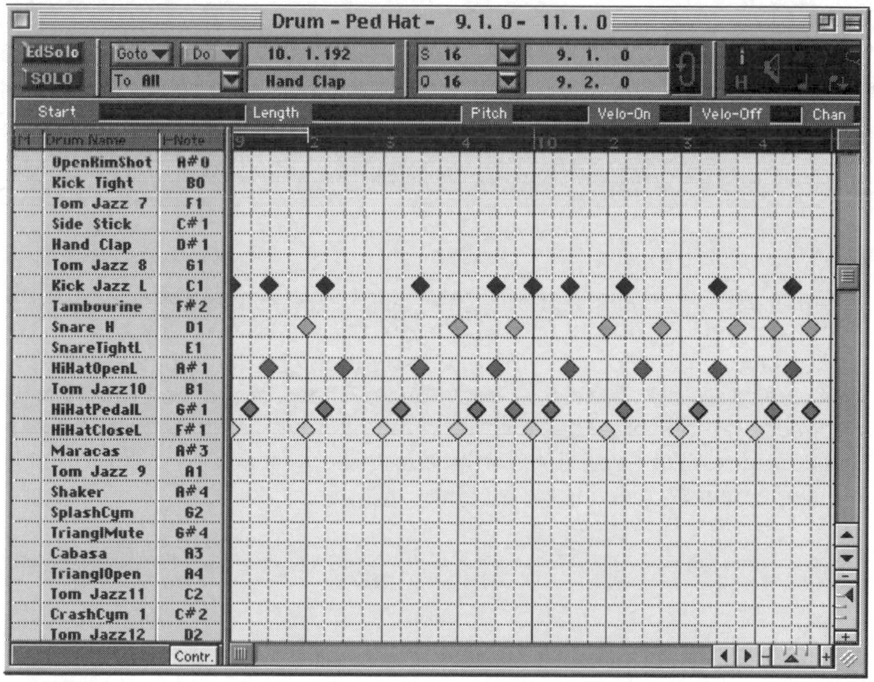

Figure 5.9
Another funky loop sped up to become a breakbeat.

The hi hat pattern in this loop is the simpler one of a closed hi hat on every beat, followed by an open hi hat on the eighth offbeat. A simple pedal hi hat placed on every first sixteenth offbeat and every fourth sixteenth offbeat in the last beat of every bar adds to the syncopated feel. In the last bar two more snares are added to the third and fourth beat to produce the snare shuffle which 'signs off' this classic breakbeat loop.

Figure 5.10
A snare shuffle is simple to program but very effective.

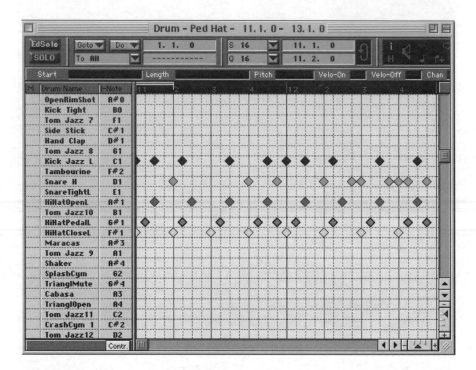

Once you have some basic breakbeat loops programmed, as in the above examples, you can start adding extra percussion to liven them up. In our last screenshot a cowbell and some congas have been played in live over the top of the first breakbeat. These could be equally well applied to all our breakbeats so far. Once you've generated simple percussion parts like these it's worth saving them to add to other loops in the same manner (see Figure 5.11).

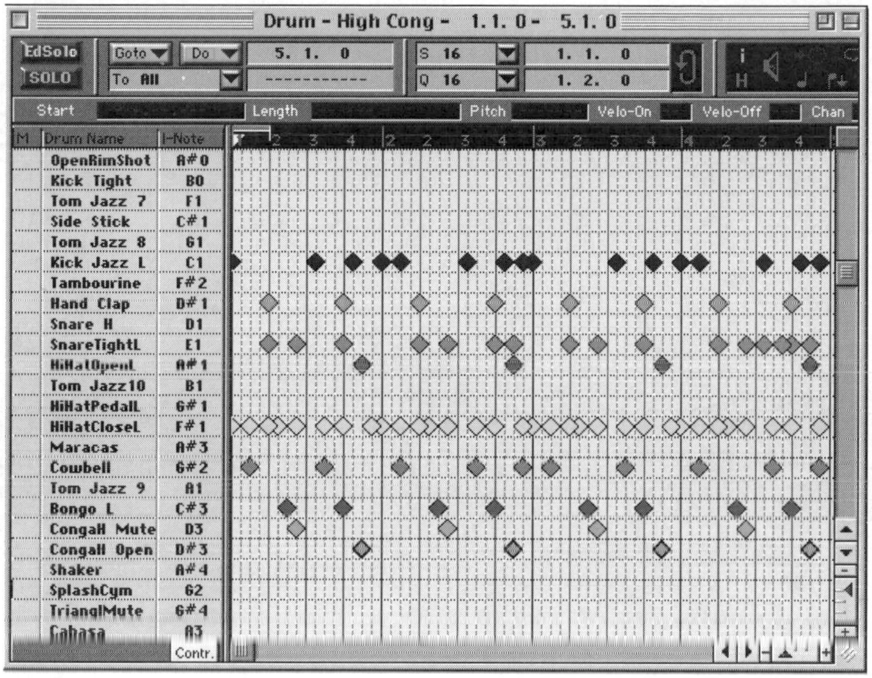

Figure 5.11
Add percussion parts you recorded earlier to liven up a basic breakbeat.

Jungle rhythms

Where Hardcore simply took breakbeats and played them faster, Jungle was where the whole process of cutting up beats into smaller parts and re-triggering them really took off. Using a sampler, this can be a time consuming process but it is one which you can easily emulate using your own MIDI loops.

Mimic the effect of re-triggering samples by the following process:

- Make a copy of a breakbeat (see Figure 5.12).

- Open the copy in the Grid editor.

- Delete the beats after anywhere from one-and-a-half to two-and-a-half beats (see Figure 5.13).

- Copy the remaining notes and paste them in where you deleted the original beats (see Figure 5.14).

Keep experimenting with this process for the best sound.

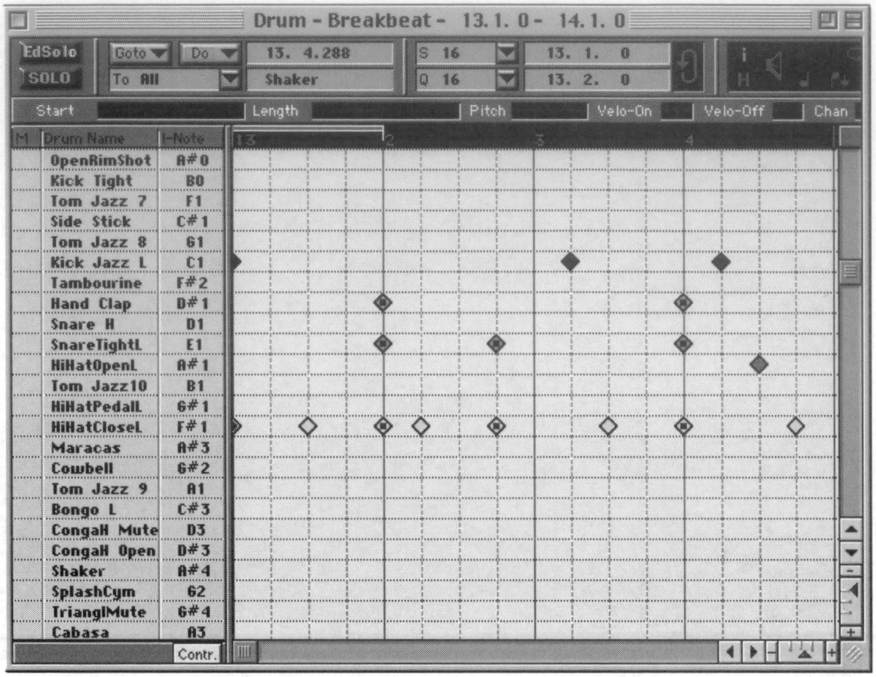

Figure 5.12
A classic breakbeat.

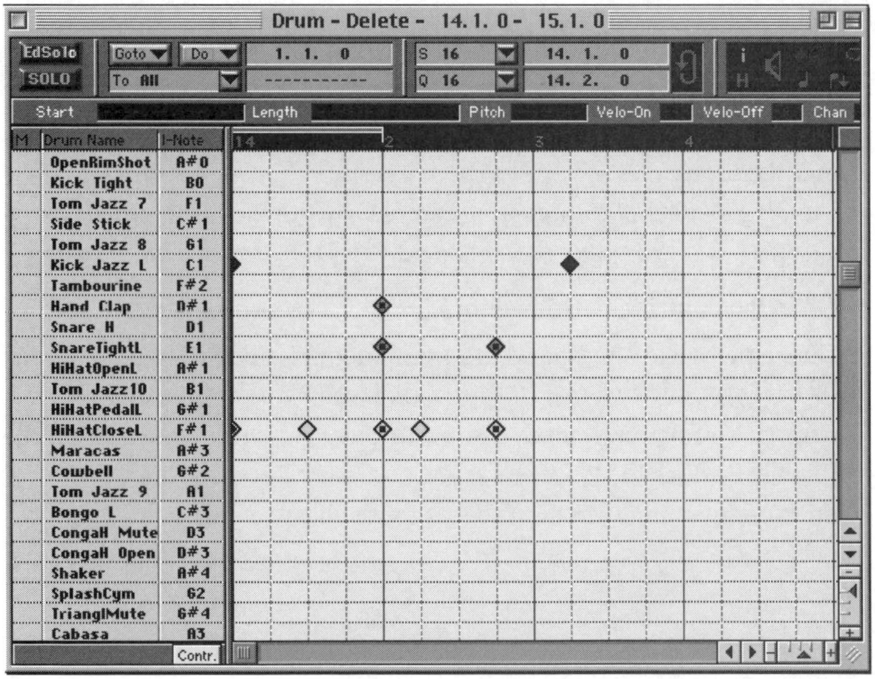

Figure 5.13
Delete everything after the second beat or so.

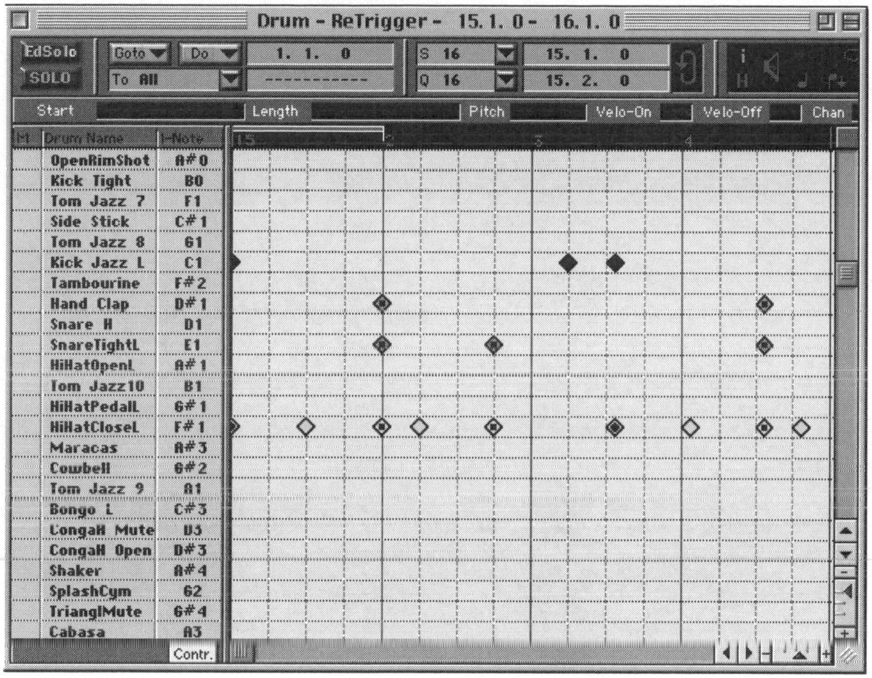

Figure 5.14
Copy the first two beats and paste into the second two.

Our first Jungle loop was programmed using this method on the snares alone combined with the 'time-stretching' method described in the previous section used on the kick drum. This has resulted in a mini-

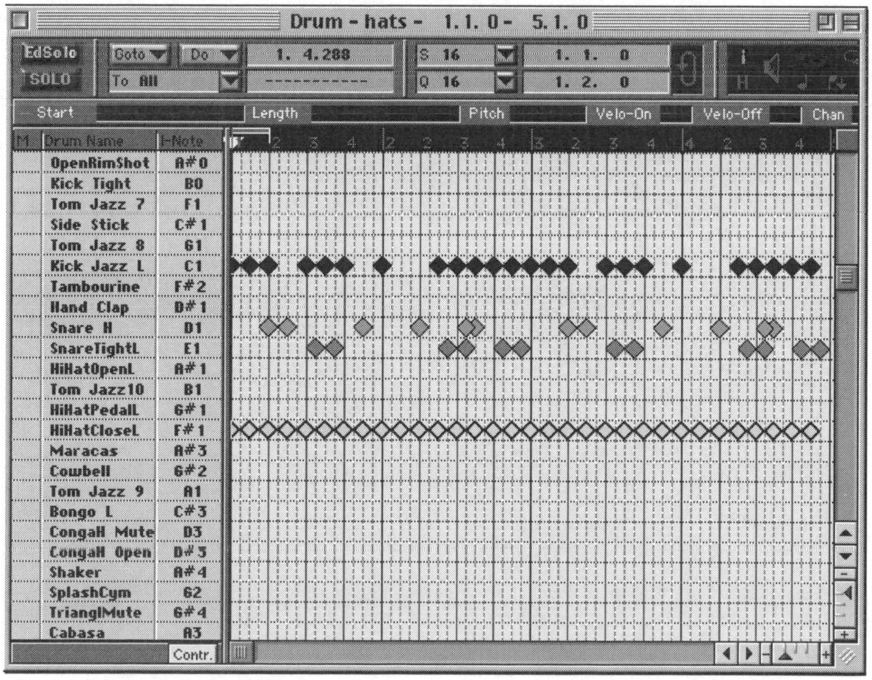

Figure 5.15
Jungle loops either feature a very busy kick drum or a very minimal one.

mal snare pattern and a busy kick drum, which have both been laid over a metronomic hi hat pattern. To add to the pitch-shifting effect some of the snares in the snare pattern have been revoiced on a different snare sound to recreate the effect of layered and re-triggered samples.

TIP

To mimic the pitched up drum sound of Jungle and Drum'n'Bass add a pitch bend command at the beginning of your drum track. Most digital drum kits can be 'tuned up' this way. For maximum effect, take one drum kit and raise its pitch by 11 or 12 semitones and put another kit on a different MIDI channel and tune it down by –6 semitones. Now all you do is set your sequencer metronome to 100–120 BPM, play in a breakbeat and then raise the speed to 160–200 BPM. This should sound correct instantly.

ON THE CD-ROM

The Jungle loops featured in this section can be found on the CD-ROM accompanying this book in the following directory: **chapter5/midifiles/drums/jungle/jungle01/2/3.mid**.

Our second Jungle loop has been programmed on two drum kits, once pitched down and the other pitched up for the sort of weird sonic distortion beloved of Junglists. In this style the drums actually begin to play

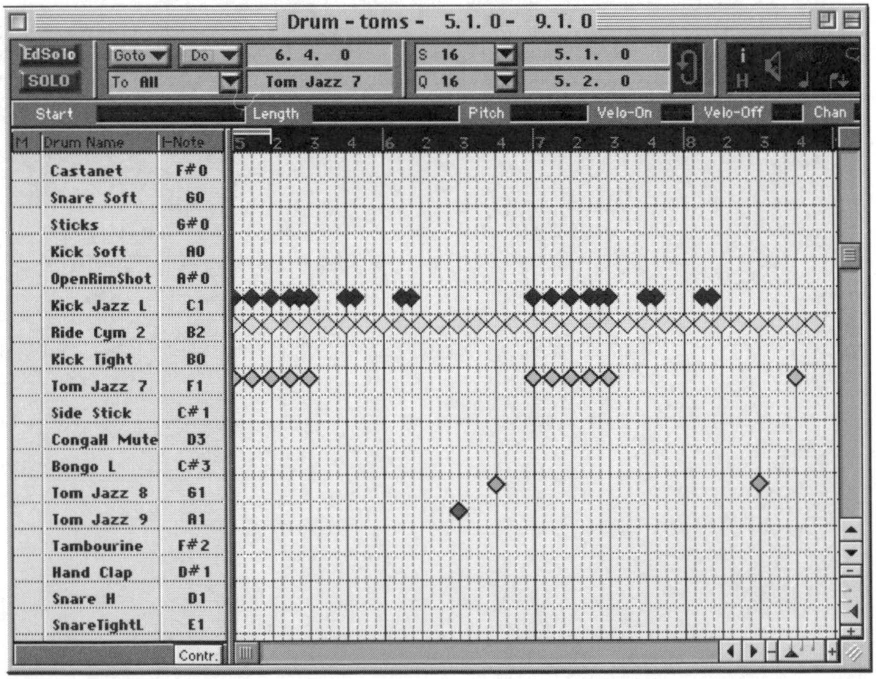

Figure 5.16

Use two drum kits to emulate the effect of playing differently pitched samples against each other.

little melodies of their own and you can often extrapolate these to form basslines. In this example the second drum kit is where most of the drum loop is played.

The loop consists of a relatively busy kick drum which is played on the Jazz kit on a dry sound. This emulates a common effect in Jungle where Pitch-shifting of samples often renders the kick drum as high and tight as a snare. This is important as it leaves room for the sub-bass in the mix. In this loop there is percussive melody being played out of the three floor toms. The only other element of the loop on this kit is the metronomic ride cymbal playing a strictly quantized sixteenth pattern. The tom pattern is so melodic it has been used as the basis for the bassline as the following screen shot shows.

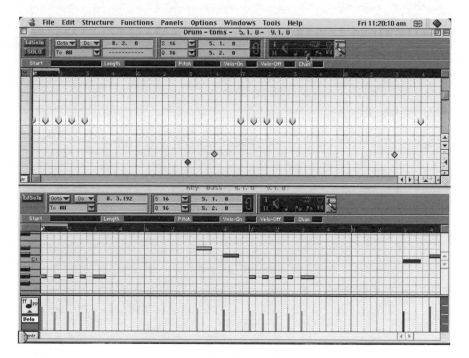

Figure 5.17
Drum patterns make a good basis for Jungle basslines.

The other part of this loop is played on a higher pitched kit for that real rattling snare sound. The snares themselves play around with the classic funky snare pattern adding 32nd fills at the end of every second bar. That is really all this part of the loop consists of except for an open hi hat that is closely followed by a closed hi hat to cut the sound off, once again in emulation of a 'real' drummer. If this loop were pitched back down and played at 96 BPM it would sound very natural indeed.

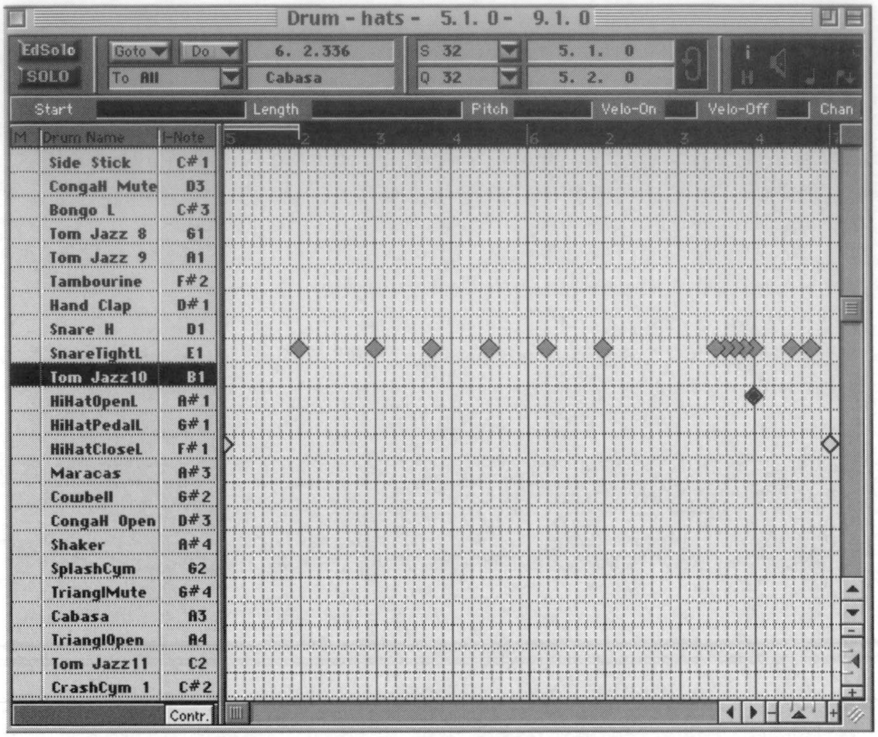

Figure 5.18
Snare fills programmed in on 32nd notes emulate the sped-up samples often heard in Jungle loops.

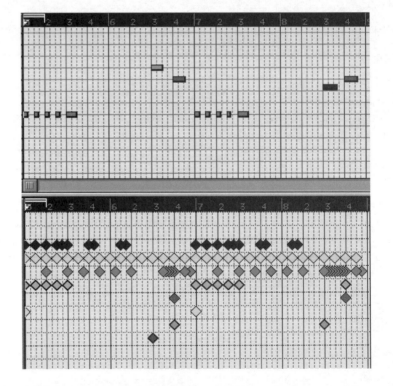

Figure 5.19
Basslines are an integral part of Jungle drum loops.

Put it all together and you have another classic Jungle loop where the pitched up drum kit sounds against the pitched down kit, emulating the effect of pitch-shifted and time-stretched samples layered on top of each other. In this loop the kick drum plays more of a snare role and the bassline becomes an integral part of the loop (see Figure 5.19).

Our final Jungle loop follows a similar pattern. It emulates the effect of re-triggering and shows this clearly with the two kick drums where one kick drum plays a standard pattern for the first two bars, then the second kick drum (in the second drum kit) takes over for some fast rolls in the third and fourth bars. The snares too are played on two kits, one kit playing a high tight snare in variations of the funky pattern, while the other snare is even higher and tighter, playing rattling snare rolls. This emulates the sound of a snare pattern pitched up and played at quadruple speed. The closed hi hat plays the familiar metronomic sixteenth pattern while pedal hi hats and the cabasa are used to provide a shuffling undercurrent that emulates the sound of a hi hat pattern pitched up and doubled in tempo. A tom has also been used to add a subtle accent to the first kick of the four bars.

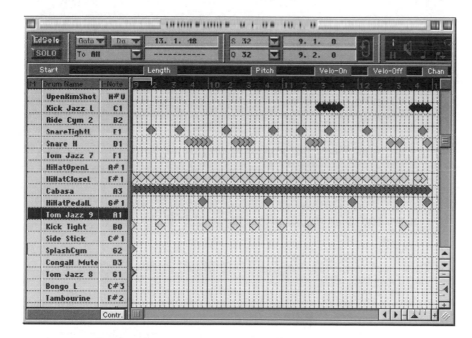

Figure 5.20
Fast 32nd snare and kick drums emulate sped up sampled loops.

Drum'n'Bass style

Drum'n'Bass sees the trick we've seen developed in Jungle reach an apogee as the practitioners of the craft perfect their skills at sample manipulation. If Jungle initiated the art of cutting up loops then Drum'n'Bass has perfected that skill. The main tool that Drum'n'Bass has programmers use is Steinberg's ReCycle!, a piece of software that allows a loop to be cut up into individual hits. Once you've done that you can time-stretch, pitch-shift and re-trigger loops at will and this skill is what lies at the heart of Drum'n'Bass beats.

ON THE CD-ROM

The Drum'n'Bass loops featured in this section can be found on the CD-ROM accompanying this book in the following directory:
chapter5/midifiles/drums/dnb/dnb01/2/3.mid.

Drum'n'Bass is much more jazz influenced than Jungle and this shows in the treatment and choice of drum loops as much as it does in the programming of string and electric piano parts. Our first Drum'n'Bass loop uses lots of shuffle rhythms, played on shakers, tambourines and maracas to give the loop a jazzy feel.

Figure 5.21
Shakers, tambourines and maracas give a jazzy feel to a loop.

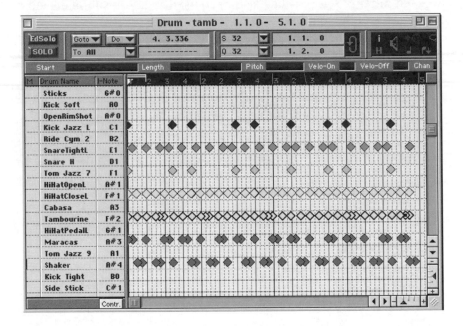

The snare is pretty busy, aping the Drum'n'Bass effect of time-stretching a snare part from a jazz loop up to a double-speed rattle. To accentuate this effect it's played on a high, tight snare sound. The more minimal kick drum pattern is given a pitch-shifted effect by doubling it up with a springy tom sound. This makes it sound as though it was a snare or kick which had been pitched down very low on an old eight-bit sampler. Pitching sounds down on low-quality samplers like this degrades the sound and gives it the classic shuddering Drum'n'Bass sound. If your drum kit doesn't include a tom with the requisite jangly sound, try pitching the kit down as low as it will go on the lowest floor tom in the kit.

Our next Drum'n'Bass loops uses a plethora of Drum'n'Bass classic effects. The first to note is the use of the triangle for a high, tinkly sound. This emulates the pitched up sound of the ride cymbal from the amen break. The shaker plays the strictly quantized sixteenth pattern which is programmed in to many a Drum'n'Bass track, usually on a GM drum kit, to provide the solidly time-locked grid that all those other sampled parts latch on to.

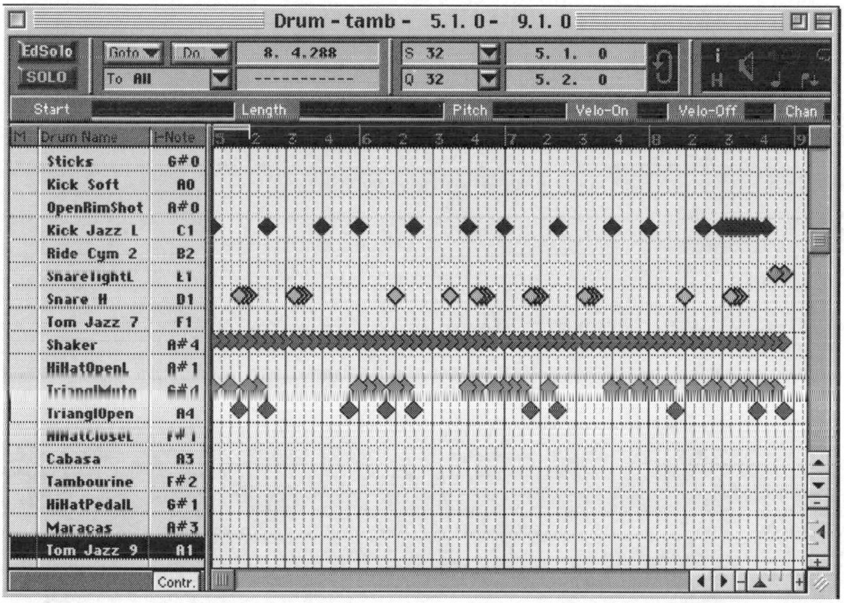

Figure 5.22
Use the triangle to emulate the pitched up sound of a ride cymbal.

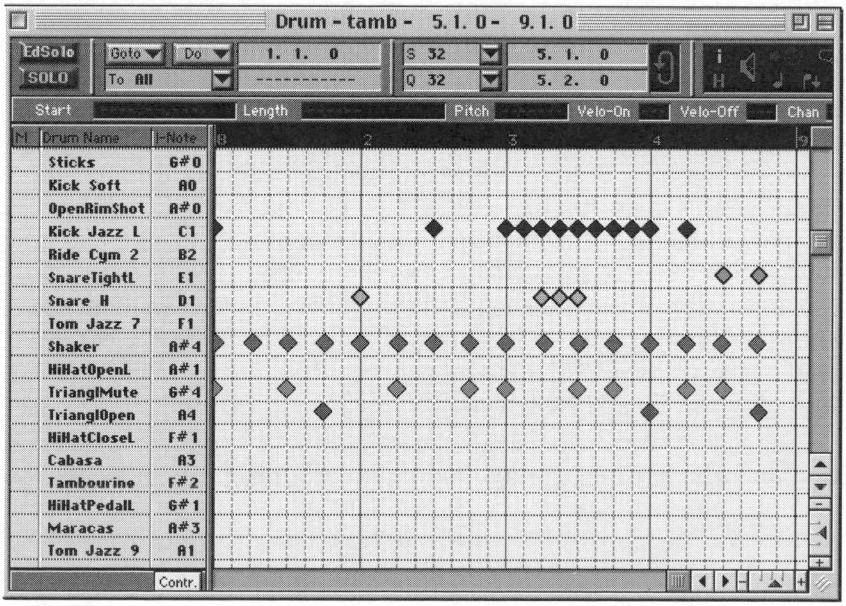

Figure 5.23
Programming 32nd snare rolls is easy and sounds effective.

Another classic effect is the fast 32nd snare rolls (see Figure 5.23). These are usually produced by sampling a slower, 16th snare pattern then pitch-shifting it up. They are then re-triggered at will throughout a loop. As you can see, they are very easy to program in. The same thing goes for the kick drum roll at the end of the four bars. It too has been programmed in and is another classic Drum'n'Bass effect originally produced by sample manipulation but now often programmed in.

Programming snare rolls

Those fast rolling snare fills are such an important element in Drum'n'Bass that it's worth having a look at how you go about programming them in. You perform the following procedure:

- Go into your grid editor with an empty part.

- Set snap and quantize values to 32 or 32T.

- Select the fill function (lots of very close together notes should appear).

- Transpose the resultant notes to the snare sound (D1 or E1).

- Adjust the velocity to create crescendos or diminuendos.

> **TIP**
>
> *Try pitch bending these fills by making the pitch bend range up to 24 semitones and then recording a pitch bend part into your sequencer. The results should sound very Drum'n'Bass. As a final touch, add a crash or splash cymbal at the end of the snare roll for a final, dramatic flourish.*

If these loops all look complicated it's worth looking closely at the next example to reorient yourself (Figure 5.24). This is the classic funky drummer loop, which often appears in Jungle and Drum'n'Bass after a certain amount of time-stretching and pitch-shifting. The familiar snare pattern is there on beats two and four with a couple of syncopated sixteenth snares, one just before beat three and the other on the last sixteenth of the bar. The important kick drum to note is on the first beat of the bar with every subsequent kick on an offbeat. The hi hat pattern is also a quantized sixteenth affair and the whole loop (or variations) can be very quickly programmed in once you've got the pattern clear in your head. Once you've done that you can start to cut it up and make variations as we've already examined.

Drum'n'Bass thrives on simple beats like these and on strange sounding fills which often sound impossible to program but on closer examination are actually very simple. Our next example is a fill that is often heard linking two sections in a Drum'n'Bass tune (see Figure 5.25).

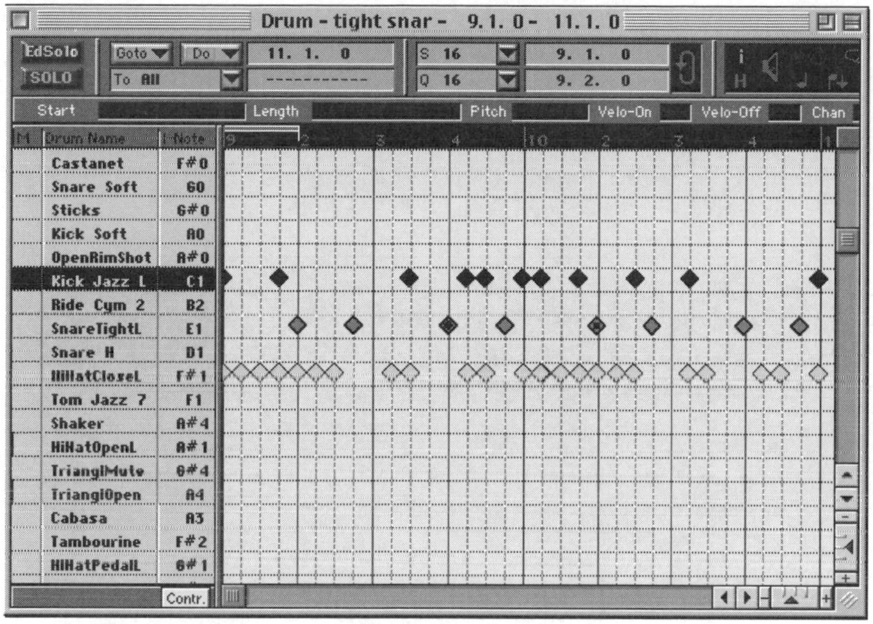

Figure 5.24
The funky drummer loop gets Drum'n'Bass wise!

ON THE CD-ROM

The Drum'n'Bass fills featured in this section can be found on the CD-ROM accompanying this book in the following directory: **chapter5/midifiles/ drums/dnb/dnbfl1/2.mid**.

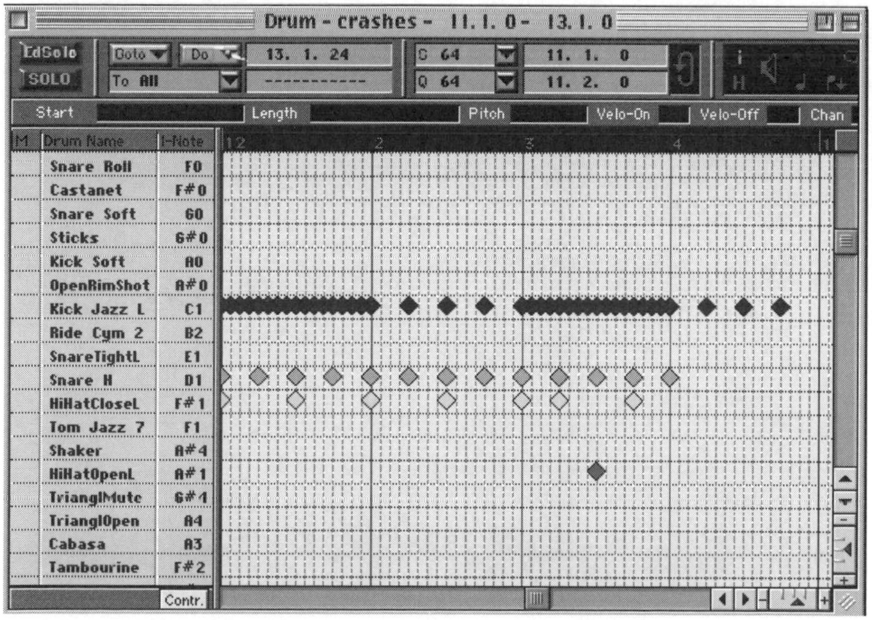

Figure 5.25
Even faster 64th kick drums for a 'machine gun' effect.

This features very fast kick drum rolls programmed in using the method outlined earlier in this section but setting snap and quantize values to 64ths for a machine gun effect. The clattering snare sound plays a strict sixteenth pattern that adds to this effect. The snare has had its sound pitched up during the course of its roll with a straight pitch bend ramp that has been programmed in while the kick drum increases in loudness by the simple use of a velocity ramp.

Figure 5.26
Pitching up a snare drum while it's playing a roll is very effective.

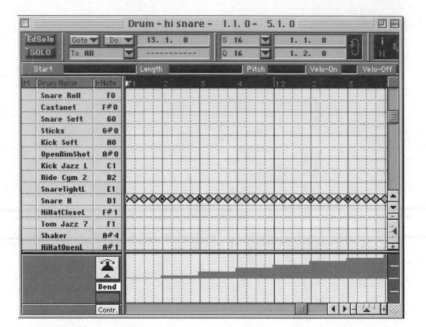

Figure 5.27
Ramping the velocity adds to the effect, making the sound grow louder in time.

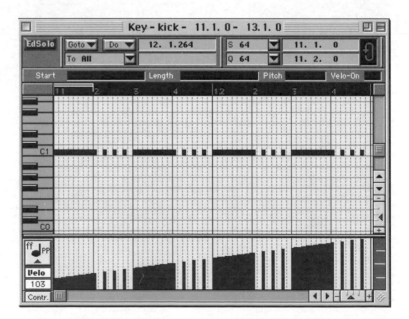

If you have a GS or XG kit you're not confined to using only pitch bend and velocity. The snare roll below, programmed in 32nds using the method outlined earlier, has had its sound affected in real time by a MIDI controller. This is combined with a velocity ramp.

Figure 5.28
Find out what MIDI controllers you can use on your drum kit and experiment with them.

Don't forget that your GM sound set includes percussion sounds as well. You can often use other parts to great effect on percussion sounds, making use of the pitches to create great effects such as the slowing down and speeding up effect produced by playing the string part below on the SynDrum (GM Program 119), as in Figure 5.29.

ON THE CD-ROM
This Drum'n'Bass fill can be found on the CD-ROM accompanying this book in the following directory: **chapter5/midifiles/drums/dnb/dnbbr1/2.mid**.

Once you've got some loops programmed, experiment with other percussion sounds and patterns. Latin percussion sounds are ideal for laying other patterns over the top as they reproduce the sound of pitched up snares and bass drums. Try out some of the patterns from the other examples in the House, Techno, Big Beat and Trip Hop sections, selecting isolated percussion tracks and playing them alongside the Drum'n'Bass grooves you've built up (see Figure 5.30).

Figure 5.29
Don't forget the percussion sounds in the standard sound set. In the Trip Hop example in the accompanying CD-ROM the SynDrum (GM Program 119) has been used to play the string patterns shown.

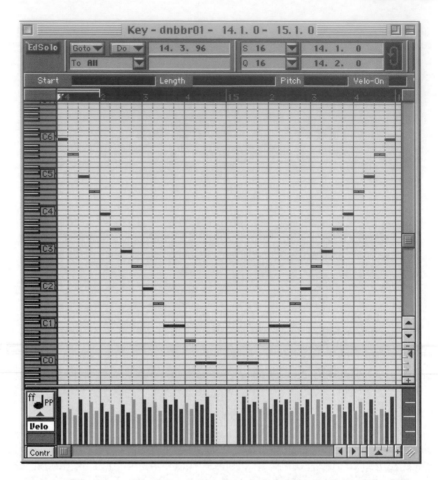

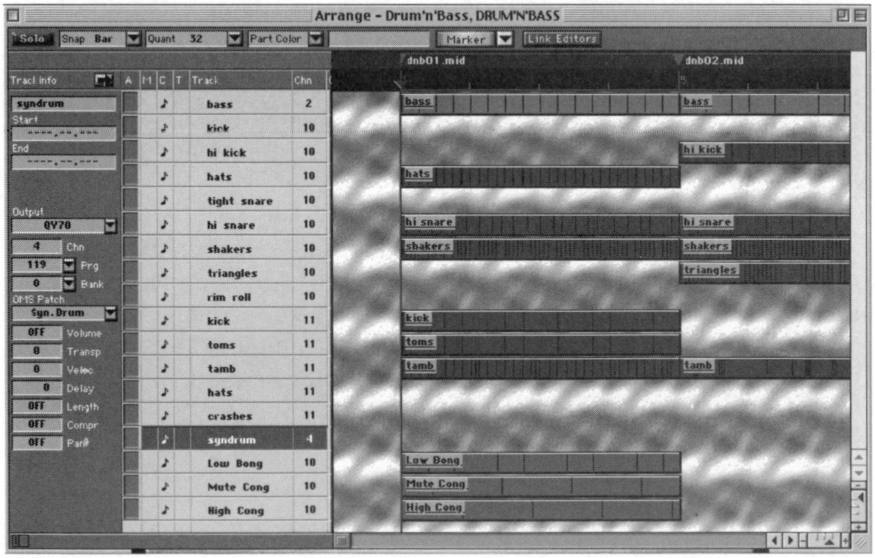

Figure 5.30
Load in other beats and play them alongside your loops.

Drum'n'Bass originated from the cut up style of mashing beats together practised by the original Hardcore and Ragga merchants who played several different records together, cutting between them to produce brand new sounds out of the resultant mish-mash of beats. The key here is the same as for Techno: experiment, play around with the voicing then experiment some more, break it all down and build it all up again.

Programming Jungle basslines

Jungle and Drum'n'Bass are full of contradictions. Mismatches between speed and slow, between pitched up, sped up breakbeats and low, slow dub basslines are the heart and soul of Drum'n'Bass. In Goldie's memorable phrase, Drum'n'Bass represents 'an abyss of ideals'. The space created by the tension between singing strings and breakbeats offers space as a point of departure. Loss and possibility meet in this new space and it is the focus on absence, rather than the fullness of those sped up beats which characterizes the best Drum'n'Bass.

The basslines in Drum'n'Bass exploit this dissonance between the harshness of the beats and the warm, enveloping sound of sub-bass (bass tones pitched so low they are barely audible but intensely physical). Dub is the starting point here. The lazy, stripped down dub bass arose as Jamaican producers from King Tubby to Lee 'Scratch' Perry used the mixing desk as an instrument, stripping away the non-essential elements of each instrument to make room for the 'toasters', Jamaican MCs, to rap over.

Dub basslines are extremely minimal, usually with only one or two beats per bar and often with whole bars with no bass at all. This all serves to focus the attention firmly on the beats. Each space where there is no bassline effectively shifts the emphasis of the mix from low to high notes. It also has the effect of the beat seemingly slowing down and speeding up as the bass draws everything back down, only for its absence in the next bar to seemingly speed everything up as the breakbeats become ascendant again.

Once you start laying down a dub bassline to a Drum'n'Bass rhythm track your attention is focused onto the construction of the beats. You'll find yourself stripping away even more as non-essential elements expose their futility. The kick drum is the first casualty in this process. Once you've laid down that slow, sensuous bassline, you'll find most of the kicks seem to disappear as they are consumed by the all-enveloping nature of the sub-bass.

Bass sounds

Drum'n'Bass almost always uses a sine wave (Program 81 Bank 65). Sub-bass isn't supported on the GM set; the nearest you can get to that rumbling, subterranean sound is the Fretless bass patch Program 36. Be careful going too low with your sine wave as your speaker cones may suffer trying to play less than 50 cycles/second. Things start to sound weird when a bass goes very low, as intervals become more difficult to hear and our brains can't distinguish pitch as well as with higher sounds. This can be used to your advantage, as almost any rumbling sub-bass line will sound good! Basslines are generally played as a single line so it's a good idea to so set your bass part to be monophonic.

The other alternative is to take a leaf out of the original junglist's book and seek out one of the Yamaha range of FM synths, the DX family. These feature bass tones which all the manuals tell you shouldn't be played below E1 but if you do you'll find the trouser-flapping bass sound you're after. Almost every Jungle producer has at least one of these machines just for those sub-bass tones.

You'll find you often have to do a lot of octave shifting to get bass sounds in the right frequency range. The bass sounds in the GM set are designed to be played at about C1 to C3, which is fine for regular basses but not low enough for rumbling bass. You need to pitch this down even lower, to the C0 to C2 range.

Dub basslines

Dub basslines are also very minimal. Our first example uses only five notes, jumping from C to two sharps, D# and A#. It then plays with that by using a semitone shift to A at the end for a dark, brooding effect. At the end of the first two bars it jumps down to G0 for a floor-shaking sub-bass wobble.

Figure 5.31
Dub basslines go as low as they can.

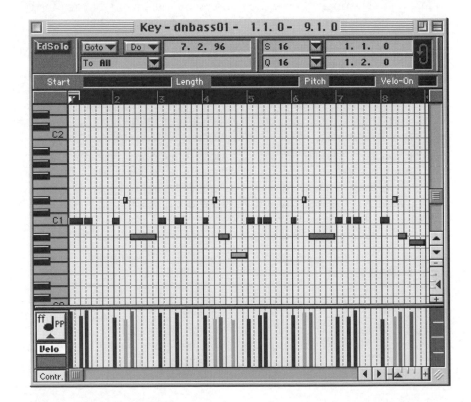

Semitone shifts give a real dark brooding vibe and our next example plays around with these even more. Don't get too hung up about scales when you're playing dub basslines. This example jumps between three different scales in its course yet still sits in well with the sort of jazzy chords that Drum'n'Bass lays over the top of lines like these. Basslines like this are useful as linking sections between different scales within a tune, something else Drum'n'Bass has borrowed from jazz.

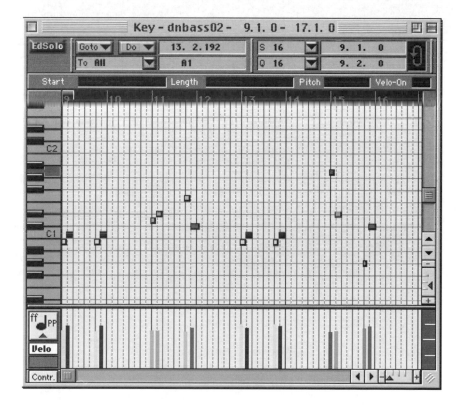

Figure 5.32
Semitone shifts add a dark and brooding vibe to dub basslines.

Blues music is a big influence on jazz of course and our next example is a simple variation on the classic walking bassline used so often for playing the blues. Repeated pitches are another common feature of dub basslines.

Figure 5.33
A variation on the classic 'walking blues' bassline.

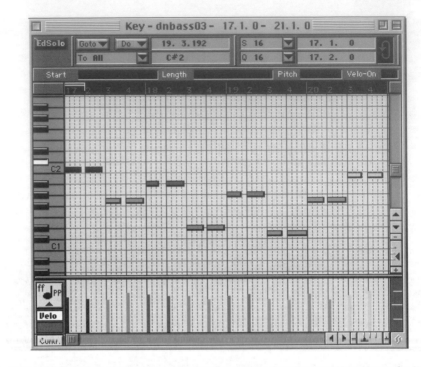

Another Blues scale for our next example. A pentatonic scale in A minor gives us a suitably dark and mournful bassline to lay under some clattering snares. The long, sustained note that occupies nearly the entire last bar is ideal for layering under a particularly busy snare fill.

Figure 5.34
Long notes are another common feature of dub basslines.

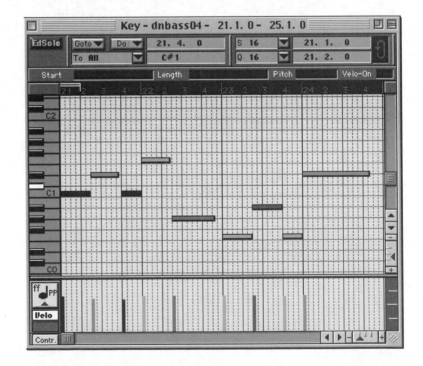

Conversely you can also use long notes like this under a breakdown for maximum dramatic effect. The octave shift in the third bar – playing F0 where F1 is expected is particularly floor-rumbling.

Our last example is another pentatonic scale in A minor. This bassline, with its two sustained notes followed by a series of stuttering short notes, can be heard in many a Drum'n'Bass tune and could be called a classic of the genre. It originated in Jungle but has found its way into Drum'n'Bass and even more recently, into pop-oriented breakbeat tunes.

Figure 5.35
The classic Jungle bassline works well in Drum'n'Bass.

Time-stretching basslines

Dub basslines are often just slowed down versions of Blues and Jazz basslines and you can generate some very useful ones by performing the same kind of MIDI time-stretching on basslines as we performed on drumbeats earlier. The procedure is the same, except this time you want to multiply the timing of the notes so the piece plays at a slower tempo.

In all cases the result is the same; the timing of a series of notes is multiplied to occupy double the amount of space and thus play in half time.

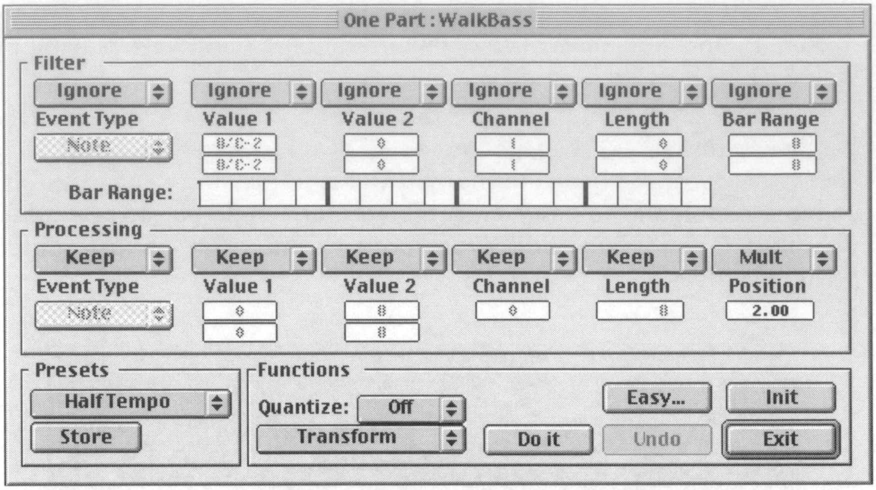

Figure 5.36
Cubase's Logical editor set to multiply the timing of the notes in a piece to play in double tempo.

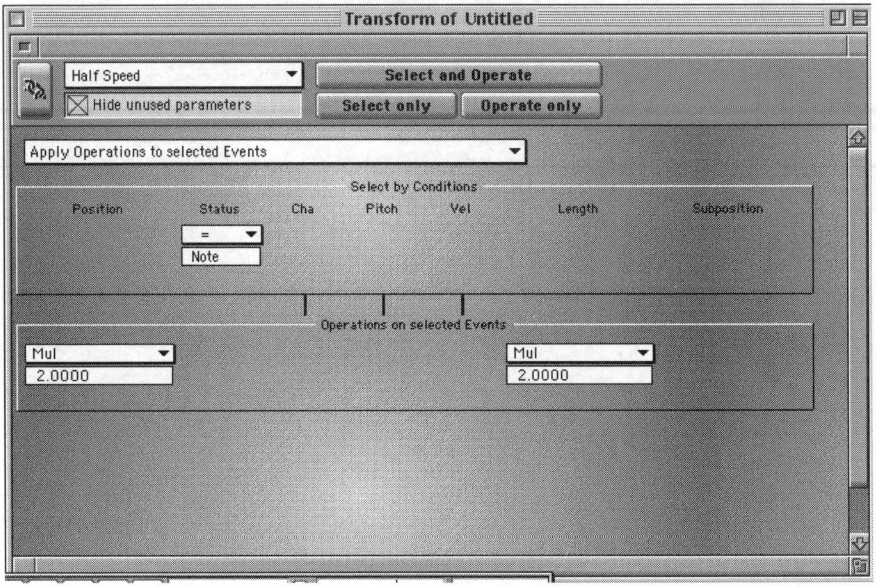

Figure 5.37
Logic's Transform function set to do the same.

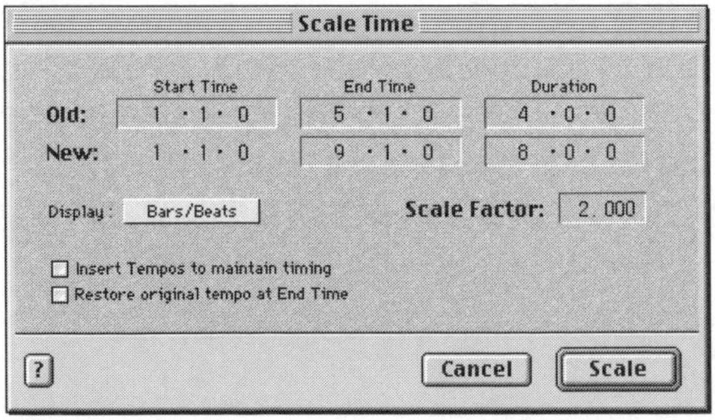

Figure 5.38
Opcode's Vision set to halve the tempo within its Scale Time function.

Figure 5.39
The Length function in Cakewalk can also halve the tempo of a part.

Figures 5.40
A walking bassline before its tempo has been reduced...

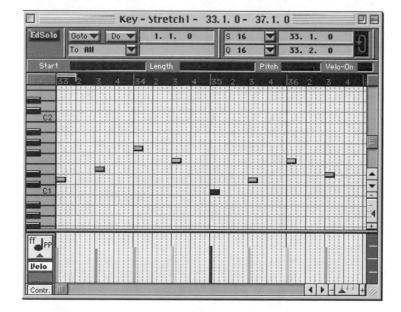

Figures 5.41
... and after.

In our example the timing position of the notes in the bassline has been multiplied by four, slowing the tempo right down – perhaps too much – leaving only two notes in every bar. Dub basslines thrive on doubled notes and, however, copying all the notes in the piece and pasting the copy in on the second beat results in a very workable bassline.

Figure 5.42
Pasting in a copy later in time transforms a simple walking bassline into a classic dub one.

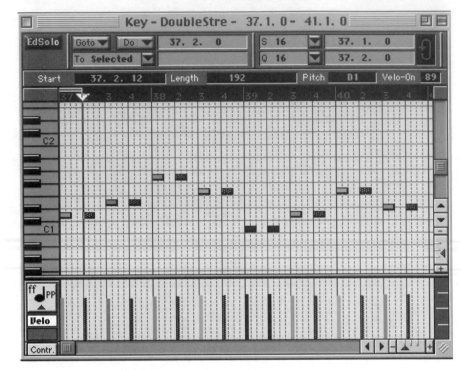

Experiment with this trick and its variations on the basslines used in the other style chapters of this book to see if you can come up with your own originals.

Arranging a Drum'n'Bass track

When you come to put a Drum'n'Bass track together you'll probably find yourself adopting a much more song-based approach, laying out some basic beats and basslines then building sections on top of that, often playing in live electric piano parts and the like. If you're programming a real jazz-based track this may soon give way to more programming as you experiment and build up different sections.

String parts

In early Drum'n'Bass and Jungle the texture was thinner with more use of string sounds and pads. This is because pads were generally playing chords that had been sampled and then played at different pitches. This process created a sound where chords jumped by intervals rather than smoothly progressing from one chord to another.

In recent times the chordal changes of Drum'n'Bass have become more subtle with cool added notes and jazzy sounding chords. Now the use of chords is much subtler. Evolving pads with added notes are the norm. Added 7th and 9th note chords are very common and have become an integral part of the style. Experiment with adding extra notes to basic chords, as the result can sound quite dark and beautiful.

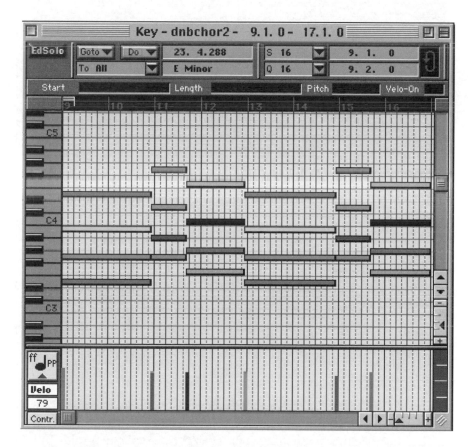

Figure 5.43
Add pitches to basic chords to transform them into dark and beautiful sounds.

ON THE CD-ROM
This string part can be found on the CD-ROM accompanying this book in the following directory: **chapter5/midifiles/chords/dnbchor2.mid**.

Electric piano

This style works well for piano parts too. Because a Jazzy style has become the norm you'll find the electric pianos fit in best with the style. On the GM set that's Programs 5 and 6 but if you've got a GS or XG set look out for the patches which emulate the classic sounds of a Rhodes or Yamaha DX piano. The jazz fraternity eagerly adopted these early electric pianos and their sound will have you playing bluesy chords in no time.

Figure 5.44
Electric piano sounds will have you playing blues and jazz style in no time.

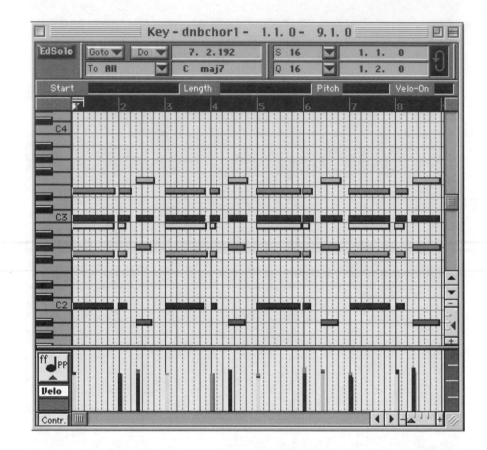

ON THE CD-ROM
This electric piano part can be found on the CD-ROM accompanying this book in the following directory: **chapter5/midifiles/chords/dnbchor1.mid**.

NOTE
Tone in Drum'n'Bass is most often minor, often switching keys in the course of a song, as in Jazz.

Putting it all together

The shift in emphasis that your chord parts produces will define those points of departure into space which will probably have you cutting up the drum patterns yet again as new ideas and possibilities suggest themselves. Hardcore and Jungle relied solely on sampled loops for their rhythms but Drum'n'Bass evolved as programmers learnt their craft. Once they learnt how to cut up sampled loops into individual hits it was a short step to programming their own drum loops, just as we've done here.

> ### ON THE CD-ROM
> *This complete Drum'n'Bass mix can be found on the CD-ROM accompanying this book in the following directory:* **chapter5/midifiles/dnb/songs/dnb.mid**. *There is also a set-up file for XG synths for the mix in the directory called* **dnbset.mid**.

Most Drum'n'Bass tracks now consist of sampled loops playing alongside programmed ones. This is a trick that *all* Electronica programmers use. Often a programmed MIDI loop doesn't sound quite right and the simple trick of sampling the loop from a drum machine, heavily compressing it and playing it alongside the MIDI loop will work wonders. If you're unsure about this, have a look at Chapter 8 for more information on using ReCycle! to cut up loops and using digital audio to add samples to your MIDI programming.

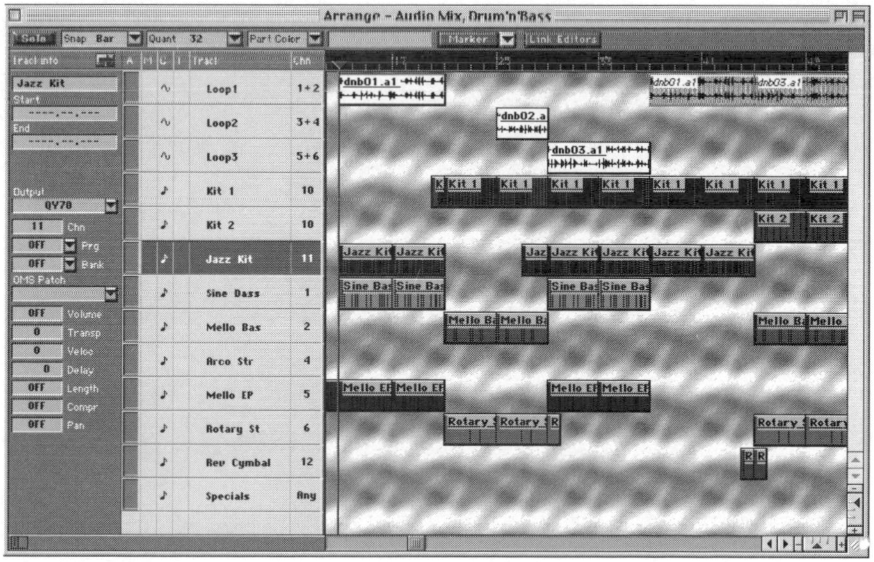

Figure 5.45
Play sampled loops alongside programmed ones.

ON THE CD-ROM

There are audio files of some extra drum loops as well as some live basslines and chord parts on the CD-ROM accompanying this book in the following directories.

Audio drum loops: **chapter5/samples/dnb/drums/dnb01/2/3.wav/ dnbbr1/2.wav**.

Live basslines: **chapter5/samples/dnb/bass/dnbass01/2.wav**.

Chords: **chapter5/samples/dnb/chords/dnbchor1/2/3.wav**.

By now you should be familiar with the intricacies of programming breakbeat loops in whatever style of Drum'n'Bass takes your fancy; Breakbeat, Hardcore, Jungle or straight Drum'n'Bass. You should also have learnt what makes a dub bassline work (sub-bass!) and how to layer that under clattering breakbeats to maximum effect. Experiment with jazz chords, adding in those 7th and 9th notes above the root for a real smoky jazz club effect and you're ready to program up your own masterpiece. Get easy, go with the flow of the rhythms and get Drum'n'Bass-wise!

6 Programming Trip Hop

Where Jungle is built on the tension between slow, dub basslines and sped up breakbeats, Trip Hop takes things to the other extreme. The slow, dubwise basslines are still there, but more accentuated, with echoes and reverb as well as the sub-bass of Jungle. The beats which have been broken down and reassembled only to be sped up to dizzying effect in Jungle, are slowed right back down in Trip Hop.

Most of them are drawn from reggae, jazz and R'n'B drum loops. With the current fashion amongst some Trip Hoppers for using 'real' drummers, the original loops are making a comeback. But Trip Hop is, above all else, electronic music and the most stunning examples of the genre owe their spaced out sound to all the tricks and effects the modern digital recording artist has at his disposal.

All those spaced out effects originated with the early reggae mixers who controlled the mixing desks and put together a whole series of dub plate classics. They pioneered the use of the mixing desk as an instrument, taking a standard reggae track, stripping out the vocals and stripping down the beats and basslines. They then treated the minimalist result to echoes and delays to rebuild a spaced out version of the original for MCs to toast over. These dub plates became respected as listening experiences in their own right and their spaced out ambience lies at the heart of Trip Hop.

If you're serious about getting an authentic Trip Hop sound, the key word is Lo-Fi. Tracks sound raw and full of energy because of their grainy Lo-Tech nature. A lot of older technology is used to create this style and sometimes the noisier and more crackly the instrument the better. Old analogue synthesizers are used as well as vintage effects and recording gear. Trip Hop is also responsible for the return of the Theremin to the musical fray.

Almost anything goes with Trip Hop; the stranger the sounds used the better and there are many good examples of utter sonic weirdness. Effects are used and abused and often overdriven to add to the rawness of the sound.

This leaves the general MIDI, XG or, GS musician with a problem; modern equipment sounds too squeaky clean. Luckily however there are a few tricks available to mimic the Trip Hop masters. We'll start by looking at the drum sounds needed for Trip Hop and then explore jazz and other drum loops you can use; then we'll examine the R'n'B and reggae basslines used in Trip Hop. Once we've laid those basics down we can explore the jazzy chordings on electric piano so beloved of Trip Hoppers. That will provide us with enough material to build up our own Trip Hop track.

Programming Trip Hop drums

Sampling breakbeat loops plays a major part in Trip Hop but these are often old vinyl recordings with many a crackle left in. Trip Hop also harks back to the days of Hip-Hop music because it relies heavily on sampled material. In those days samplers were not the clean sounding pieces of kit they are now. The sampling resolution was mainly 8-bit giving a dull grainy sound to the samples. So Trip Hop has gone retro with new samplers being forced to mimic kit with lower sound quality.

Trip Hop is basically a return to a form which developed out of Electro, called Freestyle, where DJs spun different plates together or switched rapidly between different drum grooves on their 808s. The Trip Hop edge is in the far wider palette of sounds available to the modern, GM-synth toting, sampler wielding musician.

Drum sounds

Like Big Beat, Trip Hop is more about creating the right atmosphere with your drum sounds than it is about programming the 'right' patterns. The following is a rough guide to the sort of sounds you should be looking for. In Trip Hop the golden rule is the weirder the better.

Kicks

The deeper the better. Try pure sine waves or the 808 kick and EQ it so there is only bottom end sound with no top or middle.

Snares

The more unusual the sound the better. Aside from pitching your drum kit down you could try playing snare patterns on ethnic instruments or toms for real crustiness.

Cymbals

Ride cymbals are used more than hi hats in trip hop because of their thin, sharp sound which sits well with crusty snares and kicks. Try pitching them up in your drum kit or sampler if you can for a really 'toppy' sound.

Hi hats

Make hi-hats really dirty by pitching them down or adding dirty reverb or even running them through a fuzz box. The other alternative is to go for a really thin bright sound by EQ'ing out the bottom end.

Percussion

Trip Hop percussion sounds are nearly always weird or ethnic, using things like really old analogue drum boxes or the ethnic section of the MIDI drum kit and sound set – Taiko Drum, Guiro, Kalimba etc.

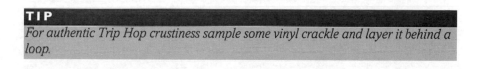

TIP

For authentic Trip Hop crustiness sample some vinyl crackle and layer it behind a loop.

Tripping on jazz loops

Trip Hop samples its loops from anywhere: old R'n'B, blues, reggae and jazz records especially. We'll start our programming by taking a few MIDI files of jazz loops and showing you how to turn them into Trip Hop loops. Once we've transformed a few of those we'll look at some classic Trip Hop loops.

ON THE CD-ROM

The two Acid jazz loops following, with their accompanying pitch bend tracks, can be found on the CD-ROM accompanying this book in the following directory: **chapter6/midifiles/drums/acidjazz/ajazzbr1.mid**.

The first thing to do with MIDI files of other styles is adjust the tempo. The selection of jazz loops here were all originally recorded at 120 BPM. By simply dropping the tempo to a more spliffed-out 90 BPM, we've transformed those loops from their original sprightly jazz tempo to something darker and mellower.

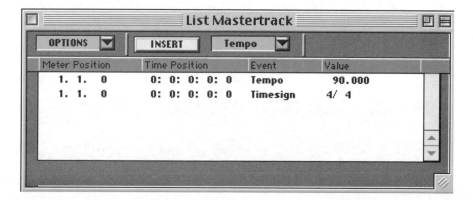

Figure 6.1
Drop the tempo for instant chill.

Our first example is a typical jazz groove, with simple use of the ride cymbal to establish a moody beat and the usual snare pattern on beats two and four supplemented by some offbeat syncopation on the brushes. The kick drum is fairly minimal with the accent on the first two kicks, both of them in beat one. This kind of loop is ideal for Trip Hop. Lowering the tempo has immediately rendered it darker and dubbier.

Figure 6.2
A basic jazz loop with a 'cool' ride pattern sets the laid-back tempo.

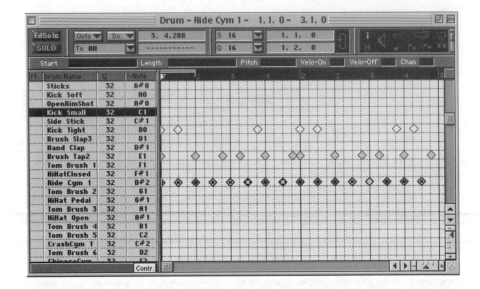

TIP

Try pitching MIDI drum kits down a few semitones to give them more graininess. With sampled loops play the loop lower down the keyboard rather than time-stretching it for maximum laid back effect.

Trip Hoppers are notoriously laid back types and the complicated business of time-stretching sampled loops doesn't seem to appeal to them at all. Consequently, to play a sampled beat slower, your average Trip Hopper will simply play it lower in pitch. This has the effect of slowing the loop all right, but it also pitches it down so that everything sounds as though it were being dragged through the aural equivalent of treacle. You can achieve the same effect on MIDI loops by pitching the drum kit down with the pitch wheel.

TIP

You can do this live and record the variations of pitch over the course of a loop for maximum tripped out weirdness. Alternatively simply insert a pitch bend command at the beginning of your drum track, thus pitching the whole loop down by the same amount.

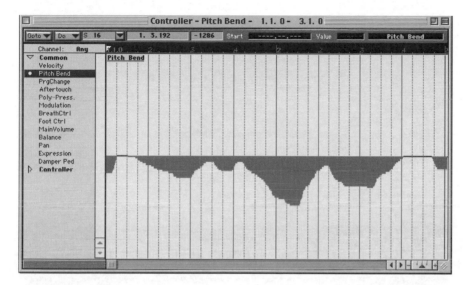

Figure 6.3
Record pitch bend information to vary the speed and graininess of a MIDI loop.

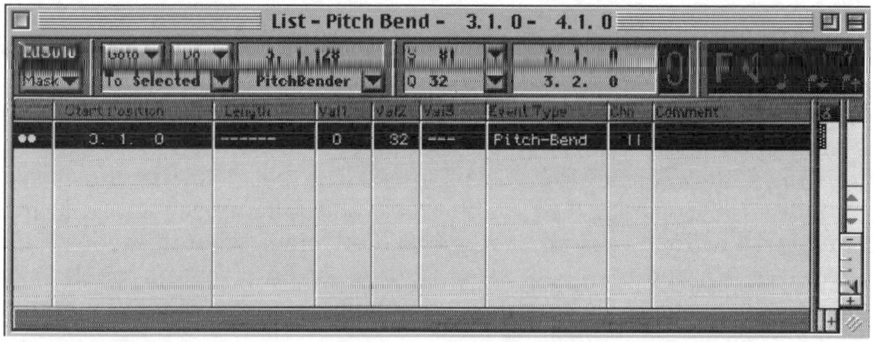

Figure 6.4
A pitch bend command at the beginning of your drum track will give loops the requisite grittiness.

The next thing to do is to revoice the drum kit. If you're just using the standard GM drum kit everything will sound too full of reverb, the snare will be far too booming and the whole thing will still sound too 'normal'. As we're using jazz loops the Jazz kit (Program 33) is a good starting point and gives the kick drum a darker hue. The snare is still very loud though. An even better option is the Brush kit (Program 41). This kit uses a brush snare which has a dirtier, more subliminal sound, well suited to Trip Hop.

NOTE
Don't be afraid to use different kits. A brush kit often sounds good in Trip Hop programming, giving the drums a cool jazzy feel.

Our second jazz loop uses hi hats instead of a ride, with minimal use being made of the Open hi hat to give the same moody jazz feel to the rhythm. The kick drum is a little busier than the last loop and is beginning to provide more of a bassline effect. Trip Hop kick drums can get very busy and take over the role of the bassline.

Figure 6.5
Pay particular attention to the sound of the hi hat when you do use it.

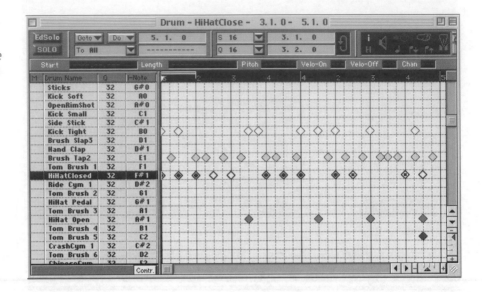

This loop sounds great on the pitched down Brush kit we used for the first loop but the hi hat is a little monotonous. The closed hi hat pattern uses lowering velocities for a fading effect. The trouble is that the closed hi hat on the Brush kit is so subtle this even subtler effect is lost. In the illustration below I've used another MIDI channel, set it to the Dark kit (Program 10) and revoiced the closed hi hat onto that channel. This works rather well as the closed hi hat now has a crusty sound, especially as that is also pitched down.

Figure 6.6
Don't put all your drum sounds on one kit; mix'n'match drum kits for textural contrast.

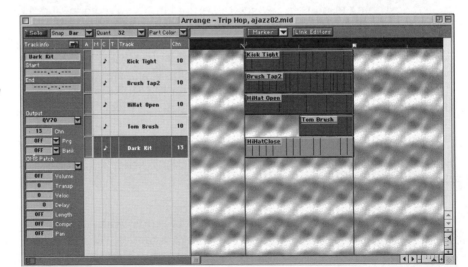

We'll finish off looking at jazz loops with a couple of breaks. The first is very minimal and reduces the kick to two notes in the first bar and three in the second. Two of the three notes in the second bar are played as a very offbeat flourish at the end. These echo the syncopated shuffle of the snares, which in its turn is echoed by a couple of tom hits. In this instance the tom hits cry out to be revoiced on a different kit. I've used the XG Jungle kit here, pitching it down while pitching the Brush kit down as low as it will go for a completely wasted feeling.

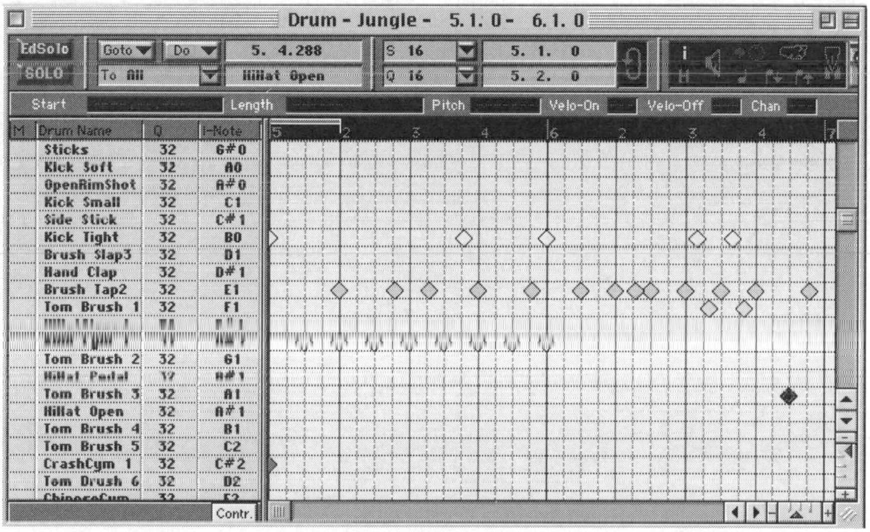

Figure 6.7
Total breakdown in a jazz style!

TIP

If you use a GS or XG synth you can tune individual drum sounds, adjust their resonance and cut-off, decay, panning, reverb etc. using a double controller. Unfortunately Yamaha and Roland don't quite agree on standard codes for these operations. Experimenting with the resonance and cut-off parameters offers the most extreme results and helps to produce Trip Hop's ringing snare sounds. You'll find a guide to XG and GS programming in Chapter 9.

Our second jazz break is very similar, with only two kick drums per bar, one at the beginning and an offbeat one at the end. It follows the same pattern as the last loop, with a bar of ride cymbals leading to a syncopated shuffle on the snare, and finishing with an open hi hat playing the part normally associated with a crash cymbal. This adds to the low-key effect and here I've exaggerated this by revoicing the ride and closed hi hat onto the XG jungle kit where the sounds are even thinner. Trip Hop has a symbiotic relationship with Jungle in that it uses a lot of the same loops, but slowed down rather than sped up, and enjoys playing around with the pitch of drum sounds.

Figure 6.8
Jazz breakdowns often change from the ride to a snare shuffle.

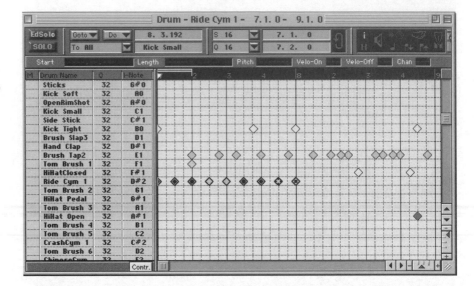

ON THE CD-ROM
You'll find this loop with its pitch bend and program change information on the CD-ROM accompanying this book in the following directory:
chapter6/midifiles/drums/acidjazz/ajazzbr2.mid.

Our final jazz break is ideal for signing off either of the two breaks we've looked at here. It's only one bar long and nothing happens until halfway through the bar when the snare does a little 32nd shuffle and finishes off with a machine gun style roll. The kick 'signs off' the bar. Try playing around with pitch bend and filter frequency on this loop to break it down further.

ON THE CD-ROM
You'll find this loop with its pitch bend and program change information on the CD-ROM accompanying this book in the following directory:
chapter6/midifiles/drums/acidjazz/ajazzbr3.mid.

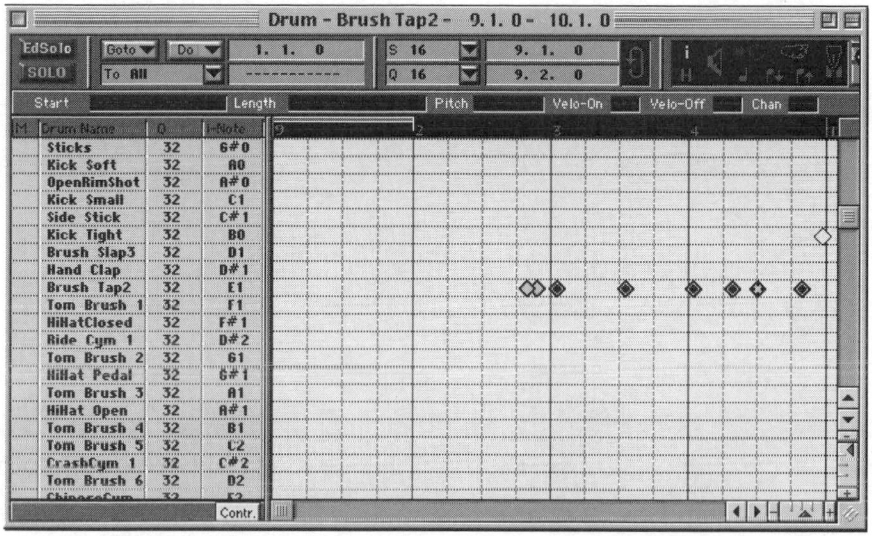

Figure 6.9
As minimal as you can get, this jazz breakdown puts it all on a snare shuffle.

TIP

You can get good Lo-Fi effects on whole drum kits by playing around with the global cut-off and resonance filters. On XG instruments the resonance filter (also called harmonic content) is control change 71 (64 being the default setting) and the cut-off frequency (also called brightness) is control change 74.

Trip Hop loops

When it comes to programming your own Trip Hop loops, it's simply a matter of playing with all the parameters we've looked at so far. Trip Hop loops can be jazz, as we've just seen, or they can be Hip-Hop, Electro or even Old School Techno loops; the real guts of a Trip Hop loop is in the sounds and how you treat them. Trip Hop does a have a fondness for 'real' drum loops so, if you're not sampling them, try playing loops in live from your keyboard or, even better, a set of MIDI drum pads.

Nice as drum pads are, you don't really need them. Just set your sequencer to loop around the number of bars you want to record and add layers of snares, hi hats and so on as your sequencer loops. The first of our Trip Hop loops was recorded that way. Don't forget to turn quantize off, as you don't want your sequencer reducing all your strange timings to strictly quantized grooves. Recording this way means you often end up with two for the price of one; certainly the next loop can be broken down into two halves.

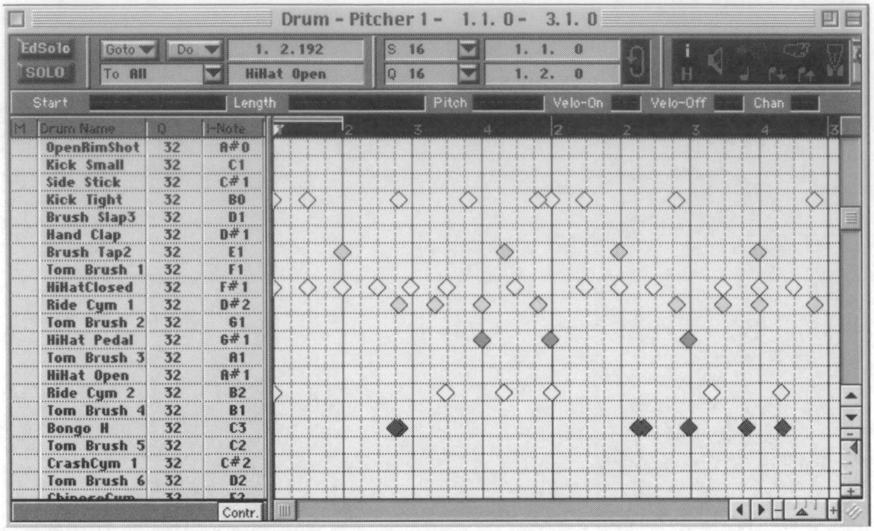

Figure 6.10
A classic Trip Hop groove with a busy kick drum.

The first two bars have worked out nicely as a classic Trip Hop groove with a relatively busy kick drum leading the whole thing and lots of percussion sitting on top of that. Note how the kicks at beats three and four in the first bar and beat three in the second bar sit just before the beat yet give the groove a laid back feel. This is one of the paradoxes of drum programming, that moving certain beats forward in time will make a loop sound more laid back. By way of contrast the second snare has been moved *back* in time and yet it too adds to the loop's laid back feel.

TIP

Try moving some kicks forward in time (but backward on the drum grid) as in the screen shot above to achieve a more laid back feel. Offbeat kicks make a groove laid back and interesting if they're moved forward in time.

The ride cymbals, once again built up over several loops of the record cycle, have a nice cool jazzy feel to them, as do the bongos, which were initially a mistake but sounded good so they were left in and built on. Finally some pitch bend was applied to the whole loop with special attention being paid to getting some pitch effects on the bongos.

ON THE CD-ROM

You'll find this Trip Hop groove along with the pitch bend track on the CD-ROM accompanying this book in the following directory: **chapter6/midifiles/ drums/triphop/triphop1.mid**.

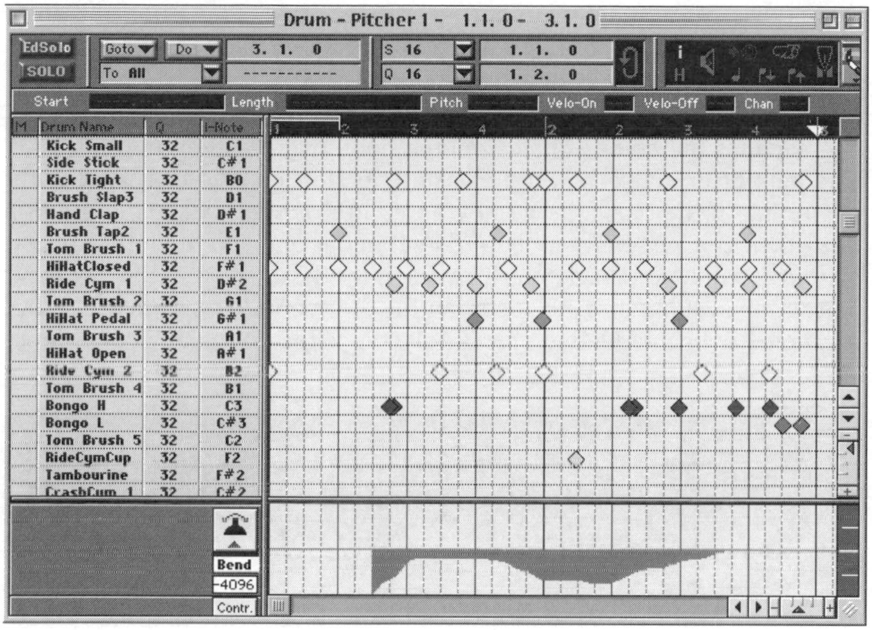

Figure 6.11
The pitch bend transforms the bongos from a simple percussion 'mistake' to a feature.

The second two bars of this loop are essentially a breakdown of the first two. The kick has been thinned out and the bongo fill 'finished off' to sign off the loop. Once again I've made use of pitch bend information to distort the bongos and, in another accident, this has added a nice slowing down and speeding up effect to the three ride cymbals at the end of the

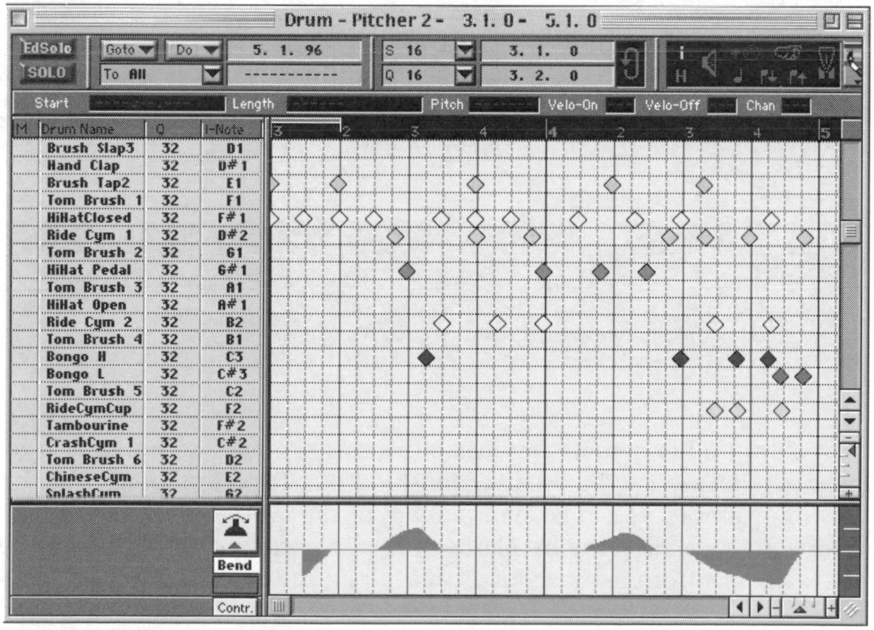

Figure 6.12
There are no such thing as 'mistakes' in Trip Hop, just carefully planned accidents.

second bar. More than any other Electronica style, Trip Hop is all about listening out for your mistakes and spotting those that are more interesting than the parts you've actually planned.

The next Trip Hop beat functions well as a breakdown for those quieter sections but could equally be built upon by adding extra percussion. The kick drum pattern is the classic Hip-Hop groove of a kick at the beginning of the bar, followed by an eighth offbeat kick. There is only one other kick, just before the third beat in bar one and the fourth beat in bar two, for that laid back feel. The ride pattern is a very simple sixteenth pattern and the pitch bend recorded for the second two bars of the first example has been added to give it a slurring effect at the end of the loop.

Figure 6.13
This groove functions well as a breakdown and could also be used as the basis for a new track.

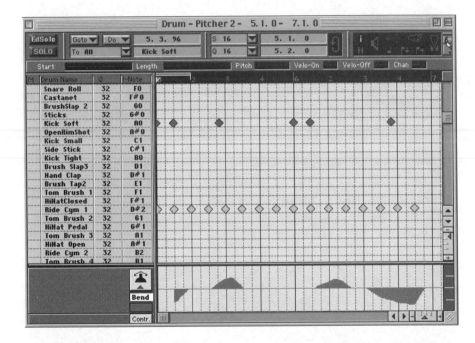

ON THE CD-ROM
You'll find this Trip Hop groove and its pitch bend track on the CD-ROM accompanying this book in the following directory:
chapter6/midifiles/drums/triphop/triphop2.mid.

We'll try adding some percussion to this groove and building it up next but first we need a break to finish off our Trip Hop loops. The following example was recorded as part of the whole loop and cut up afterward to fashion the breakdown. It's essentially a variation on the snare pattern from our jazz loops, played on the brush snare and snare roll with a crash to finish. Once again part of the pitch bend track already recorded has been called into play to give the rides some weirdness.

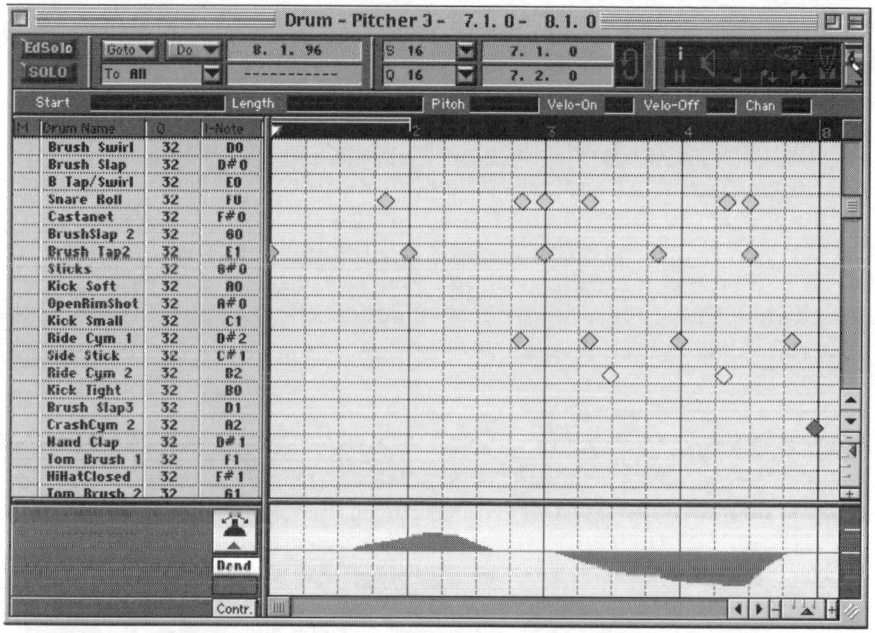

Figure 6.14
Everything comes to a halt with a crash; the pitch bend exaggerates this effect.

ON THE CD-ROM
You'll find this Trip Hop groove and its pitch bend track on the CD-ROM accompanying this book in the following directory:
chapter6/midifiles/drums/triphop/triph_fl.mid.

TIP
If your synth has built in distortion effects a little placed on a drum track can make the whole thing sound more raw.

Percussed percussion

Percussion is where there is most scope for invention when you're putting together Trip Hop grooves. In the following examples I've used the minimal beats of the second Trip Hop groove we put together in the last section as a base upon which to layer weird and wonderful percussion. The percussion grooves themselves were recorded as 'normal' percussion grooves at the standard 120 beats per minute and can be used as percussive layers in all of the electronic styles featured in this book.

To render them as strange as possible the percussion grooves were placed on a separate MIDI track and that was set to use one of the SFX kits featured on XG synths. Not all the sounds in the percussion grooves sound on the SFX kit and assembling these percussed grooves involved identifying those that did and those that didn't. Those that didn't sound on the SFX kit were revoiced back onto the regular drum kit where the pitch bend effect added to **triphop2.mid** worked its weirdness on them. Meanwhile the strange assortment of sound effects used in the SFX kit has added all manner of odd noises.

Figure 6.15
The SFX kit is the source of a number of strange sounds.

The SFX kit has been pitched up and this helps to make these sounds nothing like the originals, which are really designed as the sort of sound effects you would expect to find on a movie soundtrack, rather than the weird assortment of ethnic percussion we have here. The Tabla sound produced by the Submarine SFX is a particular surprise and quite colourful.

TIP
To use sounds from your synthesizer's SFX kit change the pitch to avoid recognition. You can either tune the whole kit up or down using your module's key shift/tune function or, if you can't access that from your sequencer, insert a pitch bend range event and set the pitch wheel low/high.

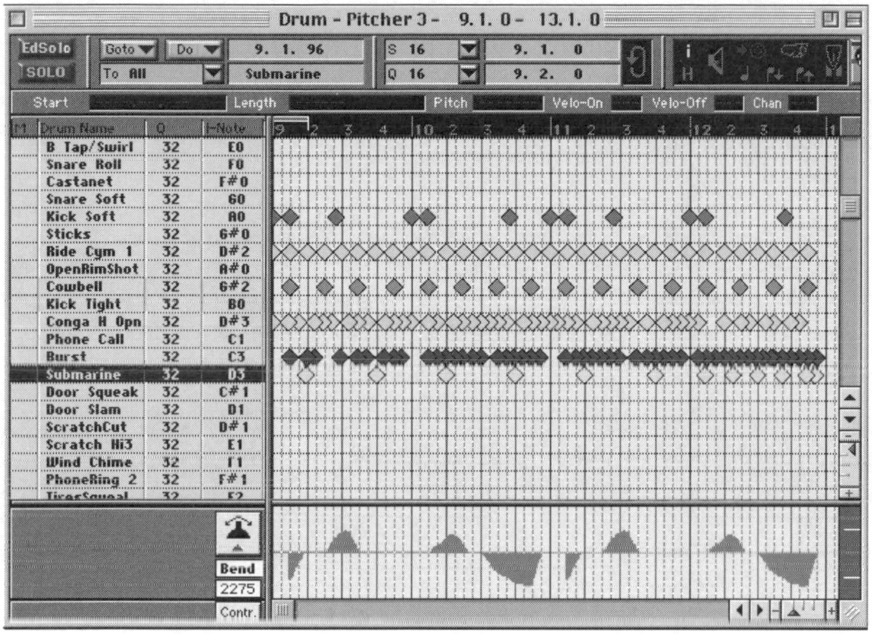

Figure 6.16
Pitch bending sound effects can yield surprisingly useful results, in this case transforming a submarine sound into one more reminiscent of a Tabla!

With sound effects, recording pitch bend commands alongside the SFX kit is usually more effective than simply pitching up or down. It helps to break up the monotony of sampled sound effects and can often add to the final effect. The wind chimes sounded monotonous until pitch bend information was added in our example here.

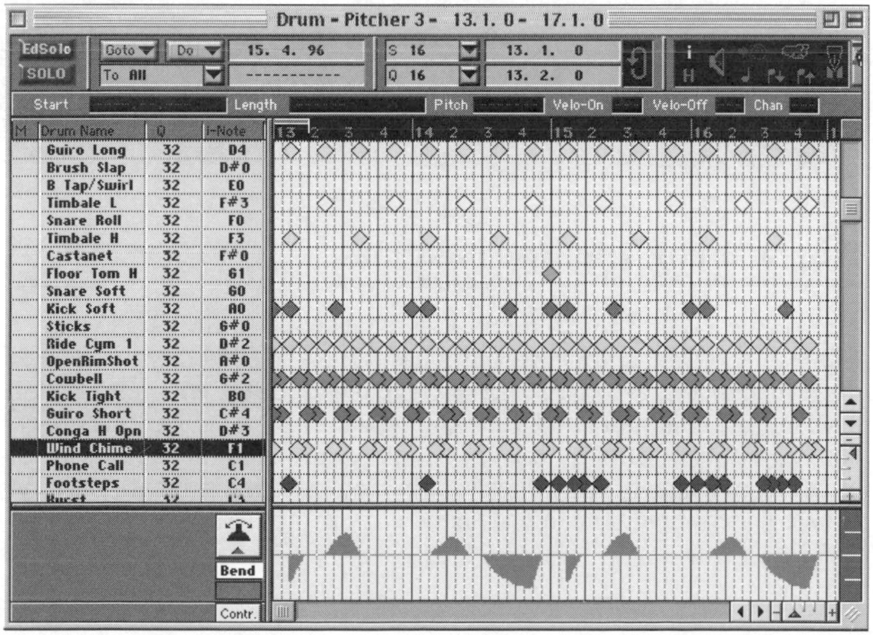

Figure 6.17
Pitch bend information adds variation to essentially static sound effects.

It's not only the SFX sounds that make these percussion grooves. The hand claps were originally part of **perc01.mid** but the pitch bend part originally recorded on the kick and ride cymbal has given the claps a 'human' quality, simply because it alters the pitch of each clap and makes them sound quite 'real'.

Figure 6.18

Not only sound effects benefit from the careful application of pitch bend; other drum sounds too are given more 'feel' by having live pitch bend information added.

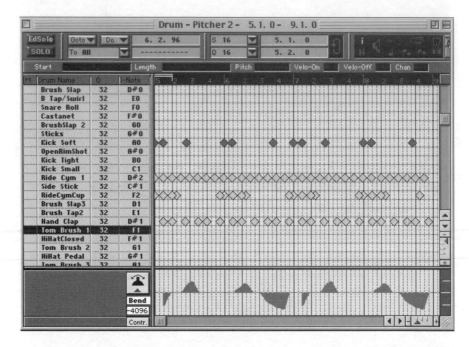

ON THE CD-ROM

The percussion loops originated here can be found on the CD-ROM accompanying this book as one file featuring all the composite loops. You'll find it in the following directory: **chapter6/midifiles/drums/perc/perked.mid**.

Programming Trip Hop basslines

Trip Hop is a return to the roots of all dance music. From Rock'n'Roll to Hip-Hop and Dance, Rhythm and Blues forms the solid bed on which all these foundations are built. Trip Hop is open to ideas and improvizations and, in this, is influenced by another spawn of R'n'B, jazz. Where the bass in jazz is often very busy, acting as a melodic interplay with the other instruments, the basslines in Trip Hop draw more on the dub style of bass underpinning the melody and beat.

Bass sounds

The bass in Trip Hop can be almost any instrument from acoustic bass to synth bass. The essential element is to get a sound that is moody and dark. Just as with the drums try to play with the character of the sound by adjusting the filters if possible. Tremolo effects are used a lot in Trip Hop and this can be reasonably well mimicked by the subtle use of vibrato on your sound module.

In the GM sound set the Acoustic Bass (Program 33), Finger (Program 34), Pick Bass (Program 35) and Fretless (Program 36) basses are particularly suitable if you're trying for a 'real' bass player sound. The other extreme is to use the Synth basses, pitched as low as you can, for dirty, menacing sounds. Synth basses usually feature lots of filter frequency and resonance tweaking while effective use can be made of pitch bend and vibrato on the 'real' basses to emulate a live player. The most effective sections of Trip Hop songs are often where these two contrasting bass sounds are layered against each other.

Blues basslines

The minimal basslines used in Trip Hop provide more space for delicate piano and synth lines to vamp over. The essential thing is that the bassline shouldn't be too busy, either rhythmically or melodically.

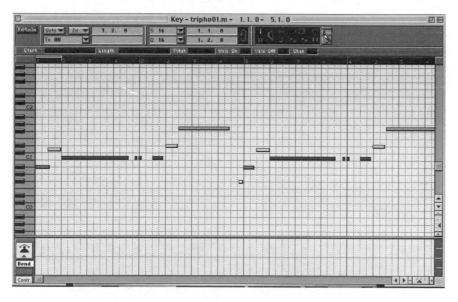

Figure 6.19
An R'n'B bassline provides plenty of space for accompaniment.

This first example is a suitably dark bassline in a blues scale and allows plenty of room to improvise piano lines over the top of it, the essential requirement in Trip Hop. The marriage of blues basslines and jazz chordings is not unique to Trip Hop; indeed this is borrowed from reggae and dub, Trip Hop's biggest influence. These minimal basslines also sit well with the sparse, laid back drumbeats we've been programming already. Large sections of Trip Hop tracks are often simply bass, drums and weird noises with plenty of space in the mix.

ON THE CD-ROM
You'll find this bassline on the CD-ROM accompanying this book in the following directory: **chapter6/midifiles/bass/tripbas1.mid**.

Our second example once again sticks to a blues scale and thins the bassline down to only three notes. Much use is again made of sustained notes, leaving plenty of space for modulation and vibrato effects. Basslines like this cry out for real time manipulation of their filters and vibrato. This can only be done in the context of an accompanying drum loop and other musical parts of course. Try matching this bassline up with a drum loop and playing around with the filter frequency and resonance.

Figure 6.20
Sustained notes are an essential element of Trip Hop basslines.

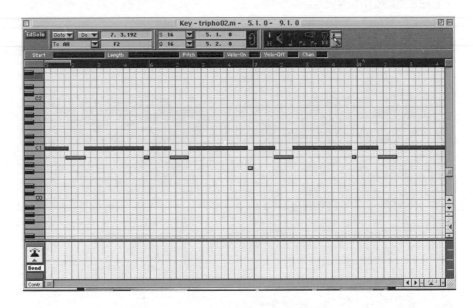

ON THE CD-ROM
You'll find this bassline on the CD-ROM accompanying this book in the following directory: **chapter6/midifiles/bass/tripbas2.mid**.

Often Trip Hop basslines will descend by semitone steps, which also gives a rather dark and melancholy sound to the music. Our next example does just that and has a suitably dark and menacing vibe. This bassline has been treated with a modicum of pitch bend that emulates a real bass player's bending of the strings. There is also a small amount of modulation on one of the sustained notes for a vibrato effect, also emulating a real bass player.

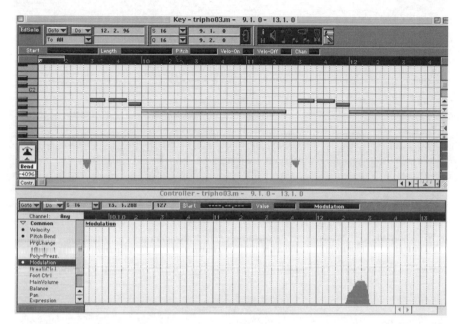

Figure 6.21
Modulation and pitch bend help to emulate the slides and string bends of a 'real' bass player.

ON THE CD-ROM
You'll find this bassline on the CD-ROM accompanying this book in the following directory: **chapter6/midifiles/bass/tripbas3.mid**.

The semitone shift is also used in our next example for that dark feel (see Figure 6.22). After the first shift from C to F# a semitone shift to F from the first bar to the next provides just the right edginess and darkness to make this deceptively simple bassline unsettling in a spooky, old sci-fi movie kind of way.

ON THE CD-ROM
You'll find this bassline on the CD-ROM accompanying this book in the following directory: **chapter6/midifiles/bass/tripbas4.mid**.

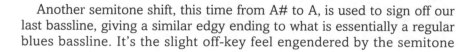

Another semitone shift, this time from A# to A, is used to sign off our last bassline, giving a similar edgy ending to what is essentially a regular blues bassline. It's the slight off-key feel engendered by the semitone shift in these two examples that gives the dark, almost menacing feel that is an essential element of Trip Hop. The moodier and darker you can make your basslines the better (see Figure 6.23).

Figure 6.22
A simple semitone shift adds just the right 'note' of darkness.

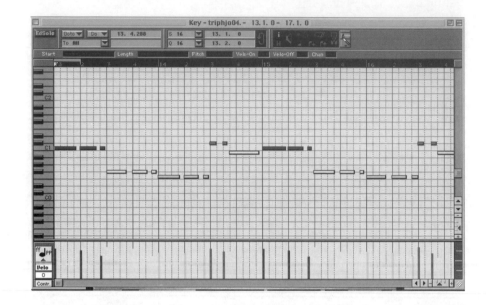

Figure 6.23
Another use of the semitone shift, this time at the end of a two bar pattern.

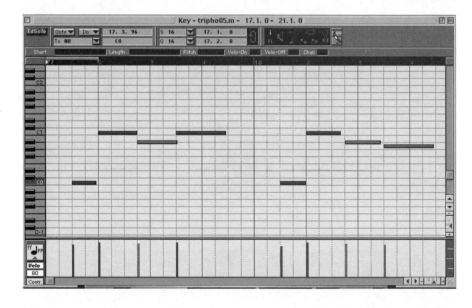

ON THE CD-ROM
You'll find this bassline on the CD-ROM accompanying this book in the following directory: **chapter6/midifiles/bass/tripbas5.mid**.

Arranging a Trip Hop Track

As Trip Hop lends itself well to sung vocals the form of the music tends to be song structured, i.e. with a verse and chorus, bridge and so on. Because Trip Hop uses more traditional song structures this is the point when you are most likely to be putting your track together. Programming Trip Hop is the reverse of programming all the other styles we've looked at up until now. With House, Techno and Big Beat you act like a DJ and assemble a load of parts then cut and paste between them. When assembling a Trip Hop track that process is reversed, with the basic structure being laid down and then the programmer finding the right loops and other weird effects to layer onto what are often live audio tracks. Once you start laying down some jazzy electric piano chords you'll have a pretty good idea of the basic structure of your track, especially if you have written some vocal parts.

ON THE CD-ROM

You'll find the MIDI file of this completed Trip Hop track on the CD-ROM accompanying this book in the following directory: **chapter6/midifiles/songs/** triphop.mid. *There's also a set up file to initialise a GS or XG synth in the same directory called* **tripset.mid**

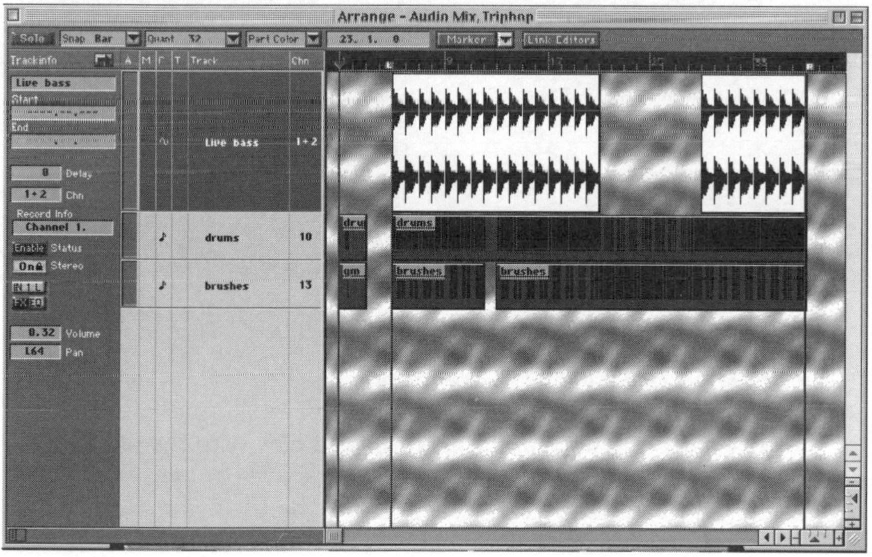

Figure 6.24
After assembling the basic drum track a bass part is recorded live onto an audio track. Trip Hop is a much more 'live' medium than most other Electronica and most of the parts will often be recorded this way with minimal MIDI sequencing.

Electric piano

When it comes to generating melodic parts for a Trip Hop track, anything spooky and mellow is what you're after. The keyboard instrument of choice is often the electric piano. If you play around with the filters and effects you could dirty up a clean sound. The electric piano usually tends to play jazzy chords with extra notes added.

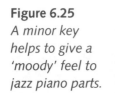

NOTE

The chords in Trip Hop are often complex with many added notes. This makes the feel of the music more jazzy. Trip Hop tracks are almost always in a minor key giving an instant dark, broody feel to the music.

Figure 6.25

A minor key helps to give a 'moody' feel to jazz piano parts.

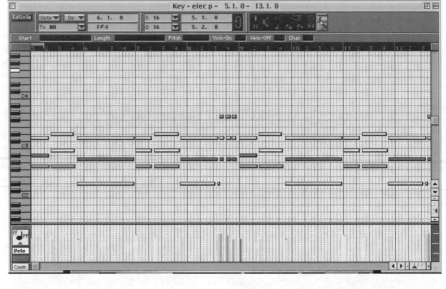

ON THE CD-ROM

You can find this pad sequence on the CD-ROM accompanying this book in the following directory: **chapter6/midifiles/chords/trippn1.mid**.

Analogue pads

Analogue sounds are also used a lot in Trip Hop so pick a sound that sounds like a basic synthesizer waveform and play with the filters in real time. Good sources for analogue type sounds are Programs 39, 40, 81 and 82. If your synth goes beyond GM then the bank variations behind these basic sounds are well worth seeking out.

Program 91, the Poly Synthesizer Pad, is just such an example of a basic synthesizer patch that emulates an analogue synth and is very useful for Trip Hop, especially since you can play it deep down and dark. To lay down a basic pad that can be used to add atmosphere to our Trip Hop piece this patch has been used and a series of dark semitone steps have been used to create an atmospheric pad sequence.

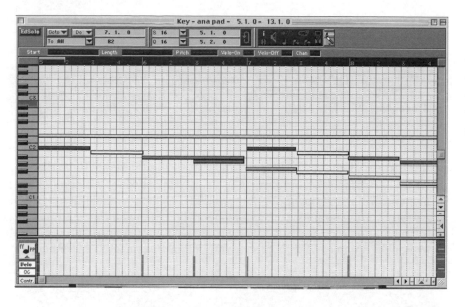

Figure 6.26
Use analogue sounds and semitone steps for an atmospheric pad sequence.

ON THE CD-ROM

You can find this pad sequence on the CD-ROM accompanying this book in the following directory: **chapter6/midifiles/chords/tripsyn1.mid**.

Keeping things dark and moody, a synthesizer bass with pitch bend and modulation can be used to vamp along with this pad and generate a dark and moody bassline. Note how the bassline simply plays around

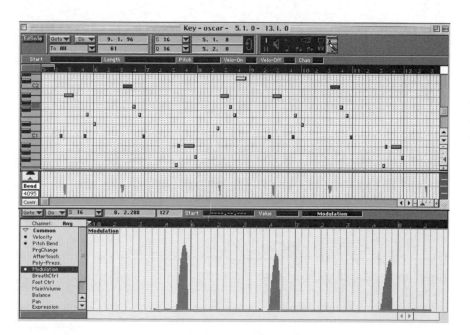

Figure 6.27
Pitch bend and modulation add atmosphere to synthesizer bass sounds as well as 'real' ones.

with the notes of the pad and makes use of pitch bend to bend the whole
thing into shape.

This style of playing, where a basic pad is sketched out and then
another instrument extemporises over the top of that, is a typical jazz
move and one that Trip Hop embraces enthusiastically, making full use of
the mood-setting sounds of jazz. This usually involves the traditional jazz
instrumentation too. In our following example a basic chord pattern is laid
down on an organ or electric piano with lots of sustain such as a Rhodes.

Figure 6.28
*Two note
chords lay
down a basic
mood to
improvise
over.*

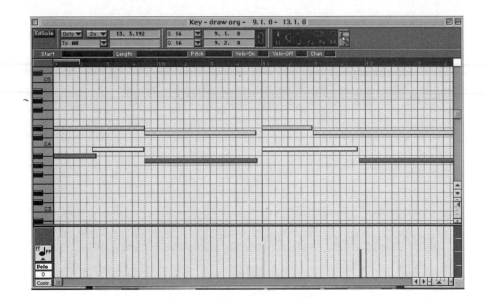

A vibe section is then vamped over the top. Note how the vibes don't
use the same notes as the chords but actually play around on the thirds,
fifths and sevenths of the organ's chord pattern. This produces a semitone shift that adds an edge to the otherwise melodic vibe part. MIDI
vibe sounds are relatively authentic sounding as the vibes are a percus-

sion instrument where as the variation in the sound which mimics the real instrument comes from the different velocity values generated by live playing.

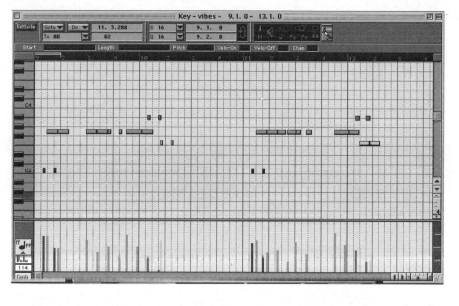

Figure 6.29
Use vibes for an authentic Jazz vibe.

ON THE CD-ROM
You'll find this melodic vibe sequence on the CD-ROM accompanying this book in the following directory: **chapter6/midifiles/melody/tripmel1.mid**.

Guitar

This does occur in Trip Hop but is often heavily effected with extreme noise or sound altering devices. The tremolo effect is also in evidence. Programming decent sounding guitars is often difficult but not impossible. Try to use more than one guitar sound for different effects, e.g. a distorted sound (maybe add some distortion effect), a feedback sound and a clean sound.

Effects

With your basic track laid out, now is the time to start playing around with the special effects rack and MIDI controllers to add atmosphere as and when the songwriter requests it. This small string part adds tension by using a volume sweep to bring the strings in suddenly just as on a thriller or sci-fi soundtrack.

Figure 6.30
Volume sweeps can add just the right amount of horror movie tension to a simple string part.

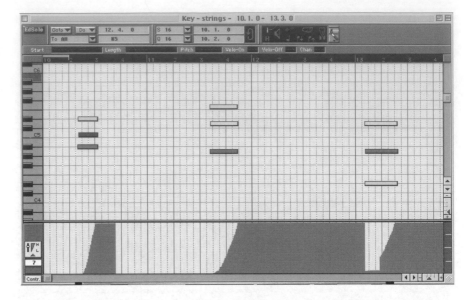

ON THE CD-ROM
You'll find this atmospheric little string snippet on the CD-ROM accompanying this book in the following directory: **chapter6/midifiles/chords/tripstr1.mid**.

TIP
For those creepy, Theremin-type sounds try a sine or square wave sound, adjust the filters to create a thinner sound and set the sound from polyphonic to monophonic. Putting portamento on the sound also gives the impression of a hand waving in front of a Theremin. Finally, detune the sound on some notes to mimic the pitching characteristics of a Theremin.

ON THE CD-ROM
The Trip Hop track arranged here and provided for as a MIDI file has also been recorded (with live bass and analogue synths) as a series of audio files. You'll find them on the CD-ROM accompanying this book in the following directory: **chapter6/samples/**. *Within the* **samples** *directory are a series of folders: bass, chords, drums and melody. Within each folder you'll find a series of WAVE files. These files feature live bass and other instruments as well as analogue synths and other special effects. All the parts that make up the completed track are there so you could reconstruct the entire track from these constituent parts. Even better, make a new arrangement yourself!*

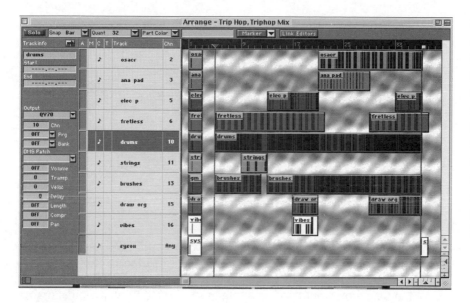

Figure 6.31
A Trip Hop track is more often constructed along traditional verse/chorus/verse lines than more dancefloor oriented Electronica.

We've now looked at programming Trip Hop drum loops, paying special attention to getting the sounds right. We've also explored the jazz and blues nature of Trip Hop basslines. Finally we've put all of that together with some jazzy chords and generated a series of weird effects to make a complete Trip Hop track. You should now be ready to record your own Trip Hop original.

With Trip Hop, Electronica has come full circle. Out of Electro came Hip-Hop then House, Garage and Techno and from Techno came Drum'n'Bass, Big Beat and Trip Hop and now we have come full circle. The words of Juan Atkins resonate: 'Jazz is the Teacher, Funk is the Preacher'.

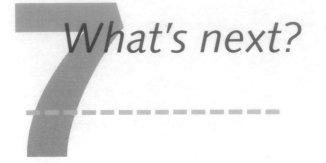

What's next?

Electronica has spawned so many styles and spanned so many genres in its assimilating romp through music's playgrounds you could be forgiven for thinking there was no answer to the perennial question, whatever next? If you assumed that the predominance of Electronica meant the end of the history of music, just as Electronica itself presaged the death of rock music, you would not be alone in thinking that all avenues of possibility had been explored. But, *la meme c'est plus, la meme c'est chose* – the more things change, the more they return to their origin.

At the time of writing Electronica is simultaneously exhausted, having explored every possible permutation of itself and invigorated, finding new life in old loops. Always a post-modern style, based upon the concept of sampling the recent past and reinventing it, Electronica now finds itself in the enviable position of being able to sample itself and represent that. Just as though there were no yesterday, all our tomorrows can now be represented by multiple, multi-layered slices of the past.

In 1989, in what many critics saw as a last, desperate attempt to reinvent itself, Electronica threw up Speed Garage – a hybrid of breakbeats, Garage vocals, Jungle basslines and House grooves. The critics sat back smugly as the inevitable signs of decay manifested themselves, along with endless arguments about what Speed Garage actually was and who originated the style, and the fervent denials of all concerned that *their* music was Speed Garage.

While the critics crowed, those of us for whom House was indeed a spiritual thing, a soul thing, heard something else. The grooves of Speed Garage were indeed familiar; they were the same shuffle beats and four-to-the-floor rhythms that had kicked the whole thing off way back in time. The R'n'B grooves of Northern Soul nights, now labelled Swingbeat but still pushing the same vibe – get out there and enjoy yourself! Further evidence of the influence of breakbeats is emerging in the various new Nu School movements. Some are based on reinventing Electro while others look to House and Garage for inspiration.

Although Electronica began in Detroit until now it has been largely a European phenomenon. The Goan Trance scene, as the first truly global

Electronica phenomenon, has shown everyone what future inspiration will be about. From Asia to South America, a truly global approach to Electronica is emerging. The crossover into Jazz is only in its infancy as Jazz musicians and composers begin to incorporate breakbeats. There are interesting collaborations to come. Once again it seems that the only rule is that there are no rules; anything goes.

As we enter the new millennium and wait for the digital clocks to melt down civilization the truth emerges, the new school *is* the old school, nothing ever changes yet nothing ever stays the same. *La meme c'est plus, la meme c'est chose – vive la difference!*

ON THE CD-ROM

You'll find a selection of Speed Garage, Swingbeat, Latin and Nu School grooves in a folder called **Chapter7** *on the CD-ROM accompanying this book. Experiment with these loops and the loops in the other style folders on the CD-ROM to evolve your own style. That's what's next!*

8 Audio Programming

Digital audio

Just when it was clear in your mind that a sequencer uses MIDI data to trigger sounds in external modules or soundcards, along comes digital audio to confuse you. Because computer processors are now faster than ever, most new computers are capable of dealing with digital audio, which is a recording of sound, just like a tape recording. The difference is that the recording is made to a sampler, DAT machine or, more commonly these days, directly to your hard drive. With support for digital audio your sequencer can run digital audio tracks alongside MIDI tracks. This greatly increases the versatility and functionality of sequencers. For electronic music makers it is a real advantage.

Figure 8.1
Cubase VST includes a sophisticated EQ section and an inline effects unit. These effects, known as 'plug-ins' are becoming a standard and are increasingly shared across the sequencer platforms. Thus Logic Audio, Vision and Cakewalk can use 'Cubase' plug-ins.

NOTE

As computer hardware has became more powerful most MIDI sequencers have added support for digital audio. There are now versions of most major sequencers with digital audio facilities for all three computer platforms. If you have a PowerMac or fast PC with a sound card, the audio versions of most sequencers give you digital audio capabilities, often with an EQ section and onboard effects.

What is digital audio?

Digital audio is simply sound which has been recorded in a digital format. A sampler is a digital recorder, as is a DAT machine, and if you're familiar with working with either of those, digital audio should hold no surprises for you. You can manipulate digital audio with the same precision as you can when manipulating MIDI data. That's what makes digital audio so powerful and exciting to work with.

NOTE

PowerMacs have a Digital Signal Processor or DSP chip that performs the A-to-D and D-to-A conversions. PCs don't come with a DSP chip inside and to record and play back digital audio you must install a sound card which will feature a DSP.

To convert natural sound into digital format a special chip known as an analogue-to-digital converter is used. This is usually abbreviated to A-to-D. To convert the digital audio back into sound requires a D-to-A, which performs the same process in reverse. This is essential if you are ever to hear the digital recording played back as anything more than digital noise, which isn't very pleasant. If you've ever played the CD-ROM section of a mixed-mode CD like the one accompanying this book on your audio CD player by mistake you'll know exactly how unpleasant and speaker-threatening that is!

NOTE

Not all D-to-A chips are the same and the quality of the playback sound depends on how good your D-to-A chip is. This is why professional studios often bypass the D-to-A converters on a cheap soundcard and run through the D-to-A chip on an outboard piece of kit like a professional DAT machine or a dedicated external unit.

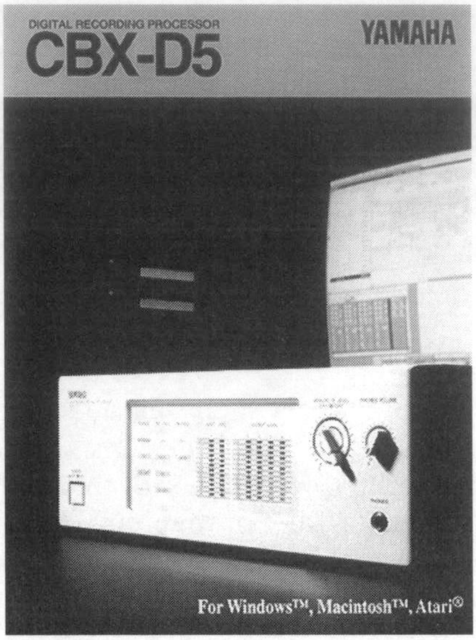

Figure 8.2
*Yamaha's
CBX D5 is a
hardware unit
that records and
plays back
digital audio in
tandem with
your sequencer.*

There are two factors that determine the quality of digital audio: sample rate and sample resolution. During recording, the incoming sound is sampled a set number of times per second. This is known as the sample rate and each sample is stored on your hard drive as a series of numbers. The more samples taken per second, the more accurate the digital representation of the sound. CDs use a sample rate of 44.1kHz which means the sound is measured 44,100 times each second. DAT machines and some sound cards can use rates up to 48kHz but for most users 44.1kHz is fine.

The sample resolution is the number of bits used to store each sample. The more bits there are, the more accurate the digital audio will be. With a resolution of 8 bits, sample values can range from 0 to 256. With 16-bit resolution, values can range up to 65,535 which means each measurement is more accurate.

NOTE

Lately, 24-bit resolutions are being utilized, giving a range of up to 16,777,216. This extra quality does make a difference in the early stages of recording but for most dance music 16-bit sound still rules.

What happens to the audio when it is digitized? In a sampler it is stored in the instrument's RAM but in digital audio recording it is saved straight to your hard disk. The digital recording process is known, therefore, as direct-to-disk or D-to-D recording. The benefits of this are enormous in terms of storage and flexibility. Hard disks are up to 100 times cheaper than RAM so you can store masses of audio material for a relatively low cost. And this is important because one minute of CD quality, stereo digital audio requires around 10Mb of storage space. A four minute song, therefore, needs about 40Mb of hard drive space.

Digital tracks

The really great thing about modern sequencers is the way they handle audio data. Audio patterns appear in the Arrange page looking very like MIDI patterns and you can edit them in much the same way. You can record as many audio tracks as you wish but the number that you can physically play back at one time depends on your computer system.

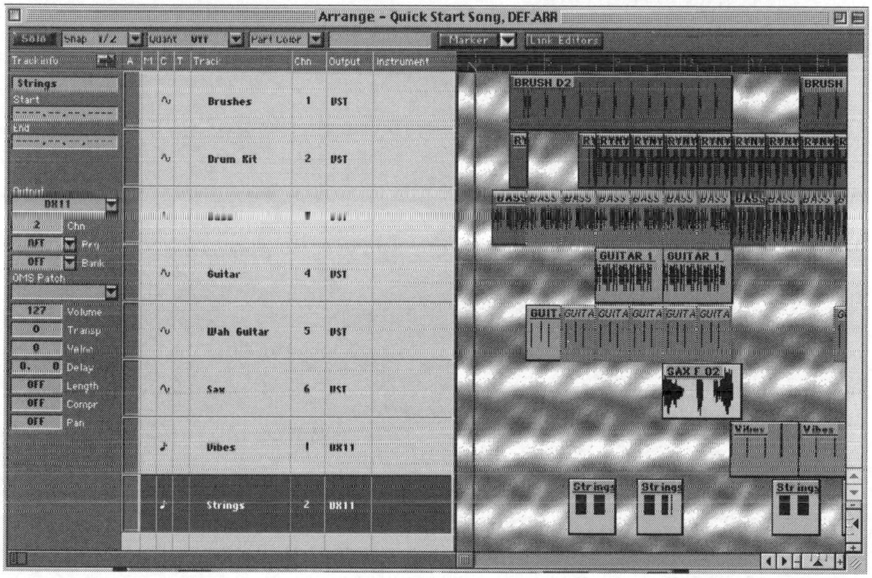

Figure 8.3
Digital tracks appear alongside MIDI tracks and can be manipulated in much the same way.

The only limit to the number of audio tracks you can use is usually the speed of your processor and the speed of the hard disk. Cubase VST on the PowerMac, for example, can handle up to 32 audio tracks but only if it's running a very, very fast Mac with lots of RAM. A more modest PowerMac will support eight or 16 tracks. On the PC, the major limitation is the hard disk speed although most systems running on a Pentium, for example, will manage six or eight tracks.

As the audio data in the patterns that appear in the audio tracks is not stored in RAM but on disk the patterns simply reference or point to the files. This means you can use the same audio recording or any section of it as many times as you wish with no additional overheads in terms of memory or disk space. All the program does is read the file more than once or, to play a segment of it, start reading the file from the point you have referenced it.

Recording digital audio

The general procedure for making a digital recording is the same in most modern sequencers although some of the details may vary. Typically an audio track is enabled for recording by selecting it and pressing 'Record'. Then a File dialogue opens prompting you to enter a name and a path for the audio file you are about to create. The only thing to watch here is that the hard drive in your record path has enough space for your intended recording. Remember: one minute of stereo audio uses 10Mb of hard disk space.

Figure 8.4
Make sure you have enough space on your record path for your digital recording.

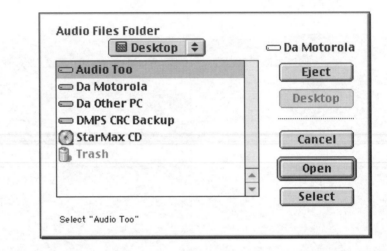

Unlike an analogue tape recording, an overloaded digital signal will distort in a very nasty manner. This means you have to watch your recording levels very carefully. Any peaks which go above the limit will produce 'digital clipping' which is very nasty indeed to the ears (see Figure 8.5).

Once you've chosen your record path and set your monitor levels, click on the Record button, wait for the count-in and record. Digital audio recording really is as simple as that. You can also import previously recorded files into an arrangement, just as you would a MIDI file. These days sample CDs are increasingly offered as CD-ROMs with the loops available as sound files for you to import directly into your arrangement. Even if they're not you can usually grab the sound files off a regular CD using a sound editor.

Figure 8.5
*Monitoring
input levels is
crucial in digital
recording.*

Changing the tempo to fit the audio

The most common scenario in Electronica is where you want to build
a track from sampled drum loops and you need to match the tempo
your sequencer is playing at to that of the loop. If you get these from
a sample CD, the vast majority tell you the tempo they were recorded
at so all you need do is set the tempo and import the audio file into
the program.

But what if you have a drum loop, bass riff or vocal hook which has no
tempo information? Then you must make the sequencer's tempo match
that of the audio. Most sequencers have a routine for doing this and you
should consult your manual to find out if your sequencer has a way of
ascertaining the BPM of a loop and set the sequencer's tempo accordingly. To do this you must first tell the sequencer how long the musical
event is in bars then select a region of the sound file corresponding to
that number of bars. Your sequencer will then calculate the BPM and
adjust the tempo of your arrangement accordingly.

Figure 8.6
Fitting the Event to the Loop range in Cubase Audio.

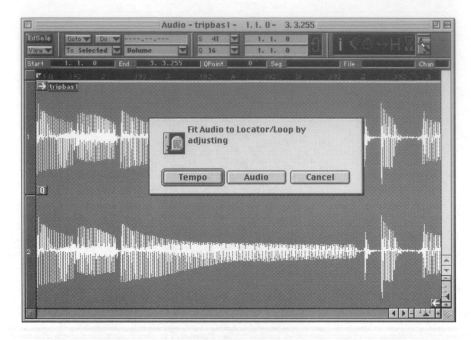

Figure 8.7
Adjust Tempo by selection and locators in Logic Audio.

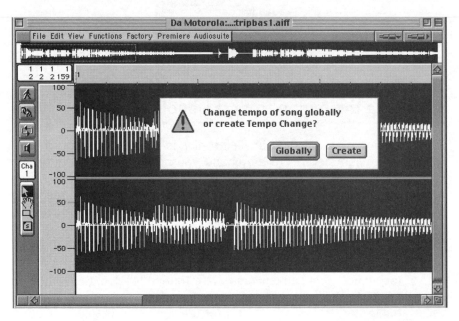

If your sequencer has no such facility you are left with the quick and dirty method. This involves looping your sequencer around the number of bars in the sample and adjusting the tempo until the audio loops cleanly. Although unsophisticated, this method does work and is used by many programmers in a hurry. You can usually tell roughly what the BPM of a loop is and then fine-tune the sequencer's tempo to match it.

Changing the audio to fit the tempo

The reverse scenario, when you must fit the audio to the tempo of a piece, happens even more frequently and is the most exciting area of modern digital recording. The solutions to this, time-stretching and pitch-shifting, are responsible for the innovations in Electronica that have led to the development of Drum'n'Bass, Trip Hop and Big Beat. Without time-stretching or pitch-shifting the sped up drum loops of Jungle and the slowed down percussion of Trip Hop simply wouldn't exist.

Time-stretching

Time-stretching is the best solution to the problem of altering the tempo of a drum loop or other musical phrase that doesn't fit with a previously recorded piece of music. Obviously if your already recorded work is in the form of a MIDI sequence you could simply change the tempo to fit the speed of the audio loop but that may not be the solution you want. If the audio loop is too slow and you want to keep your MIDI sequence at the tempo you've written it, slowing down the MIDI to match the audio is only going to ruin your composition. The solution is to time-stretch the audio piece to fit the MIDI.

You could play the sample higher up or down the keyboard of course. This has the desired effect of speeding up or slowing down the audio to match it to another tempo but also has the often unwanted effect of altering the pitch of the sound. A bass voice played an octave higher on the keyboard will be faster and higher in pitch and will cease to be a bass voice. This effect can be used to your advantage and often is in Drum'n'Bass and Trip Hop – a process we'll look at next.

The process of time-stretching involves lots of complicated mathematics but the basic concept is very simple. The computer analyzes the samples that comprise an audio loop, repositions them on a new time grid and resamples them. Thus, if you were taking the samples that made up a loop recorded at 90 BPM and time-stretching it to 120 BPM the original samples would be squeezed closer together. If the process were reversed and your loop was recorded at 120 BPM but you wanted it to run at 90 BPM the original samples would be spread out further apart. This means that you will end up with more samples if you are making the loop slower and fewer samples if you make the loop faster. The end result is that the audio loop will sound at the same pitch but a different speed.

Time-stretching used to be a complicated affair, requiring you to calculate the end length of a sample. This process meant you had to work out how long (in seconds and milliseconds) a sample would be when converted from 90–120 BPM. Not only was the maths involved hideously complicated but also, by the time you'd worked it all out, you'd often lost the inspiration that led you to alter the timing of a sample in the first place!

Fortunately, most modern sequencers make the whole process very simple these days, only asking you to input the original BPM and the target tempo. The other information is still shown and you can adjust the speed of the sounds by time or sample length if you prefer, but adjusting the start and end BPM is by far the easiest method.

Figure 8.8
Time-stretching a sound file is now a simple process.

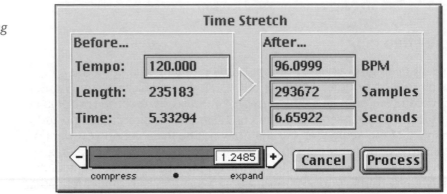

Pitch-shifting

Pitch-shifting is simpler and is, in a sense, the 'wrong' way to go about the process of fitting a loop to the tempo of a piece. Pitch-shifting originated with samplers where a sample was assigned to a fixed key on a keyboard. Playing the sample at any other key would speed up or slow down the speed of the sample by playing it at a different pitch from that originally recorded. If you assigned the range a sample could be played over as two octaves, then playing the sample an octave down from its 'correct' pitch would play it at half the speed. Conversely, playing it an octave above its assigned pitch would play it twice as fast.

While this would have the desired effect as far as speed was concerned the pitch of the sample would alter too, as the term pitch-shifting implies. The sample played an octave down would not only be half the speed, it would also sound an octave lower – turning a sprightly drum loop into a dirge-like drone. Sounds played higher up the scale would become higher-pitched versions of their original selves. Although this was often 'wrong' the effects of pitch-shifting were perceived as an effect in themselves and many creative types began to use pitch-shifting as part of the creative process.

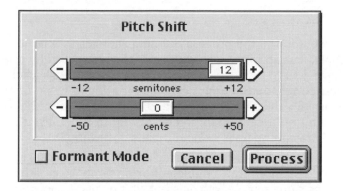

Figure 8.9
*Pitch-shifting a
sample up an
octave.*

This is most noticeable in Drum'n'Bass and Trip Hop. In the former, drum loops are often pitched up to achieve a rattling sound while Trip Hop usually slows loops down for the reverse effect, giving drum loops which sound as though time itself is slowing down. In the creative process of pitch-shifting a mixture of the two is usually the most desirable. To get the desired sound from a loop you must pitch the sample down or up. Pitch-shifting is not very precise in terms of tempo, however, and often a pitch-shifted loop will sound right but won't quite fit in to the desired tempo.

The best way to get the right combination of pitch-shifting and time-stretching is to first time-stretch your sample to fit the desired tempo. Once you've achieved that you can then pitch-shift the time-stretched sample to the desired pitch. You could do it the other way around but you would run the risk of your finished sample not quite fitting into the loop. Logic Audio has a very sophisticated function called the Time and Pitch machine that allows you to perform both operations simultaneously, adjusting the desired parameters on a visual display that graphically shows both elements.

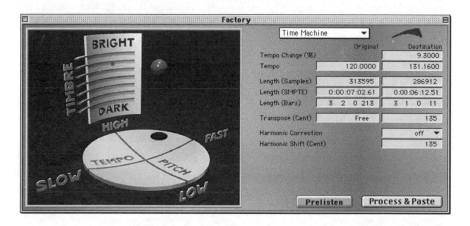

Figure 8.10
*Logic Audio's
Time and Pitch
machine allows
you to adjust
both pitch
and tempo
simultaneously.*

ReCycling

The best solution to the process of fitting samples to a tempo is to have the samples cut up into slices with each slice triggered by a MIDI note. This allows you to alter the tempo of your piece at will. Each individual slice must correspond to a musical value for this to work, of course, and these musical values must correspond to those used in the loop. Its no good cutting up a sample in pieces an eighth in length if the musical phrase you're cutting up is in 32nd triplets, for example.

In the past this process was often achieved by the painstaking process of chopping up samples in a sample editor or sampler, creating numerous copies of the same sample with different start points. Although effective this is very time-consuming which quickly leads to you losing friends and lovers as you spend long days and nights hunched over your sampler or computer finding the required start points and chopping up the samples to match.

Fortunately a software solution has arrived which does all that for you. It's called ReCycle and is used by all Drum'n'Bass programmers to give them maximum programming flexibility. With ReCycle you load a loop up into its editor and set the number of bars. ReCycle then automatically calculates the tempo for you. If you want to pitch-shift your sample you do it before loading into ReCycle.

Figure 8.11
ReCycle calculates the tempo of a loop once you enter the number of bars and/or beats.

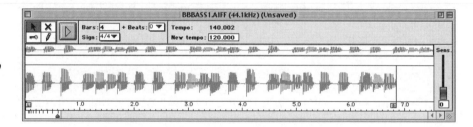

Once you've done that you simply move a slider on the right to adjust the resolution of the slices. This is a pretty easy process as the visual display makes the individual parts of a loop relatively easy to identify. You can fine-tune the process further by deleting extra slices that the software may have put in and by adding cut points where the software has missed a note. Once that's done the finished series of samples can be sent out to your sampler as a set with an accompanying MIDI file to trigger them. Then all you have to do is adjust the tempo of your sequence to play your loop at a different BPM.

Figure 8.12
ReCycle cuts your loop up into individual sounds.

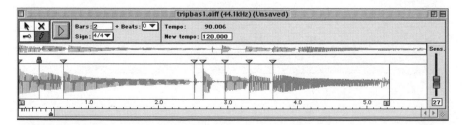

If you're using Cubase as your sequencer you can export the result as a REXX file. This is essentially the same thing as the series of samples that ReCycle sends to a sampler. It's a sound file cut up into slices of individual sounds. When you load a REXX file into Cubase you can treat that sound file as though it were a MIDI sequence, altering the tempo at will. As Cubase sees it as a series of small sound files each with their own trigger point, the loop will play faster or slower with no pitch-shifting or time-stretching necessary.

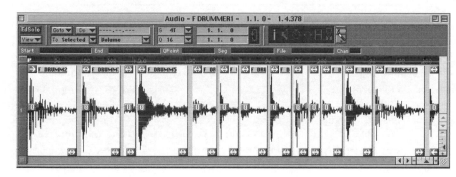

Figure 8.13
A REXX file consists of a series of sound files.

EQ and effects

The process of working with sound files doesn't end with adjusting the pitch and tempo either. Obviously if you're working with samples in a sampler you can EQ the sounds through your mixing desk and add effects from there to fine-tune the finished result. Increasingly audio sequencers allow you to do the same thing with EQ and effects from within your computer. A standard has evolved that means effects modules can be shared across sequencer platforms and this development is perhaps the most exciting in digital audio today.

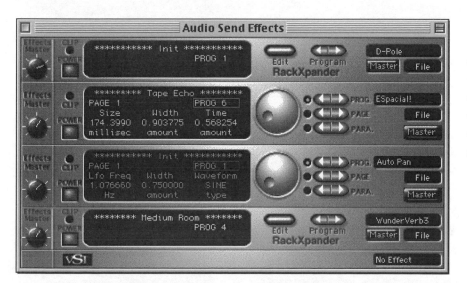

Figure 8.14
Plug-in effects are now capable of being shared across sequencer platforms.

With the ability to treat digital audio as you would regular audio it could be argued that the mixing desk and traditional recording studio are obsolete. Simply record your MIDI instruments onto digital audio tracks, EQ them and add reverb and effects to them in the computer then output the finished result to a digital file ready to burn on to a CD. The seamless integration of digital audio into the major sequencing platforms gives the home enthusiast the potential to get professional results.

Figure 8.15
Output your digital audio directly to a sound file ready for burning on to a CD.

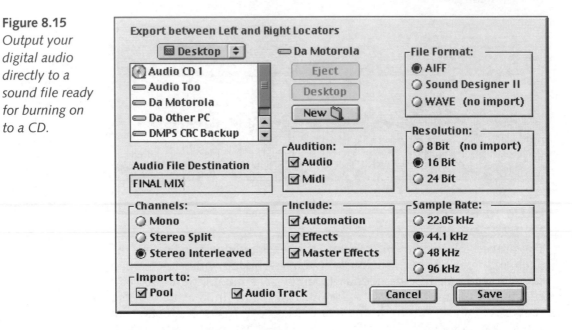

9 Getting the sound – GM, GS and XG

General MIDI

Introduction

Desktop sound modules and sound cards are now a favourite amongst songwriters. You can not only hear your arrangement instantly but also tweak the sounds so the results sound professional. As this book tells you, it's all in the programming, and an important element of programming is setting up the sounds correctly by way of the MIDI file sound set-up files.

Getting the right sound remains one of the trickiest things in MIDI file programming. The MIDI standard was first developed to make the connection of musical equipment easier, but it was soon obvious that tracks which were created on one MIDI set-up did not necessarily sound the same when played back on another. Tackling this meant the development of the General MIDI Standard that unifies certain aspects of a MIDI arrangement such as Program Selection, Volume, Reverb and Chorus set-up.

A set-up bar is placed at the beginning of an arrangement to set up your connected synths so they are playing the correct sounds for the arrangement. This is all about ease of use and portability. It will save you an enormous amount of time if you follow programming guidelines such as program selection, volume settings and drum note assignment in the first place.

A set-up bar allows you to take your data and audition it on a friend's set-up or even in a professional recording studio. Many studios have GM modules available and if you have given prior thought to proper channel assignment and track distribution during the initial programming phase of your music, it will give further production and remixing a kick start. Studio time is expensive and you don't want to spend a day just getting the sounds right.

Further enhancements to the GM standard such as GS and XG provide even more parameters to tweak the expressiveness of your data and effects. This is not only useful when trying to recreate real instrument phrases but fantastic to experiment with for creating new sounds and moods. That is what Electronica is all about.

You will see how the new standards evolve from the old ones. There are features in GS that derive from GM and you will find aspects of XG that are related to GS. It is therefore recommended that you read the whole chapter, not just the sections on the Standard you are most interested in. Specific information is given for various modules and sound cards.

Description

General MIDI allows you to select sound programs and make basic parameter settings to the sound, such as Volume and Reverb/Chorus amounts. GM also sets a standard for the key allocation of drum instruments in a drum kit set-up.

NOTE

See Appendix 3 for an overview of the GM specification.

Setup bar

The set-up bar is placed at the start of the song and its length must be at least four quarter notes. It has the same time signature as the song. When using signatures or starting your song with an up-beat you must reserve at least two bars for the setup.

The set-up sequence is clearly structured starting with the setting of the time signature, the tempo and most importantly the GM Init message.

Figure 9.1
*Starting a
set-up bar.*

Position	Event	Value
1.01.000	GM System On	F0 7E 7F 09 01 F7

The GM Init will reset your machine to a 'clean' state so that it is ready to receive events that will set the parameters for each channel.

Timing distribution

The timing distribution of the events in the set-up bar is of great importance. The most common error is trying to send all events at the same time, causing the set-up bar to malfunction. Make sure that you send the data one event after another and the data for one channel followed by the data for the next, in ascending order.

Although the timing distribution may not be such a big issue in GM, as some controllers can be sent on the same tick, we recommend that you follow the guidelines below. This will guarantee proper implementation of your set-up bars as they become more complicated or as you upgrade them to enhanced standards such as GS and XG.

The placement of the events depends on the PPQN resolution of your sequencer. PPQN stands for the number of ticks (pulses) per quarter note. The precision of capturing MIDI data such as a keyboard performance depends on the sequencer's resolution. The higher the resolution, the more precise the recording of the original data. Cubase offers a resolution of 384 PPQN while Logic goes up to 960 PPQN.

When programming a set-up bar we recommend that you keep the events at least one tick apart when working with a 96 PPQN resolution. When using a higher resolution you must multiply the number of ticks accordingly, so that in Cubase at a 384 PPQN resolution, events should be placed four ticks apart. In Logic at 960 PPQN, the gap should be 10 ticks.

When sending Sys-ex strings it is also essential that you leave enough space between the events to give the Sys-ex message time to execute. When sending the GM Init message leave at least a 200 ms gap, i.e. in a 4/4 signature at 120 BPM the next event should follow at the second quarter note position, to be on the safe side.

It is also very important to leave a big enough gap at the end of the set-up bar before the first note starts. You should leave a gap of at least 200 ms, especially after sending lots of NRPN data, explained later in this chapter. It is also recommended that you leave a 12 tick gap (384 PPQN) after sending a Program Change message.

Position	Event	MIDI Ch	Value
1.02.000	Program Change	1	0–127
1.02.012	Volume	1	0–127
1.02.016	Pan	1	0–64–127
1.02.020	Expression	1	0–127
1.02.024	Reverb Amount	1	0–127
1.02.028	Chorus Amount	1	0–127

Figure 9.2
Position examples represent Cubase at 384 PPQN.

You can use the MIDI file templates supplied on the CD-ROM and customize them to your requirements. It is, of course, possible to edit the timing distribution of the events afterwards, but it is usually simpler to use a ready-made template for a channel and adjust it to your needs in the event editor.

Figure 9.3
Example of GM set-up bar for MIDI Channel 1 as displayed in the Cubase list editor.

Start-Pos.	Length	Val.1	Val.2	Val.3	Status	Chn	Comment
0001.01.000	=====	====	===	===	Sys Ex	==	7E ,7F ,09,01,F7
0001.02.000	=====	1	===	===	Program Ch	1	
0001.02.012	=====	7	100	===	MainVolume	1	
0001.02.016	=====	10	64	===	Pan	1	
0001.02.020	=====	11	127	===	Expression	1	
0001.02.024	=====	91	40	===	Effect1Dep	1	
0001.02.028	=====	93	0	===	Effect3Dep	1	

ON THE CD-ROM

The GM set-up featured in this section can be found on the CD-ROM accompanying this book in the following directory: **chapter9/midifiles/ templates/gm/gmsetup1/2.mid**.

GM messages

In a basic GM set-up you should include the following controller messages:

Program change (#1)

The program change allows you to select one of the 128 available GM voices.

NOTE

See Appendix 3 for a detailed listing of GM sounds.

Volume (#7)

This sets the master volume for the channel and ranges from 0–127. Starting with value 100 gives you enough headroom for later adjustments.

Pan (#10)

Here you can define the placement of the sound in a stereo image, whereby value 0 corresponds to far left, 64 to centre and 127 to far right.

Expression (#11)

The expression controller is used to create volume changes within the song body. Do not use controller 7 (volume) when notes are played back. Use expression (values 0–127) instead for producing, for example, a crescendo.

Reverb amount (#91)

This controller (values 0–127) sets the Reverb Send level. Reverb effects are not part of the basic GM spec, but almost all GM units seem to have effects built in. However, the intensity of the effect amount seems to vary a lot especially among sound cards. It is therefore recommended that you use values between 0–64. Do not use values above 100.

Chorus amount (#93)

Similar rules apply to chorus as those for the reverb. Do not use values exceeding 64.

> **TIP**
>
> *Using too much chorus can make your overall mix muddled. Use it sparingly.*

Extended General MIDI

There are a number of parameters that go beyond the basic GM set-up, known as RPNs (Registered Parameter Numbers). For GM you can use Pitch Bend Sensitivity and Fine Tuning. We will discuss these parameters in more detail in the GS section.

GM messages within the song body

The majority of the messages occurring in the set-up bar should not be used in the song body. However, there are a number of controller messages which are allowed and can create some really good results.

Note On/Off

The essentials. You guessed it: the message which makes MIDI data audible.

Pitch bend

This is a very expressive parameter and can be used effectively on bass lines and guitar parts. But take care to thin out this continuous data using the relevant function in your sequencer. Too many events can cause timing problems. Make sure that you always initialize the setting by sending a Pitch Change with value 0/64 at the end of a series of pitch changes.

Position	Event	MSB	LSB
End of continuous data	Pitch Bend	0	64

Figure 9.4
Initialise the Pitch Bend value to 0 after use.

Please note that the value of the Pitch Bend data consists of a value pair of MSB (**M**ost **S**ignificant **B**it) and LSB (**L**east **S**ignificant **B**it).

Modulation (#1)

The most basic of all sound manipulating parameters, but one that often has a great effect on the basic sound.

Pan (#10)

This can be used to good effect for sequence lines. Make sure that the message is inserted between note messages. It should not be used while a note is sounding. You also should not use it for the drum channel (#10) as individual drum sounds within a kit each have their own stereo placing.

Expression (#11)

As already mentioned, this is the one to use for volume changes within the song body. Use it for gate effects and fade effects.

Hold (#64)

This is the message for the Hold pedal that is not often used in Electronica, where it is preferable to program the actual length of the notes. When using it, make sure that you switch the pedal on with value 127 and off with value 0.

Drum channel

Channel 10 is reserved for the drum kit. The GM spec provides for only one drum kit. This is why you do not find a program change message for channel 10 in the basic GM set-up bar. The lack of parameters provided for the drum kit in basic GM is its biggest drawback. However, GS and XG address this deficit and provide for additional drum kits, such as the TR808 or Analog kit essential to Electronica.

Despite its shortcomings, it is highly recommended that you follow the drum note assignment of GM, as this is the standard for many instruments and sound cards. Even if you are using a sampler make sure you assign the sounds according to the GM spec and your life will be much easier. It also makes auditioning commercial MIDI file drum loops quicker.

NOTE
See Appendix 3 for details on the GM drum kit assignment.

MIDI gates in GM

We already mentioned MIDI gate effects in Chapter 3. Here are a few more points to consider. Make sure that you use Expression (#11) data rather than Volume (#7) data within the song body. Make sure that your note and controller data are appropriately spaced and that they are not on the same tick. Experiment with varying Expression values and try different positions. Creating gates that go against the beat can make four-to-the-floor grooves much more interesting.

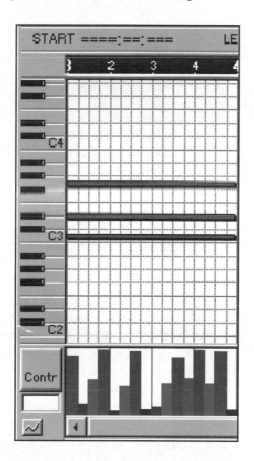

Figure 9.5
MIDI Gate template 1 in the Cubase key editor with the Expression data visible in the controller display.

ON THE CD-ROM
The gate template featured in this section can be found on the CD-ROM accompanying this book in the following directory: **chapter9/midifiles/templates/gm/gates/gmgate1.mid**.

GM implementation in sequencing software

The GM standard moved into the world of software sequencers long ago, with almost all sequencers providing some sort of program selection and basic GM controller adjustment in the track parameter list. Most now provide complete virtual mixer interfaces that allow you to mix the parameters for all 16 channels at once.

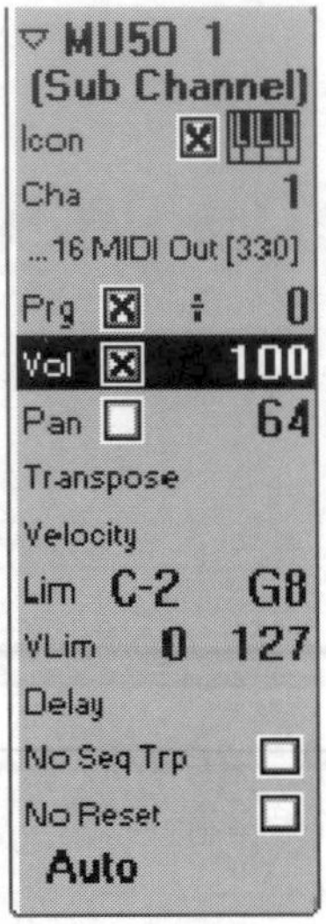

Figure 9.6
Track parameter list in Logic.

Even though it is possible to write settings straight into MIDI data, it is recommended that you use a set-up bar that follows the scheme described in this section. When exporting GM data generated by a software sequencer the timing distribution of the events might not be as required by the standard.

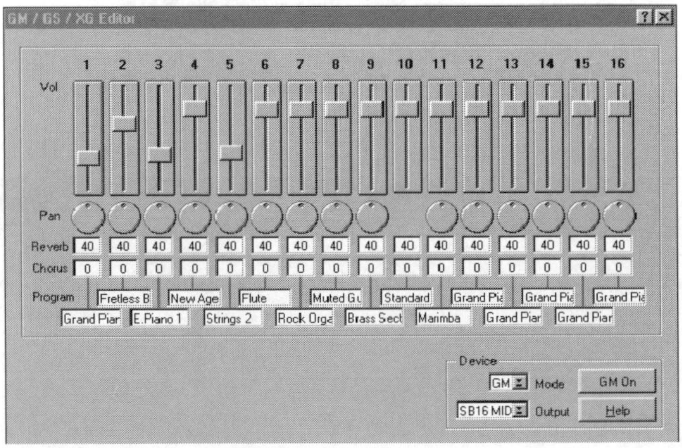

Figure 9.7
GM/GS/XG mixer in Cubase.

GS
--

Introduction

The GS format developed by Roland attempts to fill in those areas where GM falls short. It greatly enhances the programming of the drum set-up for instance, providing a greater choice of voices allowing you to edit their basic sound parameters and effect settings. Furthermore there are additional performance and sound editing parameters. The programming issues behind GS are quite complex. Here we will only deal with the actual set-up bar and additional performance parameters without going into too much detail concerning Sys-ex programming.

Description

The GS format builds on General MIDI and adds further parameters to control expressiveness of the music data. It provides additional drum kits that can be selected using the Program Change message and a great range of NRPNs (Non Registered Parameter Numbers) to edit the sounds.

NOTE

See Appendix 3 for an overview of the GS spec.

Set-up bar

Similar rules regarding length and timing distribution apply to the GS set-up bar as previously described for GM. GS bars may end up being longer, as there is a lot more data to be used. However you should always remember that you do not have to use all the possible settings for each channel and a GS set-up can be made to look reasonably uncomplicated, with only a few additions compared to a GM set-up bar.

A basic GS set-up bar starts with setting the time signature and tempo. It then includes a GS Reset message to initialize the module. Other Sys-Ex messages may follow after a gap of at least 160 ticks (384 PPQN) at 120 BPM. Additional Sys-ex data must have an eight tick space between each line (384 PPQN).

TIP

You may start the GS set-up bar with a GM Init message, which is followed by the GS Init message. This will also make your set-up bar compatible with GM equipment. The GS Init message does not take as long to execute as the GM Init message and leaving a 50 ms gap after sending it should be sufficient. Following the timing distribution shown in Figure 9.8 will allow you to use your set-up bar with tempos up to 200 BPM. All set-up bars supplied on the accompanying CD-ROM follow this timing distribution.

Figure 9.8
A string Sys-ex data starts a GS set-up bar.

Position	Event	Value
1.01.000	Sys-ex	F0 7E 7F 09 01 F7
1.01.320	Sys-ex	F0 41 10 42 12 40 00 7F 00 41 F7
1.02.000	Sys-ex	Reverb Type
1.02.008	Sys-ex	Chorus Type
1.02.016	Sys-ex	Select 2nd Rhythm Part

This is followed by the channel settings.

Figure 9.9
GM difference: Bank Select MSB+LSB are added.

Position	Event	MIDI Ch	Value
1.3.000	Bank Select MSB	1	0
1.3.004	Bank Select LSB	1	32
1.3.008	Program Change	1	0–127
1.3.020	Volume	1	100
1.3.024	Pan	1	64
1.3.028	Expression	1	127
1.3.032	Reverb	1	40
1.3.036	Chorus	1	0

ON THE CD-ROM
The GS set-up featured in this section can be found on the CD-ROM accompanying this book in the following directory: **chapter9/midifiles/ templates/gm/gssetup1.mid**. *A more enhanced set-up is:* **chapter9/ midifiles/templates/gm/gssetup2.mid**.

TIP
Sending Sys-ex data in Cubase can be a problem. If your set-up bars do not work you should check the Pre-Roll value set in Options → Synchronization. It should be set to 250. This will also cure any playback problems with audio data.

GS messages

A basic GS set-up includes the following messages.

Bank Select + Program Change

The additional voices of the GS spec are organized in banks. In order to access the additional banks the Bank Select message is used. It is comprised of two events, the Bank Select MSB followed by the Bank Select LSB. The following Bank Select settings will access bank 0, which corresponds to the 128 voices of the GM standard.

Position	Event	MIDI Ch	Value
1.3.000	Bank Select MSB #0	1	0
1.3.004	Bank Select LSB #32	1	0
1.3.008	Program Change	1	0–127

Figure 9.10
Bank Select message in GS.

Check the voice lists for your GS unit. Additional banks can be accessed changing the value of the Bank Select MSB. The following example will select Bank 8.

Position	Event	MIDI Ch	Value
1.3.000	Bank Select MSB #0	1	8
1.3.004	Bank Select LSB #32	1	0
1.3.008	Program Change	1	0–127

Figure 9.11
Selecting bank 8 with a GS Bank Select message

The normal Program Change follows after the Bank Select message and the relevant sound is selected. The other messages in the basic GS set-up are the same as in GM. The Pan controller (#10) may also be used for the rhythm part.

NOTE

See Appendix 3 for a GS voice list. Please note that this is only a basic list for the SC55 Mk1 and that newer GS-compatible modules, like the SC88, provide much greater variety in their choice of sounds.

RPNs/NRPNs

Registered Parameter Numbers (RPNs) and Non Registered Parameter Numbers (NRPNs) provide further ways to influence sound and performance aspects. Both messages consist of a number of events that must be placed in correct order to function properly. The RPNs/NRPNs follow after the GS set-up described above.

Figure 9.12
*RPN/NRPN
messages.*

Position	Event	MIDI Ch	Value
2.1.000	RPN MSB #101 NRPN MSB #99	1	1
2.1.004	RPN LSB #100 NRPN LSB #98	1	10
2.1.008	Data Entry MSB #6	1	0–127

The parameter is selected using two events (MSB/LSB). This is followed by a Data Entry message that sets the value. It is then important to lock the parameter changes with a PRN/NRPN reset for each channel, so that any Data Entry #6 or #38 received after the PRN/NRPN reset will be ignored.

Figure 9.13
*Locking the
RPN/NRPN
settings.*

Position	Event	MIDI Ch	Value
2.01.000	RPN MSB #101 NRPN MSB #99	1	1
2.01.004	RPN LSB #100 NRPN LSB #98	1	10
2.01.008	Data Entry MSB #6	1	0–127
2.01.012	RPN/NRPN Reset MSB #101	1	127
2.01.016	RPN/NRPN Reset LSB #100	1	127

Available Parameters

Pitch Bend Range

Figure 9.14
*RPN message
for Pitch Bend
Range.*

Position	Event	MIDI Ch	Value
2.01.000	RPN MSB #101	1	0
2.01.004	RPN LSB #100	1	0
2.01.008	Data Entry MSB #6	1	0–24

The default value for this parameter is two semitones, but it can be adjusted to greater ranges. This can be used for slide effects that are often used in Trance and Trip Hop tracks.

Fine Tune

Position	Event	MIDI Ch	Value
2.01.000	RPN MSB #101	1	0
2.01.004	RPN LSB #100	1	1
2.01.008	Data Entry MSB #6	1	0–127
2.01.012	Data Entry LSB #38	1	0–127

Figure 9.15
RPN message for Fine Tune.

When using the Fine Tune parameter you must send an additional Data Entry LSB message (#38) in order to set the value for the LSB.

These two RPN messages can also be used in an extended GM set-up, as most units will understand them.

Examples using NRPNs

Real time filter effects

Sweeping filters and 'squelchy' bass lines are widely used in Electronica. Techno would not have evolved without the filters on the legendary TB303. The GS format allows you to recreate these filter effects for both the Cut-Off Frequency and Resonance using NRPNs. When creating real time filter effects the same rules apply with regard to the order of the events as described for the GS set-up bar. The difference is that in the MIDI domain you have to use a number of Data Entry #6 messages at different values when imitating the actual physical turning of a knob on an analogue synth.

NRPN for Cut-Off Frequency

Position	Event	MIDI Ch	Value
2.01.000	NRPN MSB #99	1	1
2.01.004	NRPN LSB #98	1	32
2.01.008	Data Entry MSB #6	1	14–114
	Data Entry MSB #6		
	Data Entry MSB #6		
	Data Entry MSB #6		
	Data Entry MSB #6		

Figure 9.16
NRPN message for Cut-Off Frequency including real-time changes with Data Entry message.

Note that the recommended value range is 14–114 but some sounds will not change with values greater than 64. We suggest you simply try different settings out and judge for yourself what sounds best.

Figure 9.17
Bass line with filter changes in Logic's event editor.

POSITION				STATUS	CHA	NUM	VAL	LENGTH/INFO		
				——— Start of List ———						
2	1	1	1	Note	1	C0	88	_ _	3	47
2	1	1	11	Control	1	99	1 Non-Reg. MSB			
2	1	1	21	Control	1	98	32 Non-Reg. LSB			
2	1	1	31	Control	1	6	120 Data MSB			
2	1	2	1	Control	1	6	117 Data MSB			
2	1	3	1	Note	1	C2	104	_ _	_	185
2	1	3	1	Control	1	6	114 Data MSB			
2	1	4	1	Note	1	C1	80	_ _	_	152
2	1	4	1	Control	1	6	106 Data MSB			
2	2	1	1	Note	1	C0	78	_ _	1	177
2	2	1	1	Control	1	6	93 Data MSB			
2	2	2	1	Note	1	A#1	88	_ _	_	200
2	2	2	1	Control	1	6	77 Data MSB			
2	2	3	1	Note	1	C1	78	_ _	_	120
2	2	3	1	Control	1	6	57 Data MSB			
2	2	4	1	Note	1	C0	82	_ _	1	205
2	2	4	1	Control	1	6	34 Data MSB			
2	3	1	1	Note	1	C2	109	_ _	_	207
2	3	1	11	Control	1	101	127 Reg.Par. MSB			
2	3	1	21	Control	1	100	127 Reg.Par. LSB			
				——— End of List ———						

When using NRPN messages in the song body take care that you do not insert the events on the same position as a note and follow the proper timing distribution. The Data Entry message may be used while a note is sounding in order to make real time filter changes. Try to set the last Data Entry message to a value that suits the sound that you continue to use on the channel. It is also recommended that you insert a NRPN reset after the sequence is finished.

ON THE CD-ROM
The filter template featured in this section can be found on the CD-ROM accompanying this book in the following directory: **chapter9/midifiles/ templates/gs/gsfilt1.mid**.

NRPN for Resonance

Using the Resonance parameter in conjunction with Cut-Off Frequency can result in extreme sonic effects. If you set the Resonance very high and turn the Cut-Off Frequency down you emphasize the self-oscillating effect of the filter.

2.01.000	NRPN MSB #99	1	1
2.01.004	NRPN LSB #98	1	33
2.01.008	Data Entry MSB #6	1	14–64

Figure 9.18
NRPN message for Resonance.

You can of course combine the two parameters taking controlled filter effects even a step further. However, in GS you can only send these NRPNs one after the other and therefore only make one parameter change at a time. Always be alert to following the proper timing distribution. Too much data can cause heavy MIDI traffic, which may slow down your sequencer and make it unstable.

Additional NRPN messages available in GS

Vibrato Rate

Position	Event	MIDI Ch	Value
2.1.1.000	NRPN MSB #99	1	1
2.1.1.004	NRPN LSB #98	1	8
2.1.1.008	Data Entry MSB #6	1	0–64–127

Figure 9.19
NRPN message for Vibrato Rate.

Vibrato Depth

Position	Event	MIDI Ch	Value
2.1.1.000	NRPN MSB #99	1	1
2.1.1.004	NRPN LSB #98	1	9
2.1.1.008	Data Entry MSB #6	1	0–64–127

Figure 9.20
NRPN message for Vibrato Depth.

Vibrato Delay

Position	Event	MIDI Ch	Value
2.1.1.000	NRPN MSB #99	1	1
2.1.1.004	NRPN LSB #98	1	10
2.1.1.008	Data Entry MSB #6	1	0–64–127

Figure 9.21
NRPN message for Vibrato Delay.

EG Attack Time

Figure 9.22
*NRPN message
for EG Attack
Time.*

Position	Event	MIDI Ch	Value
2.1.1.000	NRPN MSB #99	1	1
2.1.1.004	NRPN LSB #98	1	99
2.1.1.008	Data Entry MSB #6	1	0–64–127

EG Decay Time

Figure 9.23
*NRPN message
for Decay Time.*

Position	Event	MIDI Ch	Value
2.1.1.000	NRPN MSB #99	1	1
2.1.1.004	NRPN LSB #98	1	100
2.1.1.008	Data Entry MSB #6	1	0–64–127

EG Release Time

Figure 9.24
*NRPN message
for Release
Time.*

Position	Event	MIDI Ch	Value
2.1.1.000	NRPN MSB #99	1	1
2.1.1.004	NRPN LSB #98	1	102
2.1.1.008	Data Entry MSB #6	1	0–64–127

MIDI gates in GS

In GS you can enhance GM MIDI gates by adding NRPN data, for example for the Cut-Off Frequency.

ON THE CD-ROM
The filter template featured in this section can be found on the CD-ROM accompanying this book in the following directory: **chapter9/midifiles/ templates/gs/gates/gsgate1/2/3.mid**.

GS drum set-up

In Electronica it's all in the grooves and that's why it's important to spend time setting up the drums. GS allows you not only to select additional drum kits and use a second rhythm part but also to tweak the parameters for each individual drum instrument. This provides you with some very powerful ways to create an individual sound for your grooves.

Selecting drum kits

GS provides a number of additional drum kits that can be selected using a Program Change message.

Position	Event	MIDI Ch	Value
1.03.360	Bank Select MSB	10	0
1.03.364	Bank Select LSB	10	32
1.03.368	Program Change	10	26
1.03.380	Volume	10	100
1.04.000	Pan	10	64
1.04.004	Expression	10	127
1.04.008	Reverb	10	40
1.04.012	Chorus	10	0

Figure 9.25
Selecting a GS drum kit.

NOTE

Figure 9.18 shows the event positions of the GS set-up bars in Cubase at 384 PPQN resolution. These positions are relative and may change, for example when inserting additional Sys-ex events at the beginning.

The example above shows how to select the TR808 kit (Program 26). Note that all the other parameters listed are master effects and will affect all drum instruments together. In order to change the settings of single drum sounds you need to use NRPNs.

It is also possible to nominate a second rhythm part. It has become general custom to assign a second drum kit to channel 11. Include the following Sys-ex message prior to the channel settings in the set-up bar.

1.1.1.208	Sys-ex	F0 41 10 42 12 40 1A 15 02 0F F7

Figure 9.26
Sys-ex message for setting a second drum part.

TIP

You can also select the SFX kit for the second drum part, giving you a whole range of effect sounds on individual keys. In this way you keep your other channels free for other instruments.

ON THE CD-ROM

A GS set-up bar assigning the second drum part to channel 11 and selecting the SFX kit for that part can be found on the CD-ROM accompanying this book in the following directory: **chapter9/midifiles/templates/gs/gssetup3.mid**.

Changing individual drum sounds using NRPNs

With GS it is possible to change individual drum instruments for powerful customization of the rhythm part using NRPNs. The usual rules for setting up NRPNs apply. The following parameters are available.

Drum Instrument Pitch Coarse

Figure 9.27
NRPN message for changing Drum Instrument Pitch Coarse.

Position	Event	MIDI Ch	Value
2.01.012	NRPN MSB #99	10	24
2.01.016	NRPN LSB #98	10	36
2.01.020	Data Entry MSB #6	10	0–127

The NRPN MSB (#99) defines the parameter to be changed, whereby the NRPN LSB (#98) defines the key number of the individual drum instrument. The value (#36) shown in the table will select Kick Drum 1 on key C1. The Data Entry message will then change the parameter for that drum instrument.

NOTE
See Appendix 3 for a complete listing of available drum instruments and their corresponding note numbers.

TIP
Some Electronica styles like Drum'n'Bass rely heavily on customized drum sounds. In order to recreate the pitching effects of a style so heavily based on sampling techniques in the MIDI domain you must use two drum kits, then you can tune up individual instruments of the second set and make your rhythm section alternate between the two parts frequently. Enjoy experimenting.

Further available NRPNs are as follows.

Drum Instrument Volume

Figure 9.28
NRPN message for changing Drum Instrument Volume.

Position	Event	MIDI Ch	Value
2.01.024	NRPN MSB #99	10	26
2.01.028	NRPN LSB #98	10	36
2.01.032	Data Entry MSB #6	10	0–127

Drum Instrument Pan

Position	Event	MIDI Ch	Value
2.01.036	NRPN MSB #99	10	28
2.01.040	NRPN LSB #98	10	36
2.01.044	Data Entry MSB #6	10	0–127

Figure 9.29
NRPN message for changing Drum Instrument Pan.

Note that a Data Entry value of 0 will put the Pan parameter into random mode.

Drum Instrument Reverb Send Level

Position	Event	MIDI Ch	Value
2.01.048	NRPN MSB #99	10	29
2.01.052	NRPN LSB #98	10	36
2.01.056	Data Entry MSB #6	10	0–127

Figure 9.30
NRPN message for changing Drum Instrument Reverb Send Level.

TIP
Remember to keep that kick dry!

Drum Instrument Chorus Send Level

Position	Event	MIDI Ch	Value
2.01.060	NRPN MSB #99	10	30
2.01.064	NRPN LSB #98	10	36
2.01.068	Data Entry MSB #6	10	0–127

Figure 9.31
NRPN message for changing Drum Instrument Chorus Send Level.

GS software

There are many GS editors available in the form of stand-alone applications, Cubase mixer maps and Logic environments. However, in order to create proper set-up bars and exciting real time changes you must not be afraid to dig deep into the data using the event editor of your sequencer.

XG

Introduction

XG by Yamaha is currently the latest standard for musical data. It is by far the most comprehensive, yet simplifies certain operations such as real time filter changes. It offers excellent effect sections that can make your MIDI files sound very professional indeed. It is not uncommon to find parts programmed on XG equipment surviving through to the mastering stage in productions.

Description

The XG standard makes use of Sys-ex data for functions such as selecting and editing built-in effects. It offers a great range of additional single controllers such as Controller #74 and #71 for changing the Cut-Off Frequency and the Resonance respectively. It simplifies the setting up of a second drum channel using Bank Select MSB, and provides a huge range of excellent sound material. XG allows you to edit single drum instruments using NRPNs, as in the GS standard.

Set-up bar

Controlling the power of XG requires some complex setting up. We have seen set-up files of 16 bars and longer, but it is not necessary to change all parameters. A few well thought out parameter changes for the effects, some filter controllers in the parts and some NPRN settings for the drums can give you amazing results.

An XG set-up bar starts with the XG system On message to initialize your sound source. You may also insert a GM On message prior to the XG On if you want to make your files compatible with GM.

Position	Type	Description
1.01.000	Time_Sign	4/4
1.01.000	Set_Tempo	120
1.01.000	Sys-ex	GM On
1.01.320	Sys-ex	XG On

Figure 9.32
Starting a XG set-up bar.

The GM On message takes at least 200 ms to execute. You must leave a sufficient gap after it before sending the XG On message. The XG On message takes about 50 ms to execute and you then can send other Sys-ex strings in the usual timing distribution. The positions here relate to a tempo of about 120 BPM. If your song is substantially faster you must increase the gap.

Position	Event	Value
1.01.000	GM On	F0 7E 7F 09 01 F7
1.01.320	XG On	F0 43 10 4C 00 00 7E 00 F7
1.02.000	Reverb Type	F0 43 10 4C 02 01 00 01 01 F7

Figure 9.33
Other Sys-ex data follow with a 50 ms gap after the XG System On message.

Then follow the channel settings for each part.

Position	Event	Ch	Value
1.02.032	Bank Select MSB #0	1	0
1.02.036	Bank Select LSB #32	1	32
1.02.040	Program Change	1	0–127
1.02.052	Volume #7	1	0–127
1.02.056	Pan #10	1	0–64–127
1.02.060	Expression #11	1	0–127
1.02.064	Reverb Send #91	1	0–127
1.02.068	Chorus Send #93	1	0–127
1.02.072	Variation Send #94	1	0–127
1.02.076	Attack Time #73	1	0–127
1.02.080	Release Time #72	1	0–127
1.02.084	Cut-Off Frequency #71	1	0–127
1.02.088	Resonance #74	1	0–127

Figure 9.34
XG Channel Settings.

Single controller messages in XG

Effect Sends (Reverb/Chorus/Variation Effect)

Figure 9.35
XG Effect Send Parameters.

Position	Event	MIDI Ch	Value
1.02.064	Reverb Send #91	1	40
1.02.068	Chorus Send #93	1	0
1.02.072	Variation Effect Send #94	1	0

NOTE
Controller #94 is only effective if you set the variation effect to 'sys'. See the section about using XG effects for further details.

In XG you can make direct sound changes using single controllers.

Attack Time/Release Time

Figure 9.36
XG EG Controllers.

Position	Event	Value
1.02.076	Attack Time #73	0–127
1.02.080	Release Time #72	0–127

Cut-Off Frequency (Brightness)/Resonance (Harmonic Content)

Figure 9.37
XG Filter Controllers.

Position	Event	Value
1.02.084	Cut-Off Frequency Time #74	0–127
1.02.088	Resonance #74	0–127

Real-time filter changes in XG

Real time filter changes are quickly programmed in XG, as you can simply include the single controllers (#71/#74), e.g. with the Hyper Draw function or Hyper editor in your sequencer.

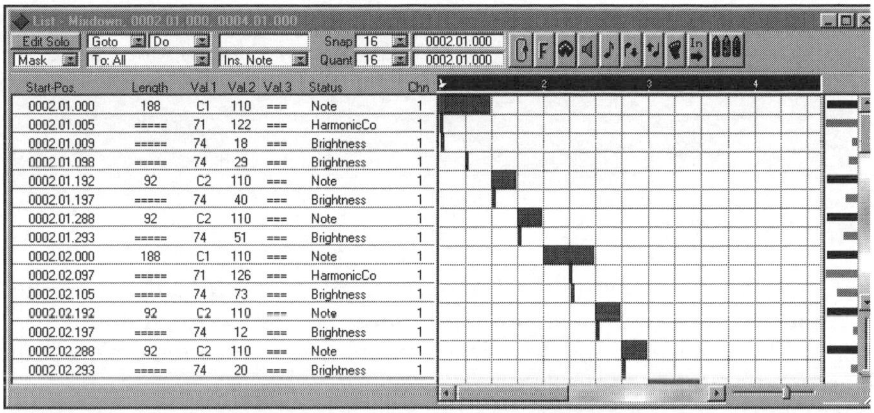

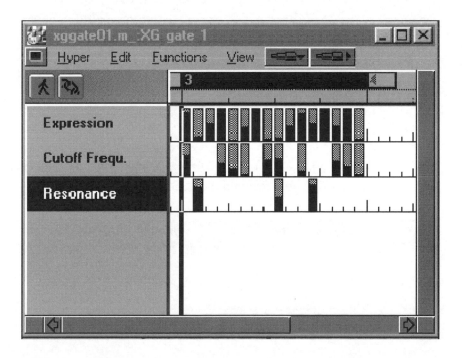

Figure 9.38
XG filter template displayed in the Cubase list editor.

ON THE CD-ROM

The filter template featured in this section can be found on the CD ROM accompanying this book in the following directory: **chapter9/midifiles/ templates/xg/filter/xgfilt1.mid**.

MIDI gates in XG

In XG you can enhance GM MIDI gates by adding single controllers to change the Cut-Off Frequency and Resonance.

Figure 9.39
XG enhanced MIDI gate template in Logic's Hyper editor.

TIP

When programming gate effects it can be useful to have a drum beat playing in the back while editing the positions of the gates. You may also experiment with filter parameter changes that can make your template suitable for more ambient Electronica styles.

NRPNs in XG

All NRPNs described in the GS section are also available in XG and require no further explanation. There are a range of additional NRPNs available for customizing drum instruments. See the section on XG Drum Setup on page 239 for further details.

Using XG effects

The XG standard accounts for three different effect units. All can be customized in detail using Sys-ex data.

Figure 9.40
XG effect set-up.

Position	Event	Value
1.01.000	GM On	F0 7E 7F 09 01 F7
1.01.320	XG On	F0 43 10 4C 00 00 7E 00 F7
1.02.000	Reverb Type	F0 43 10 4C 02 01 00 01 01 F7
1.02.008	Chorus Type	F0 43 10 4C 02 01 20 43 01 F7
1.02.016	Variation Type	F0 43 10 4C 02 01 40 49 00 F7
1.02.024	Var. Connection	F0 43 10 4C 02 01 5A 01 F7

Selecting a Reverb Effect

Figure 9.41
XG Reverb Type selection.

1.02.000	Reverb Type	F0 43 10 4C 02 01 00 **01 00** F7

The numbers in bold are the data bytes (MSB/LSB). Changing the MSB will select another Reverb Effect and the LSB a different Reverb type.

NOTE

See Appendix 3 for a description of available effects in XG.

Figure 9.42
XG Reverb Type selection (plate).

The example below will select the plate effect:

1.02.000	Reverb Type	F0 43 10 4C 02 01 00 **04 00** F7

Selecting a Chorus Effect

The example below will select the Flanger 2 effect. Note that the Flanger type is selected with the LSB.

1.02.008	Chorus Type	F0 43 10 4C 02 01 20 **43 01** F7

Selecting the Variation Effect

This will select the Distortion effect. The second Sys-ex message defines if the effect is used as an insert effect (default) or a system effect. When set to 'Sys' (Value 1) the effect is available for all 16 parts and its send level can be adjusted using controller #94.

1.02.016	Variation Type	F0 43 10 4C 02 01 40 **49 00** F7
1.02.024	Var. Connection	F0 43 10 4C 02 01 5A **01** F7

When the variation effect is switched to 'Ins' you must define the part the effect should be used for. Note that you do not need to insert the 'Var. Connection' message as described above, since the Variation effect is set to insert by default.

1.02.016	Variation Type	F0 43 10 4C 02 01 40 **49 00** F7
1.02.024	Var. Part	F0 43 10 4C 02 01 5B **01** F7

The example assigns the insert effect to Part 1.

For further details on Sys-ex programming for XG refer to the manufacturer's manual or the Yamaha XG sites on the web.

ON THE CD-ROM

The extended XG set-ups featured in this section can be found on the CD-ROM accompanying this book in the following directory: **chapter9/midifiles/templates/xg/xgsetup2.mid** *(Variation effect set to 'Sys') and* **chapter9/midifiles/templates/xg/xgsetup3.mid** *(Variation assigned to Part 1 as insert effect).*

XG drum set-up

XG allows you to mix your drum kits thoroughly. A drum part is selected using the following Bank Select message.

Figure 9.46
XG drum part selection.

Position	Event	MIDI Ch	Value
1.03.188	Bank Select MSB (#0)	10	127
1.03.192	Bank Select LSB (#32)	10	0
1.03.196	Program Change	10	0–127

You can use a second drum kit on any channel. The example below assigns Channel 11 as the second rhythm part.

Figure 9.47
XG second drum part selection.

Position	Event	MIDI Ch	Value
1.03.248	Bank Select MSB (#0)	11	127
1.03.252	Bank Select LSB (#32)	11	0
1.03.256	Program Change	11	0–127

You can also assign a SFX kit to the channel using the Bank Select MSB. The example below assigns SFX Kit 1 to Channel 11.

Figure 9.48
XG SFX kit selection.

Position	Event	MIDI Ch	Value
1.03.248	Bank Select MSB (#0)	11	126
1.03.252	Bank Select LSB (#32)	11	0
1.03.256	Program Change	11	0

Additional NRPNs for drum instruments in XG

You can tweak the individual drum sounds detailed in XG. XG provides a range of additional NRPNs for the drum instruments compared to GS.

Drum Instrument Cut-Off Frequency

Figure 9.49
Drum Instrument Cut-Off Frequency.

Position	Event	MIDI Ch	Value
1.04.224	NRPN MSB #99	10	20
1.04.228	NRPN LSB #98	10	36
1.04.232	Data Entry MSB #6	10	64

Drum Instrument Resonance

Position	Event	MIDI Ch	Value
1.04.236	NRPN MSB #99	10	21
1.04.240	NRPN LSB #98	10	36
1.04.244	Data Entry MSB #6	10	64

Figure 9.50
Drum Instrument Resonance.

Drum Instrument Attack Time

Position	Event	MIDI Ch	Value
1.04.248	NRPN MSB #99	10	22
1.04.252	NRPN LSB #98	10	36
1.04.256	Data Entry MSB #6	10	64

Figure 9.51
Drum Instrument Attack Time.

Drum Instrument Decay Time

Position	Event	MIDI Ch	Value
1.04.260	NRPN MSB #99	10	23
1.04.264	NRPN LSB #98	10	36
1.04.268	Data Entry MSB #6	10	64

Figure 9.52
Drum Instrument Decay Time.

Drum Instrument Fine Tune

Position	Event	MIDI Ch	Value
1.04.284	NRPN MSB #99	10	25
1.04.288	NRPN LSB #98	10	36
1.04.292	Data Entry MSB #6	10	64

Figure 9.53
Drum Instrument Fine Tune.

Drum Instrument Variation Effect Send

Position	Event	MIDI Ch	Value
1.04.344	NRPN MSB #99	10	31
1.04.348	NRPN LSB #98	10	36
1.04.352	Data Entry MSB #6	10	64

Figure 9.54
Drum Instrument Variation Effect Send.

NOTE

The same thing applies to XG and GS: the NRPN LSB #98 defines the note number of the drum instrument to be changed. Appendix 3 gives a detailed account of drum instrument and the SFX sounds available in XG.

XG Software (XG Editors, Mixer Maps, Environments)

The complex nature of XG has caused a range of utilities to emerge that help you in mixing XG. But be aware that most of them cannot save a proper XG set-up bar, so you must do some of the groundwork as described above to make your music data portable. Do not be afraid to look into the specification provided by the manufacturers and explore your unit in depth. XG is very powerful and an ideal vehicle to produce Electronica.

10 The mixing desk, EQ and effects

When you first start building a home recording set-up the mixing desk will probably figure low in your list of 'must have' items. Synthesizers, sound cards and drum machines are all more exciting than mixers and effects units. After all, they make sounds don't they? Those acid basslines and sweeping soaring strings don't come out of a desk or an effects rack, do they?

Actually they do. The mixing desk and effects units are what makes the difference between a standard arrangement of preset sounds and a carefully sculpted set of timbres which interplay with each other and produce those spine-tingling moments we all know and love. In this chapter we'll study all the aspects of a mixing desk and the effects units that are often attached to it. Finally we'll have a look at the various types of EQ and effects, and where and how to apply them.

The mixing desk explored

The first problem you'll encounter if you're trying to put together a track using just the sound card in your PC, or a single GM module with a pair of stereo outputs, is that the sound is all mashed up when you come to record it. Everything in the mix sounds the same and it's difficult to hear a snare pattern or bassline clearly against the other instruments. Robbed of their own individual space in the mix, instruments are forced to share frequencies with their neighbours and the result is a muddy-sounding collage of noise rather than the bright and sparkling track you envisaged.

The problem is that the sounds are all running through one set of stereo connections with no opportunity for you to individually EQ them. EQing is akin to the bass and treble adjustment on most home stereos; indeed many home stereos now feature a Graphic EQ section where you can drastically alter the sound of a record, dropping out the bass frequencies for a brighter, poppier sound or trimming away the highs to produce a darker, more physical sound. What you need to be able to do in a mix is to apply this process to each individual sound in that mix, thus cutting or accentuating those elements that have the most 'kick' to them. You need a mixing desk!

At first sight a mixing desk is a daunting prospect – loads of buttons, knobs (called 'pots' for potentiometer) and sliders adorn its fascia with indecipherable abbreviations like 'AUX 1/PRE' written above them – yet its basic functions are very simple.

Each row of pots, buttons and faders represents an audio channel and if we look at the functions of one of these we will come to an understanding of most of the mixing desk as, obviously, these functions are simply repeated for however many channels your desk is equipped with.

Channels on mixing desks used to be strictly mono affairs. If you were plugging a stereo sound source into them, as on most modern synths, you needed to use two channels, panning one hard left and the other hard right. Now, thankfully, most desks aimed at the home recording market feature at least a couple of stereo channels.

If you look at the front of the desk you can easily identify these channels as the pan pots will be marked 'Balance' instead of 'Pan'. Plugging a pair of audio jacks into one of these channels from your sound card or module, you then set the balance to the centre position and the stereo imaging of your input signal is preserved.

NOTE

Stereo synths don't use the common single stereo jack of domestic appliances with two dark rings on its tip but two mono jacks, each with one dark ring. See Figure 10.1 below for a comparison.

Figure 10.1
A stereo jack below, a mono one above.

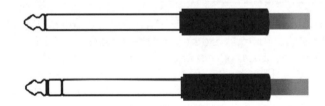

Mono channels still predominate, though, as many people use older, mono output synthesizers and, most importantly for dance music, drum machines that output their sounds through individual connections. These are mono connections and you use the 'Pan' pot here to position the sound in the stereo field, from hard left to hard right and anywhere in between.

If you have a look at the illustration opposite you'll see a graphic of one channel strip from a mixing desk. Mixing desks are simply made up of multiples of these strips so we'll look at each individual function in turn and then we will have explored most of the important aspects of a mixer.

The fader

Starting at the bottom, we have a sliding control for the output of that channel to the mix. This is pretty self-explanatory; it's a volume control for that channel. Sliding the fader right down to the bottom will silence that sound, while pushing it up to the top will probably deafen you as the sound will be output at maximum volume.

Most mixers have the output level marked in dB with 0dB at the halfway level, ∞dB at the bottom and up to +15dB at the top. You could be forgiven for thinking that 0dB would indicate silence, but the reverse is true. What the mixer is saying here is that, at that position, no extra decibels will be added to the original volume level of your sound. In engineering terms this setting means that 0dB is the level on this channel at which absolute silence will be experienced. Any sound coming through must be higher in dBs than zero or it won't be heard.

If that seems confusing consider the bottom setting, ∞dB. Now we're being told that sounds infinitely high in dBs will still be absolutely silent at this setting. Mixers measure things in terms relative to absolute silence, indicating just how much signal is needed for a sound to be heard. The faders on a mixing desk do not amplify the volume of a sound but simply let less or more of it through, depending on the setting. To amplify the signal you need to find the 'Gain' pot.

Gain and loss

To set up the sound of a synth coming into a mixer the first stage is to set the channel fader to 0dB and then adjust the amplification on that channel. This is done using the Gain pot, usually at the top of the channel pots as in our illustration. Synthesizers can vary wildly in their output levels and some sounds may need more gain applied to them, while others will need their levels cut. Most Gain pots operate as in our example, with the centre setting indicating no amplification. Turning the pot to the right will increase the amount of amplification applied to the sound, while turning it to the left will cut some amplification from that channel.

Don't confuse the amplification here with the amplifier that is used to power your speakers. This amplification is a very minor affair and only amplifies the levels of sounds in the mixer's internal channels. Without an amplifier attached to its main outputs a mixer produces very little volume. There are powered mixers which incorporate output amplification but, as this invariably adds signal noise or 'hum' to the mixer's circuitry, they're really only suitable for live performances where the resulting 'noise' is lost in the surrounding ambience.

Figure 10.2
A single mixer channel.

NOTE

If you've spent all your money on a computer, synthesizers and a mixer you can plug the output of your desk into a domestic stereo system so that you can monitor the sound. Just don't crank those levels up too high! Synthesizers put out a much stronger signal than domestic stereos – the dynamic levels in tapes, records and CD's are all they were really designed for – so be careful with this approach. As long as you don't try and push the LEDs into the red this provides a workable, if short term, solution to the problem and many a masterpiece has been monitored on a domestic system.

The usual process of setting up a series of synths and drum machines through a mixer is to set the channel output fader to 0dB, then use the gain control to set all the sounds so they are at the same volume. You can check to see if too much gain has been applied to any channel by listening to that channel without any sound being input. If you can hear background noise and hum, there's too much gain as the amplification is being applied to the circuit noise you're not supposed to hear. Some older synths may simply have hum all the time and you'll have to resort to other methods to get rid of the unwanted hum but generally, once you've got a good level of sound coming out of a channel set at 0dB and no circuit noise when there is no sound, you can rest assured that you're all set up and ready to record.

Mute and solo

The next mixer function, usually immediately above the channel fader, is a button marked Mute/Solo. As its name implies, this button has two positions. The first will cut the volume from that channel entirely, dropping it out of the mix, while the second will solo all the other channels, allowing you to listen to that channel on its own.

Some mixers might be marked PFL/Solo. In this case there will be another button elsewhere which determines whether you hear a Post Fade Level, i.e. according to the level of the fader, or Solo of that particular channel. This will be dependent on the position of the main PFL/SOLO button, usually found on the main section of the mixer. Mixers like this will typically have a separate Mute button.

All about busses

Next up on our channel strip is a button simply marked 'Buss'. This isn't a spelling mistake and pressing this will not summon a number 28 to your studio. Busses, in mixer parlance, are internal routing channels that allow you to send the sound from a channel or channels out through a separate pair of outputs to a multitrack tape recorder or effects loop. As the sound is separate from the main mix it will not be heard until it is brought back into the mix, usually through extra inputs available on each channel, called insert points. Buss channels have their own faders, often in the main section so you can control the level of their output when recording in this fashion.

Busses are traditionally used to record groupings of channels onto a multitrack and then bring that grouped mix back in on one channel alongside the remaining channels. This is very useful if you have to record using overdubs and don't have enough MIDI channels to play everything at once or enough mixer channels to mix it all down in one go. Using the busses you can send, say, the drum and bass parts out and record them onto a tape recorder then, with the tape synched to your MIDI sequencer, play them back using only one channel along with the rest of the MIDI instruments.

You can also use the Buss buttons to drop channels in and out of a mix if your mixer doesn't boast a Mute button. With the faders for the buss channel down to ∞dB, flicking the output of a channel over to that buss will effectively mute that channel. Conversely you can use preset groupings of tracks which are sent out to the different busses and control their levels in the main mix using the dedicated buss faders.

Balance and pan

Next up we come to the first of the seemingly endless array of pots on our mixer. This is marked either Pan or Balance depending on whether that channel is a mono or stereo channel. There would appear to be very little difference between the two, but consider the following scenario:

You have a stereo synth hooked up via a stereo channel. The sound coming out of that synth has been panned to the left of the stereo field. With the Balance set to the centre position the sound still appears to be coming from your left. If that were a mono channel and a mono synth connected you would have to turn the Pan pot to the left to place that instrument in the same place in the stereo field. If we turn the Balance pot to the right on our stereo hook-up the sound will disappear as it is set from the synth to appear toward the left. Turning the mono Pan pot to the right will simply shift the sound to your right speaker.

Most stereo synths use the subtleties of the stereo separation process to align sounds, most noticeably in the drum kit where sounds are usually preset to appear in the part of the stereo spectrum where a real snare or hi hat exists, so the snare and closed hi hat will be slightly to the right while the crash cymbal might appear on the left. Stereo synths, too, use auto panning on many sounds and obviously this effect can be lost if you turn the balance control too far to the left or right.

You may still want to adjust the stereo position of a stereo channel however, depending on the position of other instruments in the mix and so the Balance pot exists. You can also use it creatively to swing between sounds which you have previously panned left and right via

MIDI. As you turn the Balance pot to the right the sound panned left will disappear, and reappear when you swing the Balance to the left. Pan can also be used creatively in this way during a mix to shift a mono sound around as the sound plays. This is especially effective on hi hats and string sections.

Auxiliary sends

Immediately above the Pan pot there's usually a selection of pots, all marked variously, Aux Send 1, Aux Send 2 and so forth. If you have a look around the back of your mixer you'll find a corresponding series of output and input jacks labelled Aux Output 1, 2, etc. and Aux Return 1, 2 and so on. These are for connecting effects units. You make a connection from an auxiliary output to the input on an effect unit and then plug the output from that effects unit into the corresponding auxiliary return jack or jacks.

The Auxiliary Send pots then, will send that sound out to the effects unit where it will have reverb, delay or chorus added to it and sent back to your mix via the Auxiliary Return level setting, found on the main section of your mixer. The hard left position of the Auxiliary Send pot means no sound will be sent out from that channel to the effects unit, while turning the pot in degrees to the right will send increasingly more of the signal to the effects unit.

Effects are an integral part of producing electronic music. Initially effects such as reverb, chorus and delay were designed to replicate the ambient sounds that occur when a real instrument is played. A bass guitar sounds completely different in a large hall than it does in a small room, for instance, and reverb was designed to mimic this. Increasingly, electronic musicians use effects as part of the mix in their own right, as in the phased snare rolls in Jungle or the delays added to a synth sound in Techno. The more auxiliary sends a desk has the more useful it is to the modern electronic musician.

EQ, pump up the bass!

Finally we come to the EQ section, comprising a series of pots with cryptic messages such as 2.5K or 500Hz. These refer to the frequency ranges those pots are dedicated to boosting or cutting. Just as the Graphic EQ on a domestic stereo system divides the sound spectrum up into High, Middle and Low, the EQ pots make divisions between the various frequency ranges. The bottom one always controls the bass frequencies and the top one the high sounds while the ones in between control the various stages between those two. This will vary from mixer to mixer.

For dance music you need an EQ section that will provide you with plenty of boost in the bass range, which is 25Hz to 40Hz. If a mixer only offers EQ as low as 80Hz, forget it. You simply won't be able to muster up that big booming kick sound out of it.

The mid-ranges are also an important focus in dance music. Some mixers offer sweepable mid-range settings where one pot determines the centre frequency of that band and the pot above it controls the amount of boost applied. This provides a very flexible way of boosting those all-important frequencies where that acid bassline or piano riff is the most active, frequency-wise. Pay particular attention to this set of pots when looking for a mixer. If they only offer one mid-range pot with no sweep at all then it simply won't offer you enough control.

The EQ pots all work in the same way, except of course for the sweepable setting pot, applying either cut or boost to a frequency range. The centre setting means no cut or boost is being applied to that range while turning the pot to the right will boost the frequencies and, conversely, turning the pot to the left will cut frequencies. The principle of cutting frequencies is often overlooked – everyone naturally thinks in terms of addition, but if you're got two sounds which are both pretty busy in the same frequency range the mix can get a little crowded. If you cut one sound at the bottom of the range in which it is busiest, and cut the other at the top of that range both sounds will be heard more distinctly.

The EQ section is rightly considered by many to be the most important feature of a desk and many artists will find the sound of one desk suits them and their style of writing more than another. Your mixing desk is a very important instrument in your music-making armoury so listen to as many as you can and talk to other people making the same kind of music about their preferences before you decide what to spend your hard-earned money on!

The master section

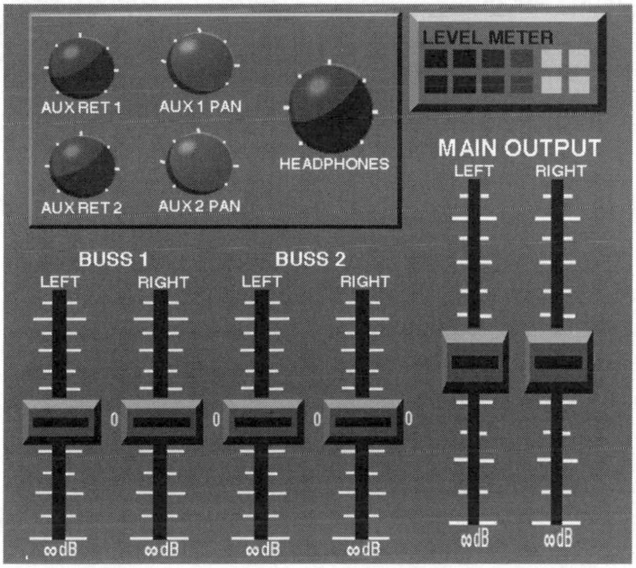

Figure 10.3
The master section of a mixer.

Figure 10.3 shows you where you find all those other sections we've been referring to throughout our exploration of the channel strip. They are as follows:

- The main faders – this is where you control the level of the whole mix output to your amplifier;

- The group faders – these control the level of the grouped outputs to a tape machine;

- The Auxiliary Return levels – these are usually pots and determine how much of the effected signal you bring into the mix;

- Auxiliary Pan – a good mixer will allow you to pan the returning effects; and

- Headphone monitor – this section will normally include a stereo headphone jack and a volume level pot for close listening or working late at night. If your mixer features buss outputs you should be able to choose which buss you are monitoring from here as well.

All about EQ

Equalization is one of the most useful and creative devices in the studio, and its creative use lies at the heart of producing electronic grooves. Just as a painter mixes the three basic hues of red, yellow and blue to achieve an infinity of colours so a sound engineer manipulates a mix of low, mid and high frequencies to achieve the subtle colourings of tone a mix demands.

Often when you come to listen back to a piece you have written, two or more sounds operating in the same frequency range will combine to produce a new sound which neither makes on its own. This blending of sounds creates new timbres and as well as forcing sounds apart you can use EQ creatively to force sounds from your arrangement to sit together so that they produce a new sound.

Other sounds you'll want to keep distinct, however. In dance music a lot of time is spent EQ'ing basslines and kick drums to get the bottom section grooving along with each component distinct from its neighbour. This extends upward into the mid range too with snares, hi hats and other percussion like bongos and congas, all occupying a part of this range and all needing to stand out a little from each other.

EQ can vastly affect the character of a sound but, used subtly, the presence of a sound can be changed in the mix without making noticeable changes to its tonal quality. Vocals are an ideal candidate for this. Boosting the high frequencies on them will help a weak vocal sound cut through the mix. Alternatively cut the amount of boost applied to the instruments in the top end.

On a decent mixing desk or outboard EQ unit you'll find more than one type of EQ or filter at your disposal. They perform differently and offer distinctive ways in which to manipulate sounds. Here's a guide to the most common ones you'll come across.

The different types of EQ

Graphic equalizers

A graphic equalizer is usually one of the first serious EQs that people encounter, now that most home stereo systems boast them. All the frequency bands are clearly labelled, with dedicated faders for each stage.

The individual sliders have a zero centre setting and usually provide +12dB of boost/cut. Graphic equalizers are useful if your desk doesn't offer very good EQ or hasn't got the output that you want.

High pass filter (HPF)

A high pass filter lets all the high frequencies pass through it unaffected but lowers the boost of the low frequencies progressively the lower they are. Exactly how low a frequency will be allowed to go before it is cut off completely varies between different types and makes of filter.

Low pass filter (LPF)

A low pass filter employs the same principles as a high pass filter except that it operates at the other end of the audio spectrum, allowing all the low frequencies to pass through and 'rolling off' or cutting the high frequencies.

Parametric equalization

This type of equalization allows you to choose the frequency range that you want to boost or cut. There are usually two controls, one to select the frequency to be cut or boosted and another to add or lower the amount of gain.

This type of equalizer is extremely flexible, and allows you to remove unwanted resonance. Sweeping through the frequency spectrum, you can track down unwanted frequencies and then lower them by reducing the gain. If you need to emphasize an instrument, you can find the frequency that makes it stand out and apply some boost to it.

There is an additional control that helps you to focus even more closly on a particular frequency. When you boost a frequency with a parametric equalizer, you're not boosting that frequency alone. If you set a parametric EQ to work at 1kHz you'll usually boost a range from 500Hz to 2000Hz with 1000Hz as the peak. That range is called the bandwidth.

The Q control on an equalizer will vary the bandwidth that is being boosted or cut. Low- or broadband Q values affect a wider range of frequencies than high, narrow band values.

Tonal EQing

No EQ set up is 'right' and another 'wrong'. Particular musical styles require distinct differences in approach. A Garage piano is typically bright, whereas House and Trip Hop piano recordings tend towards softer, warmer tones.

Following are some generalizations you can apply to certain instruments. Synth sounds aren't covered here as they fall into so many categories. That classic filter-swept TB303 sound can be treated as though it was a brass or saxophone sound or even as a piano sound as well as the bass sound it aspires to.

Generally you can identify a synth sound as being brassy or vocal or whatever and treat it accordingly. Remember these are only guidelines. You may come up with an original sound all your own by EQ'ing a piano sound as though it were a flute, so read the following with caution and never doff your experimentalist's cap to anyone!

EQing vocals

Usually, the mid-range is where to start when EQ'ing vocal sounds. However, adding some boost at the top end will introduce a sense of space. If you have two vocal sounds try different amounts of mid and top gain on each to make them distinct.

EQing brass and wind sounds

How you EQ these sounds is dictated by the range in which they're played. A baritone sax will require more attention to the bottom end while an alto sax obviously demands some attention be paid to the top. Brass and wind instruments have a quality similar to vocal sounds and similar treatments apply. Saxophones are very powerful in the mid-range, so try cutting rather than applying any gain to those frequencies.

EQing string sounds

If you're working on a solo sound such as a violin, then you probably need to fatten it up by adding some gain at the top of the mid-range. String ensembles, or pads, on the other hand, cover such a broad range that you'll need to cut all the frequencies except for a very narrow range, to prevent the resonance produced by masses of frequencies. Just what frequency range you boost on pads is dependent on the rest of your mix. The resonant beating of string sounds is often used as an effect in its own right by Techno and Jungle fiends so remember rules are made to be broken.

EQing bass sounds

Bass sounds are the most difficult to EQ. It's usually best to avoid doing anything too drastic. Try to check bass sounds out on small speakers as well as big bass bins. This will give you some idea of the huge frequency range your bass sound is hogging, often inaudibly as it hugs up to other sounds like kick drums and low piano tones.

EQing piano sounds

Synthesizers' piano patches usually emphasize the high frequencies and attack timbres, but often lack the warm mid-tones of the original. Try boosting the lower mid range to bring that 'natural' piano sound to your mix. Conversely, you can make piano sounds even brighter and cheesier by adding some gain in the high frequencies. Perfect for ravey chord patterns, adding bright tops brings that 'hands in the air' effect into full play.

EQing drum sounds

The kick drum is the most problematic sound to EQ in dance music, not least because differing styles demand often completely different approaches. As with bass sounds, try and listen to your mix on everything from trouser flapping bins down to those home hi-fi speakers to see just how wide a range this thump is occupying. For Techno, Garage and House you'll probably want to emphasize the lower frequencies while Trip Hop and Jungle tend to cut the bottom end and boost the lower mids for a more woody sound.

Snare drums usually respond best to a little gain in the mid-range. Add some gain on the higher frequencies and cut the mid-range and you'll get a more rattly sound. This can be useful for producing distinctive sounds like Jungle snares. Toms also benefit from a touch of top, as this helps to pronounce their attack, but a low-end boost will often give them more presence in a mix.

Boosting the upper mid-range will add more definition to stick sounds and rides. Vary the EQs applied to the different cymbals in your mix, ride, crash, splash and so on. Panning is essential for clarity when it comes to drums; closed and open hi hats sound more distinct if they are panned slightly left and right of the centre. Check the pan position of every drum sound in your mix and try and position them so they all occupy their own part of the stereo spectrum.

All about effects

Effects units were originally designed to replicate the natural acoustics of live venues in the recording studio. Adding delays, echoes and chorusing to the raw sounds, they create the effect of the sound being recorded in a 'real' environment. Using a series of different effects on each of the sounds in your mix will make each sound stand out more from those around it as the various reverbs create an individual space for each instrument.

Initially digital reverbs were used to replicate natural reverbs but the experimental nature of all electronic music has seen a new generation take these units and use them as sounds in their own right, pumping up the levels beyond those previously considered acceptable to produce whole new sound vistas. What follows is a guide to the basic types of reverb and their origin in the real world. Use them as a guide to exploring your effects units.

Types of reverb

Real acoustic rooms and chambers

Those presets on your reverb unit marked Room, Hall etc. are designed to reproduce the reverberations of their namesakes. As such they are pretty self-explanatory. Experiment with different sized rooms to see what the effect sounds like on pads, strings and brass sounds. Room reverbs are generally too boomy for drum tracks with the exception of the 'Small Room' or 'Club' reverbs. Of course a big booming set of toms may be just what your Techno track needs.

Plate reverbs

Before digital reverbs there were only two means of reproducing the sound of a large hall in a recording studio – spring reverbs and plate reverbs. Plate reverbs were initially a huge plate of metal stuck behind the drummer for the sound of his kit to bounce off. Mikes placed in the drum booth and on the surface of the plate itself recorded the reverb.

With digital plate reverbs, you have far more control. The reverberation time can be varied from less than a second to around four seconds allowing you to cut off the boomy tail of the plate reverb. They work well on drum sounds but can also add a metal edge to basslines and synth lead lines.

Spring reverbs

Spring reverbs are the other way of emulating the sound of natural reverb. Basically they consist of a coiled spring inside a tube. The sound is fed into one end of the tube and the reverberations of the spring are added to it and recorded at the output. Most digital spring reverbs don't really do a great job of emulating the real thing; instead they add a slightly vocoder-ish sound. The original spring reverbs were abandoned by the early studio pioneers for their 'unrealistic' sound, but are being rediscovered by Junglists and Techno fiends alike as their wild, mechanical-sounding reverb is applied to vocals and drum sounds.

Reverb parameters

Digital reverbs are the virtual reality of acoustics. No longer limited to level, EQ and decay time, you can now set pre-delays, EQ crossovers, density, reflections and a lot of other confusing parameters. Just as you experiment with different synth sounds, you can tweak a digital reverb to produce entirely new sounds.

Digital reverbs are actually samplers, converting the analogue sounds at the input into digital information that can then be manipulated by a dedicated sound chip called a Digital Signal Processor or DSP. Once in the digital domain, they are subjected to various algorithms to add echoes and the like. These can include emulations of plate reverbs, as well as the usual rooms and halls. Within each algorithm are various parameters and it's these you alter to produce your own, original sound.

What follows is a guide to the most common parameters to be found on digital effects units. As these vary enormously from unit to unit, use this only as a guide and refer to the manual of your effects unit for more complete information.

Pre-delay
This parameter is measured in milliseconds, and decides the length of the gap between the original unaffected sound and hearing the effected sound.

Size
Size is measured in metres, and simply sets the dimensions of the 'room' or 'hall' the effects unit is trying to replicate.

Reverb time or decay
Adjusting this parameter varies the time it takes for a reverb sound to die away. This is usually shown in seconds and milliseconds or sometimes more simply as an arbitrary range.

Equalization
Many multi-effect units include an EQ section as part of their effects chain, allowing you to shape just which frequencies a reverb, chorus or delay will operate on.

High and low pass filters

Just as with EQ, high and low pass filters let you filter a range of frequencies before passing them onto the effects processor.

Echoes

Digital delays

Echoes and delays are a more pronounced effect than reverb and can produce all manner of surprising results. The feedback control determines how many repeats you get. Set this to one or zero, and you'll get a single echo. The delay time is for setting the interval between echoes. Set this to 100ms or less, and echoes become reverb-like in effect. If you make the delay shorter still, you won't hear distinct echoes at all.

Chorus

Chorus is actually a delay, doubled up and detuned to produce a fatter sound. Go for an even mix of the original sound and the chorus effect, as they work against each other. The delay feedback control will make the sound more dense.

Flanging

If you program two bass kicks, one on the beat and another just a few ticks before or after the beat, you'll get what is known as a 'flanging' effect where the closeness of the two sounds produces a noticeable 'thwoosh'. You've probably heard this effect at a club when the DJ fluffs the beat matching of two records and the two bass kicks become flanged. Digitally speaking, flanging is the halfway house between phasing and chorus, using a copy of the sound offset in time to produce the effect.

Phasing

Phasing is the whooshing effect produced from panning a sound very quickly from side to side. Digital effects units replicate this by panning very quickly back and forth between two versions of a sound. Very short delay times produce the best results.

Built-in synth effects

Most modern synths feature onboard effects, built in reverb units. Initially rather basic versions of outboard effects, these are now often as sophisticated as the real thing. If you're only going to use one sound from your synth, then these are great and will save you the expense of buying another effects unit.

Problems arise when you're using the synth in Multi or Combination modes. These feed all the sounds into the same onboard DSP, hence, all your sounds are swathed in the same effect. Reverbs that sound great on strings will make a bass mushy and turn out hissing hi hats. Newer synths offer a little more control over this process, often with a choice of two different effect types with control over the amount of effect on each sound.

Some synths feature extra outputs besides the stereo pair, thus enabling you to route sounds away from the internal effects processors and out to your desk where other reverbs can be applied. Unfortunately not many modern synths offer this option. One solution is to use your sequencer's audio functions and record parts individually. Although this old fashioned 'overdubbing' process is very tedious, the plus side is that you can record with all the effects you have available.

If you don't have a digital audio sequencer, or a large enough hard drive to make full use of it, a sampler offers another way of getting all the effects you need. Sample a sound with the reverb on it then replay the treated sound from the sampler. Then you can use that effects unit on another sound. Dealing with the limitations of your recording equipment in this way is an integral part of the creative process. Original sounds are often born out of working around such limitations. When it comes to experimenting with music, the golden rule is: there are no golden rules.

We've now looked at what a mixing desk is and what it does. By now you should also understand how to use EQ to fine-tune your mix. The descriptions of the various kind of effects units you can plug into a mixing desk apply equally to the effects plug-ins which process the digital audio tracks in your sequencer and you now have a clear idea of how to use these to add reverb, delay, chorus and echoes to your creations.

Now you should be ready to produce a finished track. In Chapter 11 we'll look at getting your work published, whether by landing a record deal or by doing it yourself, and getting your own pressings made up and getting them distributed. We'll also cover the most important aspect of getting your work published – protecting your copyright.

Getting your work published

These days, it's harder than ever to have a hit with a dance record. After ten years of the rave revolution, making your mark amongst the Techno tunes, Drum'n'Bass builders and Big Beat merchants is harder than ever.

The key element is originality. For your tune to make an impact it must offer something different to the thousands of tunes already out there. As well as revolutionizing the way music is made, the electronic dance explosion has also drastically altered the way records impact upon peoples' consciousness and ultimately the charts.

Submitting tunes to record companies

The traditional route used to be sending your demo tape to the A&R department at a major label in the hope someone would pick up on it. That died out with the onset of the dance explosion and now your best bet is to seek out small independent labels. Not only will they be more interested in hearing your tune, they'll also be in touch with the DJs and record stores who specialize in stocking dance tunes. Find one whose releases seem to be in the same vein as your tunes and approach them. The big companies are only interested in a dance tune once it's a proven commodity; i.e. when it's already filling the dancefloors. That's the point at which the majors step in and license your tune off the independent label for a chart push.

Choosing the right independent label to sign to is of major importance. Make sure they are well respected and connected in the clubs and record shops which specialize in whatever style of dance your tune is. Talk to the DJs in the clubs that play the music you're producing and find out which labels and shops they rate. The more friends and contacts you can make among the club runners and record shop owners, the better your chance is of people paying attention to your tune and the better placed you are to make an impact.

Once you've got a contract the record label should be able to do more than simply pressing up your track on vinyl. A good label will be in touch with the tastemakers in the clubs and magazines to spread the word about your masterpiece. They should have money to invest in press promotion and ads in the dance magazines. If they haven't, then they're probably not doing that well. At this stage your tune needs all the help it can get to stand out from the crowd.

If the label is doing well they should also be able to offer you an advance. Advances are just that – an advance against future earnings – and shouldn't be regarded as a signing fee. Only megastars command fees simply for signing to a label, and that's because they've got a track record for selling records in large quantities. Remember, until the record company has sold enough records to cover the advance, you won't begin to see any more earnings from your dancefloor filler.

Some of the smaller, independent labels offer 'profit-share' deals. Instead of the smaller royalty rate offered by bigger labels they will offer you a 50% share in the profits once the costs of pressing and distributing your tune are met. There's no question of an advance with this sort of deal and unless your tune is a massive success you won't make a fortune. This route is not to be sniffed at however; many of the biggest dance classics were released with just such a deal.

Deciding which deal is the best is down to you and your impression of how much investment in time and money a label seems to be offering. Whatever you decide, make sure you read the contract thoroughly and understand every word. If you can afford it seek professional advice from a music lawyer, especially if large sums of money are involved.

Doing it yourself – the white label route

The other approach is doing it yourself. The cost of pressing 500 12" singles is currently around £500. Sell half of them for around £2.50–3.50, and mail out the rest to DJs, magazines and radio stations that specialize in your type of music. Most independent dance record shops will stock a record on a sale or return basis. If you can't sell 500 copies of your record, you'll never sell a million.

Choosing the right shops is essential. Visit the shops, see what they're playing, ask them to listen to your tune and tell you what they think. The major labels pay the owners of independent dance shops to look out for potential hits and, once again, many a dance hit has been discovered this way.

Getting 500 copies pressed up and distributing them to DJs, shops and radio stations which play your kind of music is the best way to gain attention in the underground dance scene. If your track is any good it should do well enough for a record label to track you down in their quest for a chart climber. Or you could take the returns from selling half the pressings and reinvest it in some more and carry on until you have enough cash to form your own label.

If you decide to get your own white labels pressed up, choose the cutting and pressing plants carefully. Once again, ask around for recommendations. Check out the comments in the run-in track of your favourite tunes. The cutting engineer usually scratches a comment onto the master, and you can usually find out who they are by asking around. Find out who's made a reputation for themselves cutting your sort of music. It's the cutting engineer who decides how the finished vinyl will sound.

It will be up to him to decide how best to lay out the grooves. Careful mastering means choosing the minimum groove spacing to ensure all the recorded peak volumes are safely contained within the groove. Wider grooves give a louder pressing but a shorter playing time. If the track is too long to fit, more compression will have to be applied to the master. For this reason many people choose to press their singles at $33\frac{1}{3}$ RPM for maximum dynamic range.

If you can't afford to press up 500 records you might want to consider getting a dub plate pressed. This term originated from the independent studios in Jamaica like King Tubby's that first put out reggae and dub releases as one-offs for MCs to 'toast' over.

The conventional record is pressed from two metal stamps, one for each side. Dub plates, or acetates to give them their proper name, are made from soft plastic that has a record groove cut directly into it. The advantage is cost. You get a record that a DJ can play straight away on the turntables. Because the disc is such soft material, it'll start to deteriorate in quality after 20 plays but with luck you will have secured some interest by then.

Promotion

Once you have your tune out in clubs and the DJs are going crazy it's time to press the promotion switch. As small labels have blossomed, a complete promotion industry has grown up to support them. If you've signed to a label they should look after this for you but if you're releasing your own records you'll need to get a list of the promotion companies which deal in your kind of music. Ask magazine editors and shop owners for contact names and numbers and also for advice on which companies are doing a good job. Choosing the right promotion company can be as important as choosing the right shops to stock your tune.

Promotion companies charge around £400 to £500 for mailing out around 100 records to journalists, DJs and radio stations. Though your tune might be going down a storm in the clubs on dub plate or white label, you're going to need press promotion to bring it to the attention of a wider audience. Creating an interest in your tune in the month or two before it's released on a label can make the difference between a Top 40 smash and an also ran.

Copyright control – protecting your assets

Before you get involved in releasing your tunes make sure you copyright your music. The legal rights of your tune reside in both the song and the way in which it has been recorded. Music industry law is almost entirely based around the publishing copyright which exists in a song and the sound recording copyright, which exists in the recorded version of the song.

For copyright to exist in either of these, the song or recording must be set down in a permanent and repeatable form. For a song this can be the music manuscript, a sequence of notes stored on a floppy disk from a sequencer, or even a clear enough Dictaphone recording of the melody. For a sound recording copyright, you must have made some sort of permanent recording of a performance.

The cheapest method of copyrighting your tune is to mail yourself, by recorded delivery, a copy of the manuscript or sequencer file and a copy of the DAT or master on which it was recorded. Don't open the parcel when it arrives and then you have positive proof that you recorded that tune on or before the date shown on the postmark.

The traditional approach is to use the services of a copyright lawyer. This is usually a lawyer who specializes in the music industry and he'll be able to work with you and your record company in securing your copyright. He'll also come in useful if you intend to release a record which uses someone else's bassline, drum break, vocal stab, or even their original song, making sure that you get an agreement from the artist concerned and their record label. Failure to do this could end up costing you a lot of money.

Recommended reading

The Music Week Directory

Comprehensive lists of labels, cutting houses, pressing plants, press companies and club promoters.

Available from: Spotlight Publications Ltd, 120–126 Lavender Avenue, Mitcham, Surrey, CR4 3HP. RRP: £30.00.

The New Music Seminar Booklet

A useful reference for the American Music Industry.

Contact: The New York office: (001) 212 473 4343. RRP $40.00.

Music Business Agreements

A good beginner's guide to all the legal side of things.

Published by Waterlow, it's available in specialist bookshops. RRP: £45.00–£55.00.

The BPI Year Book

All the latest UK record industry statistics. Published every year in March.

Available from: BPI Roxburghe House, 273–287 Regent Street, London W1R 7PB. RRP: £15.00.

NOTE

All contract rates, fees, sale prices, and methods of trade described here are intended as guidelines only, and should not be taken as authoritative figures or recommended methods of business.

12 Sequencing and the Internet

MIDI is part of the whole digital communications medium using MIDI (Musical Instrument Digital Interface) to connect your synthesizers so they can talk to each other. Computers also connect and talk to each other in networks. The largest network of all is the Internet and the connectivity it offers provides resources and points of contact for the modern electronic musician beyond anything ever conceived of before.

What is the Internet?

The Internet is a network of computers worldwide that are connected over phone lines. First initiated by American defence programmers who needed to exchange information, the Internet grew exponentially, as computer programmers everywhere discovered the benefits of communicating with colleagues all over the world. Once you are connected, you can send e-mail to other people on the net, log on to newsgroups and discussion forums, and access the World Wide Web.

What is the World Wide Web?

The World Wide Web (WWW) is a GUI (Graphical User Interface) for the Internet, which has been responsible for the huge growth in net activity since its inception. You use a browser such as Netscape Navigator or Internet Explorer to access all the parts of the Web via simple point-and-click methods, just like any other program on your Mac or PC.

What use is all this to me?

Quite simply, the Internet is the largest source of information in the world. For musicians and multimedia programmers, connection to the Internet is essential if you want to keep abreast of current developments in software and hardware. Most manufacturers maintain web sites, where you can download the latest version of software, or information about new hardware, and there are also a wealth of sites where you can download MIDI files and transcriptions of popular songs and original compositions.

What do I need to get online?

You will need a computer, modem, Internet account and communications software. Most Internet Service Providers (ISPs) have all the software you need, so it's really just a matter of buying a modem and computer. Mac, PC, Atari, Amiga and Archimedes computers all have Internet software available and can be connected.

Where do I get an Internet account?

There are an increasing number of service providers out there, and many now offer free Internet access and e-mail: all you have to pay are telephone charges. The major phone companies are now getting in on the act with AT&T in America and BT in Britain offering web accounts alongside a regular phone service.

Web jargon explained

Surfing

Surfing is the term used to describe the activity of exploring different sites around the world. Netscape Navigator and Internet explorer incorporate search facilites whereby you simply type in a keyword, 'music' for example, and any sites featuring that word in their description will appear as a series of links for you to click on and thus 'surf' to that site.

Links

World Wide Web pages are full of links – highlighted text or graphics which take you somewhere else when you click on them. Some links are to other pages within an individual web site, others will take you to the other side of the world, logging on to events such as Sony's launch of the Playstation from a site in New Zealand.

E-mail

E-mail or electronic mail is simply a message from your word processor that you send to another e-mail address. Once you have an individual Internet account you will be given an e-mail address and can communicate with like-minded correspondents all over the world. Your e-mail address usually consists of a personal name followed by the @ symbol then the name of your service provider. Thus Newtronic is accessible at: sales@newtronic.com.

Newsgroups

Newsgroups are the best means of contacting people with whom to communicate. They're much like e-mail, except the message is posted to a newsgroup that is accessible by anyone logging on to that group. You can continue a public discussion here with everyone or communicate with individuals who wish to carry on a discussion via e-mail. There are many groups covering all aspects of the music industry. Once you have an Internet account you also have access to a list of newsgroups maintained by your service provider and can follow discussions on them.

Internet Relay Chat (IRC)

Internet Relay Chat (or IRC) is much like a newsgroup except everything is live! You could take part in a discussion with a group of people from all over the world. Many businesses use this facility to gather together executives from far-flung locations for group meetings. Video conferencing over the Internet is also rapidly passing the stage of expensive plaything and becoming an everyday reality. If development continues at this pace it is entirely possible that the Internet will supersede television as the mass communication medium of the world.

Web browsers

There are many web browsers out there, programs which interpret the data sent over the Internet and turn it into word and pictures for your enjoyment. It all began with a free program called Mosaic that became Netscape and is still going strong. Microsoft leapt into the fray with their own browser, Internet Explorer – also distributed for nothing, which now has as many users as Netscape. You (don't) pay your money and you take your choice …

The Internet – the music connection

So the Internet is a huge network of computers and the world's largest source of information, but what use is all this to the modern electronic musician? Plenty, that's what! Most of the sources used in computer sequencing, MIDI files, .WAV files and other sound files and even software are available for you to download directly to your computer's hard drive. Are you sequencing up a piece and fancy using a section of the Moonlight Sonata? Just download a MIDI file of the piece in question and you're ready to start! Need the latest upgrade to Cubase or the latest version of Logic? Software developers all operate web sites worldwide that operate ftp (File Transfer Protocol) sites containing the latest versions for registered users to download.

There's also a load of freeware and shareware MIDI software out there. Shareware is computer software, usually written by computer enthusiasts, for which you pay a token fee to the author if you like it and continue using it. This is entirely based on trust and the fees involved are usually very small (£10–£20) for which you'll often receive upgrades to the program (when available) and a manual, so they're well worth supporting. Whatever synth you've got, the chances are that someone, somewhere has written a shareware editor for it which you can download and try out.

Commercial programs such as Cubase also offer demo versions of their software for you to try before you buy. The demos of the sequencers on the CD-ROM accompanying this book are available at the various sites and it's well worth a visit to check out new programs. You can even purchase software over the net with your credit card. CD-ROMs, sample CDs and musical instruments can all be located and purchased over the web. If you're interested in old synths there are numerous sites with full specs on all the various models ever made and which often a guide to current prices. Many of these feature a buyers' bulletin board where you can read adverts from other readers selling their gear and contact them by e-mail to arrange a purchase.

Sources of music on the Internet

There are numerous sites on the web that feature MIDI files, sound files and MIDI software for you to download. Listed below are some of the millions out there. Go to a web search engine like Yahoo (*http://www.yahoo.com*) where you can type in a keyword like 'MIDI' and locate thousands of sites all over the world which feature MIDI in some way or another.

You could also be more precise and search for a particular song, or simply 'surf' all the MIDI sites you find; it's up to you. There are also sites with information about everything from MIDI specifications to analogue synths and you'll find them in the section on other interesting sites on page 268.

Commercial software sites

Yamaha
http://www.yamaha.com/
Roland USA
http://www.rolandcorp.com/

Korg
http://www.korg.com
Akai
http://www.akai.com/akaipro/index.html
Novation
http://www.nova-uk.com/

MIDI file sites

MIDI files
http://www.newtronic.com
http://www.midifarm.com
http://www.themidicity.com
Classical MIDI files
http://www.prs.net

Sound file sites

Dancetech
http://www.dancetech.com
Time+Space
http://www.timespace.com
AMG
http://www.amguk.co.uk/
SampleNet
http://www.samplenet.com

MIDI software sites

Steinberg
http://www.steinberg.de
Emagic
http://www.emagic.de
Opcode
http://www.opcode.com
Cakewalk
http://www.cakewalk.com
Newtronic
http://www.newtronic.com

Record labels

Ninja Tune
http://www.ninjatune.net
Detroit Record Labels
http://www.hyperreal.com:80/music/lists/313/labels/index.html
Irdial Discs
http://Penny.ibmPCUG.CO.UK:80/~irdial/catalo.htm
Moonshine Records
http://www.moonshine.com/
Mute Liberation Technologies
http://www.mutelibtech.com/mute/
R&S Records
http://www.rsrecords.com/
Virgin Music Group
http://www.vmg.co.uk/index.html

Other interesting sites

The Mobeus
http://www.u-net.com/~cev/
Hyperreal
http://hyperreal.com/
Music Machines
http://www.hyperreal.com:80/music/machines/
Musical Web Connections
http://www.columbia.edu/~hauben/music/
Progression – The Future of Music
http://www.progression.co.uk
System 7 (777 in the USA)
http://www.easynet.co.uk/Pages/system7/sys7.htm
Techno Online
http://www.techno.de/index.html
Transmat Worldwide
http://www.transmat.com
Detroit 313 WWW Site
http://www.hyperreal.com:80/music/lists/313/
The Black Dog's Home Page
http://www.feedback.com/tbd/

Newsgroups – make contact

The Internet is about more than just surfing the World Wide Web, and by far the most attractive aspect of the Internet to modern musicians is the chance to make contact with like-minded musicians worldwide.

The best way to do this is through *newsgroups*, which are like public e-mail postings, where like-minded individuals post messages to be read and replied to by anyone else subscribing to that group.

Subscribing to a newsgroup simply means downloading the postings to a particular newsgroup from your Internet Service Provider. Most service providers maintain all or most of the current newsgroups.

There are newsgroups covering every aspect of music and music-making from composing to recording to distribution and live gigs. The list below is not comprehensive, as new groups are appearing every day and older ones often simply die away as people gravitate to new or different groups, but it is a listing of the main groups.

MIDI and music newsgroups

alt.binaries.sounds.cartoons

alt.binaries.sounds.d

alt.binaries.sounds.erotica

alt.binaries.sounds.midi

alt.binaries.sounds.misc

alt.binaries.sounds.mods

alt.binaries.sounds.mods.d

alt.binaries.sounds.movies

alt.binaries.sounds.music

alt.binaries.sounds.samples.music

alt.binaries.sounds.tv

alt.binaries.sounds.utilities

alt.emusic

alt.music

alt.music.dance

alt.music.gangsta.rap

alt.music.hardcore

alt.music.house

alt.music.makers.dj

alt.music.makers.electronic:

alt.music.midi

alt.music.midiweb

alt.music.misc

alt.music.mods

alt.music.producer

alt.music.synth.roland.u20

alt.music.techno

alt.music.uk

aus.music

austin.music

ba.music

cl.kultur.musik

comp.music.midi

comp.music.misc

comp.music.research

dc.music

de.alt.binaries.sounds

de.alt.binaries.sounds.d

de.rec.music.elektronisch

de.rec.music.misc

fido.ger.musik

fido.ger.musiker

fido.music

fido.musik-ger

fido7.music

fido7.music.lyrics

fj.comp.music

fj.rec.music.j-pop

fj.rec.music.progressive

francom.musique

han.music.artrock

houston.music

it.arti.musica

maus.midi

microsoft.public.music.products

misc.business.records-mgmt

nctu.club.midi

nlnet.muziek

no.musikk

osu.music

othernet.demi-monde.music

pdaxs.ads.music

pdaxs.arts.music

pdaxs.services.music

phl.music

rec.arts.anime.music

rec.audio.marketplace

rec.audio.misc

rec.audio.opinion

rec.audio.pro

rec.audio.tech

rec.audio.tubes

rec.music.ambient

rec.music.collecting.cd

rec.music.collecting.misc

rec.music.collecting.vinyl

rec.music.compose

rec.music.funky

rec.music.hip-hop

rec.music.industrial

rec.music.info

rec.music.makers

rec.music.makers.marketplace

rec.music.makers.songwriting

rec.music.makers.synth

rec.music.marketplace.cd

rec.music.marketplace.misc

rec.music.marketplace.vinyl

rec.music.misc

rec.music.movies

rec.music.promotional

rec.music.reggae

rec.music.video

relcom.music

sdnet.music

slac.rec.music

swnet.musik

tamu.music

tw.bbs.comp.midi

uiuc.org.music.cmp

uk.music.makers.dj

uk.music.misc

uk.music.rave

um.music

umich.music

umn.general.music

MIDI jamming on the Internet

Using the connectivity provided by the Internet, several forward-thinking individuals have been developing software which allows you to link your MIDI set-up to other musicians anywhere in the world and jam with them, all for the price of a local phone call! This is perhaps the most exciting aspect of the Internet for musicians and is certainly a great source of inspiration for the modern electronic musician, who is often to be found working alone late at night. Just the right time to log on, connect to a bass player in Budapest and play your ideas to them for a little feedback when inspiration fails you! All this is made possible by a program called ResRocket.

ResRocket software is under constant development and new developments in the offing are the transmission of audio tracks alongside MIDI ones and the ability to run the ResRocket software as a plug-in for Cubase. ResRocket Surfer members are to be found worldwide engaging in real time jamming sessions. You can join them at ***http://www.resrocket.com/***.

Online distribution

The Internet also promises the possibility of universal distribution for the musician. The development of the MP3 (MPEG-1 Layer 3) format, a sound format which delivers CD-quality sound in a file a tenth of the size of an equivalent audio CD file has seen a massive growth in the online distribution of music, not all of it legal. Pirate sites have sprung up offering commercial tracks lifted from CDs and converted to MP3 format. Because of their illegal status these sites are closed down as quickly as they spring up.

Other variations on the MP3 format have sprung up, attempting to capitalize on the new markets offered by the Internet. Macromedia have their own Shockwave format, which is essentially MP3 encoded in their own file format, and this is used by many sites to enhance the web surfing experience. Check it out at: ***http://www.macromedia.com***.

Another variation of the format is Liquid Audio. This format requires you to download a special player. You then download tracks in the Liquid Audio format (after paying for them with your credit card) and can listen to them on your computer. George Michael was the first commercial artist to embrace the Liquid Audio concept and you can check out his songs and those of other artists at ***http://www.aegean.net***. Download the Liquid Audio player and check out a list of sites at ***http://www.liquidaudio.com***.

Real Audio is another variation on the theme which uses a compressed audio format to send audio over the net in real time. The Real Player is a piece of software which then plays back these streaming sound files on your computer. The Real Audio format has been eagerly adopted as an alternative to pirate radio, and a number of sites have sprung up, offering all kinds of online music from Abba to Zappa. Download the Real Player and check out a list of sites at ***http://www.real.com***.

Recently, hardware players have begun to appear which allow you to listen to MP3 songs away from your computer. This is the final development which has seen the MP3 format escape the boundaries of the Internet and has forced the record companies to take MP3 seriously. The record companies' response has been mixed – the Beastie Boys were forced to remove some live tracks from their 1998 tour off their web site after their record company objected. Follow their progress at ***http://www.beastieboys.com***.

Public Enemy were also blocked from distributing tracks online and responded by issuing an MP4 file called Swindlers Lust which is a lyrical call to arms over the artists' right to distribution of their own material. MP4 is a variation on MP3 where an MP3 file is bundled with its own player as an executable file. Check it out at ***http://www.public-enemy.com***.

The interesting consequence of this is a proliferation of legal MP3 sites, where new bands distribute their tracks for free or for a minimal fee. At the time of writing, record companies are beginning to join the fray, distributing MP3 or similar files for a nominal fee. You can find many of the legal MP3 files on the Internet and more information about MP3 hardware and software at ***http://www.mp3.com***.

Appendix 1
Computer basics

Understanding computers

Computers, we are constantly being told, are powerful machines that are changing our lives. Yet, placed in front of a computer keyboard for the first time, most people's reaction is one of bewilderment followed closely by frustration. Once the basic skills of navigating the mouse and opening programs and documents are mastered, understanding most of the menu commands in a program depends on detailed knowledge of the subject the application was designed to process. It is then that the flaw in the 'computers are powerful machines' argument is exposed. Computers *are* powerful, but only when they are controlling other machines. Understanding what any given program is designed to do is rendered doubly difficult if the computer isn't connected to an appropriate piece of hardware. A word processing program is useless to most of us without a printer to output our typing in paper form.

In the case of music sequencing that truth is even more fundamental to an understanding of how the whole thing works. Without at least a drum machine and a synthesiser connected via MIDI to your computer a sequencer is a useless piece of software, but with a minimum set-up it is transformed into an interactive music learning and composing tool. Understanding this is the first step in overcoming any apprehension about using a computer, and making you the master of a powerful tool, rather than the slave of a technological master.

In keeping with the philosophy outlined in the Introduction any feature of either the computer or the software is only introduced as and when it is useful. The following sections describe basic computing concepts, principles and terms used in computing.

Computer/CPU

It may seem an obvious place to start but many people are still confused as to what a computer actually *is* and are terrified of breaking it as a consequence. It helps to realize that a computer is a chip, known as a *CPU*

(Central or Computer Processing Unit). This CPU in your PC, Mac or Atari is a more complicated version of the chip that powers a tool most of us are now familiar with; the pocket calculator. What your pocket calculator chip does is to perform simple addition and subtraction, and display the result to you on a small LCD (Liquid Crystal Diode) display.

What about multiplication and division, I hear you ask? It is a sobering fact to realise that computers, including the most powerful, are actually incapable of these two most basic mathematical skills that we take for granted. I myself am not naturally mathematically minded but can still work out 8×112 or $112 \div 8$, even if I have to resort to a scrap of paper. And that is exactly what a computer does when presented with a multiplication problem. It calls upon its own version of a scrap of paper, a RAM chip (see next section), to scribble on while it works out the solution to multiplication and division problems by a series of additions and subtractions.

Without getting bogged down in mathematics, the output you see on a personal computer's screen is achieved by a series of commands, called a program, which use the number-crunching ability of the CPU to output text and pictures in binary format to a monitor or other device, such as a printer or MIDI instrument. Binary is the numbering system computers talk in and its use arises from the fact that a computer chip is just a series of on/off switches that are manipulated in series to output their results. This means that computers only recognize two states of any one digit, 0 or 1, and so the binary system, which depends upon each digit in a row being potentially worth twice its predecessor, reading from right to left, is used.

A computer program is written in these binary digits, or bits, and manipulates the output of the CPU to produce for instance a visual display on the screen. If you look closely at your computer screen you'll see that the picture is composed of tiny dots called pixels. Each one of these can be thought of as equivalent to a series of bits, their on/off states signalling what colour any given pixel should be. MIDI is a binary system for musical notes as opposed to text or pictures and allows your sequencer to talk to your synth or drum machine in much the same way, except in this case the series of bits indicate the pitch and timing of a note rather than the colour of a pixel on a screen.

RAM/memory

To do all this the CPU must have some memory in which to store the data it is working on. This is what RAM is. RAM stands for Random Access Memory and a RAM chip is a storage device for all those series of 0s and 1s we looked at in the previous paragraph. RAM chips are electrostatically charged pieces of silicon and therefore can not only hold the position of a row of binary digits but can, with a flick of their electrical switches, change the state of any of those digits to reflect the additions and subtractions which constitute the CPU's calculating process. RAM draws its electrostatic charge from the current in the machine in which it is installed and so loses any information once your computer is switched off. To store information for future use the computer must use another device, a disk drive. This, and other hardware, is discussed in the following sections.

Bits, bytes, kilobytes and megabytes

We've already discussed bits (binary digits). Bytes, kilobytes (K) and megabytes (Mb) are computer terminology for groupings of binary data larger than single digits. A byte is the term for eight bits, the smallest meaningful piece of binary data. It takes a byte to represent a single letter on screen, for instance. The next meaningful measurement is the kilobyte. Because of the way the binary number system works, a K or kilobyte stands for 1,024 not 1,000 and a kilobyte is 1,024 bytes. Similarly a megabyte is 1,024 kilobytes or 1,048,576 bytes. These terms are usually abbreviated to K or Kbyte and Mb or Mbyte. A megabyte is the term most commonly used to measure the amount of RAM and hard disk storage in a computer. It was not long ago that computer memory and storage was measured in kilobytes and with the ever-increasing use of memory and storage space by modern applications the basic hard drive is already at least 2 Gigabytes (Gb) in size.

Hardware

The physical devices we have been looking at, computer parts like the CPU and RAM chips and other devices like disk drives are what's known as *hardware*. This is to differentiate them from the software described in the next section. It is important to realize that, just as your pocket calculator contains a specialized CPU, so do MIDI instruments. Just as in a personal computer, the CPU is connected to RAM chips to store settings' data and provide memory for the CPU to process the MIDI data sent to it from your sequencer. For this reason synthesizers, samplers and other MIDI devices are also referred to as hardware.

Software

Software is the magic bit you can't see, the computer program, which transforms the basic, mathematical functions of a CPU into the colourful screen display and complicated processing that we now know as the PC. There are two types of software, the *operating system* and *applications*. We'll have a look at these two next.

Operating systems

The *operating system* is the basic core program that does all the things we associate with PCs today. It is a program that handles the basic tasks of presenting text and images to the screen and transforms a box of chips into a useful tool. All modern computers have an operating system. In the case of the PC it is DOS or Disk Operating System, on the Mac it is the Mac O/S or Mac operating system, while the Atari has TOS, for The Operating System. Usually operating systems are loaded into a computer's RAM from a hard disk or floppy disk and this is why the PC's system is called a Disk Operating System. The Atari, by contrast, stores its operating system in another form of memory called a ROM chip. A ROM chip acts exactly like a RAM chip except that it is not dynamic and cannot alter the state of any of its bits, ROM standing for Read Only Memory. This means if you want to change the operating system in an Atari you must remove the old ROM chip and insert a new one containing the new operating system. Loading an operating system from disk does allow for easier upgrades and is the most common method because of this. In any case, once the operating system has taken care of basic tasks the PC is able to run programs that perform more useful functions, like word processing or sequencing. These are known as applications and we'll look at them next.

Applications

Computer programs written to do specific tasks, such as a sequencer, take advantage of the fact that the operating system has done the job of drawing windows and menus, displaying information to the screen and sending out binary data through the printer or MIDI socket. The operating system has also provided them with a means of accessing the CPU to do specific jobs, such as the aforementioned multiplication and division. Freed from these cumbersome chores an *application* can not only concentrate on its own tasks but can also exchange data with other programs using the same operating system. This depends on whether the operating system will allow that, of course, and application developers are often responsible for improvements in operating systems through their calls for more functionality to be added to the basic tools that they are given to work with when they write programs. Sometimes programmers of operating systems aren't interested in developing these special features and so the applications developer is forced to write his own, supplementary, operating system to handle data specific to the task. Steinberg's MROS (MIDI Realtime Operating System) and Opcode's OMS (Open Music System) are two examples of these supplementary operating systems.

Applications such as sequencers are often stored in their own folder, or directory, along with files containing settings and other data the program may need. To differentiate between these files and the actual application, the PC and the Atari add a three-character extension to the file name to identify it. Thus an application on the Atari has the letters .PRG, for program, or .APP for application, written after the file name, as in CUBASE.PRG. On the PC the same system is used but DOS uses the extension .EXE, for Executable File, indicating that this is a file which will execute a task rather than a simple text file which has the extension .TXT for Text.

The Mac uses colourful icons to indicate a file's status but you can choose to view its files in text format where you will find the word application written next to a file to indicate if it is an executable program. On the Atari an icon in the form of the Atari desktop indicates an executable file and Windows uses a very similar one. The Mac uses custom icons but in all cases double-clicking on their icons with the mouse starts executable programs such as sequencers. On the PC you can also start an application by choosing Run... from the Start menu and typing in the name of the program. Similarly on the Mac and Atari, highlighting an application's icon by clicking once on it and selecting Open from the File Menu will start that program as in Figure A1.1 below.

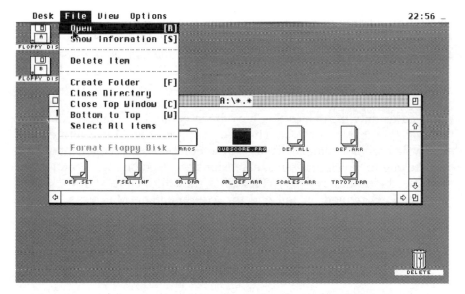

Figure A1.1
Selecting Open from the File menu.

Files

All data, including operating systems and applications, are stored on your hard drive or floppy disk in the form of *files*. This can often cause confusion when first trying to run an application or open a document so it's worth taking a look at the various file types and how to recognize them on the PC, Mac or Atari.

The operating system on your computer actually consists of a whole series of files, designed to handle all the different tasks that you may ask the computer to do. Because they're so important they're stored in a separate section all to themselves. This is known as a *folder* on the Mac and Atari, and a *directory* on the PC (more on these below). This is so that you don't have to see them unless you need to (and know what you're doing!) and so the operating system can find them when it needs them. On the Mac they're stored in a folder called System, while the PC stores its system software in a directory called DOS and another called Windows. The Atari, of course, has its system in ROM and so you can't see it at all. Operating systems load into your computer's memory at start-up and you shouldn't have to worry about them at all. Only try to alter operating system files if you know what you're doing!

Documents

Anything that isn't an operating system file or an application file is called a *document*. Documents come in many forms. There are text documents, to save the output from a word processing Application; graphics documents, for saving pictures created in a drawing program and, of course, MIDI files, which store all the information from a song created with a sequencer. In addition, many applications and operating systems use documents to keep track of system settings. These are usually hidden away in the system folder or, in the case of applications, in the application's own special folder. Documents such as MIDI files and text files are designed to be opened from within applications and, when you choose Open from that application's File menu, a file requester will appear. In most cases only those files that have been created by that program will be available for you to open, since the computer will have filtered out any which are not suitable. To assist the computer in recognizing which files belong to which programs, extensions are used on the PC and Atari, text files being indicated by .TXT after their file name and MIDI files having .MID tagged on the end for example. The Mac uses its own system and does not need extensions but the principle is the same.

Folders/directories

If you've checked out the files on your computer you will have noticed these folders and directories we've been talking about. In DOS they're identified by a DIR in the file listing and on the Mac and Atari desktops and Windows File Manager they're shown as little icons in the shape of a manila folder. This is because that concept represents exactly the function they fulfill. Folders, or directories, are files which group all files below them in something called a directory tree. If you think of opening up an ordinary manila folder to see the individual documents inside then you've grasped the concept. You can even create a new folder within an existing folder, so your top folder could be called My Song with several folders inside that called Mix 1, Mix 2 and so on. Folders are useful things for keeping related documents in, separate from other files, for your clarity and the computer's. That is why your computer's operating system stores all the files it needs in separate folders and why most applications store all their essential files in separate directories. It's a good idea to keep your documents away from essential files like operating systems and applications, so explore creating folders for your song files on your computer's hard disk.

Directory tree/structure

Computers need a highly organized system to keep track of all the data stored on their hard drive. They use a structure called a directory tree which is just like an upside down family tree (see Figure A1.2), with the root directory layer, your hard drive, at the top, and all the folders and nested folders branching out the further down you go. Here we see the folders and directories discussed above represented as nodes in the directory structure, pointing to the files contained below/within them.

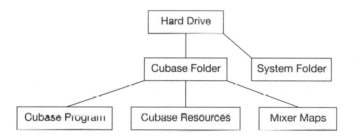

Figure A1.2
A directory tree.

Menus

Modern software has become very sophisticated and contains more functions than could be comfortably displayed on your screen, so applications make use of something called a *menu bar*. This normally runs along the top of the screen. By moving your mouse to the top edge of your screen you cause the menus hidden there to appear. Then you drag the mouse down to the command you want and release it to activate that function. Most of these commands will be marked with key combinations such as Ctrl/M and these are the keyboard versions of the commands you see on the menu (in this case pressing the Control key, followed by the M key on your keyboard) – see Figure A1.3. It's a good idea to learn these as you go, using the menu commands until you know your way around the program and then using the keyboard equivalents for faster operation later on when speed will become more important to you.

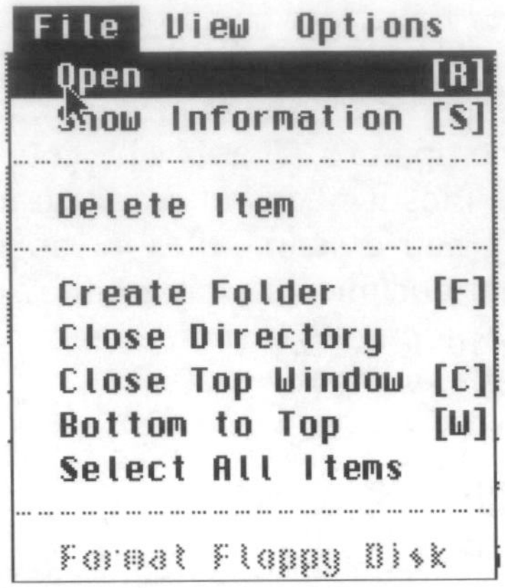

Figure A1.3
*Drop-down
menus show the
key commands.*

```
┌─────────────────────────────────┐
│ File  View  Options             │
├─────────────────────────────────┤
│ ▌Open                    [R]    │
│ Show Information         [S]    │
│ ································· │
│ Delete Item                    │
│ ································· │
│ Create Folder           [F]    │
│ Close Directory                │
│ Close Top Window        [C]    │
│ Bottom to Top           [W]    │
│ Select All Items               │
│ ································· │
│ Format Floppy Disk             │
└─────────────────────────────────┘
```

Commands/functions

The processes a computer program carries out on data loaded into its memory are called *functions* or *commands*. This could be something like altering the font of a text document or transposing a piece of music up or down in semitones. An application is really just a lot of related functions grouped together in one single program designed to work together. As more functions are added to an application, usually at the request of users like you and me, developers release new versions, or upgrades, of their original program.

Floppy disk drive

The *floppy disks* that come with your computer usually contain copies of the system software for backup should your hard drive crash. Once upon a time computers didn't have hard drives attached and had to load their operating system from a floppy disk. As the amount of data increased hard drives became more common on computers – today a computer without a hard drive is considered an anachronism. Essentially a floppy disk is made of the same magnetic media as a cassette tape except that the ferrous particles are spread over a disk instead of along a length of tape. When you format a floppy disk the magnetic particles are divided up into sectors for the data to be stored on. Your computer's floppy disk drive reads the floppy disk in a circular fashion, spinning the disk at thousands of revolutions per second.

Hard disk drive

A *hard drive* is like many floppy disks stacked on top of one another, each with its own read/write head. This makes them much faster to operate than floppy disks and, of course, means they can store much more data. For this reason they have become essential and, if you want to achieve any meaningful amount of work, it is certainly the first item you Atari owners out there should consider investing in. PC and Mac owners are lucky enough to have built-in hard disks but, if your hard disk is any less than one gigabyte in size, you'll soon need to invest in a larger one.

CD-ROM disk drive

CD-ROMs can be thought of as one step up from a floppy disk, in terms of storage space. ROM stands for Read Only Memory, just like ROM chips, although perhaps a less confusing term would be Read Only Storage as neither a CD-ROM, hard drive or floppy disk adds any memory to your computer, only storage space. CD-ROMs can store much more data (650 Mb) and are faster to access than floppies but not as fast as a hard drive. Faster CD-ROM drives are now being manufactured, and they are fast becoming the default storage medium for games and multimedia applications. The large storage space makes them ideal for storing large amounts of data such as encyclopaedias or MIDI files and sequencing software as on the CD-ROM attached to this book.

Appendix 2
Program Change Tables

MIDI Program Changes offer 128 possible numbers, starting at 0. Manufacturers and sequencer programmers often ignore the zero start convention of computers and MIDI and usually number Program Changes from 1–128. The following conversion table lists the most common variations and should help you to find the Program Change number to send to a device to access the required patch. The first column shows the 0–127 numbering method used by the MIDI standard. Column two shows the 1–128 numbering method used by most sequencers. Column three, by contrast, shows the octal method of breaking programs down into 16 banks of eight as used on the Roland D-series. The fourth column is also octal but each bank is defined by a letter rather than a number, as on the Kawai K1. Finally, the fifth column uses eight banks of 16 as on the Yamaha DX and SY series.

Program Change Table

Column	Column	Column	Column	Column
1	2	3	4	5
0	1	1-1	A-1	A-1
1	2	1-2	A-2	A-2
2	3	1-3	A-3	A-3
3	4	1-4	A-4	A-4
4	5	1-5	A-5	A-5
5	6	1-6	A-6	A-6
6	7	1-7	A-7	A-7
7	8	1-8	A-8	A-8
8	9	2-1	B-1	A-9

Column	Column	Column	Column	Column
9	10	2-2	B-2	A-10
10	11	2-3	B-3	A-11
11	12	2-4	B-4	A-12
12	13	2-5	B-5	A-13
13	14	2-6	B-6	A-14
14	15	2-7	B-7	A-15
15	16	2-8	B-8	A-16
16	17	3-1	C-1	B-1
17	18	3-2	C-2	B-2
18	19	3-3	C-3	B-3
19	20	3-4	C-4	B-4
20	21	3-5	C-5	B-5
21	22	3-6	C-6	B-6
22	23	3-7	C-7	B-7
23	24	3-8	C-8	B-8
24	25	4-1	D-1	B-9
25	26	4-2	D-2	B-10
26	27	4-3	D-3	B-11
27	28	4-4	D-4	B-12
28	29	4-5	D-5	B-13
29	30	4-6	D-6	B-14
30	31	4-7	D-7	B-15
31	32	4-8	D-8	B-16
32	33	5-1	E-1	C-1
33	34	5-2	E-2	C-2
34	35	5-3	E-3	C-3
35	36	5-4	E-4	C-4
36	37	5-5	E-5	C-5
37	38	5-6	E-6	C-6
38	39	5-7	E-7	C-7

Column	Column	Column	Column	Column
39	40	5-8	E-8	C-8
40	41	6-1	F-1	C-9
41	42	6-2	F-2	C-10
42	43	6-3	F-3	C-11
43	44	6-4	F-4	C-12
44	45	6-5	F-5	C-13
45	46	6-6	F-6	C-14
46	47	6-7	F-7	C-15
47	48	6-8	F-8	C-16
48	49	7-1	G-1	D-1
49	50	7-2	G-2	D-2
50	51	7-3	G-3	D-3
51	52	7-4	G-4	D-4
52	53	7-5	G-5	D-5
53	54	7-6	G-6	D-6
54	55	7-7	G-7	D-7
55	56	7-8	G-8	D-8
56	57	8-1	H-1	D-9
57	58	8-2	H-2	D-10
58	59	8-3	H-3	D-11
59	60	8-4	H-4	D-12
60	61	8-5	H-5	D-13
61	62	8-6	H-6	D-14
62	63	8-7	H-7	D-15
63	64	8-8	H-8	D-16
64	65	9-1	I-1	E-1
65	66	9-2	I-2	E-2
66	67	9-3	I-3	E-3
67	68	9-4	I-4	E-4
68	69	9-5	I-5	E-5

Column	Column	Column	Column	Column
69	70	9-6	I-6	E-6
70	71	9-7	I-7	E-7
71	72	9-8	I-8	E-8
72	73	10-1	J-1	E-9
73	74	10-2	J-2	E-10
74	75	10-3	J-3	E-11
75	76	10-4	J-4	F-12
76	77	10-5	J-5	E-13
77	78	10-6	J-6	E-14
78	79	10-7	J-7	E-15
79	80	10-8	J-8	E-16
80	81	11-1	K-1	F-1
81	82	11-2	K-2	F-2
82	83	11-3	K-3	F-3
83	84	11-4	K-4	F-4
84	85	11-5	K-5	F-5
85	86	11-6	K-6	F-6
86	87	11-7	K-7	F-7
87	88	11-8	K-8	F-8
88	89	12-1	L-1	F-9
89	90	12-2	L-2	F-10
90	91	12-3	L-3	F-11
91	92	12-4	L-4	F-12
92	93	12-5	L-5	F-13
93	94	12-6	L-6	F-14
94	95	12-7	L-7	F-15
95	96	12-8	L-8	F-16
96	97	13-1	M-1	G-1
97	98	13-2	M-2	G-2
98	99	13-3	M-3	G-3

Column	Column	Column	Column	Column
99	100	13-4	M-4	G-4
100	101	13-5	M-5	G-5
101	102	13-6	M-6	G-6
102	103	13-7	M-7	G-7
103	104	13-8	M-8	G-8
104	105	14-1	N-1	G-9
105	106	14-2	N-2	G-10
106	107	14-3	N-3	G-11
107	108	14-4	N-4	G-12
108	109	14-5	N-5	G-13
109	110	14-6	N-6	G-14
110	111	14-7	N-7	G-15
111	112	14-8	N-8	G-16
112	113	15-1	O-1	H-1
113	114	15-2	O-2	H-2
114	115	15-3	O-3	H-3
115	116	15-4	O-4	H-4
116	117	15-5	O-5	H-5
117	118	15-6	O-6	H-6
118	119	15-7	O-7	H-7
119	120	15-8	O-8	H-8
120	121	16-1	P-1	H-9
121	122	16-2	P-2	H-10
122	123	16-3	P-3	H-11
123	124	16-4	P-4	H-12
124	125	16-5	P-5	H-13
125	126	16-6	P-6	H-14
126	127	16-7	P-7	H-15
127	128	16-8	P-8	H-16

Most modern synths and sequencers use the Bank Change command which uses MIDI Controllers 0 and 32 to select a bank of 128 sounds thus:

Control 0   Bank Change

Control 32   Number of Bank (1–9,999)

Program Change Number   1–128

Most synths manufactured since 1994 support this standard.

Appendix 3
GM/GS and XG
sound sets

GM sound sets

Program No.	Instrument	Program No.	Instrument	Program No.	Instrument
1	Grand Piano	44	Contrabass	87	Lead 7 Fifths
2	Bright Piano	45	Tremelo Strings	88	Lead 8 Bass+Lead
3	Electric Grand	46	Pizzicato Strings	89	Pad 1 New Age
4	Honky-Tonk	47	Harp	90	Pad 2 Warm
5	Electric Piano 1	48	Timpani	91	Pad 3 Polysynth
6	Electric Piano 2	49	String Ensemble 1	92	Pad 4 Choir
7	Harpsichord	50	String Ensemble 2	93	Pad 5 Bowed
8	Clavichord	51	Synth Strings 1	94	Pad 6 Metallic
9	Celeste	52	Synth Strings 2	95	Pad 7 Halo
10	Glockenspiel	53	Choir Aahs	96	Pad 8 Sweep
11	Music Box	54	Choir Oohs	97	FX 1 Rain
12	Vibraphone	55	Synth Voice	98	FX 2 Soundtrack
13	Marimba	56	Orchestra Hit	99	FX 3 Crystal
14	Xylophone	57	Trumpet	100	FX 4 Atmosphere
15	Tubular Bells	58	Trombone	101	FX 5 Brightness
16	Dulcimer	59	Tuba	102	FX 6 Goblins
17	Drawbar Organ	60	Muted Trumpet	103	FX 7 Echoes
18	Percussive Organ	61	French Horn	104	FX 8 Sci Fi
19	Rock Organ	62	Brass Section	105	Sitar

Program No.	Instrument	Program No.	Instrument	Program No.	Instrument
20	Church Organ	63	Synth Brass 1	106	Banjo
21	Reed Organ	64	Synth Brass 2	107	Shamisen
22	Accordian	65	Soprano Sax	108	Koto
23	Harmonica	66	Alto Sax	109	Kalimba
24	Accordian	67	Tenor Sax	110	Bagpipe
25	Nylon Guitar	68	Baritone Sax	111	Fiddle
26	Steel String Guitar	69	Oboe	112	Shanai
27	Jazz Guitar	70	English Horn	113	Tinkle Bell
28	Clean Guitar	71	Bassoon	114	Agogo
29	Muted Guitar	72	Clarinet	115	Steel Drums
30	Overdrive Guitar	73	Piccolo	116	Woodblock
31	Distortion Guitar	74	Flute	117	Taiko Drum
32	Guitar Harmonics	75	Recorder	118	Melodic Drum
33	Accoustic Bass	76	Pan Flute	119	Synth Drum
34	Finger Bass	77	Blown Bottle	120	Reverse Cymbal
35	Picked Bass	78	Shakuhachi	121	Guitar Fret Noise
36	Fretless Bass	79	Whistle	122	Breath Noise
37	Slap Bass 1	80	Ocarina	123	Seashore
38	Slap Bass 2	81	Lead 1 Square	124	Bird Tweet
39	Synth Bass 1	82	Lead 2 Sawtooth	125	Telephone
40	Synth Bass 2	83	Lead 3 Calliope	126	Helicopter
41	Violin	84	Lead 4 Chiff	127	Applause
42	Viola	85	Lead 5 Charang	128	Gunshot
43	Cello	86	Lead 6 Voice		

GM Drum Kit

The GM standard drum kit, with each drum sound assigned to a specific note. This is always on MIDI channel 10.

NN	Note	Drum Sound	NN	Note	Drum Sound
27	D#0	High Q	58	A#2	Vibra Slap
28	E 0	Slap	59	B 2	Ride 2
29	F 0	Scratch Push	60	C 3	Hi Bongo
30	F#0	Scratch Pull	61	C#3	Lo Bongo
31	G 0	Sticks	62	D 3	Mute Conga
32	G#0	Square Click	63	D#3	Hi Conga
33	A 0	Metronome-Click	64	E 3	Lo Conga
34	A#0	Metronome Bell	65	F 3	Hi Timbale
35	B 0	Kick Drum 2	66	F#3	Lo Timbale
36	C 1	Kick Drum 1	67	G 3	Hi Agogo
37	C#1	Side Stick	68	G#3	Lo Agogo
38	D 1	Snare 1	69	A 3	Cabasa
39	D#1	Hand Clap	70	A#3	Maracas
40	E 1	Snare 2	71	B 3	Short Whistle
41	F 1	Low Tom 2	72	C 4	Long Whistle
42	F#1	Closed Hi Hat	73	C#4	Sort Guiro
43	G 1	Low Tom 1	74	D 4	Long Guiro
44	G#1	Pedal Hi Hat	75	D#4	Claves
45	A 1	Mid Tom 2	76	E 4	Hi Wood Block
46	A#1	Open Hi Hat	77	F 4	Lo Wood Block
47	B 1	Mid Tom 1	78	F#4	Mute Cuica
48	C 2	High Tom 2	79	G 4	Open Cuica
49	C#2	Crash 1	80	G#4	Mute Triangle
50	D 2	High Tom 1	81	A 4	Open Triangle
51	D#2	Ride 1	82	A#4	Shaker
52	E 2	Chinese Cymbal	83	B 4	Jingle Bell
53	F 2	Ride Bell	84	C 5	Bell Tree
54	F#2	Tambourine	85	C#5	Castanets
55	G 2	Splash	86	D 5	Mute Surdo
56	G#2	Cowbell	87	D#5	Open Surdo
57	A 2	Crash 2			

GS sound sets

PGM	Bank	Instrument	PGM	Bank	Instrument
1	0	Acoustic Grand	22	0	Accordian
2	0	Bright Acoustic		8	Accordian 2
3	0	Electric Grand	23	0	Harmonica
4	0	Honky-Tonk	24	0	Tango Accordion
5	0	Electric Piano1	25	0	Nylon Guitar
	8	Detuned EP1		8	Ukelele
6	0	Electric Piano2	26	0	Steel Guitar
	8	Detuned EP2		8	12 String Gt
7	0	Harpsichord	27	0	Jazz Guitar
	8	Coupled Hps		8	Hawaiian Gt.
8	0	Clav	28	0	Mute Guitar
9	0	Celesta		8	Chorus Gt.
10	0	Glockenspiel	29	0	Electric Guitar
11	0	Music Box		8	Funk Gt.
12	0	Vibraphone	30	0	Overdrive Guitar
13	0	Marimba	31	0	Distortion Guitar
14	0	Xylophone		8	Feedback Gt.
15	0	Tubular Bells	32	0	Guitar Harmonics
	8	Church Bell		8	Gt. Feedback
16	0	Dulcimer	33	0	Acoustic Bass
17	0	Drawbar Organ	34	0	Finger Bass
	8	Detuned Or.1	35	0	Pick Bass
18	0	Percussive Organ	36	0	Fretless Bass
	8	Detuned Or.2	37	0	Slap Bass 1
19	0	Rock Organ	38	0	Slap Bass 2
20	0	Church Organ	39	0	Synth Bass 1
	8	Church Organ 2		8	Synth Bass 3
21	0	Reed Organ	40	0	Synth Bass 2

PGM	Bank	Instrument	PGM	Bank	Instrument
	8	Synth Bass 4	65	0	Soprano Sax
41	0	Violin	66	0	Alto Sax
42	0	Viola	67	0	Tenor Sax
43	0	Cello	68	0	Baritone Sax
44	0	Contrabass	69	0	Oboe
45	0	Tremolo Strings	70	0	English Horn
46	0	Pizzicato Strings	71	0	Bassoon
47	0	Orchestral Strings	72	0	Clarinet
48	0	Timpani	73	0	Piccolo
49	0	String Ensemble 1	74	0	Flute
	8	Orchestra	75	0	Recorder
50	0	String Ensemble 2	76	0	Pan Flute
51	8	SynthStrings 3	77	0	Blown Bottle
	0	SynthStrings 1	78	0	Skakuhachi
52	0	SynthStrings 2	79	0	Whistle
53	0	Choir Aahs	80	0	Ocarina
54	0	Voice Oohs	81	0	Lead 1 (square)
55	0	Synth Voice	82	0	Lead 2 (sawtooth)
56	0	Orchestra Hit	83	0	Lead 3 (calliope)
57	0	Trumpet	84	0	Lead 4 (chiff)
58	0	Trombone	85	0	Lead 5 (charang)
59	0	Tuba	86	0	Lead 6 (voice)
60	0	Muted Trumpet	87	0	Lead 7 (fifths)
61	0	French Horn	88	0	Lead 8 (bass+lead)
62	0	Brass Section	89	0	Pad 1 (new age)
	8	Brass 2	90	0	Pad 2 (warm)
63	0	SynthBrass 1	91	0	Pad 3 (polysynth)
	8	SynthBrass 3	92	0	Pad 4 (choir)
64	0	SynthBrass 2	93	0	Pad 5 (bowed)
	8	SynthBrass 4	94	0	Pad 6 (metallic)

PGM	Bank	Instrument	PGM	Bank	Instrument
95	0	Pad 7 (halo)	114	0	Agogo
96	0	Pad 8 (sweep)	115	0	Steel Drums
97	0	FX 1 (rain)	116	0	Woodblock
98	0	FX 2 (soundtrack)		8	Castanets
99	0	FX 3 (crystal)	117	0	Concert BD
100	0	FX 4 (atmosphere)		8	Taiko Drum
101	0	FX 5 (brightness)	118	0	Melodic Tom
102	0	FX 6 (goblins)		8	Melodic Tom 2
103	0	FX 7 (echoes)	119	0	Synth Drum
104	0	FX 8 (sci-fi)		8	808 Tom
105	0	Sitar	120	0	Reverse Cymbal
106	0	Banjo	121	0	Guitar Fret Noise
107	0	Shamisen	122	0	Breath Noise
108	0	Koto	123	0	Seashore
	8	Taisho Koto	124	0	Bird Tweet
109	0	Kalimba	125	0	Telephone Ring
110	0	Bagpipe	126	0	Helicopter
111	0	Fiddle	127	0	Applause
112	0	Shanai	128	0	Gunshot
113	0	Tinkle Bell			

GS Drum Kits PGMs 1, 8, 16 and 24

NN	Key	PGM 1 Standard	PGM 8 Room	PGM 16 Power	PGM 24 Elec
27	D#0	High Q			
28	E0	Slap			
29	F0	ScrPush			

NN	Key	PGM 1 Standard	PGM 8 Room	PGM 16 Power	PGM 24 Elec
30	F#0	ScrPull			
31	G0	Sticks			
32	G#0	SqarClck			
33	A0	MetrClck			
34	A#0	MetrBell			
35	B0	BassDr2			
36	C1	BassDr1		Mondo	Elec BD
37	C#1	SideKick			
38	D1	SnareDr1		Gated	Elec SD
39	D#1	HandClap			
40	E1	SnareDr2			Gated SD
41	F1	LowTom2	RLoTom2	RoLoTom2	E LoTom2
42	F#1	Cl-HH			
43	G1	LowTom1	RLoTom1	RoLoTom1	E LoTom1
44	G#1	Pedal-HH			
45	A1	MidTom2	RMiTom2	RoMiTom2	E MiTom2
46	A#1	Open-HH			
47	B1	MidTom1	RMiTom1	RoMiTom1	E MiTom1
48	C2	HighTom2	RHiTom2	RoHiTom2	E HiTom2
49	C#2	Crash 1			
50	D2	HighTom1	RHiTom1	RoHiTom1	E HiTom1
51	D#2	RideCym1			
52	E2	Chinese			RevrsCym
53	F2	RideBell			
54	F#2	Tamburin			
55	G2	Splash			
56	G#2	Cowbell			
57	A2	Crash 2			
58	A#2	Quijada			

NN	Key	PGM 1 Standard	PGM 8 Room	PGM 16 Power	PGM 24 Elec
59	B2	RideCym2			
60	C3	Hi Bongo			
61	C#3	Lo Bongo			
62	D3	Mt Conga			
63	D#3	Hi Conga			
64	E3	Lo Conga			
65	F3	HTimbale			
66	F#3	LTimbale			
67	G3	Hi Agogo			
68	G#3	Lo Agogo			
69	A3	Cabasa			
70	A#3	Maracas			
71	B3	S Whistl			
72	C4	L Whistl			
73	C#4	Sh Guiro			
74	D4	Lg Guiro			
75	D#4	Claves			
76	E4	HWodBlck			
77	F4	LWodBlck			
78	F#4	Mt Cuica			
79	G4	Op Cuica			
80	G#4	MtTriang			
81	A4	OpTriang			
82	A#4	Shaker			
83	B4	JingBell			
84	C5	Belltree			
85	C#5	Castanet			
86	D5	Mt Surdo			
87	D#5	Op Surdo			
88	E5	--------			

GS Drum Kits PGMs, 1, 25, 40 and 49

NN	Key	Standard	PGM 25 Analog	PGM 40 Brush	PGM 49 Orch
27	D#0	High Q			Close-HH
28	E0	Slap			Pedal-HH
29	F0	ScrPush			Open-HH
30	F#0	ScrPull			HideCymb
31	G0	Sticks			
32	G#0	SqarClck			
33	A0	MetrClck			
34	A#0	MetrBell			
35	B0	BassDr2			
36	C1	BassDr1	BassDr		ConcBD 2
37	C#1	SideKick	RimSht		ConcBD 1
38	D1	SnareDr1	Snare	BrshTap	CncertSD
39	D#1	HandClap		Br Slap	Castanet
40	E1	SnareDr2		Br Swirl	CncertSD
41	F1	LowTom2	LoTom2		Timpan F
42	F#1	Cl-HH	Cl-HH1		TimpanF#
43	G1	LowTom1	LoTom1		Timpan G
44	G#1	Pedal-HH	Cl-HH2		TimpanG#
45	A1	MidTom2	MiTom2		Timpan A
46	A#1	Open-HH	OpenHH		TimpanA#
47	B1	MidTom1	MiTom1		Timpan B
48	C2	HighTom2	HiTom2		Timpan c
49	C#2	Crash 1	Cymbal		Timpanc#
50	D2	HighTom1	HiTom1		Timpan d
51	D#2	RideCym1			Timpand#
52	E2	Chinese			Timpan e
53	F2	RideBell			Timpan f

NN	Key	Standard	PGM 25 Analog	PGM 40 Brush	PGM 49 Orch
54	F#2	Tamburin			
55	G2	Splash			
56	G#2	Cowbell	Cowbel		
57	A2	Crash 2			Cymbal 2
58	A#2	Quijada			
59	B2	RideCym2			Cymbal 1
60	C3	Hi Bongo			
61	C#3	Lo Bongo			
62	D3	Mt Conga	HConga		
63	D#3	Hi Conga	MComga		
64	E3	Lo Conga	LConga		
65	F3	HTimbale			
66	F#3	LTimbalc			
67	G3	Hi Agogo			
68	G#3	Lo Agogo			
69	A3	Cabasa			
70	A#3	Maracas	Maracs		
71	B3	S Whistl			
72	C4	L Whistl			
73	C#4	Sh Guiro			
74	D4	Lg Guiro			
75	D#4	Claves	Claves		
76	E4	HWodBlck			
77	F4	LWodBlck			
78	F#4	Mt Cuica			
79	G4	Op Cuica			
80	G#4	MtTriang			
81	A4	OpTriang			
82	A#4	Shaker			

NN	Key	Standard	PGM 25 Analog	PGM 40 Brush	PGM 49 Orch
83	B4	JingBell			
84	C5	Belltree			
85	C#5	Castanet			
86	D5	Mt Surdo			
87	D#5	Op Surdo			
88	E5	Applause			

GS SFX kit

NN	Key	Standard	PGM 57 SFX Set
27	D#0	High Q	
28	E0	Slap	
29	F0	ScrPush	
30	F#0	ScrPull	
31	G0	Sticks	
32	G#0	SqarClck	
33	A0	MetrClck	
34	A#0	MetrBell	
35	B0	BassDr2	
36	C1	BassDr1	
37	C#1	SideKick	
38	D1	SnareDr1	
39	D#1	HandClap	High Q
40	E1	SnareDr2	Slap
41	F1	LowTom2	ScrPush
42	F#1	Cl-HH	ScrPull
43	G1	LowTom1	Sticks
44	G#1	Pedal-HH	SqarClck

NN	Key	Standard	PGM 57 SFX Set
45	A1	MidTom2	MetrClck
46	A#1	Open-HH	MetrBell
47	B1	MidTom1	Gt.Fret Noise
48	C2	HighTom2	Gt.Cut Noise
49	C#2	Crash 1	String Slap
50	D2	HighTom1	StrSlapAcBass
51	D#2	RideCym1	Fl. Key Click
52	E2	Chinese	Laughing
53	F2	RideBell	Screaming
54	F#2	Tamburin	Punch
55	G2	Splash	Heart Beat
56	G#2	Cowbell	Footsteps1
57	A2	Crash 2	Footsteps2
58	A#2	Quijada	Applause
59	B2	RideCym2	Door Creaking
60	C3	Hi Bongo	Door
61	C#3	Lo Bongo	Scratch
62	D3	Mt Conga	Windchimes
63	D#3	Hi Conga	Car Engine
64	E3	Lo Conga	Car Stop
65	F3	HTimbale	Car Pass
66	F#3	LTimbale	Car Crash
67	G3	Hi Agogo	Siren
68	G#3	Lo Agogo	Train
69	A3	Cabasa	Jet Plane
70	A#3	Maracas	Helicopter
71	B3	S Whistl	Star Ship
72	C4	L Whistl	Gun Shot
73	C#4	Sh Guiro	Machine Gun
74	D4	Lg Guiro	Laser Gun

NN	Key	Standard	PGM 57 SFX Set
75	D#4	Claves	Explosion
76	E4	HWodBlck	Dog
77	F4	LWodBlck	Horse Gallop
78	F#4	Mt Cuica	Bird
79	G4	Op Cuica	Rain
80	G#4	MtTriang	Thunder
81	A4	OpTriang	Wind
82	A#4	Shaker	Seashore
83	B4	JingBell	Stream
84	C5	Belltree	Bubble
85	C#5	Castanet	
86	D5	Mt Surdo	
87	D#5	Op Surdo	
88	E5	--------	

XG sound sets

PGM	BNK	Instrument	PGM	BNK	Instrument
1	0	GrandPno		40	ElGrPno1
	1	GrandPnoK		41	ElGrPno2
	18	MelloGrP	4	0	HnkyTonk
	40	PianoStr		1	HnkyTnkK
	41	Dream	5	0	E.Piano1
2	0	BritePno		1	El.Pno1K
	1	BritPnoK		18	MelloEP1
3	0	E.Grand		32	Chor.EP1
	1	ElGrPnoK		40	HardEl.P
	32	Det.CP80		45	VX El.P1

PGM	BNK	Instrument	PGM	BNK	Instrument
	64	60sEl.P		98	Log Drum
6	0	E.Piano2	14	0	Xylophon
	1	El.Pno2K	15	0	TubulBel
	32	Chor.EP2		96	ChrchBel
	33	DX Hard		97	Carillon
	34	DXLegend	16	0	Dulcimer
	40	DX Phase		35	Dulcimr2
	41	DX+Analg		96	Cimbalom
	42	DXKotoEP		97	Santur
	45	VX El.P2	17	0	DrawOrgn
7	0	Harpsi.		32	DetDrwOr
	1	Harpsi.K		33	60sDrOr1
	25	Harpsi.2		34	60sDrOr2
	35	Harpsi.3		35	70sDrOr1
8	0	Clavi.		36	DrawOrg2
	1	Clavi.K		37	60sDrOr3
	27	ClaviWah		38	EvenBar
	64	PulseClv		40	"16+2" "2/3"
	65	PierceCl		64	Organ Ba
9	0	Celesta		65	70sDrOr2
10	0	Glocken		66	CheezOrg
11	0	MusicBox		67	DrawOrg3
	64	Orge1	18	0	PercOrgn
12	0	Vibes		24	70sPcOr1
	1	VibesK		32	DetPrcOr
	45	HardVibe		33	LiteOrg
13	0	Marimba		37	PercOrg2
	1	MarimbaK	19	0	RockOrgn
	64	SineMrmb		64	RotaryOr
	96	Balafon		65	SloRotar
	97	Balafon2		66	FstRotar

PGM	BNK	Instrument	PGM	BNK	Instrument
20	0	ChrchOrg		64	CleanGt2
	32	ChurOrg3	29	0	Mute.Gtr
	35	ChurOrg2		40	FunkGtr1
	40	NotreDam		41	MuteStlG
	64	OrgFlute		43	FunkGtr2
	65	ReedOrgn		45	Jazz Man
21	0	ReedOrgn		96	Mu.DstGt
	40	Puff Org	30	0	Ovrdrive
22	0	Accordion		43	Gt.Pinch
	32	AccordIt	31	0	Dist.Gtr
23	0	Harmnica		12	DstRhtmG
	32	Harmo 2		24	DistGtr2
24	0	TangoAcd		35	DistGtr3
	64	TngoAcd2		36	PowerFt2
25	0	NylonGtr		37	PowerGt1
	16	NylonGt3		38	Dst.5ths
	25	NylonGt3		40	FeedbkGt
	43	VelGtHrm		41	FeedbGt2
	96	Ukulele		43	RkRythm2
26	0	SteelGtr		45	RockRthm
	16	SteelGt2	32	0	GtrHarmo
	35	12StrGtr		64	AcoHarmo
	40	Nyln&Stl		65	GtFeedbk
	41	Stl&Body		66	GtrHrmo2
	96	Mandolin	33	0	Aco.Bass
27	0	Jazz Gtr		40	JazzRthm
	18	MelloGtr		45	VXUprght
	32	JazzAmp	34	0	FngrBass
	96	PdlSteel		18	FingrDrk
28	0	CleanGtr		27	FlangeBa
	32	ChorusGt		40	Ba&DstEG

PGM	BNK	Instrument	PGM	BNK	Instrument
	43	FngrSlap		19	SynBa2Dk
	45	FngBass2		32	SmthBa 2
	64	JazzBass		40	ModulrBa
	65	ModAlem		41	DX Bass
35	0	PickBass		64	X WireBa
	28	MutePkBa	41	0	Violin
36	0	Fretless		8	Slow Vln
	32	Fretles2	42	0	Viola
	33	Fretles3	43	0	Cello
	34	Fretles4	44	0	Contrabass
	96	SynFretl	45	0	Trem.Str
	97	Smooth		8	SlowTrStr
37	0	SlapBas1		40	Susp Str
	27	ResoSlap	46	0	Pizz Str
	32	PunchThm	47	0	Harp
38	0	SlapBas2		40	YangChin
	43	VeloSlap	48	0	Timpani
39	0	SynBass1	49	0	Strings1
	18	SynBa1Dk		3	S.Strings
	20	FastResB		8	SlowStr
	24	AcidBass		24	ArcoStr
	35	Clv Bass		35	60sStrng
	40	TeknoBa		40	Orchestr
	64	Oscar		41	Orchstr2
	65	SqrBass		42	TremOrch
	66	RubberBa		45	VeloStr
	96	Hammer	50	0	Strings2
40	0	SynBass2		3	S.SlwStr
	6	MelloSB2		8	LegatoSt
	12	Seq Bass		40	Warm Str
	18	ClkSynBa		41	Kingdom

PGM	BNK	Instrument	PGM	BNK	Instrument
	64	70sStr		32	WarmTrp
	65	Str Ens3		96	FluglHrn
51	0	Syn.Str1	58	0	Trombone
	27	ResoStr		18	Trmbone2
	35	Syn Str 3	59	0	Tuba
	64	Syn Str4		16	Tuba 2
	65	SS Str	60	0	Mute.Trp
52	0	Syn.Str2		64	MuteTrp2
53	0	ChoirAah	61	0	Fr.Horn
	3	S.Choir		32	FrHorn2
	16	Ch.Aahs2		37	HornOrch
	32	MeiChoir	62	0	BrasSect
	40	ChoirStr		6	FrHrSolo
	64	StrngAah		14	SfrzndBr
	65	Male Aah		35	Tp&TbSec
54	0	VoiceOoh		39	BrssFall
	64	VoiceDoo		40	BrssSec2
	96	VoiceHmm		41	HiBrass
55	0	SynVoice		42	MelloBrs
	40	SynVox2	63	0	SynBras1
	41	Choral		12	QuackBr
	64	AnaVoice		20	RezSynBr
56	0	Orch.Hit		24	PolyBrss
	35	OrchHit2		27	SynBras3
	64	Impact		32	JmpBrss
	65	BrssStab		45	AnaVelBr
	66	DoublHit		64	AnaBrss1
	67	BrStab80	64	0	SynBras2
57	0	Trumpet		18	Soft Brs
	16	Trumpet2		40	SynBrss4
	17	BriteTrp		41	ChoirBrs

PGM	BNK	Instrument	PGM	BNK	Instrument
	45	VelBrss2		64	Mellow
	64	AnaBrss2		65	SoloSine
65	0	SprnoSax		66	SineLead
66	0	Alto Sax	82	0	Saw.Lead
	40	Sax Sect		6	Saw 2
	43	HyprAlto		8	ThickSaw
67	0	TenorSax		18	DynaSaw
	40	BrthTnSx		19	DigiSaw
	41	SoftTnr		20	Big Lead
	64	TnrSax 2		24	HeavySyn
68	0	Bari.Sax		25	WaspySyn
69	0	Oboe		40	PulseSaw
70	0	Eng Horn		41	Dr. Lead
71	0	Bassoon		45	VeloLead
72	0	Clarinet		96	Seq Ana
	96	BassClar	83	0	CalipLd
73	0	Piccolo		64	Vent Syn
74	0	Flute		65	Pure Pad
75	0	Recorder	84	0	Chiff Ld
76	0	PanFlute		64	Rubby
	64	PanFlut2	85	0	CharanLd
	96	Kawala		64	DistLead
77	0	Bottle		65	WireLead
78	0	Shakhchi	86	0	Voice Ld
79	0	Whistle		24	SynthAah
80	0	Ocarina		64	VoxLead
81	0	SquareLd	87	0	Fifth Ld
	6	Square 2		35	Big Five
	8	LMSquare	88	0	Bass & Ld
	18	Hollow		16	Big&Low
	19	Shmoog		64	Fat&Prky

PGM	BNK	Instrument	PGM	BNK	Instrument
	65	SoftWurl		66	Celstial
89	0	New AgePd	97	0	Rain
	64	Fantasy2		45	ClaviPad
90	0	Warm Pad		64	HrmoRain
	16	ThickPad		65	AfrcnWnd
	17	Soft Pad		66	Caribean
	18	SinePad	98	0	SoundTrk
	64	Horn Pad		27	Prologue
	65	RotarStr		64	Ancestrl
91	0	PolySyPd		65	Rave
	64	PolyPd80	99	0	Crystal
	65	ClickPad		12	SynDrCmp
	66	Ana Pad		14	Popcorn
	67	SquarPad		18	TinyBell
92	0	ChoirPad		35	RndGlock
	64	Heaven2		40	GlockChi
	65	Lite Pad		41	ClearBel
	66	Itopia		42	ChorBell
	67	CC Pad		64	SynMalet
93	0	BowedPad		65	SftCryst
	64	Glacier		66	LoudGlok
	65	GlassPad		67	XmasBell
94	0	MetalPad		68	VibeBell
	64	Tine Pad		69	DigiBell
	65	Pan Pad		70	AirBells
95	0	Halo Pad		71	Harp
96	0	SweepPad		72	GameImba
	20	Shwimmer	100	0	Atmosphr
	27	Converge		18	WarmAtms
	64	PolarPad		19	HollwRls
	65	Sweepy		40	NylonEP

PGM	BNK	Instrument	PGM	BNK	Instrument
	64	NylnHarp		32	DetSitar
	65	Harp Vox		35	Sitar 2
	66	AtmosPad		96	Tambra
	67	Planet		97	Tamboura
101	0	Bright	106	0	Banjo
	64	FantaBel		28	MuteBnjo
	96	Smokey		96	Rabab
102	0	Goblins		97	Gopichnt
	64	GobSyn		98	Oud
	65	50sSciFi	107	0	Shamisen
	66	Ring Pad		96	Tsugaru
	67	Ritual	108	0	Koto
	68	ToHeaven		96	T Koto
	69	MilkyWay		97	Kamoon
	70	Night	109	0	Kalimba
	71	Glisten		64	BigKalim
	72	Puffy	110	0	Bagpipe
	96	BelChoir	111	0	Fiddle
103	0	Echoes	112	0	Shanai
	8	EchoPad2		64	Shanai2
	14	Echo Pan		96	Pungi
	64	EchoBell		97	Hichriki
	65	Big Pan	113	0	TnklBell
	66	SynPiano		96	Bonang
	67	Creation		97	Gender
	68	Stardust		98	Gamelan
	69	Reso Pan		99	S.Gamlan
104	0	Sci-Fi		100	Rama Cym
	64	Starz		101	AsianBel
	65	Odyssey	114	0	Agogo
105	0	Sitar		96	Atrigane

PGM	BNK	Instrument	PGM	BNK	Instrument
115	0	SteelDrm		64	Rev Cym2
	96	Tablas		96	RevSnar1
	97	GlasPerc		97	RevSnar2
	98	ThaiBell		98	RevKick1
116	0	WoodBlok		99	RevConBD
	96	Castanet		100	Rev Tom1
117	0	TaikoDrm		101	Rev Tom2
	96	Gr.Cassa	121	0	FretNoiz
118	0	MelodTom	122	0	BrthNoiz
	64	Mel Tom2	123	0	Seashore
	65	Real Tom	124	0	Tweet
	66	Rock Tom	125	0	Telephone
119	0	Syn.Drum	126	0	Helicptr
	64	Ana Tom	127	0	Applause
	65	ElecPerc	128	0	Gunshot
120	0	RevCymbl			

XG drum kits

BNK PGM NN	Key	127 1 *Standard Kit*	127 2 *Standard Kit 2*	127 9 *Room Kit*	127 17 *Rock Kit*
13	C# -1	Surdo Mute			
14	D -1	Surdo Open			
15	D# -1	High Q			
16	E -1	Whip Slap			
17	F -1	Scratch Push			
18	F# -1	Scratch Pull			
19	G -1	Finger Snap			
20	G# -1	Click Noise			
21	A -1	MetrClick			
22	A# -1	MetrBell			
23	B -1	Seq Click L			
24	C0	Seq Click H			
25	C#0	Brush Tap			
26	D0	Brush Swirl L			
27	D#0	Brush Slap			
28	E0	Brush Swirl H			
29	F0	Snare Roll	Snare Roll 2		
30	F#0	Castanet			
31	G0	Snare L	Snare L 2		SD Rock M
32	G#0	Sticks			
33	A0	Bass Drum L			Bass Drum M
34	A#0	Open Rim Shot	Open Rim Shot 2		
35	B0	Bass Drum M	Bass Drum M 2		Bass Drum H3
36	C1	Bass Drum H	Bass Drum H 2	BD Room	BD Rock
37	C#1	SideKick			
38	D1	Snare M	Snare M 2	SD Room L	SD Rock

BNK PGM NN	Key	127 1 Standard Kit	127 2 Standard Kit 2	127 9 Room Kit	127 17 Rock Kit
39	D#1	HandClap			
40	E1	Snare H	Snare H 2	SD Room H	SD Rock Rim
41	F1	LowTom2		Room Tom 1	Rock Tom 1
42	F#1	Cl-HH			
43	G1	LowTom1		Room Tom 2	Rock Tom 2
44	G#1	Pedal-HH			
45	A1	MidTom2		Room Tom 3	Rock Tom 3
46	A#1	Open-HH			
47	B1	MidTom1		Room Tom 4	Rock Tom 4
48	C2	HighTom2		Room Tom 5	Rock Tom 5
49	C#2	Crash 1			
50	D2	HighTom1		Room Tom 6	Rock Tom 6
51	D#2	RideCym1			
52	E2	Chinese			
53	F2	RideBell			
54	F#2	Tamburin			
55	G2	Splash			
56	G#2	Cowbell			
57	A2	Crash 2			
58	A#2	Vibraslap			
59	B2	RideCym2			
60	C3	Hi Bongo			
61	C#3	Lo Bongo			
62	D3	Mt Conga			
63	D#3	Hi Conga			
64	E3	Lo Conga			
65	F3	HTimbale			
66	F#3	LTimbale			
67	G3	Hi Agogo			

BNK PGM NN	Key	127 1 Standard Kit	127 2 Standard Kit 2	127 9 Room Kit	127 17 Rock Kit
68	G#3	Lo Agogo			
69	A3	Cabasa			
70	A#3	Maracas			
71	B3	S Whistl			
72	C4	L Whistl			
73	C#4	Sh Guiro			
74	D4	Lg Guiro			
75	D#4	Claves			
76	E4	HWodBlck			
77	F4	LWodBlck			
78	F#4	Mt Cuica			
79	G4	Op Cuica			
80	G#4	MtTriang			
81	A4	OpTriang			
82	A#4	Shaker			
83	B4	Jingle Bell			
84	C5	Bell Tree			
85	C#5				
86	D5				
87	D#5				
88	E5				
89	F5				
90	F#5				
91	G5				

BNK PGM NN	Key	127 1 Standard Kit	127 25 Electro Kit	127 26 Analog Kit	127 33 Jazz Kit
13	C# -1	Surdo Mute			
14	D -1	Surdo Open			
15	D# -1	High Q			
16	E -1	Whip Slap			
17	F -1	Scratch Push			
18	F# -1	Scratch Pull			
19	G -1	Finger Snap			
20	G# -1	Click Noise			
21	A -1	MetrClick			
22	A# -1	MetrBell			
23	B -1	Seq Click L			
24	C0	Seq Click H			
25	C#0	Brush Tap			
26	D0	Brush Swirl L			
27	D#0	Brush Slap			
28	E0	Brush Swirl H	Rev Cymbal	Rev Cymbal	
29	F0	Snare Roll			
30	F#0	Castanet	High Q	High Q	
31	G0	Snare L	Snare M	SD Rock H	
32	G#0	Sticks			
33	A0	Bass Drum L	Bass Drum H4	Bass Drum M	
34	A#0	Open RimShot			
35	B0	Bass Drum M	BD Rock	BD Analog L	
36	C1	Bass Drum H	BD Gate	BD Analog H	BD Jazz
37	C#1	SideKick		Analog Stick	
38	D1	Snare M	SD Rock L	AnalogSnr L	
39	D#1	HandClap			
40	E1	Snare H	SD Rock H	Analog Snr H	
41	F1	LowTom2	E Tom Tom 1	Analog Tom 1	Jazz Tom 1

BNK PGM NN	Key	127 1 Standard Kit	127 25 Electro Kit	127 26 Analog Kit	127 33 Jazz Kit
42	F#1	Cl-HH		AnalogCHH 1	
43	G1	LowTom1	E Tom Tom 2	Analog Tom 2	Jazz Tom 2
44	G#1	Pedal-HH		AnalogCHH 2	
45	A1	MidTom2	E Tom Tom 3	Analog Tom 3	Jazz Tom 3
46	A#1	Open-HH		Analog OHH	
47	B1	MidTom1	E Tom Tom 4	Analog Tom 4	Jazz Tom 4
48	C2	HighTom2	E Tom Tom 5	Analog Tom 5	Jazz Tom 5
49	C#2	Crash 1		Analog Cymbal	
50	D2	HighTom1	E Tom Tom 6	Analog Tom 6	Jazz Tom 6
51	D#2	RideCym1			
52	E2	Chinese			
53	F2	RideBell			
54	F#2	Tamburin			
55	G2	Splash			
56	G#2	Cowbell		Analog Cowbell	
57	A2	Crash 2			
58	A#2	Vibraslap			
59	B2	RideCym2			
60	C3	Hi Bongo			
61	C#3	Lo Bongo			
62	D3	Mt Conga		Analog Conga H	
63	D#3	Hi Conga		Analog Conga M	
64	E3	Lo Conga		Analog Conga L	
65	F3	HTimbale			
66	F#3	LTimbale			
67	G3	Hi Agogo			
68	G#3	Lo Agogo			
69	A3	Cabasa			
70	A#3	Maracas		Analog Maracas	

BNK PGM NN	Key	127 1 Standard Kit	127 25 Electro Kit	127 26 Analog Kit	127 33 Jazz Kit
71	B3	S Whistl			
72	C4	L Whistl			
73	C#4	Sh Guiro			
74	D4	Lg Guiro			
75	D#4	Claves		Analog Claves	
76	E4	HWodBlck			
77	F4	LWodBlck			
78	F#4	Mt Cuica	Scratch Push	Scratch Push	
79	G4	Op Cuica	Scratch Pull	Scratch Pull	
80	G#4	MtTriang			
81	A4	OpTriang			
82	A#4	Shaker			
83	B4	Jingle Bell			
84	C5	Bell Tree			
85	C#5				
86	D5				
87	D#5				
88	E5				
89	F5				
90	F#5				
91	G5				

BNK		127	127	127
PGM		1	41	49
NN	Key	Standard Kit	Brush Kit	Classic Kit
13	C# -1	Surdo Mute		
14	D -1	Surdo Open		
15	D# -1	High Q		
16	E -1	Whip Slap		
17	F -1	Scratch Push		
18	F# -1	Scratch Pull		
19	G -1	Finger Snap		
20	G# -1	Click Noise		
21	A -1	MetrClick		
22	A# -1	MetrBell		
23	B -1	Seq Click L		
24	C0	Seq Click H		
25	C#0	Brush Tap		
26	D0	Brush Swirl L		
27	D#0	Brush Slap		
28	E0	Brush Swirl H		
29	F0	Snare Roll		
30	F#0	Castanet		
31	G0	Snare L	Brush Slap L	
32	G#0	Sticks		
33	A0	Bass Drum L		Bass Drum L2
34	A#0	Open Rim Shot		
35	B0	Bass Drum M		Gran Cassa
36	C1	Bass Drum H	BD Soft	Gran Cassa Mute
37	C#1	SideKick		
38	D1	Snare M	Brush Slap	Marching Snare M
39	D#1	HandClap		
40	E1	Snare H	Brush Tap	Marching Snare H
41	F1	LowTom2	Brush Tom 1	Jazz Tom 1

BNK PGM NN	Key	127 1 Standard Kit	127 41 Brush Kit	127 49 Classic Kit
42	F#1	Cl-HH		
43	G1	LowTom1	Brush Tom 2	Jazz Tom 2
44	G#1	Pedal-HH		
45	A1	MidTom2	Brush Tom 3	Jazz Tom 3
46	A#1	Open-HH		
47	B1	MidTom1	Brush Tom 4	Jazz Tom 4
48	C2	HighTom2	Brush Tom 5	Jazz Tom 5
49	C#2	Crash 1		Hand Cym.Open L
50	D2	HighTom1	Brush Tom 6	Jazz Tom 6
51	D#2	RideCym1		Hand Cym.Closed L
52	E2	Chinese		
53	F2	RideBell		
54	F#2	Tamburin		
55	G2	Splash		
56	G#2	Cowbell		
57	A2	Crash 2		Hand Cym.Open H
58	A#2	Vibraslap		
59	B2	RideCym2		Hand Cym.Closed H
60	C3	Hi Bongo		
61	C#3	Lo Bongo		
62	D3	Mt Conga		
63	D#3	Hi Conga		
64	E3	Lo Conga		
65	F3	HTimbale		
66	F#3	LTimbale		
67	G3	Hi Agogo		
68	G#3	Lo Agogo		
69	A3	Cabasa		
70	A#3	Maracas		

BNK PGM NN	Key	127 1 Standard Kit	127 41 Brush Kit	127 49 Classic Kit
71	B3	S Whistl		
72	C4	L Whistl		
73	C#4	Sh Guiro		
74	D4	Lg Guiro		
75	D#4	Claves		
76	E4	HWodBlck		
77	F4	LWodBlck		
78	F#4	Mt Cuica		
79	G4	Op Cuica		
80	G#4	MtTriang		
81	A4	OpTriang		
82	A#4	Shaker		
83	B4	Jingle Bell		
84	C5	Bell Tree		
85	C#5			
86	D5			
87	D#5			
88	E5			
89	F5			
90	F#5			
91	G5			

XG SFX kits

BNK PGM NN	Key	127 1 Standard Kit	126 1 SFX 1	126 2 SFX 2
13	C# -1	Surdo Mute		

BNK PGM NN	Key	127 1 Standard Kit	126 1 SFX 1	126 2 SFX 2
14	D -1	Surdo Open		
15	D# -1	High Q		
16	E -1	Whip Slap		
17	F -1	Scratch Push		
18	F# -1	Scratch Pull		
19	G -1	Finger Snap		
20	G# -1	Click Noise		
21	A -1	MetrClick		
22	A# -1	MetrBell		
23	B -1	Seq Click L		
24	C0	Seq Click H		
25	C#0	Brush Tap		
26	D0	Brush Swirl L		
27	D#0	Brush Slap		
28	E0	Brush Swirl H		
29	F0	Snare Roll		
30	F#0	Castanet		
31	G0	Snare L		
32	G#0	Sticks		
33	A0	Bass Drum L		
34	A#0	Open Rim Shot		
35	B0	Bass Drum M		
36	C1	Bass Drum H	Gtr Cutting Noise	Dial Tone
37	C#1	SideKick	Gtr Cutting Noise 2	Door Creaking
38	D1	Snare M	Dist. Cut Noise	Door Slam
39	D#1	HandClap	String Slap	Scratch
40	E1	Snare H	Bass Slide	Scratch 2
41	F1	LowTom2	Pick Scrape	Windchimes

BNK PGM NN	Key	127 1 Standard Kit	126 1 SFX 1	126 2 SFX 2
42	F#1	Cl-HH		Telephone Ring 2
43	G1	LowTom1		
44	G#1	Pedal-HH		
45	A1	MidTom2		
46	A#1	Open-HH		
47	B1	MidTom1		
48	C2	HighTom2		
49	C#2	Crash 1		
50	D2	HighTom1		
51	D#2	RideCym1		
52	E2	Chinese	Fl. Key Click	Engine Start
53	F2	RideBell		Tire Screech
54	F#2	Tamburin		Car Passing
55	G2	Splash		Crash
56	G#2	Cowbell		Siren
57	A2	Crash 2		Train
58	A#2	Vibraslap		Jetplane
59	B2	RideCym2		Starship
60	C3	Hi Bongo		Burst Noise
61	C#3	Lo Bongo		Coaster
62	D3	Mt Conga		SbMarine
63	D#3	Hi Conga		
64	E3	Lo Conga		
65	F3	HTimbale		
66	F#3	LTimbale		
67	G3	Hi Agogo		
68	G#3	Lo Agogo	Rain	Laughing
69	A3	Cabasa	Thunder	Screaming

BNK PGM NN	Key	127 1 Standard Kit	126 1 SFX 1	126 2 SFX 2
70	A#3	Maracas	Wind	Punch
71	B3	S Whistl	Stream	Heart Beat
72	C4	L Whistl	Bubble	Footsteps
73	C#4	Sh Guiro	Feed	Applaus 2
74	D4	Lg Guiro		
75	D#4	Claves		
76	E4	HWodBlck		
77	F4	LWodBlck		
78	F#4	Mt Cuica		
79	G4	Op Cuica		
80	G#4	MtTriang		
81	A4	OpTriang		
82	A#4	Shaker		
83	B4	Jingle Bell		
84	C5	Bell Tree	Dog	Machine Gun
85	C#5		Horse Gallop	Laser Gun
86	D5		Bird 2	Explosion
87	D#5		Kitty	Fire Work
88	E5		Growl	
89	F5		Haunted	
90	F#5		Ghost	
91	G5		Maou	

Appendix 4
Control Change events

MIDI Control Change events are a very powerful element of MIDI which is becoming more important within the GS and XG sound sets. In contrast to the disagreement on the original protocol many of the 128 Control Change events available have never been standardized, and the effect they produce varies from one synth to another.

Certain MIDI Control Changes do have common functions, however. The MIDI implementation chart in the manual for your synth is the place to see what Control Change events the manufacturer has used on your synth. The following list contains the 128 Control Changes and the common functions which have been agreed upon.

0	Not defined
1	Modulation
2	Breath control
3	Not defined
4	Foot control
5	Portamento time
6	Data entry MSB
7	Volume
8	Balance
9	Not defined
10	Pan
11	Expression
12-15	Not defined
16	General purpose 1
17	General purpose 2
18	General purpose 3
19	General purpose 4
20-32	Not defined

33	Modulation LSB
34	Breath control LSB
35	Not defined
36	Foot control LSB
37	Portamento LSB
38	Data entry LSB
39	Main volume LSB
40	Balance LSB
41	Not defined
42	Pan LSB
43	Expression LSB
44-47	Not defined
48	General purpose 1 LSB
49	General purpose 2 LSB
50	General purpose 3 LSB
51	General purpose 4 LSB
52-63	Not defined
64	Damper pedal
65	Portamento pedal
66	Sostenuto
67	Soft pedal
68	Not defined
69	Hold 2
70-90	Not defined
91	Effect depth
92	Tremelo depth
93	Chorus depth
94	Celeste depth
95	Phaser depth
96	Data increase
97	Data decrease
98	Non regulation LSB
99	Non regulation MSB
100	Regulation LSB
101	Regulation MSB
102-120	Not defined
121	Reset control
122	Local control

123	All note off
124	Omni mode off
125	Omni mode on
126	Mono mode on
127	Poly mode on

Appendix 5
Synchronization

Practical synchronization

If you want to run your sequencer in synch with an external MIDI device such as a drum machine, multi-track tape recorder or another computer running another MIDI sequencing program you'll need to use the synchronization functions. This Appendix outlines most of the synchronization methods in use today.

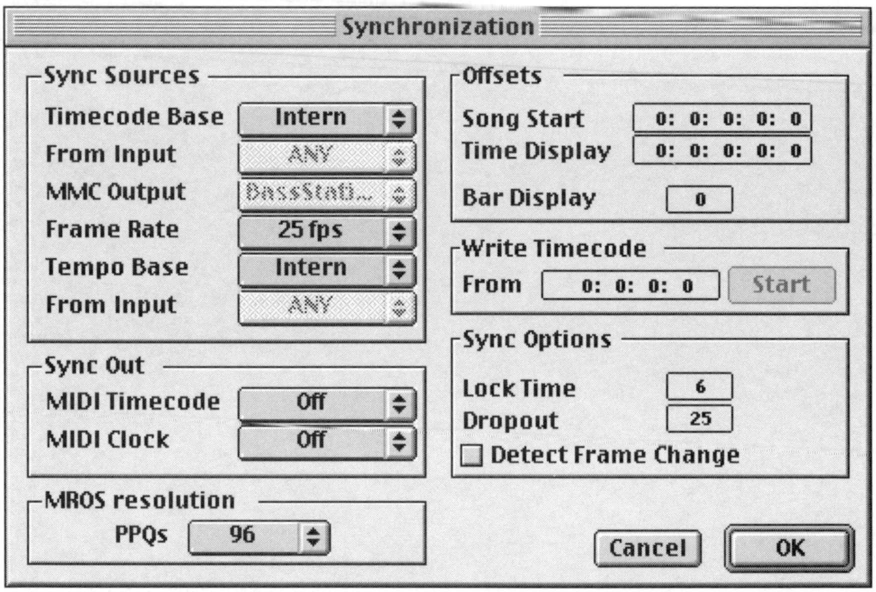

Figure A5.1

Cubase's Synchronization dialogue box.

The two main methods of synchronizing machines are MIDI synchronization and SMPTE. All the settings needed for simple MIDI synchronization are displayed on the left hand side of the screen shot above, while the right hand side is mostly concerned with settings for SMPTE synchronization. SMPTE stands for the Society of Motion Picture and Television Engineers and is a standard developed for synchronization in the film and television world, as its title suggests. SMPTE is used in studios to synch together non-MIDI devices (such as a multi-track tape machine) with MIDI devices (such as a computer running a sequencer).

MIDI clocks

By far the easiest method of synchronization is MIDI synchronization in which one MIDI device is designated as the master and any other MIDI machines are connected to it as slaves. For ease of use, it's simplest to use your sequencer as the master for MIDI synchronization.

MIDI synchronization uses a MIDI timing interval known as MIDI clocks. When you press Play on a master device it sends a Start command to the slave. This starts the slave device which moves forward one beat for every successive MIDI clock received.

The tempo setting in your sequencer determines the speed at which MIDI clocks are sent. The sequence is terminated by a Stop command that is sent when you press the Stop button in your sequencer.

To synchronize a MIDI device to your sequencer, select 'Synchronization', usually to be found on the 'Options' menu. Click the arrow next to the box marked 'MIDI Clock' and select the output to which you wish to send MIDI clocks.

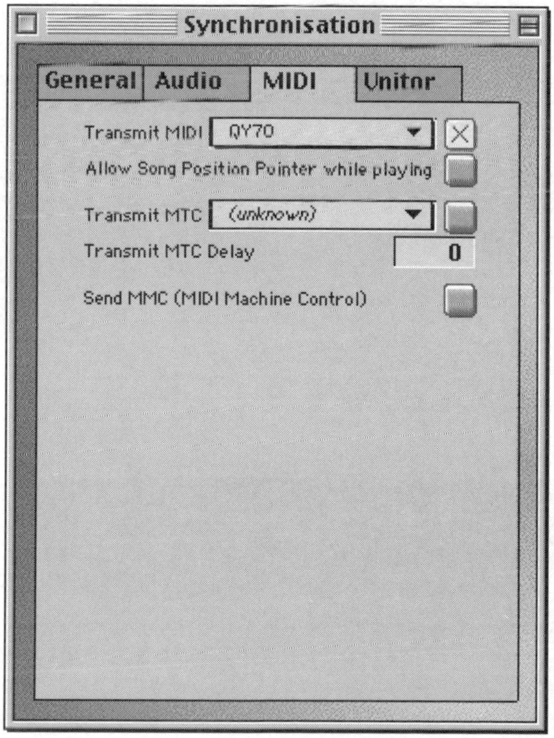

Figure A5.2
Choosing an output in Logic. This display will vary depending on which hardware you have.

NOTE

MIDI timing information is extremely data-intensive. To prevent the MIDI data flow from becoming clogged up, you should attach the connected device to a separate MIDI output from the other receiving devices in your set-up, if at all possible.

Once you've set your sequencer as the master, set the slave machine to External sync. This is usually done from the front panel of the drum machine or MIDI device under 'Sync'. If in doubt consult the manual of the device. Setting your sequencer to be the slave is almost as easy. In the Sync Source section simply set Tempo Sync to MIDI Clocks. Don't forget to turn off the MIDI Clock option in the Send Sync section. With these settings your sequencer is ready to receive incoming MIDI clocks.

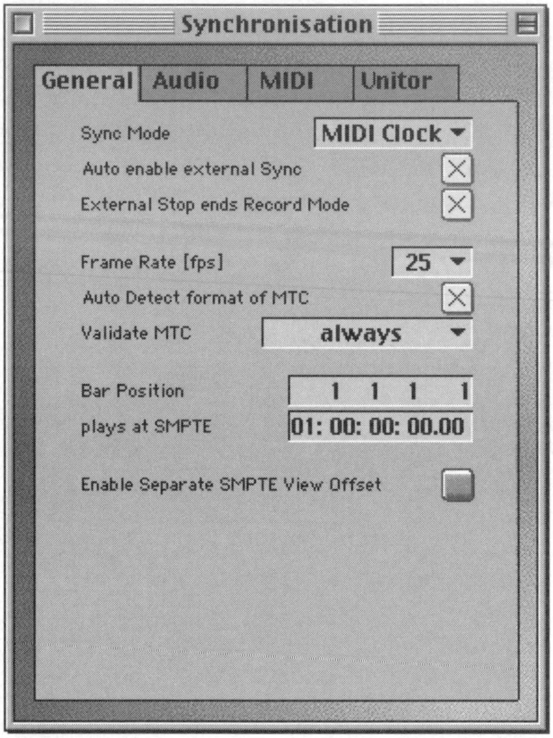

Figure A5.3 *The settings to synchronize Logic to an external MIDI device.*

TIP

If you are lucky enough to have two computers, set one to be the slave and the other to be the master. Then with the MIDI Out of the master connected to the MIDI In of the slave you have two sequencers that will run in sync. As well as expanding the number of MIDI channels available to you there are numerous creative possibilities. With two-way MIDI connections data can be exchanged between the two sequencers; or you might want to record the output from another MIDI program such as Koan Pro into your sequencer for further editing.

MIDI time code

MIDI clocks simply consist of a Start and Stop command, with the intervening MIDI clocks used as a timing base. For more accurate timing and to enable playback from half way through a song there is a variation on MIDI clocks called MIDI Time Code or MTC.

Although MTC isn't used by many drum machines it is increasingly being offered as a synchronization option by digital recording devices. Once again the settings for your sequencer to act as the master or slave in an MTC set-up are accessed from the Synchronization page.

If you wish to control external MTC devices from your sequencer the settings are very similar to the setting for MIDI Clocks. In the 'Send Sync' section choose the MIDI output your device is connected to from the drop-down menu next to the legend 'MIDI Timecode'. Set the external machine to be the slave and it will only start when you press Play or Record in your sequencer.

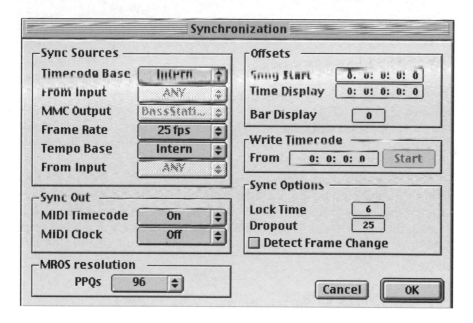

Figure A5.4
Setting Cubase to send MIDI Time Code.

To slave your sequencer to an external MTC device, first turn off any 'Send Sync' settings, then click the arrow next to the box marked 'SMPTE Sync' in the 'Sync Source' section. Unless you have a SMPTE device connected, there are only two options here, Internal sync and MTC. Select the latter to ready your sequencer to receive incoming MIDI Time code.

Figure A5.5
*Cubase set to
receive MIDI
Time code.*

Synchronization	
Sync Sources	**Offsets**
Timecode Base [MTC ▾]	Song Start [0: 0: 0: 0: 0]
From Input [ANY ▾]	Time Display [0: 0: 0: 0: 0]
MMC Output [BassStati... ▾]	Bar Display [0]
Frame Rate [25 fps ▾]	**Write Timecode**
Tempo Base [Intern ▾]	From [0: 0: 0: 0] [Start]
From Input [ANY ▾]	**Sync Options**
Sync Out	Lock Time [6]
MIDI Timecode [Off ▾]	Dropout [25]
MIDI Clock [Off ▾]	☐ Detect Frame Change
MROS resolution	
PPQs [96 ▾]	[Cancel] [OK]

SMPTE

SMPTE timing protocol was established to synchronize devices in the film world. It is also used to synchronize multi-track recorders and this is its most common application in recording studios. TV studios use SMPTE to sync video machines to sequencers for accurate positioning of musical events on a soundtrack.

SMPTE works by recording a track of SMPTE timecode on a 'silent' track on a multi-track tape machine or video recorder. This track is then used as the master timing track on which all other timing is based. We'll look at the most common operation, 'striping' one track of a multi-track tape machine with SMPTE code and then syncing your sequencer with the tape machine.

Writing SMPTE code

Connect the MIDI Out of your tape machine to your computer's MIDI In and the computer's MIDI Out to the tape machine's MIDI In. Unless you have a MIDI merge box to merge incoming MIDI signals you'll have to disconnect the MIDI In from your keyboard and won't be able to record from it while your sequencer is synchronized to the multitrack device.

If you want to record MIDI tracks alongside tracks recorded on a multi-track tape recorder you'll need a MIDI merge. With a MIDI unit like the Studio 64, multiple MIDI In ports allow you to record from your keyboard with your sequencer simultaneously receiving sync input from a SMPTE device.

Connect the SMPTE output from your SMPTE device to your tape machine's audio input. Finally, connect the tape machine's output to the SMPTE device's SMPTE input. Select a track on the multi-track to record the time code onto. This is commonly the 'last' track (4/8/16/32). If the tape machine features any kind of noise reduction system such as Dolby make sure this is turned off as this will interfere with the recording and subsequent playback of the SMPTE code.

NOTE

SMPTE is an audio signal. Be especially careful not to set the levels too high or low, as this will also cause problems in reading the code. Audio 'leakage' to other tracks may also lead to problems.

Once you've connected all the cables, you're ready to record the SMPTE code to tape. This is what is known as 'striping' the tape.

NOTE

The frame rate box at the bottom of the 'Sync Source' section indicates which rate of SMPTE time code to use. There are varying standards in force, according to whether you are working with American devices (24 FPS) or European (25 FPS). Other options are for other differing standards. The important thing is to ensure the frame rate setting here matches the setting on your SMPTE device. You'll have to consult its manual for this. The default setting of 25 FPS is the most commonly used, however, and you shouldn't experience too many problems setting this up.

Start recording on the tape machine. Then click 'Start' in the 'Write SMPTE' section of the Synchronization page. The input indicator on the tape machine should now indicate that it is receiving SMPTE code from the SMPTE device. Wait for about 15 seconds to allow a decent 'run in' on the tape then press 'Start' again in the 'Write SMPTE' section. Now your sequencer sends out MTC to the connected device that translates it into SMPTE code and sends it on to the tape machine where it is recorded.

NOTE

Record more code than you need as you cannot add more code to the end of a section of SMPTE code. It's usually best to record code over the entire tape length.

After you've recorded enough time code, press the 'Stop' in the 'Write SMPTE' section.

Syncing your sequencer to SMPTE

Set your sequencer to slave to MTC. Rewind the tape recorder and press Play. As soon as the time code you have just 'striped' on the tape starts, the SMPTE interface will generate MTC and your sequencer will begin playback from position 1.1.0. It's usually best to offset the start in your sequencer to allow a few seconds for the interface to start generating MTC. Do this in the 'Song Start' box in the 'Offsets' section of the Synchronization page.

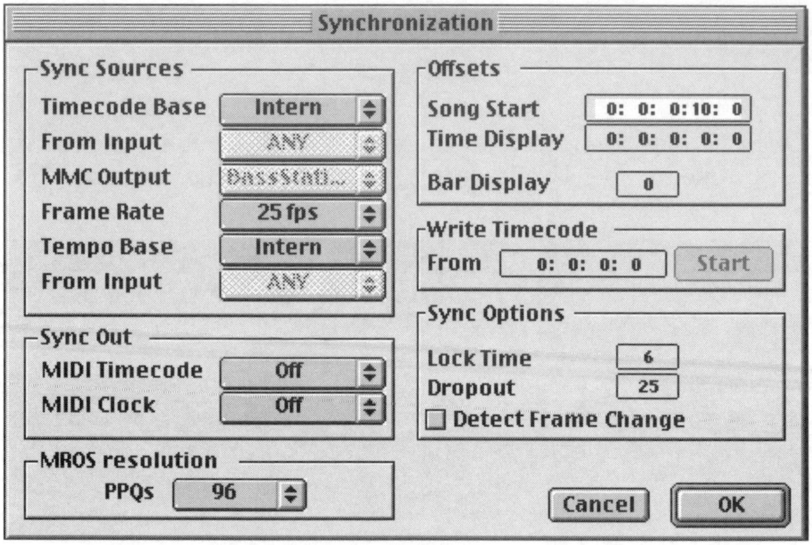

Figure A5.6
Set an offset to allow a SMPTE interface time to read the 'lead in' from a SMPTE track.

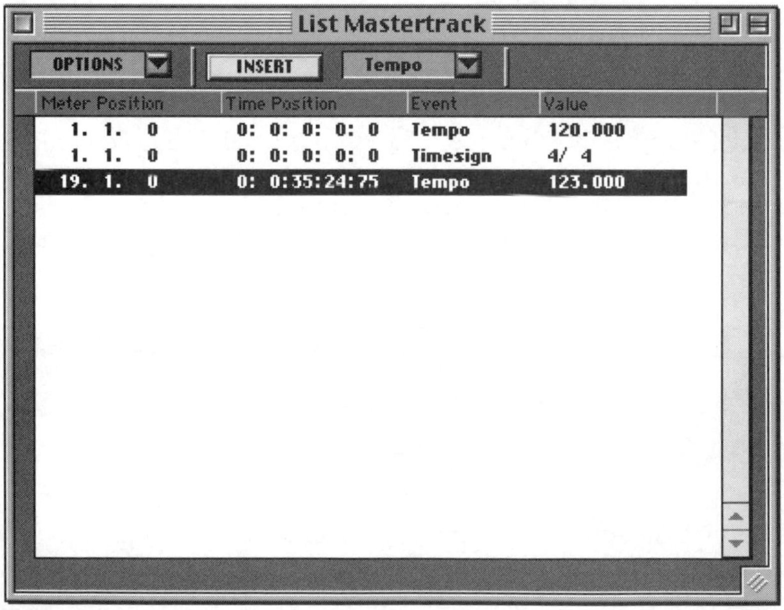

Figure A5.7
Differing tempos can be programmed in the Mastertrack to 'match' the timing of audio events on tape.

SMPTE time code does not control the sequencer tempo; it just synchronizes the tape machine and sequencer. Your sequencer will still play at the tempo in the Master track. This means you can adjust the tempo of a song within the Master track page to match timing where a 'live' track on the tape is not as precise as your sequencer. This feature is also commonly used when syncing to a video to move the timing of a soundtrack to match the visuals. See Figure A5.7.

DIN synchronization

Older synths used a variety of synchronization systems, the most common being the DIN sync used by Roland for the TR909, 808 and TB303. There are now devices available that take incoming MIDI clocks and convert them into DIN sync, thus enabling you to incorporate these older devices in your sequencing set-up.

All you need do is take a MIDI Out from your computer and plug it into the device's MIDI In and set your sequencer to send out MIDI clocks, just as you would for simple MIDI synchronization. The DIN sync device translates the incoming MIDI clocks into the appropriate timing signal and sends this out through another lead to the synth or drum machine.

Frequency Shift Keying

Older multi-track tape machines don't feature MIDI ports and rely on a system called FSK or Frequency Shift Keying. In a similar process to SMPTE, a track is striped with FSK code which is then used to drive all the connected devices. Once again there are devices available which convert MIDI Time Code or Clocks to FSK. Connection with these is similar to the procedure for a SMPTE translator. Connect a MIDI Out from your computer to the unit's MIDI In and vice versa. Then connect the audio Out from the FSK unit to the audio In of your multi-track and the audio Out to the FSK unit's audio In.

Set your sequencer to generate MIDI Time Code or MIDI Clocks, whichever the unit works with, on the output to which the FSK unit is connected via MIDI. Press record on the tape machine then, after allowing 15 seconds for 'run in'; press Play on your sequencer. Your sequencer will send MIDI Clocks or Time Code out to the FSK unit, that will translate it into FSK and send it as an audio signal to the tape machine. Once you've recorded enough code simply stop the tape machine and your sequencer.

Now set your sequencer to either incoming MIDI clocks or Time Code, whichever the device uses, and press the sync button on the transport bar. Rewind the tape and press Play. Your sequencer will start when the FSK code on the tape begins playback. Use the 'Song Start' offset in the 'Offsets' section of the Synchronization page to adjust any discrepancies in timing at the start caused by delays between the start of the FSK track and the FSK unit's translation of the code.

Appendix 6
Other computer music software

Excellent as sequencers are at sequencing and musical manipulations, there *are* other approaches to creating music using computers and MIDI. While these other programs may lack a sequencer's arrangement and editing functions they often provide other stimulating ways of producing original ideas.

Adopting radically different approaches to generating new musical patterns can often be the source of that one hook or riff you're looking for. If you really want to capture the authentic sequencing feel of step write sequencers like the Roland TB303 there are programs which replicate those mechanical functions. Alternatively you might find the idea of software which takes the whole process of time-stretching samples out of your hands creatively stimulating.

Both these approaches and a hundred in between are available from a vast selection of software. There are far too many software applications to cover in this book but the following run-down of some of the different software available for the Mac and PC will give you some idea of the different approaches available.

ON THE CD-ROM

*You'll find demo versions of most of the software mentioned in the following sections on the CD-ROM accompanying this book. Applications for the PC are all in a folder called **win_apps** and those for the Mac in a folder called **mac_apps**. Each description is accompanied by a file reference to help you locate them. Generally they're in a folder which is named after the manufacturer.*

Once you've come up with new ideas from these programs, the full versions usually offer you the option of saving your work as a MIDI file. This means you can then import that file into your sequencer for a final arrangement or further tweaking. If you have two computers you might want to experiment with running a sequencer on one and one of these 'freestyle' sequencers on the other, using a MIDI link between the two to record the results of one into the other. The limit, when it comes to generating music using computers, is only the limit of your imagination.

PC software

Acid

Sonic Foundry's Acid has caused a revolution of sorts in the world of sequencing and music-making. Acid has no MIDI tracks, concentrating solely on audio. Unlike other dedicated audio sequencers, it makes the whole process easy and fun. Instead of requiring you to work out tempos and time-stretch your samples accordingly, Acid does all of that for you. Just drop a sample onto your arrangement and Acid will automatically work out the original BPM and time-stretch the sample. Acid also syncs to MIDI clocks so you can run it in tandem with your sequencer for maximum versatility.

ON THE CD-ROM

There's a demo version of the Acid In the **Sonic Foundry** *folder on the CD-ROM accompanying this book. You can also download the latest version from Sonic Foundry's web site at:* **http://www.sonicfoundry.com**.

ReBirth

One of the most used synthesizers in Electronica is the Roland TB303. This little silver box was originally designed as a bass accompaniment for guitarists but never caught on. Then some electronic musicians were playing around with it one day and discovered that, if you tweaked the filter, it produces some amazing squealing sounds which became famous as the 'acid' sound after the release of Phuture's 'Acid Trax'.

You can expect to pay a lot of money for a TB303 these days, as they have become the most-used instrument in all fields of Electronica. That's assuming you can find one. Roland withdrew the little silver box after only a few thousand were made and despite many attempts since to replicate them, no one has managed to completely duplicate one in hardware. There are many honourable contenders for the TB303's crown including the Novation BassStation and Roland's own, sample-based, MC303 but none of them has managed to replace the sound of the original; that is, until a Swedish team of programmers, operating under the collective sobriquet of Propellerheads, developed ReBirth.

ReBirth wasn't the first software synth but it was the first to convincingly copy the crunchy filters of the TB303 and ally that with a sequencer that also replicated the unique programming facilities of the original. Programming a TB303 is a hit and miss affair, requiring you to input pitch values from a dinky keyboard followed separately by note lengths. Slides and accents are also entered separately. What happens in reality is that you punch buttons until everything returns to the start, and then check out your chaotically generated sequence.

ReBirth was so successful at replicating the sound of the TB303 and its unique sequencer that Steinberg bought it and made it compatible with Cubase. The program is under constant development. It originally paired a 'soft' TB303 with a sample-based Roland TR808 drum machine and now features two TB303s and has added a TR909 to the drum machine section. Some people consider it to be all you need to make Electronica, and the program has developed into a whole scene in itself. With the facility to load your own drum samples into the drum machine section and the capability to customize its appearance, ReBirth's popularity shows no signs of waning.

ON THE CD-ROM
There's a demo version of the PC version of ReBirth in the **rebirth** *folder located in the* **Steinberg** *folder. You can also download the latest version and a host of Mods – customized versions with new drum samples – from their web site at:* **http://www.propellerheads.se**.

ReCycle!

ReCycle! is a program from Steinberg which has revolutionized the process of cutting up samples and has been enthusiastically adopted by the most avid of sample choppers, the Drum'n'Bass fraternity. Indeed if it wasn't for ReCycle! Goldie's classic 'Timeless' probably would be!

What ReCycle! does is simple but effective, and you find yourself wondering why no one thought of it before. You load a sample in to ReCycle! and tell it how long in bars and/or beats the sample is. Next you set a level of sensitivity with a simple slider so that ReCycle! can calculate where to chop the sample. This is made visually intuitive by a visual display of the sample. Once that's done ReCycle! chops the sample up into a series of smaller samples.

It can then send those samples out to your sampler and generate a MIDI file to trigger them. Each sample will have been allocated a different note to trigger it and you can then load the MIDI file into your sequencer and replay the loop at whatever tempo you desire with no time-stretching or pitch-shifting necessary. There is also the option to save the chopped up sample as a ReCycle! REXX file. This is essentially the same thing but can be loaded into Steinberg's sequencing program, Cubase, for replay in the same way. At the time of writing, it looks as though the REXX format is going to be adopted as a standard by other sampling and sequencing programs.

ON THE CD-ROM
There's a demo version of the PC version of ReCycle! In the **recycle** *folder located in the* **Steinberg** *folder. You can also download the latest version from Steinberg's web site at* **http://www.steinberg.de**.

Koan Pro

If you're looking for an alternative method of composition you should check out Koan Pro. Koan Pro can be used to add music to web sites and is popular because it works and it is fun. The fact that Brian Eno has chose to release an album as a Koan Pro file rather than an audio recording can't have hurt either.

The reason Eno likes Koan Pro is its ability to generate ever-changing music from a few simple parameters. You set up rules for pitch ranges, rhythmic pulses and changes in a similar fashion to the IPS section in Cubase but with an even more intuitive interface of virtual sliders and colour bands.

Koan Pro was originally designed to produce ambient music and is excellent at that. Recently the designers have added features that also make it suitable for producing dance music. The results can be saved as a MIDI file for further work in a sequencer or as a Koan file that will never play the same way twice.

ON THE CD-ROM

There's a demo version of Koan Pro in the **Koanpro** *folder located in the* **Sseyo** *folder. You can download the latest version and plug-ins for your web browser from* **http://www.sseyo.com**.

The Jammer

Ever wished that you had some other musicians to play some funky basslines and drum patterns that go with the chord pattern you just discovered? That's what The Jammer was designed to do. It comes with lots of style settings and parameters for generating different musical styles for everything from drumbeats to pads.

All you have to do is choose the musical style in which you want your virtual band to play and they will 'play' along with your chord patterns, basslines or whichever instrument you choose to pick up. As with Koan Pro, you can save the results as a standard MIDI file and load it into your sequencer later.

The Jammer was designed in a modular fashion so new musical styles can be added to its repertoire in future. You can also make your own style templates or even load a MIDI file from a previous work into it and use that to make new style settings. Now when you write a track that has got that certain something, you can use it to make your own Jammer style sheets and produce the elusive follow-up, the tune with the same groove as your first big hit.

XG Ace

XG Ace is the latest editing software for Yamaha XG synths by Newtronic. It has a range of outstanding editing features and full midifile compatibility, i.e. you can save your XG setups as midifiles and import them into any sequencer package. The XG Ace Lite version has been included on the CD-ROM.

Mac software

ReBirth

Everything you've already read about ReBirth for the PC stands for the Mac version. The PC version was developed first but, in keeping with Steinberg's cross-platform compatibility, the Mac version mirrors developments on the PC version and ReBirth songs are compatible between the two versions.

ReCycle!

Everything you've already read about ReCycle! for the PC applies to the Mac version. The Mac version was actually developed first but, in keeping with Steinberg's cross-platform compatibility, the PC version mirrors developments on the Mac version and ReCycle! REXX files are compatible between the two versions.

ProTools

Long the preferred tool of the professionals for post-production treatment of sound files, ProTools used to be ignored by everyone else because of two things: you needed extra hardware to run it and it didn't have direct MIDI support. Although you could sync it up to a MIDI sequencer ProTools itself didn't feature MIDI tracks. All that has now changed with the introduction of a version of ProTools which doesn't require an AudioMedia card to function and which includes MIDI tracks running alongside audio ones. ProTools scores above other audio sequencers for the number of audio plug-ins it has available and for its advanced audio editing functions.

Appendix 7
Table of contents of CD-ROM

Chapter 1

Midifile data for Chapter 1

Directory	File Name
	4square.mid
chapter1/midifiles/	
	jazzy.mid

Chapter 2

Midifile data for Chapter 2

Directory	Filename
chapter2/midifiles/	
bass/dreamho/	dhbass1.mid
	dhbass2.mid
	dhbass3.mid
	dhbass4.mid
	dhbass5.mid
bass/garage/	2bass.mid
	disco1.mid
	disco2.mid

Directory	Filename
	disco3.mid
	disco4.mid
	garabas1.mid
	garabas2.mid
	garage1.mid
bass/house/	house01.mid
	house02.mid
	house03.mid
	house04.mid
	house05.mid
	walkfnk1.mid
	walkfnk2.mid
	walkfnk3.mid
	walkfnk4.mid
chords/dreamho/	dhguit1.mid
	dhguit2.mid
	dhpiano1.mid
	dhpiano2.mid
	dreamp1.mid
	dreamp2.mid
	dreamp3.mid
chords/garage/	dpiano1.mid
	dpiano2.mid
	pgroove1.mid
	pgroove2.mid
	pgroove3.mid
	pgroove4.mid
	pgroove5.mid

Directory	Filename
drums/dreamho/	dreambr1.mid
	dreambr2.mid
	dreambr3.mid
	dreamh01.mid
	dreamh02.mid
	dreamh03.mid
	dreamh04.mid
	dreamh05.mid
	dreamh06.mid
drums/garage/	gar_01.mid
	gar_02.mid
	gar_fl.mid
drums/house/	club01.mid
	club02.mid
	club03.mid
	club04.mid
	club_br.mid
	clubreak.mid
	clubroll.mid
	congas.mid
	houseg01.mid
	houseg02.mid
	houseg03.mid
	houseg04.mid
seqs/	dhseq1.mid
	drmarp1.mid
songs/	dreamh.mid
	dreamset.mid

Audio data for Chapter 2

Directory	File Name	bpm
chapter2/samples/		
bass/dreamho/	dhbass1.wav	125
	dhbass2.wav	125
bass/garage/	garabas1.wav	125
	garabas2.wav	125
chords/	dhguitr1.wav	125
	dhguitr2.wav	125
	dhpiano1.wav	125
	dhpiano2.wav	125
drums/dreamho/	dreambr1.wav	125
	dreambr2.wav	125
	dreambr3.wav	125
	dreamh04.wav	125
	dreamh05.wav	125
	dreamh06.wav	125
drums/garage/	garage1.wav	125
drums/house/	houseg01.wav	125
seqs/	dhseq1.wav	125
vocs/	dh_light.wav	125
	dh_ahh.wav	125

Chapter 3

Midifile data for Chapter 3

Directory	File Name
chapter3/midifiles/	
bass/techno/	tekdnc01.mid
	tekdnc02.mid
	tekdnc03.mid
	tekdnc04.mid
	tekdnc05.mid
bass/trance/	trance01.mid
	trance02.mid
	trance03.mid
	trance04.mid
	trance05.mid
drums/eurobeat/	euro01.mid
	euro02.mid
	euro_fl.mid
drums/oldtechno/	oldtec01.mid
	oldtec02.mid
	oldtec03.mid
drums/techno/	techno01.mid
	techno02.mid
	techno03.mid
drums/trance/	trance01.mid
	trance02.mid
	trance03.mid
	trance04.mid
	trance05.mid

Directory	File Name
	trancfl1.mid
	trancfl2.mid
seqs/	trseq01.mid
	trseq02.mid
songs/	trance.mid
	trancset.mid

Audio data for Chapter 3

Directory	File Name	bpm
chapter3/samples/		
bass/	trbass01.wav	135
	lrbass06.wav	135
drums/techno/	techno01.wav	135
	techno02.wav	135
drums/trance/	trance04.wav	135
	trance05.wav	135
	trance06.wav	135
	trance07.wav	135
	trance08.wav	135
	trance09.wav	135
	trance10.wav	135
	trance11.wav	135
	trance12.wav	135
seqs/	trseq01.wav	135
	trseq02.wav	135
	trseq03.wav	135
	trseq04.wav	135

Chapter 4

Midifile data for Chapter 4

Directory	File Name
chapter4/midifiles/	
bass/	bigbass1.mid
	bigbass2.mid
	bigbass3.mid
	bigbass4.mid
	bigbass5.mid
drums/bigbeat/	bigbeat1.mid
	bigbeat2.mid
	bigbeat3.mid
	bigbeat4.mid
	bigbe_fl.mid
	big_br01.mid
drums/electro/	electro1.mid
	electro2.mid
	electro3.mid
drums/hiphop/	hiphop01.mid
	hiphop02.mid
	hiphop03.mid
seqs/	bigseq01.mid
	bigseqal.mid
songs/	bigbeat.mid
	bigset.mid

Audio data for Chapter 4

Directory	File Name	bpm
chapter4/samples/		
bass/	bassa.wav	140
	basse.wav	140
	bassf.wav	140
	bassg.wav	140
	bbbass1.wav	140
	bbbass2.wav	140
	bbbass3.wav	140
	bbbass4.wav	140
chords/	bbgt1C.wav	140
	bbgt2C.wav	140
	bbgt3Bb.wav	140
	bbgt4Bb.wav	140
drums/	bigbeat3.wav	140
	bigbeat5.wav	140
	bigbeat6.wav	140
	bigbeat7.wav	140
	bigbeat8.wav	140
	big_br01.wav	140
seqs/	bigseq01.wav	140
	bigseq02.wav	140
	bigseq03.wav	140
	bigseq04.wav	140
	bigseq05.wav	140
	bigseq06.wav	140

Chapter 5

Midifile data for Chapter 5

Directory	File Name
chapter5/midifiles/	
bass/	dnbass01.mid
	dnbass02.mid
	dnbass03.mid
	dnbass04.mid
	dnbass05.mid
chords/	dnbchor1.mid
	dnbchor2.mid
drums/breakbeat/	breakb01.mid
	breakb02.mid
	breakb03.mid
drums/dnb/	dnb01.mid
	dnb02.mid
	dnb03.mid
	dnbfl1.mid
	dnbfl2.mid
	dnbbr01.mid
	dnbbr02.mid
drums/jungle/	jungle01.mid
	jungle02.mid
	jungle03.mid
songs/	dnb.mid
	dnbset.mid

Audio data for Chapter 5

Directory	File Name	bpm
chapter5/samples/		
bass/	dnbass01.wav	160
	dnbass02.wav	160
chords/	dnbchor1.wav	160
	dnbchor2.wav	160
	dnbchor3.wav	160
drums/	dnb01.wav	160
	dnb02.wav	160
	dnb03.wav	160
	dnbbr01.wav	160
	dnbbr02.wav	160

Chapter 6

Midifile data for Chapter 6

Directory	File Name
chapter6/midifiles/	
bass/	tripbas1.mid
	tripbas2.mid
	tripbas3.mid
	tripbas4.mid
	tripbas5.mid
chords/	tripcho1.mid
	trippn1.mid

Directory	File Name
	tripstr1.mid
	tripsyn1.mid
drums/acidjazz/	ajazz01.mid
	ajazz02.mid
	ajaz_br1.mid
	ajaz_br2.mid
	ajaz_br3.mid
drums/perc/	perc01.mid
	perc02.mid
	perc03.mid
	perked.mid
drums/triphop/	tripdr01.mid
	tripdr02.mid
	tripdr03.mid
	tripdr04.mid
	tripdr05.mid
	tripdr06.mid
	tripdr07.mid
	tripdr08.mid
	triphop1.mid
	triphop2.mid
	triph_fl.mid
melody/	tripmel1.mid
songs/	triphop.mid
	tripset.mid

Audio data for Chapter 6

Directory	File Name	bpm
chapter6/samples/		
bass/	tripbas1.wav	90
	tripbas2.wav	90
chords/	tripcho1.wav	90
	trippn1.wav	90
	tripstr1.wav	90
	tripsyn1.wav	90
drums/	tripdr01.wav	90
	tripdr02.wav	90
	tripdr03.wav	90
	tripdr04.wav	90
	tripdr05.wav	90
	tripdr06.wav	90
	tripdr07.wav	90
	tripdr08.wav	90
melody/	tripmel1.wav	90

Chapter 7

Midifile data for Chapter 7

Directory	File Name
chapter7/midifiles/	
bass/	wnebass.mid
chords/	wnclav.mid
	wngate.mid

	wnstr.mid	
	wnstrbig.mid	
drums/	wn_conga.mid	
	wn_tamb.mid	
	wnbig.mid	
	wnhse.mid	

Audio data for Chapter 7

Directory	File Name	bpm
chapter7/samples/		
bass/	wnbass.wav	130
	wnebas2.wav	130
	wnebass.wav	130
chords/	wnclav.wav	130
	wngate.wav	130
	wnstr.wav	130
	wnstrbig.wav	130
drums/	wn_conga.wav	130
	wn_tamb.wav	130
	wn01.wav	130
	wn02.wav	130
	wnbig.wav	130
	wnhse.wav	130
melodys/	wn_mel1.wav	130
	wn_mel2.wav	130
	wn_syn_d.wav	130
vocs/	dh_ahh.wav	130
	wn_voc_rev.wav	130

Chapter 9

Midifile data for Chapter 9

Directory	Filename
chapter9/templates/	
gm/	gmsetup1.mid
	gmsetup2.mid
gates/	gmgate1.mid
	gmgate2.mid
	gmgate3.mid
gs/	gssetup1.mid
	gssetup2.mid
	gssetup3.mid
filter/	gsfiltr1.mid
gates/	gsgate1.mid
	gsgate2.mid
	gsgate3.mid
xg/	xgsetup1.mid
	xgsetup2.mid
	xgsetup3.mid
	xgsetup4.mid
filter/	xgfiltr1.mid
gates/	xggate1.mid
	xggate2.mid
	xggate3.mid

Appendix 8
Newtronic – Dance
Kit Lite

We are proud to provide additional midifile data to the programming examples from Newtronic. The Dance Kit Lite features professionally programmed midifiles in a variety of styles featured in this book. Go and check them out, what are you waiting for?

Midifile Data

Directory	File Name	Length
newtronic/		
Dance Kit Lite/		
acid jazz/	acjazz_demo.mid	
bass/	bs2_01.mid	8 bars
	bs2_02.mid	4 bars
	bs2_03.mid	5 bars
	bs2_04.mid	8 bars
chords/	org2_01.mid	4 bars
	pad2_01.mid	8 bars
drums/	loop2_01.mid	8 bars
	loop2_02.mid	2 bars
melody/	sax2_01.mid	4 bars
	sax2_02.mid	6 bars
	sqr2_01.mid	8 bars

Directory	File Name	Length
bigbeat/	bigbeat_demo.mid	
bass/	bs0_01.mid	2 bars
	bs0_02.mid	2 bars
drums/	loop0_01.mid	2 bars
	loop0_02.mid	2 bars
	loop0_03.mid	2 bars
	loop0_04.mid	4 bars
	loop0_05.mid	2 bars
	fill0_01.mid	1 bar
seqs/	git0_01.mid	4 bars
	git0_02.mid	4 bars
dreamhouse/	dreamhouse_demo.mid	
bass/	bs1_01.mid	2 bars
	bs1_02.mid	8 bars
	bs1_03.mid	2 bars
chords/	pad1_01.mid	8 bars
	pad1_02.mid	8 bars
	pn1_01.mid	2 bars
	pn1_02.mid	8 bars
drums/	break1_01.mid	
	break1_02.mid	
	loop1_01.mid	1 bar
	loop1_02.mid	2 bars
	loop1_03.mid	2 bars
melody/	pn1_01.mid	1 bar
	gt1_01.mid	2 bar

Directory	File Name	Length
seqs/	seq1_02.mid	1 bar
	seq1_02.mid	8 bars
	seq1_03.mid	1 bar
drum'n'bass/	drumnbass_demo.mid	
bass/	bs0_01.mid	2 bars
	bs0_02.mid	2 bars
chords/	pad0_01.mid	2 bars
	pad0_02.mid	2 bars
	pad0_03.mid	8 bars
	pad0_04.mid	8 bars
drums/	loop0_01.mid	2 bars
	loop0_02.mid	2 bars
	loop0_03.mid	2 bars
	loop0_04.mid	2 bars
	loop0_05.mid	2 bars
	loop0_06.mid	2 bars
	loop0_07.mid	2 bars
	loop0_08.mid	2 bars
	loop0_09.mid	1 bar
	loop0_10.mid	2 bars
	loop0_11.mid	2 bars
	loop0_12.mid	2 bars
	loop0_13.mid	2 bars
	loop0_14.mid	2 bars
	loop0_15.mid	2 bars
	loop0_16.mid	2 bars
	loop0_17.mid	4 bars

Directory	File Name	Length
fx/	fx0_01.mid	1 bar
	fx0_02.mid	2 bars
melody/	ep0_01.mid	2 bars
	ep0_02.mid	2 bars
	ep0_03.mid	4 bars
trance/	trance_demo.mid	
bass/	bs4_01.mid	4 bars
	bs4_02.mid	2 bars
drums/		
	loop4_01.mid	4 bars
	loop4_02.mid	1 bar
	loop4_03.mid	4 bars
lx/	fx4_01.mid	10 bars
seqs/	scq4_01.mld	2 bars
	seq4_02.mid	2 bars
	seq4_03.mid	2 bars
	seq4_04.mid	2 bars
	seq4_05.mid	1 bar
	seq4_06.mid	1 bar
	seq4_07.mid	1 bar
	seq4_08.mid	2 bars
trip hop/	triphop_demo.mid	
bass/	bs1_01.mid	4 bars
chords/	pad1_01.mid	8 bars
	pad1_02.mid	4 bars

Directory	File Name	Length
drums/	loop1_01.mid	4 bars
	loop1_02.mid	4 bars
phrases/	seq1_01.mid	4 bars
	seq1_02.mid	2 bars
melody/	vib1_01.mid	4 bars
	vib1_02.mid	4 bars

Index